Paul and Imperial Divine Honors

PAUL AND IMPERIAL DIVINE HONORS

Christ, Caesar, and the Gospel

———

D. Clint Burnett

WILLIAM B. EERDMANS PUBLISHING COMPANY

GRAND RAPIDS, MICHIGAN

Wm. B. Eerdmans Publishing Co.
4035 Park East Court SE, Grand Rapids, Michigan 49546
www.eerdmans.com

Book design by Lydia Hall

Printed in the United States of America

30 29 28 27 26 25 24   1 2 3 4 5 6 7

ISBN 978-0-8028-7985-1

Library of Congress Cataloging-in-Publication Data

A catalog record for this book is available from the Library of Congress.

To my daughter and heartstring,
Joanna Grey,
from Papa with love

Contents

Contents

Figures

Tables

Foreword

"Religion in the Cities" might be an engaging miniseries or virtual-reality tour developed from the picture that Rev. D. Clint Burnett paints of first-century Philippi, Thessalonica, and Corinth. Unlike the standard tourist guidebooks or broad generalizations repeated in many New Testament texts, he has immersed himself in the archaeological remains dated to each city when Paul founded churches there. An extensive archive that includes many of his own photos draws on inscriptions, statuary, and coin images to illustrate local differences in divine honors paid to deceased or, occasionally, living members of the Julio-Claudian imperial family.

Most clergy received only superficial sketches of religious life in the first-century urban context of earliest Christianity from their seminary training. Recently college-educated participants in my parish Bible study group were surprised to learn that altars in Corinth were outside the temples and to be reminded of the bloody facts of sacrificing oxen and cows as well as the complex civic hierarchy associated with such events. Look carefully at coin images in this book to educate the visual imagination (figs. I.1; 1.5). Other coins fill out our pictures of imperial statues in temples that no longer survive (figs. I.2; 4.12; 4.14). Women are not absent from the male-dominant picture. A coin depicting a female figure enthroned in a temple could represent the divinized Livia/Augusta in Corinth's temple honoring the Julian family (fig. 4.14). One from Thessalonica represents *thea Livia* (fig. 3.8). While women were not permitted to hold "priesthoods" that required blood sacrifices, the inscription on a monument from Philippi lists those who were *sacerdotes* of the divinized Livia (figs. 2.5; 2.6). An inscription from Thessalonica introduces readers to Avia Posilla, another female civic benefactor from one of the city's most prominent families, who was responsible for a complex of temple, pool, and portico dedicated to Augustus, Hercules, and the divine personification of the city ("Appendix 1: Inscriptions" §3.5).

Along with public honors accorded divinized imperial family members on the occasion of annual athletic contests, an industrious sleuth can land another surprise from Corinth. A certain civic benefactor Gn. Cornelius Pulcher, who bankrolled Isthmian games, honored *Diva Julia Augusta* with poetry and female chariot races ("Appendix 1: Inscriptions" §4.16). Another inscription found at Delphi dated to the mid-first century honors a certain Helena as winner of an "armed chariot race" during Isthmian games sponsored by Cornelius Pulcher. In a setting of large-scale celebration and excitement, whether or not some insignificant group of Christian house-based churches could be seen in the cheering crowds hardly mattered. As Burnett points out, Paul chides the church in Corinth for being all too comfortably integrated in the social customs of the city. There is no evidence in 1–2 Corinthians of harassment by authorities or neighbors as the routine fact of life. Issues in Philippi and Thessalonica prove to be quite different.

Before engaging the evidence from the three Pauline churches to investigate differences in how each city paid divine honors to members of the imperial family and the social position of Christians in each case, Burnett treats readers to an orientation video. An inscription from Gythium, a city at the southern end of mainland Greece, details the procedures for an eight-day festival that honors five Julio-Claudians, a Roman general, and two local benefactors of their city. After conquering Greece, the Roman general gave Gythium a grant of freedom in 196 BC. The local benefactors—a certain Eurycles followed by a son, Laco—held imperial appointment of "ruler" over Sparta that included Gythium. At various points in the processions, sacrifices, and incense offerings, the honors accorded these deceased humans were distinct from, but associated with, those accorded the gods and goddesses revered by the city. When the procession ended at the theater where the contests would begin, all civic officials would approach painted images of *theos* Augustus, Julia Augusta, and Tiberius to offer incense to traditional gods "on behalf of the health of the rulers."

That qualification sets up a complaint about the habits of much New Testament scholarship, which Burnett hammers home throughout this book even against such popular scholars as N. T. Wright: the assumption that there was a universal "emperor cult" by which living Roman emperors expected their subjects to worship them as "gods." That presumption has fueled extensive scholarly discussion about Christian resistance to Roman imperial politics that has accelerated in the academic adoption of postcolonial hermeneutics. The Gythians themselves provided a caution against the using divine epithets and sacrificial actions in ways that would confuse the honor given to a Julio-Claudian with the worship due to deities. The city dispatched an embassy to inform the emperor Tiberius and his mother, Livia, of the honors in question. And then the city recorded Tiberius's reply, which praised the piety of "honors fitting for the gods" for Augustus but insisted that he himself should receive only honors due humans ("Appendix 1: Inscriptions" §I.1).

Given how difficult it is for nonspecialists to access or interpret the records of archaeological finds, inscriptions, statues, and coin images, scholars cannot be blamed for taking what has been uncovered and published about one city to represent what was the case for others. Nor is their habit of passing general conclusions of major scholars on from one book to the next a surprising feature of any academic disciple. But Burnett has adopted a rigorous logic of exclusion. Each city must be investigated on its own terms. Philippi, Thessalonica, and Corinth each have a distinctive civic history, population mix, and—in the case of Philippi and Corinth—relationship to their re-founding as Roman colonies. For New Testament students, this methodological restriction will pay off with new insights about the churches to which Paul writes along with some new puzzles for our inherited images. We typically do not highlight the Roman orientation with its "official Latin language" that differentiates Philippi and Corinth from Thessalonica's Greek orientation. Students used to singling out the fuss of women praying and prophesying in 1 Corinthians as evidence of women in liturgical roles may be surprised to learn that in Philippi priestesses celebrated divine honors for our sole Julio-Claudian *diva*, Augusta, while no evidence for *sacerdotes* has been found in Corinth. However, as this learned foray into the world of classical archaeology reminds us, all conclusions come with the caveats of incomplete evidence, a jigsaw puzzle missing major pieces as well as the photo on the box.

PHEME PERKINS
Joseph Professor of Catholic Spirituality at Boston College
Pentecost Sunday, 2023

Preface

This book has two main goals. The first is to provide contextual reconstructions of imperial divine honors (more commonly known in New Testament circles as "imperial cult") in the three cities in mainland Greece in which Paul established Christian churches and to which he composed letters: Philippi, Thessalonica, and Corinth. By "contextual," I mean using the latest Philippian, Thessalonian, and Corinthian archaeological, epigraphic, numismatic (which means the study of coins), and statuary evidence as well as the ancient literary record (when such literature is available) to reconstruct for which Julio-Claudians Philippi, Thessalonica, and Corinth established divine honors; who in these communities administered them; and how and when these cities offered such honors. This book's second goal is to bring these contextual reconstructions to bear on the relationships of early Christians in the cities in question with imperial divine honors, which in my estimation differed from city to city. My prayer is that by this book's end, the reader will see that imperial divine honors were embedded into the public fabric of Philippi, Thessalonica, and Corinth, what we today would call the social, political, economic, and religious spheres of these cities, and that any suffering that early Christians experienced was not due to these honors alone but was for a more complex reason, the overturning of Greco-Roman pagan culture.

While I hope that many of my New Testament colleagues will benefit from this book, I have written this work with clergy in mind as well for two reasons. First, I have presented my overall reconstructions of imperial divine honors in Philippi, Thessalonica, and Corinth to the scholarly guild in academic publications.[1] Second, after I began writing this book, I was ordained into the diaconate

---

1. D. Clint Burnett, "Divine Titles for Julio-Claudian Imperials in Corinth," *CBQ* 82 (2020): 437–55; Burnett, *Studying the New Testament through Inscriptions: An Introduction* (Peabody, MA: Hendrickson, 2020), 97–120; Burnett, "Imperial Divine Honors in Julio-Claudian Thessalonica and the Thessalonian Correspondence," *JBL* 139 (2020): 570–72; Burnett, "Imperial Divine Honors in Julio-Claudian Thessalonica and the Thessalonian Correspondence," in *Thessalonica*, vol. 7

and priesthood in the Anglican Church in North America, and I have begun to serve as a priest in my parish, Old North Abbey (Knoxville, TN USA). These events have shifted my academic interests and goals, to the point that I believe that scholarship worth pursuing should be in service of the church. In consideration of this audience, I have made four accommodations.

First, I have attempted to interact with New Testament and classical scholarly works that are readily available to the parish priest or congregational pastor. That is, studies in English that the average clergyperson might have in his or her personal library, his or her church library, or, at the very least, that he or she might have access to at the nearest theological library. As for works by classicists, I have tried to use English sources that are open access, available online through digital databases such as JSTOR, and works that classicists have uploaded to their academia .edu web pages. However, the use of classical studies in English was impossible for my chapters on Philippi (chapter 2) and Thessalonica (chapter 3), because the archaeologists who excavate at these cities and many of the historians who focus on them are mostly French and Greek. Therefore, most of the archaeological publications associated with these two cities are in French and Greek, respectively.

Second, I have kept footnotes to a minimum. Therefore, in the following pages, I have not engaged with as many scholars, both New Testament and classical, as I would have liked, because I did not wish to overwhelm my intended audience. If someday a publisher requests a more detailed scholarly portrait of Philippian, Thessalonian, and Corinthian imperial divine honors and their relationship with Christianity in these cities, I am happy to oblige, for the preparation of this book left much material on the cutting-room floor.

Third, given that much of the evidence for Philippian, Thessalonian, and Corinthian imperial divine honors is from inscriptions and coins, I must say a word about how I reference these sources. I know that most clergy have not been initiated into the mysteries of epigraphy and numismatics. To aid the reader in penetrating these arcane ancient sources, I have included the most relevant inscriptions from Philippi, Thessalonica, and Corinth in an appendix. For epigraphs not in the appendix, I have tried to aid the reader in accessing them by providing references to inscriptional collections online. For Greek epigraphs, I have provided the numbering system from the largest online database of Greek epigraphy, that of the

---

of *The First Urban Churches*, ed. James R. Harrison and L. L. Welborn, WGRWSup 21 (Atlanta: SBL Press, 2022), 63–92; Burnett, *Christ's Enthronement at God's Right Hand and Its Greco-Roman Cultural Context*, BZNW 242 (Berlin: de Gruyter, 2021), 111–56; Burnett, "The Interplay between Indigenous Cults and Imperial Cults in the New Testament World," in *Inscriptions, Graffiti, Documentary Papyri*, ed. James R. Harrison and E. Randolph Richards (Grand Rapids: Zondervan, forthcoming).

Packard Humanities Institute, when I can.[2] These references begin with "PH," for example, PH146221, and the reader can search such references online and easily find the epigraphs in question. For inscriptions from Thessalonica, *IG* 10.2.1; 10.2.1s, the reader can access these, along with German translations of them, through the "Inscriptiones Graecae" project.[3] If the reader cannot find any epigraphs in either of the two above databases, he or she can access most of them from older inscriptional collections, *SIG* and *IGR*, which have been digitized and placed on archive.org. For this reason, I have included references to those collections when possible.

Most Latin epigraphs from Corinth (Meritt, *Corinth* 8.1; West, *Corinth* 8.2; Kent, *Corinth* 8.3) can be found digitized on the website of the Corinthian excavations by the American School of Classical Studies at Athens.[4] Unfortunately, the latest publication of inscriptions from Corinth's Julian Basilica, Roncaglia, *Corinth* 22, and the epigraphic collections from Philippi, Pilhofer 2; *CIPh*, are unavailable online. Moreover, the inscriptions from Philippi have been edited in not English but German and French, respectively. To aid the reader in accessing these epigraphs, when possible, I reference older editions of them that one can find in the digitized version of *CIL*.[5] However, *CIL* provides little information about the epigraphs in question, and this information is in Latin. Thanks be to God that the reader will have no trouble accessing every coin that I discuss in the following pages whose image is not included in this book, for they, along with descriptions and images, can be found on *RPC*'s amazing website.[6]

Finally, to aid the average clergyperson in the reading of this book, I have adopted the Latinized spelling of all Greek names and terms. This is an Anglo-American convention that has a long tradition in modern scholarship, and, as an American from British descent who is Anglican, I see no reason to alter it.

Christmas 2022

---

2. "Searchable Greek Inscriptions," Packard Humanities Institute, https://epigraphy.pack hum.org.

3. "Inscriptiones Graecae," Berlin-Brandenburgische Akademie der Wissenschaften, http:// telota.bbaw.de/ig/.

4. "Ancient Corinth," American School of Classical Studies at Athens, https://www.ascsa.edu .gr/excavations/ancient-corinth.

5. Corpus Inscriptionum Latinarum, https://cil.bbaw.de.

6. Roman Provincial Coinage Online, https://rpc.ashmus.ox.ac.uk.

Acknowledgments

This book would not be possible without a number of people to whom I am indebted. Professor Richard E. Oster (Harding School of Theology, Memphis, TN USA) introduced me to imperial divine honors in the Spring 2010 semester. Professors Pheme Perkins (Boston College, Chestnut Hill, MA USA) and Kendra Eshleman (Boston College) altered the way that I approach imperial divine honors in particular but also the study of antiquity in general. Professor Yonder M. Gillihan (Boston College) procured and maintained my status as a visiting scholar at Boston College, which has enabled me to conduct the necessary research to complete this book as well as my other publications. I am grateful to the following friends and colleagues who read portions of this book and provided indispensable feedback: Yonder: chapter 4; Rusty Moorman (Knoxville, TN USA) and postdoctoral fellow Christoph Heilig (University of Basel, Basel, Switzerland): the entire manuscript; Dean Allen Black (Harding School of Theology, Memphis, TN USA): the introduction and conclusion; Professor James "Jim" R. Harrison (Sydney College of Divinity, Macquarie Park, Australia) and Professor Cédric Brélaz (University of Fribourg, Fribourg, Switzerland): chapter 2; and Professor Daniel Vos (Central College, Pella, IA USA): chapter 3. I must thank Eleonora Melliou (Archaeological Museum of Thessaloniki), the Hellenic Organization of Cultural Resources Development, and the Archaeological Museum of Thessaloniki; Georgios Spyropoulos (head of Department of Prehistoric, Classical Antiquities and Museums of the Ephorate of Antiquities of Corinth; deputy director of the Ephorate of Antiquities of Corinth; and the many other academic positions that he holds across the world), the Archaeological Museum of Corinth, the Archaeological Site of Corinth, James A. Herbst (Corinth Excavations architect), and Corinth Excavations; and the Archaeological Site of Philippi for allowing me to reproduce images and pictures from and associated with Philippi, Thessalonica, and Corinth and their respective museums. I owe a debt of gratitude to Professor Margaret Laird (University of Delaware, Newark, DE USA) for graciously allowing me to use her reconstruction of the *Augustales*'s monument from Corinth, to Professor Michel Sève (University of Lorraine, Nancy, France) and the École française d'Athènes for the kind use of the site maps from Philippi and the reconstruction of the monument of the *sacerdotes* of *Diva* Livia, to Professor Paul Scotton (chair of the Department of Archaeology California State University, Long Beach, CA USA and research fellow at the Costen Institute of Archaeology at the University of California Los Angeles, Los Angeles, CA USA) and Carol Stein (director of publications of the American School of Classical Studies at Athens) for the use of the reconstruction of the Julian Basilica, to Dane Kurth at wildwinds.com for benevolently allowing me to use a number of images of coins in this book, and to Chloe Dyar (student at the University of Tennessee at Knoxville, Knoxville, TN USA) for creating the site map of Thessalonica. I am thankful to Trevor Thompson (Eerdmans, Grand Rapids, MI USA) for piloting this book from idea to final publication. Finally, I am forever grateful to my wife, Gerilyn Burnett, and daughter, Joanna Grey Burnett. I, like so many of my younger New Testament colleagues, am not a full-time academic. In his wisdom, God did not see fit to place me in a university setting, and being a parish priest and a full-time financial advisor leaves little time for researching and writing, much less spending time with the two people in the world who mean the most to me, my wife and daughter. Thus, Gerilyn and Joanna Grey have kindly, though sacrificially, given me time away from them to complete this book.

Abbreviations

AB	Anchor Bible
ABRL	Anchor Bible Reference Library
ABSA	*Annual of the British School at Athens*
ANRW	*Aufstieg und Niedergang der römischen Welt: Geschichte und Kultur Roms im Spiegel der neueren Forschung*. Part 2, *Principat*. Edited by Hildegard Temporini and Wolfgang Haase. Berlin: de Gruyter, 1972–
ANTC	Abingdon New Testament Commentaries
AYB	Anchor Yale Bible
BBR	*Bulletin of Biblical Research*
BCH	*Bulletin de correspondance hellénique*
BDAG	Danker, Frederick W., Walter Bauer, William F. Arndt, and F. Wilbur Gingrich. *Greek-English Lexicon of the New Testament and Other Early Christian Literature*. 3rd ed. Chicago: University of Chicago Press, 2000
BECNT	Baker Exegetical Commentary on the New Testament
BICS	Bulletin of the Institute of Classical Studies
BTB	*Biblical Theology Bulletin*
BZNW	Beihefte zur Zeitschrift für die neutestamentliche Wissenschaft
CBQ	*Catholic Biblical Quarterly*
CIL	*Corpus Inscriptionum Latinarum*. Berlin, 1862–
CIPh	*La colonie romaine: La vie publique de la colonie*. Vol. 2, part 1 of *Corpus des Inscriptions grecques et latines de Philippes*. Edited by Cédric Brélaz. Athens: École française d'Athènes, 2014
ClQ	*Classical Quarterly*
CP	*Classical Philology*
EC	*Early Christianity*
GRBS	*Greek, Roman, and Byzantine Studies*
GRNSC	Greece and Rome New Surveys in the Classics

Hesperia	*Hesperia: The Journal of the American School of Classical Studies at Athens*
HTR	*Harvard Theological Review*
HTS	Harvard Theological Studies
IAph	*Inscriptions of Aphrodisias.* Edited by Joyce Reynolds, Charlotte Roueché, and Gabriel Bodard. 2007. https://insaph.kcl.ac.uk/insaph/iaph2007/index.html
IBC	Interpretation: A Bible Commentary for Teaching and Preaching
IBeroia	*Επιγραφές Κάτω Μακεδονίας: Μεταξύ του Βερμίου όρους και του Αξιού ποταμού; Τεύχος Α´ Επιγραφές Βέροιας.* Edited by Loukretia Gounaropoulou and Miltiades B. Hatzopoulou. Athens: Diffusion de Boccard, 1998
IG	*Inscriptiones Graecae.* Editio Minor. Berlin: de Gruyter, 1924–
IGR	*Inscriptiones graecae ad res romanas pertinentes.* Edited by René Cagnat et al. 3 vols. Paris: Leroux, 1906–1927
IKnidos	*Die Inschriften von Knidos I.* Edited by Wolfgang Blümel. Inschriften griechischer Städte aus Kleinasien 41. Bonn: Rudolf Habelt, 1992
ILS	*Inscriptiones Latinae Selectae.* Edited by Hermann Dessau. 3 vols. Berlin: Weidmann, 1892–1916
IPergamon	*Die Inschriften von Pergamon.* Altertümer von Pergamon 8.1, 2. Edited by Max Fränkel. Berlin: Spemann, 1890–1895
IPriene	*Inschriften von Priene.* Edited by F. Hiller von Gaertringen. Berlin, 1906
IvO	*Die Inschriften von Olympia.* Edited by Wilhelm Dittenberger and Karl Purgold. Olympia 5. Berlin: Asher, 1896
JAJ	*Journal of Ancient Judaism*
JBL	*Journal of Biblical Literature*
JHS	*Journal of Hellenic Studies*
JRA	*Journal of Roman Archaeology*
JRS	*Journal of Roman Studies*
JSNT	*Journal for the Study of the New Testament*
JSNTSup	Journal for the Study of the New Testament Supplement Series
LCL	Loeb Classical Library
LSJ	Liddell, Henry George, and Robert Scott, Henry Stuart Jones. *A Greek-English Lexicon.* 9th ed. with revised supplement. Oxford: Clarendon, 1996
LTQ	*Lexington Theological Quarterly*
NIB	*The New Interpreter's Bible.* Edited by Leander E. Keck. 12 vols. Nashville: Abingdon, 1994–2004
NICNT	New International Commentary on the New Testament
NovTSup	Supplements to Novum Testamentum

NTS	*New Testament Studies*
OCD	*Oxford Classical Dictionary*. Edited by Simon Hornblower and Antony Spawforth. 4th ed. Oxford: Oxford University Press, 2012
OGIS	*Orientis Graeci Inscriptiones Selectae*. Edited by Wilhelm Dittenberger. 2 vols. Leipzig: Hirzel, 1903–1905
Phil	*Philologus: Zeitschrift für das klassische Altertum*
Pilhofer 2	Pilhofer, Peter. *Katalog der Inschriften von Philippi*. Vol. 2 of *Philippi*. WUNT 119. Tübingen: Mohr Siebeck, 2000
PNTC	Pillar New Testament Commentary
P.Oxy.	*The Oxyrhynchus Papyri*. Edited by Bernard P. Grenfell et al. London: Egypt Exploration Fund, 1898–
PW	*Paulys Real-Encyclopädie der classischen Altertumswissenschaft*. New edition by Georg Wissowa and Wilhelm Kroll. 50 vols. in 84 parts. Stuttgart: Metzler and Druckenmüller, 1894–1980
RevPhil	*Revue de philologie*
RGRW	Religions in the Graeco-Roman World
RPC	*Roman Provincial Coinage*. Edited by Andrew Burnett et al. London: British Museum Press; Paris: Bibliothèque Nationale, 1992–
RRE	*Religion in the Roman Empire*
SALOP	The Society of Antiquaries of London Occasion Papers
SBLDS	Society of Biblical Literature Dissertation Series
SEG	*Supplementum epigraphicum graecum*
Sel. Pap.	*Select Papyri*. Translated by Arthur S. Hunt and Campbell C. Edgar. 5 vols. LCL. Cambridge: Harvard University Press
SIG	*Sylloge Inscriptionum Graecarum*. Edited by Wilhelm Dittenberger. 4 vols. 3rd ed. Leipzig: Hirzel, 1915–1924
SNTSMS	Society for New Testament Studies Monograph Series
TDNT	*Theological Dictionary of the New Testament*. Edited by Gerhard Kittel and Gerhard Friedrich. Translated by Geoffrey W. Bromiley. 10 vols. Grand Rapids: Eerdmans, 1964–1976
WBC	Word Biblical Commentary
WGRWSup	Writings from the Greco-Roman World Supplement Series
WUNT	Wissenschaftliche Untersuchungen zum Neuen Testament
ZNW	*Zeitschrift für die neutestamentliche Wissenschaft und die Kunde der älteren Kirche*
ZPE	*Zeitschrift für Papyrologie und Epigraphik*
ZST	*Zeitschrift für systematische Theologie*

Epigraphic Conventions

Throughout this book, the reader will notice numerous symbols, called *sigla*, associated with the Greek and Latin inscriptions that I cite, especially in "Appendix 1: Inscriptions." For this reason, this section provides a short explanation for each *siglum* (the singular of *sigla*) that I use:

[ ]	A letter or letters within brackets are not present in the epigraph but are ones that an editor has restored.
( )	Letters within parentheses are part of the abbreviated form of a word and were omitted by the stonecutter to save space.
< >	Letters within angular brackets have been omitted or substituted by the stonecutter.
[[ ]]	Letters within double brackets have been erased in antiquity.
{ }	Letters within curved brackets are superfluous and have been inscribed by the stonecutter by mistake.
[. . .]	Brackets with dots inside represent instances in which, while letters are missing, the number of them is known.
[- - -]	Brackets with dashes inside represent instances in which, while the letters are missing, the number of them is unknown.
ạ	A letter with a dot under it means that it is only partially preserved in the inscription.
a̲	A letter with a line under it means that the letter is no longer visible, but an older editor of the epigraph noted its presence.
vacat	This Latin verb, which means "it is empty or vacant," indicates that the stonecutter has intentionally left a space in the epigraph in question.

Introduction

In August AD 1923, laborers working near the ancient theater in the Greek city of Gythium, a city on the southern end of modern-day mainland Greece, discovered a gray stone stele on which a Greek "sacred law" (*hieros nomos*) dating to AD 15 had been inscribed.[1] The top of the stele had been broken off, and thus the inscription's beginning is lost. However, the remaining text contains the fullest known portrait of an imperial cultic festival ever discovered.[2] According to this *hieros nomos*, the leaders of Gythium instituted an eight-day festival to honor three groups of benefactors: five Julio-Claudians, a Roman general, and two local patrons of their city. The first group, that of Julio-Claudians, consists of Augustus, who had recently died on August 19, AD 14; his adopted son Tiberius, who, upon his father's passing, ascended to the imperial throne; Augustus's wife and Tiberius's mother, Livia, also known as Augusta; Tiberius's adopted son Germanicus Caesar; and Tiberius's son Drusus Caesar. The Roman general in question is Titus Quinctius Flamininus who, in 197 BC, led Rome's armies into Greece and, in 196 BC, after conquering Greece, granted many of its cities, including Gythium, "freedom" (*eleutheria*), which consisted mainly of exemption from taxes and the ability to live by their own laws.[3] The final group consists of two local benefactors, the first of whom is Gaius Julius Eurycles. Augustus had appointed him as dynast (*hēgemōn*) of Sparta—a position that gave him political oversight of Gythium—and he had died between 7 and 2 BC. The second is Eurycles's son, Gaius

---

1. "Appendix 1: Inscriptions" §I.1. For an informed discussion of the inscription, see Elena Calandra and Maria Elena Gorrini, "Cult Practice of a Pompé in the Imperial Age: S. E. G. XI.923," *Sparta* 4 (2008): 3–22.

2. Simon R. F. Price, *Rituals and Power: The Roman Imperial Cult in Asia Minor* (Cambridge: Cambridge University Press, 1984), 210.

3. Livy, *History of Rome* 33.32; Suetonius, *Nero* 24; Plutarch, *Comparison of Philopoemen and Flaminius* 12. An inscription from Gythium dated to 195 BC calls Flamininus its "savior" (σωτήρ) (*IG* 5.1.1165 = PH31581).

Julius Laco, whom Tiberius appears to have appointed to the same position after Eurycles's passing.[4]

The eight-day festival consisted of a combination of "theatrical games" (*agōnes*), a "sacred procession" (*pompē*), and sacrifices of animals and incense, with each day being devoted to one of the aforementioned benefactors.[5] The festival's first day was dedicated to Augustus, whom the sacred law calls a "god" (*theos*), "savior" (*sōtēr*), and "deliverer" (*eleutherios*). The second was in honor of Tiberius. The third day was devoted to Julia (Livia) Augusta, whom the inscription identifies as "the Good Fortune" (*Tychē*), the goddess of fortune who offers protection, of Gythium and other nearby cities under the authority of Sparta. The fourth and fifth days were dedicated to Germanicus Caesar and Drusus Caesar, respectively. These two are associated in an unclear way with two local goddesses, for the epigraph refers to them as the "Victory of Germanicus Caesar" and the "Aphrodite of Drusus Caesar."[6] The sixth day was in honor of Flamininus. Finally, the seventh day was devoted to the "memory" (*mnēmē*) of Eurycles, and the eighth to the "honor" (*timē*) of Laco.[7]

Either on the first day of the festival or on each of the eight days, Gythium's civic leaders and citizens—both male and female, young and old—dressed in white and other sacred garb and joined a *pompē* that began at the city's temple of the healing god Aesculapius and his consort, the divine personification of Health or Well-being. Thence, the cortege winded its way to Gythium's imperial temple, which the sacred law calls the *Kaisarēon* (*sic*) after Caesar Augustus, where certain civic officials sacrificed a bull "on behalf of the well-being of the rulers, the gods, and their continual eternal governance."[8] In the context of the epigraph, the magistrates directed this offering to the city's traditional gods for the benefit of the five

---

4. For a history of Gaius Julius Eurycles and Gaius Julius Laco, see G. W. Bowersock, "Eurycles of Sparta," *JRS* 51 (1961): 112–18. The reader would do well to remember Laco because, as we shall see, he held public offices in Corinth and the province of Achaia, including ones devoted to imperial divine honors.

5. The inscription calls these games thymelic, which typically included drama, music, poetry, dance, and other vocal performances. For more on thymelic ἀγῶνες, see Angelos Chaniotis, "Festivals and Contests in the Greek World," *Thesaurus Cultus et Rituum Antiquorum* (*ThesCRA*) *VII: Festivals and Contests*, ed. Antoine Hermary (Los Angeles: The J. Paul Getty Museum, 2011), 3–172, esp. 24–25.

6. Γερμανικοῦ Καίσαρος τῆς Ν[ί]κης . . . Δρούσου Καίσαρος τῆς Ἀφροδείτης ("Appendix 1: Inscriptions" §I.1, lines 10–11).

7. The sacred law distinguishes between the first six days of the festival and the last two. See "Appendix 1: Inscriptions" §I.1.

8. ὑπὲρ τῆς τῶν ἡγεμόνων καὶ θεῶν σωτηρίας καὶ ἀϊδίου τῆς ἡγεμονίας αὐτῶν διαμονῆς ("Appendix 1: Inscriptions" §I.1, line 29).

Julio-Claudians in question, whom the text calls "rulers" (*hēgemones*) and appears to hail as "gods" (*theoi*).[9] Once this sacrifice was completed, the procession moved to Gythium's *agora* or "marketplace" where the city's magistrates and parties of citizens who were divided into groups for dining purposes offered another bull to the traditional gods for the exact same reason. The participants of the procession ended their journey at the city's theater to observe a set of theatrical games. Before the contests began, however, all Gythium's civic officials approached three painted images of *theos* Augustus, Julia Augusta, and Tiberius and offered incense to the traditional gods "on behalf of the well-being of the rulers."[10] The final portion of the *hieros nomos* notes the reason that Gythium decreed this festival, placed the decision in its public archives, and engraved the decree on the stone stele, which was discovered in 1923: "so that in public, under the open sky, and evident to all, this deposited law will demonstrate to all people the perpetual gratitude of the citizen body of the Gytheates for their rulers."[11]

For this city, the institution of this sacred law, the depositing of it in its archives, and the engraving of this decision on stone was not enough to show appreciation to the Julio-Claudians. Another gray stone stele, found at the same time as the *hieros nomos* and that was probably originally part of it, records a letter that Tiberius composed and sent to Gythium.[12] This missive was in response to an embassy from the city that had gone to Rome and informed the emperor and Livia of Gythium's imperial festival. In the letter, Tiberius thanks the city for its "piety" (*eusebeia*)—which in this context is duty, reverence, and divine honor—toward Augustus and the *timē* toward Livia and himself. The emperor then praises Gyth-

9. Given that the Καισάρηον existed at the time of the sacred law's passing (AD 15), it must have been built during Augustus's reign (31 BC–AD 14). The epigraph calls Augustus θεός four times. Livia is not named one explicitly in the ἱερὸς νόμος, but it equates her with the Τύχη of Gythium and Laconian cities. Another inscription from Gythium indicates that the city dedicated an object to Livia as θεὰ Τύχη (see "Appendix 1: Inscriptions" §I.2) and after her divinization in Rome (AD 42); a third epigraph from Gythium calls her Σεβαστὴ θεά (*IG* 5.1.1208 = PH31624). As noted, Germanicus and Drusus are associated in an unclear way with Victory and Aphrodite. The only Julio-Claudian who was not associated directly and explicitly with a god is Tiberius. The closest the sacred law comes to calling Tiberius a god are vague references to "the rulers and the gods," which probably include Tiberius. It may be that the original ἱερὸς νόμος included references to Tiberius as divine, but when he declined such honors (see "Appendix 1: Inscriptions" §I.3), Gythium edited its decision before engraving it on stone.

10. ὑπὲρ τῆς τῶν ἡγεμόνων σωτηρία[ς] ("Appendix 1: Inscriptions" §I.1, line 6).

11. ἵνα καὶ ἐν δημοσίωι καὶ ἐν ὑπαίθρῳ καὶ πᾶσιν ἐν φανερῷ κείμενος ὁ νόμος [διηνε]κῆ τὴν τοῦ δήμου τοῦ Γυθεατῶν εὐχαριστίαν εἰς τοὺς ἡγεμόνας ("Appendix 1: Inscriptions" §I.1, lines 38–39).

12. "Appendix 1: Inscriptions" §I.3.

ium for its *eusebeia* for Augustus because "the greatness of his benefactions for all the world" deserves "honors fitting for the gods."[13] However, Tiberius declines such honors for himself, asks the city to provide him honors appropriate for humans, and informs Gythium that it will be hearing from his mother about the honors that the city had voted her. Despite Tiberius's protestation, Gythium did not heed his request but celebrated the festival in AD 15 and even continued celebrating it after the emperor's death.[14] Moreover, the city engraved the *hieros nomos* and the emperor's letter declining the very honors it had voted for him in the sacred law on the same stone stele that Gythium set up probably in its theater, near where the workers discovered both epigraphs in 1923.

About nine hundred miles west of Gythium in the city of Rome, the Roman Senate met a few months before Gythium passed its *hieros nomos* to debate how best to honor the recently deceased Augustus for the benefactions, including peace and prosperity, that his long reign had brought Rome and her empire.[15] After some deliberation, on September 17, AD 14 it decreed that Augustus had been numbered among the Roman gods. Thus, the senate granted him a new title, the Latin term *divus*, which is an epithet acknowledging that the deceased was a human who had been made a divinity of the Roman state; a new temple with a cultic image inside it and altar in front of it; and priests to offer the deceased emperor regular sacrifices on behalf of the Roman Senate and people.[16] These honors were put into effect immediately and Tiberius and Livia began to construct the temple, which was not completed until early in the reign of Caligula (AD 37–41). When the temple was finished, Caligula presided over its consecration on August 30, AD 37. To commemorate the event, Rome minted a coin series depicting the scene (see fig. I.1).[17]

The reverse or tails side of the coin pictures *Divus* Augustus's temple garlanded for the occasion. Caligula stands in front of it in a Roman toga, part of which is

13. τῶι μεγέθει τῶν τοῦ ἐμοῦ πατρὸς εἰς ἅπαντα τὸν κόσμον εὐεργεσιῶν τὰς θεοῖς πρεσπούσας τιμάς ("Appendix 1: Inscriptions" §I.3, lines 18–20).

14. An inscription from Gythium dating to AD 42 notes that the festival has been shortened to three days. See Kaja Harter-Uibopuu, "Trust Fund of Phaenia Aromation (IG 5.1 1208) and Imperial Gytheion," *Studia Humaniora Tartuensia* 5 (2004): 1–17.

15. For Augustus's summary of his munificent deeds, see the *Res gestae divi Augusti*, an inscription that the emperor composed and had inscribed on his mausoleum in Rome, which also has been found engraved on monuments in Asia Minor. See Alison E. Cooley, *Res gestae divi Augusti: Text, Translation, and Commentary* (Cambridge: Cambridge University Press, 2009), 1–55. For a reconstruction of Tiberius's funeral speech highlighting Augustus's beneficent rule, see Dio Cassius, *Roman History* 56.35.1–56.41.9.

16. Dio Cassius, *Roman History* 56.46.1–4.

17. Dio Cassius, *Roman History* 59.7.1–2.

Fig. I.1 Coin, minted in Rome during Caligula's reign (AD 37–41), depicting the emperor presiding over the consecration of *Divus* Augustus's temple in the same city | *Courtesy of Yale University Art Gallery*

pulled atop the back and top of his head in a posture known in Latin as *capite velato*.[18] The emperor holds a shallow bowl known as a *patera* in his left hand whence he pours a libation of wine presumably to *Divus* Augustus. This coin depicts two other figures standing behind Caligula. The one on the left is a special slave known in Latin as a *victimarius*. This was the individual who was actually responsible for slaughtering and carving up the sacrificial victim. Due to the bloody nature of his work, a *victimarius* tended to be naked from the waist up, which is how the coin in question pictures him. In addition, he holds the bull about to be sacrificed, once again, presumably to *Divus* Augustus. The figure to Caligula's right is unknown, but he may be a priest of the divinized emperor.

Gythium's sacred law and the divinization of Augustus in Rome are examples of two different imperial cults, what I prefer to call grants of imperial divine honors, associated with Augustus. These two historical episodes highlight one of this book's main goals: to demonstrate the specific, historical nature of grants of imperial divine honors and thus the necessity of approaching such honors contextually. For my purposes, I will demonstrate this goal as it relates to imperial divine honors in the three cities of mainland Greece in which the apostle Paul established nascent Christianity and to which he composed letters, Philippi, Thessalonica, and Corinth. I have chosen the examples of Gythium's *hieros nomos* and *Divus* Augustus's divinization in Rome because they are excellent contrasting

18. The covering of the back and top of the head by a Roman was part of a sacrificial method that the Romans called "the Roman rite." This differed from "the Greek rite" in which a Roman did not cover his or her head. See Valerie Warrior, *Roman Religion* (Cambridge: Cambridge University Press, 2006), 21–22.

examples of the two main types of imperial divine honors that Paul and the early Christians in these cities encountered: Greek civic and Roman imperial divine honors. By "Greek civic," I mean the type of imperial divine honors that occurred in Greek communities of mainland Greece like Gythium and, for our purposes, Thessalonica.[19] By "Roman," I do not mean the Roman Empire in general but the official cults of Julio-Claudians that were part of the public life of the city of Rome and, of import for us, the Roman colonies of Corinth and Philippi. Even though these cities were located in mainland Greece and distant from the city on the Tiber River, they were founded to be centers of Roman thought, ideology, and culture. To this end, Gythium's sacred law and the consecration of *Divus* Augustus in Rome allow us to compare Roman and Greek civic imperial divine honors detailing how each type resembles and, equally as important, differs from the other.

Broadly speaking, Gythium's imperial festival and *Divus* Augustus's consecration in Rome have a similar origin and thus nature: they are public in both the ancient and modern senses of the term. In the ancient sense of "public," these two grants of imperial divine honors stem from the legislative processes of the political bodies of Gythium and Rome. These public entities oversaw and administered daily life in the two respective cities and, in the case of Rome, the empire that it controlled.[20] This means that Roman and Greek civic imperial divine honors, like all cults in the Roman Empire, were intertwined with the public lives of Greco-Roman communities and had political, economic, social, and religious components that one cannot neatly separate. This fact will become patently clear in the following pages, as we shall see that the ruling bodies of Philippi, Thessalonica, and Corinth determined to which Julio-Claudians to grant public divine honors, and local aristocrats who sat or would later sit on these bodies politic oversaw imperial sacrifices in these cities. Another way that Gythium's imperial festival and *Divus* Augustus's divine honors in Rome were "public" in the ancient definition of the term is that the two cities paid for and offered sacrifices connected to them on behalf of the citizens of these respective communities. This is clearest in that Gythium's sacred law stipulates a strict accounting of public funds used for the imperial festivities, including the provision that any citizen could bring charges of malfeasance against the magistrate who oversaw the festival. Similarly, Roman

---

19. Greek civic imperial divine honors occurred in cities that were founded as Greek city-states and remained such in the Roman period.

20. Provincial imperial divine honors, which I introduce in the next chapter, also stem from the legislative processes of provincial administration, which included members of the leading cities of the province or, in the case of Achaia, smaller clusters of cities. The exceptions to the public nature of imperial divine honors are ones that private individuals bestowed on Julio-Claudian family members (see pp. 45–49).

public funds supported *Divus* Augustus's temple, and even the coin depicting its inauguration has the backing of the Roman Senate, for it bears the Latin abbreviation *S C*, which means "by senatorial decree" (*senatus consulto*) and that the senate stands behind and backs the coin's monetary value (see fig. I.1).

Gythium's imperial festival and Rome's temple of *Divus* Augustus were "public" in the modern sense of the term in that Gythium's festivities and Caligula's sacrifices to *Divus* Augustus occurred amid these respective cities in full view of anyone who wished to see. The procession detailed in Gythium's sacred law began at the city's temple of Aesculapius and Health/Well-being, made its next stop at Gythium's imperial temple, moved to the most public place in the city, the *agora*, and ended at Gythium's theater where its citizens had gathered to watch theatrical competitions. Archaeologists have yet to locate *Divus* Augustus's temple in Rome, but it was probably in the city's ancient forum, which, like the Greek *agora*, was the political, social, and religious heart of the so-called eternal city.[21] The scene of Caligula sacrificing before this temple on the coin probably depicts the end result of a sacred procession similar to the one in Gythium, though in the Roman custom, that had winded its way through ancient Rome (see fig. I.1).[22]

The above grants of imperial divine honors in Gythium and in Rome share the same motivation for their establishment: gratitude for benefaction. The leaders of Gythium stated their purpose in the passing, archiving, and inscribing of their sacred law on stone: to demonstrate "to all humans" (*pasin anthrōpois*) the citizen body's "perpetual gratitude" (*diēnekē eucharistian*) for the rule of the five Julio-Claudians whom the city honored. One of the contributing factors behind the Roman Senate's decision to divinize Augustus was his benevolent rule. According to the third-century AD Roman historian Dio Cassius, various divine honors for emperors in Rome "are given to those who rule rightly after they have ceased (to live)."[23] Thus, divinization in Rome was neither dynastic nor mandatory. In fact, the senate divinized only half the Julio-Claudian emperors, Julius Caesar,

21. Filippo Coarelli, *Rome and Environs: An Archaeological Guide*, trans. James J. Clauss and Daniel P. Harmon (Berkeley: University of California Press, 2008), 74, suggests that *Divus* Augustus's temple is south of the Julian Basilica in Rome's forum in an unexcavated area.

22. I am not claiming that all imperial divine honors were public in nature. Divine honors were given to Julio-Claudians on the private level in neighborhoods of ancient Roman cities and in homes of ancient Romans and Greeks (see pp. 43–44).

23. μεταλλάξασι . . . τοῖς ὀρθῶς αὐταρχήσασιν ἄλλαι τε ἰσόθεοι τιμαὶ δίδονται (Dio Cassius, *Roman History* 51.20.7–8). See Ittai Gradel's *Emperor Worship and Roman Religion* (Oxford: Clarendon, 2002), 109–16, a discussion where he argues convincingly that Dio has in mind official state-sponsored imperial divine honors in Rome and Italy, for there is an abundance of evidence for private imperial divine honors in Rome and municipal imperial divine honors in Italy to living Julio-Claudians.

Augustus, and Claudius. As we shall see, when the context of specific grants of divine honors in Philippi, Thessalonica, and Corinth is known, it coheres to this portrait. Thessalonica honored divinely mostly living Julio-Claudians to show appreciation for munificence, while Philippi and Corinth waited until the deaths of Julio-Claudians and tended to follow the Roman Senate's determination of whether their reign benefited the empire before bestowing divine honors on any Julio-Claudian, though there are exceptions in both colonies.

Gythium's imperial festival and *Divus* Augustus's divinization in Rome resemble each other in that they mirrored honors that the inhabitants of these cities gave to their gods: temples, sacred images, altars, festivals, processions, priests/ priestesses, and sacrifices. The inscription from Gythium describes the institution of the imperial festival as a *hieros nomos*, *hieros* being a term that Greeks often used to describe items associated with and dedicated to the gods.[24] This sacred law prescribes the eight-day festival with a *pompē*, *agōnes*, and sacrifices offered to the gods on behalf of certain Julio-Claudians. One of the procession's stopping points was Gythium's imperial temple, the *Kaisarēon*, which must have been built during Augustus's reign (31 BC–AD 14). Inside this building, there was probably a cultic image of Augustus, and given that Gythium provided divine honors for Tiberius, Livia, Germanicus, and Drusus, the city may have erected cultic statues of some or all of them in the *Kaisarēon*, too.[25] In front of this temple, there was an altar, for when the procession reached this location, certain magistrates were to sacrifice a bull to the gods on behalf of the Julio-Claudians. Even though he appears to have had no part in the imperial festival, the sacred law indicates that there was a priest of *theos* Augustus Caesar in Gythium.[26] The scene on the reverse of the Roman coin in question depicts Caligula offering a libation of wine as he is poised to sacrifice a bull on *Divus* Augustus's altar in front of his temple presumably to the divinized emperor. As noted, these cultic activities probably occurred at the end of a sacrificial procession resembling but not identical to the one detailed in Gythium's sacred law.[27] The *victimarius* depicted on the coin who is about to slaughter the bull for Caligula to offer to *Divus* Augustus is the same cultic official who aided priests in their blood sacrifices to Roman gods (see fig. I.1). Moreover, this entire ritual was conducted under the eye of *Divus* Augustus as his

24. LSJ 822; BDAG 470.

25. It was common for Greco-Roman cities to have collections of cultic images of multiple Julio-Claudians in the same temple or shrine. See my discussion of Corinth's Julian Basilica, where a total of twelve statues of Julio-Claudians were set up (see pp. 207–9).

26. "Appendix 1: Inscriptions" §I.1, lines 33–34.

27. Roman sacrificial rituals tended to occur at the end of processions. See Warrior, *Roman Religion*, 21–24.

Fig. I.2 Coin, minted in Rome during the reign of Antoninus Pius (AD 138–161), depicting *Divus Augustus's* cultic image in his temple in the same city | *Courtesy of Yale University Art Gallery*

cultic statue, seated and in the guise of Jupiter, gazed out from inside the temple to oversee sacrifices at his altar (see fig. I.2).

On the other hand, there are notable differences between Gythium's imperial festival and Augustus's divinization in Rome. The state of the Julio-Claudians to whom these two cities provided divine honors differs. Gythium's sacred law prescribes an imperial festival for mostly living Julio-Claudians: Tiberius, Livia, Germanicus, and Drusus. Even though the city included the deceased Augustus in the festival, it had already established divine honors for him while he was alive, for the sacred law attests to the existence of a priest and temple dedicated to the emperor.[28] The reason that Gythium provided such honors to these living Julio-Claudians is to show its gratitude for their benefaction, which, as noted, is found in the rationale for the sacred law's publication, archiving, and engraving on the stone stele. The city, however, did not keep its decision to itself. Rather, Gythium sent an embassy to Tiberius and Livia informing them of its *hieros nomos*. Such a move was an attempt on the city's part to secure the goodwill of these two Julio-Claudians and to court future beneficence from them.[29] Therefore, divine honors for Julio-Claudians in Greek communities tended to function as a quid pro quo.

28. "Appendix 1: Inscriptions" §I.1, lines 28, 33–34. Outside official state-sponsored imperial divine honors in Rome, Romans and Italians granted such honors to living Julio-Claudians, too. See the lists of ancient sources in Gradel, *Emperor Worship*, 375–79.

29. It is interesting to note that the next historical reference to this festival indicates that it was for only three days, which suggests that it no longer included the two Julio-Claudians who had died, Germanicus and Drusus in AD 19 and AD 23, respectively. See Harter-Uibopuu, "Trust Fund," 1–17.

Divus Augustus's temple in Rome was dedicated to him only after his death and divinization by the Roman Senate, which included the official title *divus*. While this epithet meant that the deceased Augustus was divine, that he had ascended to heaven, and that he was a Roman divinity deserving of sacrifices, it did not mean that he was equal to the gods. To the contrary, there appears to have been a distinction in official Roman thought between a *divus* and a *deus* or "god" in Latin. In the words of an ancient Roman commentator on Virgil's *Aeneid*, the Roman Senate make *divi* (the Latin plural of *divus*) because *divi* are humans who die, while *dei* (the Latin plural for *deus*) are immortal.[30] This distinction is evident in Roman public sacrifice, for the only known ancient documents recording sacrifices that were consistently made in Rome on behalf of the city, the *Acts of the Arval Brothers*, attest that offerings were made to the *dei* first and *divi* second, in that order.[31] The different state of Julio-Claudians on whom Greco-Roman communities bestowed divine honors, whether they were living or dead, will be evident in the discussions of these honors in Philippi, Thessalonica, and Corinth. Philippi and Corinth granted postmortem divine honors exclusively to *divi* or deceased Julio-Claudians whom the Roman Senate did not divinize, while Thessalonica established such honors mostly for living Julio-Claudians.

Some aspects of Gythium's imperial festival and Rome's divinization of Augustus differ from each other because both cities granted divine honors to Julio-Claudians according to local customs. The civic offices mentioned in Gythium's sacred law—*archontes, synedroi, agoranomos, ephoroi, stratēgos*, and members of the common mess (*phideitia*)—were traditional to the city and that region of mainland Greece, which had long been in Sparta's sphere of influence.[32] Moreover, the leaders of Gythium mapped divine honors for Julio-Claudians onto the public, that is, the social, political, and religious, fabric of their city. The *hieros nomos* indicates that the imperial festival began at Aesculapius's temple, the god of health and well-being, probably because of the type of offering made during the festival: a bull sacrificed "on behalf of [the Julio-Claudians'] well-being" (*hyper sōtērias*). Thus, a connection existed between Aesculapius and the rationale for sacrificing, the welfare of the Julio-Claudians. The imperial procession ended in Gythium's theater, the area over which Dionysus held sway, and included theat-

---

30. Maurus Servius Honoratus, *Servii grammatici qui ferunter in Vergilii carmina commentarii*, ed. Georgius Thilo and Hermannus Hagen (Leipzig: Teubner, 1881), 5.45, *deos perpetuos dicamus, divos ex hominibus factos*.

31. For a discussion of the *Acts of the Arval Brothers*, see p. 42.

32. All these were under the oversight of a ἡγεμών in charge of the "League of the Free Laconians," which Augustus instituted (Pausanias, *Description of Greece* 3.21.6–9). At the time of the sacred law's passing, Laco was the ἡγεμών.

rical performances of some kind. The sacred law associates three Julio-Claudians with three of Gythium's gods: Germanicus with Victory, Drusus with Aphrodite, and Livia is identified as Gythium's *Tychē*. Finally, Gythium's *hieros nomos* incorporated divine honors for Julio-Claudians into an already existing framework. The inscription notes that after the imperial festival was over, the city was to celebrate "the games for the goddess" (*tous agōnas apo tēs theou*), which appears to be a reference to a traditional, though unnamed, goddess of Gythium. Moreover, the city probably had granted divine honors for Flamininus, after he provided Gythium with limited freedom in 196 BC, and, at the very least, Eurycles, who died between 7 and 2 BC.[33] Thus, the city created an imperial festival and fused it with already existing grants of divine honors for other civic benefactors, all of which occurred before games for a traditional goddess.

Divus Augustus's postmortem divine honors in Rome reflect the character and custom of the city of Rome itself, which had its own unique traditions. The senate patterned Augustus's divinization after Julius Caesar's in 42 BC, which made him *Divus* Julius, and one of Rome's founders, Romulus, who became Quirinus. According to Roman tradition, Romulus, along with his brother Remus, founded Rome. The former ruled the city until his mysterious disappearance, which some legends interpreted as his ascension into heaven as the new Roman god Quirinus.[34] The cultic officials on the coin depicting *Divus* Augustus's temple are traditional Roman ones. As noted, the *victimarius* was the person responsible for slaughtering and carving up the sacrificial animal. Caligula's clothing, the toga, is the traditional dress of a Roman, and the way he wears it, *capite velato*, is a unique Roman way of sacrificing.

Finally, while Gythium's sacred law and the coin picturing the consecration of *Divus* Augustus's temple in Rome indicate that bulls were offered in association with Julio-Claudians, the objects to whom they were directed differed. In Gythium, the civic magistrates were to sacrifice bulls only to the gods *hyper* or

---

33. Bowersock, "Eurycles of Sparta," 114, notes that the sacred law "records an already flourishing benefactor cult of Eurycles."

34. The second-century AD historian Appian, *Civil Wars* 2.148, acknowledges that the divinization of Julius Caesar in Rome set a precedent that Rome continued to follow even into his own day: emperors who did not rule like tyrants were divinized after their deaths. For a discussion of the Roman traditions on which the divinization of emperors was based, see Simon Price, "From Noble Funerals to Divine Cults: The Consecration of the Roman Emperor," in *Rituals of Royalty: Power and Ceremonial in Traditional Societies*, ed. David Cannadine and Simon Price (Cambridge: Cambridge University Press, 1987), 56–105. For more on Quirinus and Romulus, see Herbert Jennings Rose and John Scheid, "Quirinus," *OCD* 1253; Herbert Jennings Rose and John Scheid, "Romulus, Remus," *OCD* 1296–97.

"on behalf of" Augustus, Tiberius, Livia, Germanicus, and Drusus, despite the fact that the city's sacred law outrightly calls Augustus a *theos*, that the city had an imperial temple dedicated to him, and that the *hieros nomos* intimates that the other Julio-Claudians are divine, too.[35] It seems that for the leaders of the city, the Julio-Claudians occupied a liminal space between gods and humans. They were humans and thus subject to disease and death. Hence, the need to sacrifice to the deities associated with health and well-being on their behalf. However, the Julio-Claudians possessed power and authority resembling that of the Olympians, which the former could use to benefit the empire in general and Gythium in particular. To ensure that they retained this ability, Gythium's citizen body attempted to propitiate their gods.[36] Nevertheless, it would be a mistake to assume that this complex relationship between Greek gods and Julio-Claudians was universal in the Greek East, for often Greeks sacrificed to, not on behalf of, Julio-Claudians, which, as we shall see, was probably the case in Thessalonica.[37]

Unlike the liminal place of Julio-Claudians in Gythium, the status of *Divus* Augustus in Rome was more straightforward. The Roman Senate had debated, voted, decreed, and thus declared that he had been numbered among the gods and that he was a *divus*, an official divinity of the state. From that point on, priests offered state-sponsored sacrifices to, not on behalf of, *Divus* Augustus. For this reason, the coin depicting the consecration of *Divus* Augustus's temple in Rome probably pictures Caligula sacrificing to, not on behalf of, the deceased and divinized emperor (see fig. I.1).[38] As we shall see, Philippi and Corinth followed Rome in this regard, making similar sacrifices most often to Julio-Claudian *divi*.

In sum, Gythium's imperial festival and Rome's divinization of Augustus not only introduce Greek civic and Roman divine honors for Julio-Claudians but also illustrate their complexity. These two cases demonstrate that while similarities existed between grants of such honors, there was no uniform, centrally controlled

35. The complexity of treating Julio-Claudians like gods, even calling them such, yet sacrificing to the gods on their behalf is not unique to Gythium. See Price, *Rituals and Power*, 227–33; however, he incorrectly argues that "most imperial sacrifices" were offered in this manner.

36. Price, *Rituals and Power*, 233, concludes, "Standing at the apex of the hierarchy of the Roman empire the emperor offered the hope of order and stability and was assimilated to the traditional Olympian deities. But he also needed the divine protection which came from sacrifices made to the gods on his behalf. The emperor stood at the focal point between human and divine." This observation applies equally to Greeks living in mainland Greece.

37. See the critique of Price's conclusion that sacrifices were mostly offered to the gods on behalf of emperors, by Steven J. Friesen, *Twice Neokoros: Ephesus, Asia and the Cult of the Flavian Imperial Family*, RGRW 116 (Leiden: Brill, 1993), 142–68, esp. 146–52.

38. This object of sacrifice is confirmed by the records of sacrifices of the Arval Brothers (see p. 42).

"imperial cult" in the Roman Empire, much less one in which provincials were required to participate.[39] Rather, like the cults of the gods, individuals, groups, cities, and provinces worshiped the Julio-Claudians according to their local customs.[40] Because of this situation, one must approach imperial divine honors in the same manner that one should approach Paul's letters, in light of their specific occasions and historical and theological contexts. In short, if one wishes to understand imperial divine honors in Philippi, Thessalonica, and Corinth, one must do the hard work of delving into the particulars of such honors in these cities and building contextualized profiles of them. This goal is one that will encompass the bulk of this book.[41]

Imperial Divine Honors, Paul, and His Churches in Greece

Interpreting imperial divine honors like Paul's letters brings me to this book's second and final goal: to use these contextual profiles of imperial divine honors in Philippi, Thessalonica, and Corinth to reconstruct what relationship, if any, Paul and the earliest Christians in these cities had with the honors in question. The need for such an approach is evident from a survey of scholarship on this topic. New Testament scholars often use divine honors for Julio-Claudians to interpret various passages and to reconstruct the social, political, and religious backgrounds of 1–2 Thessalonians, Philippians, and mostly 1 Corinthians. However, many interpreters do so inappropriately and oftentimes incorrectly. Frequently, they wrongly assume the presence of a uniform centrally controlled Julio-Claudian "imperial cult" in the Roman Empire, and some scholars even contend that emperors desired, even demanded, their subjects sacrifice to them.

39. In the words of Mary Beard, John North, and Simon Price, *Religions of Rome* (Cambridge: Cambridge University Press, 1998), 1:318, "There was no such thing as *'the* imperial cult.'"

40. Elias J. Bickerman, "*Consecratio*," in *Le culte des souverains dans l'Empire romain*, ed. Willem den Boer (Geneva: Fondation Hardt, 1973), 9, notes, "Each city, each province, each group worshiped this or that sovereign according to its own discretion and ritual." Greg Woolf and Miguel John Versluys, "Empire as a Field of Religious Actions," in *Religion in the Roman Empire*, ed. Jörg Rüpke and Greg Woolf, Die Religionen der Menschheit (Stuttgart: Kohlhammer, 2021), 26, conclude, "The collective rituals in which individuals [in the Roman Empire] participated were almost always conducted at the local scale, whether it was the worship of the gods . . . ; the worship of Roman emperors, living and dead; and eventually rituals performed at the tombs of Christian martyrs."

41. One would not read the historical and theological context of 1 Thessalonians into Galatians, for example, or vice versa. In the same way, one cannot interpret imperial divine honors in a generalized manner.

One major consequence of this incorrect presumption is that many New Testament scholars fail to consider the diversity of grants of divine honors for Julio-Claudians and that they all have specific contexts, as is evident in the two examples from Gythium and Rome. To this end, interpreters tend to generalize evidence for these honors, taking one grant of them for one Julio-Claudian or even one source attesting to such honors from one city and using it as the canon by which to judge all others. In the process, scholars often make broad conjectures about imperial divine honors. One of the commonest is that "the imperial cult" was the fastest-growing religion in the Roman Empire, or that all pagans in Rome's sphere of influence believed the reigning emperor was a god. Some New Testament scholars attempt a degree of contextualization of the honors in question most often by noting that grants of them were diverse. This contextualization, however, is often limited to an emperor-by-emperor presentation of select evidence "demonstrating" that each emperor received divine honors, which in their minds justifies a generalized use of the data in question as an interpretive lens to read Paul's letters. While more appropriate, this approach generalizes too much, because it still assumes that if one city offered divine honors to one Julio-Claudian, then all cities did. Finally, because of this flawed approach to imperial divine honors, some scholars conclude that Paul, his converts, or both singled out and opposed these honors sometimes clandestinely, at other times openly. One prominent New Testament interpreter has coined the saying that has become axiomatic not only in the academy but also in today's church, "Jesus is Lord; Caesar is not." The underlying assumption is that early Christianity resisted and opposed an empire that and an emperor who promoted and demanded its and his subjects worship the reigning monarch.

As we shall see, the actual evidence for imperial divine honors in Philippi, Thessalonica, and Corinth—inscriptions, coins, statues, archaeological finds, and in a few cases literary testimony—paints a different, more complex picture than the one just described. The data that I have gathered and present in the following chapters demonstrate the contextual nature of such honors in these cities and that Philippi, Thessalonica, and Corinth established divine honors in keeping with their own unique traditions. Moreover, the evidence in question shows that local leaders of these cities made the conscious decision to interweave divine honors for Julio-Claudians into the public fabric of their communities in ways that made them inseparable from the spheres that today we would call political, religious, economic, and social. For this reason, one cannot isolate such honors, much less claim that imperial divine honors are the main opponent for early Christianity in Philippi, Thessalonica, and Corinth. As will be evident, while these honors were well known to Paul and his converts in those cities, their relationship to early

Christianity varied from city to city because each community and each group of Christians in these cities were unique.

OUTLINE

For this book's remainder, I reconstruct imperial divine honors in mid-first-century AD Philippi, Thessalonica, and Corinth—thus divine honors associated with the Julio-Claudians—in the order in which the apostle Paul first established Christianity in these cities, on what is known as his second missionary journey (Acts 15:36–18:22: Philippi, Thessalonica, and Corinth). Then, I unpack my theses about their relationship to earliest Christianity in those cities as exemplified by the letters that Paul composed to the churches in those cities, Philippians, 1–2 Thessalonians, and 1–2 Corinthians, supplemented by information culled from Acts of the Apostles. Before I can accomplish this task, I must introduce imperial divine honors and delve deeper into the contextual approach that I advocate. Thus, chapter 1 defines the honors in question, discuss where one should look to find them, survey how New Testament scholarship has tended to interpret imperial divine honors, and present a more appropriate method of approaching them. My second chapter focuses on imperial divine honors in Philippi and their relationship to earliest Christianity in the Roman colony. In this chapter, I present all the available evidence to date for divine honors for Julio-Claudians in the city, demonstrating which Julio-Claudians were given such honors, their Roman character, and their interconnection with Philippi's public life. Because of this last point, the honors in question are not the sole cause of the suffering that the letter to the Philippians indicates some Philippian Christians were experiencing from their pagan counterparts (Phil 1:27–30). Rather, the pagan Philippians mistreated Christians in the colony because they interpreted Christianity as an un-Roman custom that advocated atheism and threatened the safety and security of their city and the empire that the mother city's gods and Julio-Claudian *divi* ensured.

In the third chapter, I reconstruct divine honors for Julio-Claudians in Thessalonica and their relationship to the first Christians there. I argue that these honors were Greek civic in character but influenced by the Roman custom of postmortem divinization. Thus, while the Thessalonians established divine honors for living Julio-Claudians, they tended to wait until these individuals passed before they hailed them as gods. Moreover, the leaders of Thessalonica embedded the honors in question into the public life of their city. It is evident from the Thessalonian correspondence that Christians in the city were suffering mistreatment, but imperial divine honors were not the sole cause of their misfortune. Rather, because the pagan Thessalonians interpreted Christianity as calling for the abandonment of the city's gods and their divinely sponsored rulers, the Julio-Claudians, for the God of Israel and his divine vice-regent, Jesus the Messiah, Christians threatened Thessalonica's coveted status of a "free city," which was a gift with economic, political, and social benefits that the Julio-Claudians had bestowed on the city and just as easily could take away.

The fourth chapter focuses on divine honors for Julio-Claudians in Corinth and their relationship with nascent Christianity in that Roman colony. In the process, I demonstrate the Roman character of these divine honors and their interwovenness into the city's public life. Unlike at Philippi and Thessalonica, there is no evidence that divine honors for Julio-Claudians or, for that matter, traditional Corinthian cults caused any adversity for early Christians, even though the Corinthian correspondence indicates that Christians and pagans in the city interacted frequently, that pagans entered at will into Christian assemblies, and that Corinthian believers were married to nonbelievers. This does not mean, however, that divine honors for Julio-Claudians did not cause problems for the nascent Corinthian church. The participation of some Corinthian Christians in pagan rituals, which were stumbling blocks to other Corinthian Christians, probably included but were not limited to the honors in question.

In my conclusion, I summarize the findings of these chapters and discuss how they allow us to construct a more complex understanding of the association among Paul, his converts, and divine honors for Julio-Claudians as well as how my approach to such honors relates to Paul's positive comments about the Roman Empire in Rom 13:1–7. Finally, I provide two appendixes. The first contains fresh translations of the main inscriptions from Philippi, Thessalonica, and Corinth that I discuss throughout this book. I have labeled these sources after the chapter in which they are found and the sequence in which they appear in said chapters. Thus, I.1 stands for the first inscription in the introduction, 3.3 the third epigraph of the third chapter, and so on. The second appendix is a hypothetical reconstruction of the cultic imperial calendars of Philippi and Corinth that I have reconstructed from two Roman sources, an inscription and a papyrus document, that attest to divine honors that Romans provided for Julio-Claudians. Given that we do not possess the cultic calendar of either of these cities (or the full calendar of any ancient city!), I must stress that this appendix is fragmentary and approaches nothing like completeness. The purpose of these appendixes is to provide the reader easy access to the evidence I have collected, while allowing for smoother prose with less interruptions.

SOURCES

In this introduction's final portion, I must say a few words about the biblical and nonbiblical sources that I use. The reader will notice that references to pagan literary sources in this book are not as frequent as in other books that reconstruct various aspects of the Greco-Roman world. This is not a value judgment upon Greco-Roman literary sources but reflects the fact that most (by no means all) literary references to imperial divine honors relate to those offered in the city of Rome. The reason is that our surviving ancient historians and biographers were most concerned with events that changed the course of history of the Mediterranean world. Given that Rome was the superpower in this world from the second century BC onward and that decisions made in that city affected hundreds of other cities and millions of people, these authors tended to focus on that city, which means divine honors for Julio-Claudians there. These writers were less concerned with events in other places in the empire, such as Philippi, Thessalonica, and Corinth.[42] To reconstruct imperial divine honors in these cities, we must turn to sources with which many students of the New Testament are unfamiliar: archaeology (including statues), inscriptions, and coins. Thus, it is worthwhile to provide definitions of these sources and concise introductions to them with an eye to Philippi, Thessalonica, and Corinth.

Archaeology is the study of past material remains for the purpose of preserving them for the future and using these sources to reconstruct antiquity.[43] To achieve this goal, archaeologists dig up the past in controlled scientific excavations, documenting what they find and collecting these artifacts for further study. We are fortunate that extensive systematic excavations have occurred in Philippi and Corinth. Some excavations have occurred in Thessalonica, but they have been piecemeal, because the site has been inhabited since its founding in 316/315 BC and the modern city of Thessaloniki lies atop its Greco-Roman counterpart. Excavations in all these cities have turned up physical, concrete evidence of divine honors for Julio-Claudians in the form of inscriptions, temples, altars, and cultic statues of Julio-Claudians.

The ancient coins (the study of which is called numismatics) on which I focus in this book are mostly pieces of bronze that the local governments of Philippi,

42. Unless, of course, those events affected the history of Rome, such as the Battle of Philippi in 42 BC that left Octavian Caesar (later called Augustus) and Marc Antony rulers of most of the Roman Empire.

43. For a concise introduction to archaeology, see Kristian Kristiansen, "The Discipline of Archaeology," in *Oxford Handbook of Archaeology*, ed. Barry W. Cunliffe, Chris Gosden, and Rosemary A. Joyce (Oxford: Oxford University Press, 2009), 3–46.

Thessalonica, or Corinth issued. These coins had an ancient monetary value, and the inhabitants of these cities used them for buying and selling goods and services. Ancient coins, however, were not merely pieces of metal facilitating commerce and trade. Rather, the images and legends on them functioned as vehicles of propaganda advertising local cults, festivals, myths, and building projects.[44] Therefore, coins are indispensable for reconstructing imperial divine honors in Philippi, Thessalonica, and Corinth because they attest to the important place that the Julio-Claudians had in these cities, the titles by which their respective citizens hailed them, the monuments that Philippi, Thessalonica, and Corinth dedicated to the Julio-Claudians, and the sites in these cities at which imperial divine honors occurred. All translations of coin legends in this book are my own unless otherwise noted.

Inscriptions or epigraphs are messages most often engraved, incised, or scratched on durable materials, such as marble and limestone, that local governments, groups, and individuals set up, often attached to monuments or buildings. There are, however, exceptions to this definition, such as graffiti, which, while not necessarily etched on durable materials, are classified as inscriptions. This qualification notwithstanding, unlike most surviving ancient literature that scribes have copied and recopied throughout the centuries (sometimes making changes to texts!), inscriptions are direct, unaltered primary witnesses to the past. The inhabitants of the Greco-Roman world produced millions of inscriptions and somewhere between five hundred thousand and eight hundred thousand survive to this day, and more are discovered every year. Thus, with good reason, the world of the earliest Christians has been called "a civilization of epigraphy."[45] Two reasons that epigraphs are so important for imperial divine honors are that (1) they are contextual documents and (2) they are one of our main sources of evidence for such honors in Philippi, Thessalonica, and Corinth. These epigraphs attest to the actual titles by which Philippians, Thessalonians, and Corinthians acclaimed Julio-Claudians, the names of imperial priests and priestesses in these cities, and other important facets of imperial divine honors. As with coins, all translations of inscriptions in this book are mine unless otherwise noted.

Finally, I must address the early Christian sources that I use. I have chosen to reconstruct earliest Christianity in Philippi, Thessalonica, and Corinth from the

---

44. For a concise treatment of numismatics, see William E. Metcalf, "Numismatics," in *The Oxford Handbook of Roman Studies*, ed. Alessandro Barchiesi and Walter Scheidel (Oxford: Oxford University Press, 2010), 135–45. For examples of the benefits of numismatics in interpreting the New Testament, see Richard E. Oster, "Numismatic Windows into the Social World of Early Christianity: A Methodological Inquiry," *JBL* 101 (1982): 195–223.

45. D. Clint Burnett, *Studying the New Testament through Inscriptions: An Introduction* (Peabody, MA: Hendrickson, 2020), 11.

letters that Paul composed to the early Christian congregations in those cities. I hypothesize that Philippians consists of one letter that Paul composed with Timothy as coauthor (Phil 1:1) from an Ephesian imprisonment (Phil 1:7, 12–18) unrecorded in Acts of the Apostles, probably around AD 56/57. I consider 1 and 2 Thessalonians to be authentically Pauline with Silvanus and Timothy as co-authors (1 Thess 1:1; 2 Thess 1:1).[46] These missives were written six months apart around AD 50/51 from Corinth. I believe that 1 Corinthians was written from Ephesus (1 Cor 16:8) before Paul's probable Ephesian imprisonment in AD 56/57 with Sosthenes as coauthor (1 Cor 1:1). I contend that the bulk of 2 Corinthians (chapters 1–7, 10–13) consists of a letter that Paul composed with Timothy as co-author in AD 57. Paul probably dictated this epistle from Philippi after his release from his hypothetical Ephesian imprisonment. However, I am uncertain about whether 2 Corinthians consists of one, two (2 Cor 1–7, 10–13 and 2 Cor 8–9), or three (2 Cor 1–7, 10–13; 2 Cor 8; and 2 Cor 9) letters. To be forthright, I change my mind about this issue every time I read 2 Corinthians. In the end, this matters little for our purposes, and so any references to 2 Corinthians in this book will be to the canonical letter as we have it now. Concerning Acts of the Apostles, I consider Luke, the physician and traveling companion of Paul (Col 4:14; Phlm 24; 2 Tim 4:11), to be its author, and generally I hold to the historicity of Luke's narrative as it concerns Paul's itinerary and the founding of the churches in Philippi (Acts 16:11–40), Thessalonica (Acts 17:1–9), and Corinth (Acts 18:1–22).[47] As with coins and inscriptions in this book, all translations of early Christian texts are my own unless otherwise noted.

46. For an epigraphic and archaeological argument that lends credence to the authenticity of 2 Thessalonians, see D. Clint Burnett, "'Seated in God's Temple': Illuminating 2 Thess 2:4 in Light of Inscriptions and Archaeology Related to Imperial Divine Honors," *LTQ* 48 (2018): 69–94.

47. For a discussion of these introductory issues, see Raymond E. Brown, *An Introduction to the New Testament*, ABRL (New York: Doubleday, 1997), 225–332, 456–66, 483–501, 511–58, 590–98.

CHAPTER 1

Imperial Divine Honors

A s we saw in this book's introduction, imperial divine honors in the Roman Empire were diverse and in keeping with local customs. For us to interpret such honors properly, we must approach them as we approach Paul's letters, contextually. The main purpose of this chapter is to lay the groundwork for this method of interpreting imperial divine honors in general, which will serve our particular goal of reconstructing such honors in Philippi, Thessalonica, and Corinth so that we can adjudicate with precision what relationship, if any, these honors had with early Christianity in these cities. To this end, this chapter has four main goals. First, it defines imperial divine honors and explains my use of the phrase in question (see "Defining Imperial Divine Honors"). Second, this chapter discusses the sources for these honors, namely, inscriptions, coins, statues, and archaeological data (see "Finding Imperial Divine Honors"). Third, it addresses how most New Testament scholars approach imperial divine honors, which leads to their misrepresentation and misinterpretation. In place of this method, this chapter sets forth a more appropriate one for interpreting the honors in question, the contextual method, which considers the immediate context of these honors in Philippi, Thessalonica, and Corinth; the proper use of comparative material to fill out our fragmentary sources; the ways in which imperial divine honors were most often wedded to honors given to the gods; and how local aristocrats were responsible for mediating and promoting such honors to their cities (see "Approaching Imperial Divine Honors"). Finally, this chapter's conclusion summarizes my findings and sets the scene for the remainder of this book (see "Conclusion").

DEFINING IMPERIAL DIVINE HONORS

The first task in introducing imperial divine honors is to define them. This is an exercise that many New Testament scholars fail to undertake, which results in a lack of precision in discussions of the honors in question. At the outset, it is important to remind ourselves that Greco-Roman religion or, for reasons given below, what I prefer to call "traditional divine honors" in general, not just imperial divine honors in particular, differed markedly from modern forms of Christianity. The former was polytheistic, wedded to every aspect of life (politics, economics, society, family, etc.), predicated on correct observance of rituals, not focused on a book, and, for the most part, unconcerned with ethics.[1] In contrast, modern Christianity is monotheistic (Deut 6:4; Mark 12:29; 1 Cor 8:5–6), not as intertwined in politics (at least supposedly in Western democracies), predicated on belief (Rom 10:9), grounded in a book, the Bible, and very much concerned with ethics. In short, we might say that traditional ancient Greek and Roman religion was more concerned with orthopraxy or correct actions and rituals, while (ancient and) modern Christianity is more concerned with orthodoxy or correct beliefs.[2] What this means is that we cannot judge Greek and Roman religion, including imperial divine honors, by our own modern criteria of religiosity, as many New Testament interpreters have done in the past with some dismissing divine honors for Julio-Claudians as a debased form of ancient religion.[3]

With this warning in mind, imperial divine honors are cultic acts bestowed on certain Julio-Claudians that resembled in kind but differed in degree from those given to the Greek and Roman gods.[4] They consisted of any one or combination of the following cultic honors: priests/priestesses, prayers, sacrifices, hymns, altars, processions, festivals, games, cultic images, divine titles, shrines, and temples.[5] Let me briefly unpack these honors. Imperial priests and priestesses were aristocratic men and women from Greco-Roman communities who administered and oversaw

1. For surveys of traditional Greek and Roman divine honors, see Jan N. Bremmer, *Greek Religion*, GRNSC 24 (Oxford: Oxford University Press, 1994); John Scheid, *An Introduction to Roman Religion*, trans. Janet Lloyd (Bloomington: University of Indiana Press, 2003).

2. This does not mean that ancient and modern Christianity is unconcerned with orthopraxy. For in Christianity, one's orthodoxy should influence one's orthopraxy.

3. Martin Hengel, *Christ and Power*, trans. Everett R. Kalin (Philadelphia: Fortress, 1977), 7–10, speaks of "ruler-cult" as a "totally *political* religion."

4. I do not consider imperial virtues or abstractions such as Augustan Victory or Augustan Mercury evidence of imperial divine honors, because these were divinities in their own right and not necessarily divine honors for Julio-Claudians.

5. For informed discussions of imperial divine honors, see Simon R. F. Price, *Rituals and Power: The Roman Imperial Cult in Asia Minor* (Cambridge: Cambridge University Press, 1984); Duncan Fishwick, *The Imperial Cult in the Latin West: Studies on the Ruler Cult of the Western Provinces of the Roman Empire*, 3 vols. (Leiden: Brill, 1987–2002); Ittai Gradel, *Emperor Worship and Roman Religion* (Oxford: Clarendon, 2002); Gwynaeth McIntyre, *Imperial Cult* (Leiden: Brill, 2019).

imperial sacrifices. These imperial cultic officials made offerings on imperial altars, the most important piece of furniture for ancient divine honors. Some altars were makeshift, while others were permanent, especially those set up in front of imperial temples and shrines. Oftentimes, these officials made such sacrifices on altars at stops during or at the end of sacred processions, as in Gythium's sacred law (see pp. 1–4, 7), that included prayers, libations of wine, the burning of incense, and animal sacrifice to the Julio-Claudians, to the gods on their behalf, or to the gods and the Julio-Claudians at the same time. If appropriate, during the sacrifice of animals on behalf of or to Julio-Claudians, certain individuals sang or chanted hymns honoring imperial family members, which had the twofold effect of honoring the Julio-Claudians in question and drowning out the sounds of dying animals. Such activity often occurred during imperial festivals that included wild beast fights, gladiatorial combats, and games such as athletic, musical, and even theatrical contests, like the festival in Gythium, but were not limited to them.[6]

Imperial cultic statues were set up inside imperial temples (see figs. 3.6, 9) or shrines (see figs. 4.3–5, 9) or even outside near imperial altars (see possibly fig. 4.9). Some of these images depicted Julio-Claudians in the guise of gods, most often Zeus/Jupiter (see figs. I.2; 3.6, 9; 4.3, 7, 10), while others pictured them in pious or military fashion (see figs. 2.3, 4; 3.10). Thus, there was no one type of cultic image, and in actuality any statue of a Julio-Claudian, even one not set up in a temple, shrine, or next to an altar could have been cultic. The bestowal of divine titles on Julio-Claudians, like *divus* or "divinized" in Latin and *theos* or "god" and *sōtēr* or "savior" in Greek, is found in numerous Greco-Roman sources, especially inscriptions and coins that local communities produced. Before I leave this brief description of imperial divine honors, I must note that not every Julio-Claudian granted one of the above honors was given every one of these cultic acts. For example, one should not assume that because a city bestowed the title *theos* on a Julio-Claudian that it erected a large temple to him or her. To the contrary and because of the diversity of imperial divine honors, upon which I have already touched in this book's introduction and will discuss further below, one must not go beyond the claims of our ancient sources.

Now that we know what imperial divine honors are, I must address why I refer to grants of them as such and why I do not use the phrase that has become part

6. The names of imperial festivals varied across Italy and the eastern Roman Empire. In Rome and other Latin speaking communities, they were most often called *Augustalia*, while in Greek speaking communities *Sebasteia*, *Caesarea*, and *Actia* were commonest. This last title, *Actia*, takes its name from the battle of Actium in 31 BC that left Caesar Octavian (later Augustus) sole ruler of the Roman Empire.

of the lexicon of the New Testament academy and even the church, "the imperial cult." I avoid this term because of the unintended misconception that it leaves for readers of Paul's letters who have not been initiated into the mysteries of imperial divine honors. For the uninitiated, "the imperial cult" can imply, incorrectly, that a single, centrally controlled cult existed in the Roman world. Historians of the Greco-Roman world understand this well and tend to preface their use of "imperial cult" by noting that it is a modern term that covers a wide, diverse range of cultic acts associated with Roman emperors and their family members.[7] However, this is not something that many New Testament scholars do, or if they qualify their use of "imperial cult," their method of interpreting imperial divine honors does not track with it. To capture the diversity of these divine honors, other historians prefer to use "imperial cults" and "emperor worship."[8] I appreciate these options but consider them deficient. I avoid "emperor worship" because it can leave the false impression, however unintended, that imperial divine honors were bestowed only on emperors or other male Julio-Claudians, which, as we have seen from Gythium's sacred law, was not the case. I try not to use "imperial cults" because it is a modern term and not one that most Greeks and Romans used to refer to what they were doing when they gave cultic acts to the Julio-Claudians.

My term of choice, "imperial divine honors," reflects more closely the actual language that Greeks and Romans most often used to describe cultic acts for Julio-Claudians. Scores of examples of such imperial cultic acts being called "honors," *timai* in Greek or *honores* in Latin, or "rites," *religiones* in Latin, almost always in the plural, appear in ancient literary sources, inscriptions, and papyri. In the letter that Tiberius composed to Gythium declining divine honors that I referenced in this book's introduction, the emperor says that cultic acts that the city established for Augustus were appropriate because he deserves "honors fitting of the gods" (*tas theois prespousas timas*).[9] Frequently, Greek sources combine the adjective *isotheoi* or "godlike" with "honors" to describe the cultic acts that they bestowed on Julio-Claudians. When the third-century AD historian Dio Cassius records the creation of the temples of Augustus and Roma for the entire provinces of Asia and Bithynia, respectively, in 29 BC, he describes them, and the imperial festivities and sacrifices that occurred at these cultic buildings, as *isotheoi timai*.[10] Latin speakers

---

7. McIntyre, *Imperial Cult*, 1, points out that "the term 'imperial cult' is a modern attempt to catalogue and define a collection of related practices and has no ancient equivalent."

8. Steven J. Friesen, *Twice Neokoros: Ephesus, Asia, and the Cult of the Flavian Family*, RGRW 116 (Brill: Leiden, 1993), 1–2; Friesen, *Imperial Cults and the Apocalypse of John: Reading Revelation in the Ruins* (Oxford: Oxford University Press, 2001); Gradel, *Emperor Worship*, 4–7.

9. "Appendix 1: Inscriptions" §I.3, lines 19–20.

10. Dio Cassius, *Roman History* 51.20.6–9. Dio omits that Roma was included in these temples

tended to attach the adjective *caelestes* or "heavenly" in some form to honors or to describe them as honors resembling those given to the gods. Thus, Tacitus refers to the grant of postmortem divine honors for Augustus that the Roman Senate gave him on September 17, AD 14 as *caelestes religiones* or "heavenly rites," and one of the earliest epigraphic dedications to the divinized Julius Caesar locates him as "reckoned among the number of the gods" (*in deorum numerum rettulit*).[11]

For these reasons, I prefer to call cultic acts given to Julio-Claudians "divine honors" or variations of this phrase. To distinguish these honors from those given to the gods, I attach the adjective "imperial" to it, which is not something that ancient Romans or Greeks did. My term of choice has three advantages over "imperial cult," "emperor worship," and "imperial cults." First, as noted, it reflects more closely the vocabulary of Greeks and Romans. To borrow a term from the social sciences, "divine honors" is an "emic" phrase reflecting the language of Greeks and Romans. Second, the phrase "imperial divine honors" avoids the false impression that a single, centrally controlled imperial cult existed in the Roman Empire and the generalizations that stem from such an assumption (see pp. 31–36). Third, my preferred phrase showcases the relationship between imperial and traditional divine honors. Thus, "imperial divine honors" allows us to conceptualize better what these honors actually were: cultic acts and rituals that Greeks and Romans normally gave to their gods, which they bestowed on Julio-Claudians. This captures the continuity between the imperial and traditional divine honors and explicates the former's origin.[12]

This last point helps us to conceptualize imperial divine honors and how Greeks and Romans could bestow such honors on certain Julio-Claudians. For heirs of Christendom and the Enlightenment, the notion of humans offering other humans divine honors is ridiculous and downright blasphemous. In our worldview, a large gulf exists between divinity and humanity because divinity is absolute and connected to monotheism, which I define as belief in the exis-

---

with Augustus, but inscriptions and coins from Asia attest that, at least in Pergamum, the temple was dedicated to both Augustus and Roma. See Price, *Rituals and Power*, 252, 266.

11. Tacitus, *Annals* 1.10; *ILS* 72. This inscription is from Aesernia, Italy (modern-day Isernia).

12. Panagiotis Iossif and Catharine Lorber, "More Than Men, Less Than Gods: Concluding Thoughts and New Perspectives," in *More Than Men, Less Than Gods: Studies on Royal Cult and Imperial Worship*, ed. Panagiotis P. Iossif, Andrezj Chankowski, and Catharine Lorber (Leuven: Peeters, 2011), 697, note, "The rituals and apparatus [of imperial divine honors] were the same as those of traditional cults of the poleis, or differed only in degree." Older historians of the Greco-Roman world tended to argue that imperial divine honors arose because belief in the gods had waned among Greeks and Romans. For this outdated view, see Arnaldo Momigliano, "How Roman Emperors Became Gods," *American Scholar* 55 (1986): 181–93.

tence of only one God, the God of Israel.[13] Christians worship, follow, and devote their lives to one eternal Deity revealed in three persons—Father, Son, and Holy Spirit—who has no beginning or end, who is responsible for the creation of the cosmos (however that event happened), and who has revealed himself in human form, Jesus.[14] For ancient Greeks and Romans, such theological concepts were alien, even atheistic![15] Most ancient Greeks and Romans were polytheists, which means that their gods were numerous, far more than the Olympian pantheon, and included many deities and lesser divine beings.[16] The reason for this proliferation of deities is that the gods in ancient Greece and Rome were not omnipotent but controlled various dominions over which they held sway: Zeus/Jupiter, the earth and sky, Poseidon/Neptune, the sea, Hades/Pluto, the underworld, and so on. For most in the Greco-Roman world, these gods were neither eternal (having no beginning or end) nor the creators of the world. Pagan gods had beginnings, and Greeks and Romans even celebrated their birthdays. The Olympian gods did not create the world; an older generation of gods did that. Like the Priestly creation account in Gen 1:1–2:4, most Greeks and Romans thought that the Olympian deities made this form of our world by bringing order from chaos.[17] The main two things that separated humans from gods is that the gods were immortal (literally deathless in Greek, *athanatos*), and they possessed more power than humans. One consequence of this Greco-Roman conception of divinity is that new gods or new manifestations of already known ones could and on occasion needed to be discovered. To provide an example, in 135 BC Attalus II, the king of Pergamum, a Greek kingdom in the midst of Asia Minor in modern-day Turkey, wrote a letter

13. A sophisticated discussion of monotheism in antiquity should allow for the existence of other spiritual beings and divinities. For a nuanced, concise discussion of ancient monotheism, see Paula Fredriksen, *Paul: The Pagans' Apostle* (New Haven: Yale University Press, 2017), 10–13.

14. Many Christians affirm these theological tenets weekly in divine services as they recite the Nicene-Constantinopolitan Creed: "We believe in one God . . . maker of heaven and earth . . . We believe in one Lord, Jesus Christ . . . eternally begotten of the Father . . . through him [Jesus] all things were made . . . We believe in the Holy Spirit, the Lord, the giver of life" (*The Book of Common Prayer and Administration of the Sacraments* [Huntington Beach, CA: Anglican Liturgy, 2019], 127).

15. According to *The Martyrdom of Polycarp*, the crowd that assembled in Smyrna's stadium screamed, "Take away the atheists" (αἶρε τοὺς ἀθέους) during Polycarp's martyrdom (9.2).

16. See Keith Hopkins, *A World Filled with Gods: The Strange Triumph of Christianity* (New York: Plume, 2001). For a description of the numerous gods involved in a Roman marriage ceremony, for example, see Augustine, *City of God* 6.9.

17. The way in which they accomplished this feat was by defeating the Titans and the Giants and banishing them to the depths of Hades in a place of torment known as Tartarus. See D. Clint Burnett, "Going through Hell: TARTAROΣ in Greco-Roman Culture, Second Temple Judaism, and Philo of Alexandria," *JAJ* 4 (2013): 352–78.

to the government of the city informing its officials of his decision to erect a cultic statue of a manifestation of Zeus called Sabazius in the temple of Pergamum's patron goddess Athena Guardian of the City and to appoint a priest for the newly installed deity. The reason for this decision, the king said, was that his mother, Queen Stratonice, had brought the god from her native homeland of Cappadocia, and since she had done that, he had protected the king in the midst of war.[18]

This example highlights one of the main reasons why Greeks and Romans sacrificed to their gods, which differs from modern Christian religiosity and in turn aids further in our conceptualizing of imperial divine honors. The former sacrificed to their gods because they provided tangible benefactions: a productive growing season, victory in war, healthy children, and other gifts.[19] Historians of Greek and Roman religion use a Latin phrase to capture this foundational religious principle, *do ut des*, "I give so that you may give." We should not condemn this ancient theological tenet as some form of works-righteousness and thereby judge it by our own modern concepts of God, his gifts, and grace.[20] As Simon Price, a prominent historian of ancient Greek and Roman divine honors, notes, "Gifts to the gods were not a way of buying the gods, but of creating goodwill from which humans might hope to benefit in the future."[21] Thus, for many Greeks and Romans, divinity was connected to power and the ability to benefit suppliants.[22] What this means for imperial divine honors is that a Julio-Claudian's humanness

---

18. *OGIS* 331 = *IPergamon* 1.248 = PH301890, lines 45–61. For a discussion, see D. Clint Burnett, *Christ's Enthronement at God's Right Hand and Its Greco-Roman Cultural Context*, BZNW 242 (Berlin: de Gruyter, 2021), 50–51.

19. In the words of the third-century AD philosopher and critic of Christianity, Porphyry, *On Abstinence from Killing Animals* 2.24, "For above all there are three things for which one should sacrifice to the gods: because of honor, because of thanksgiving, and because of the need of good things" (καὶ γὰρ ἄλλως τριῶν ἔνεκα θυτέον τοῖς θεοῖς. ἢ γὰρ διὰ τιμὴν ἢ διὰ χάριν ἢ διὰ χρείαν τῶν ἀγαθῶν).

20. For an excellent discussion of the modern conception of grace and how it differs from ancient conceptions of grace, see John M. G. Barclay, *Paul and the Gift* (Grand Rapids: Eerdmans, 2015).

21. Simon R. F. Price, *Religions of the Ancient Greeks* (Cambridge: Cambridge University Press, 1999), 38–39. We find this rationale for divine honors expressed clearly by the first-century BC Stoic philosopher Cicero, *On the Nature of the Gods* 2.60–62, in his treatise on Roman religion: "Those gods therefore who were the authors of various benefits owed their deification to the value of the benefits which they bestowed" (*Utilitatum igitur magnitudine constituti sunt ei di qui utilitates quasque gignebant, atque his quidem nominibus quae paulo ante dicta sunt quae vis sit in quoque declaratur deo*; trans. H. Rackham).

22. See Price, *Rituals and Power*, 23–77; Gradel, *Emperor Worship*, 27–53. Even Cicero, *On the Nature of the Gods* 2.62, acknowledges the connection between benefaction and divine honors when he notes the origin of such honors for Hercules and Romulus: "human life and common

was not a hindrance to Greeks and Romans offering divine honors to him or her. Like the gods, Julio-Claudians were not eternal. They had birthdays, they were powerful, and, most importantly, they provided benefits. To this end, a second-century AD question to an Egyptian oracle captures well this connection among divinity, power, benefaction, and divine honors for rulers:

> "What is a god [*theos*]?" the petitioner asks.
> The oracle answers, "Power" [*kratoun*].
> "What is a king [*basileus*]?" the petitioner inquires.
> "Godlike [*isotheos*]," the oracle responds.[23]

Acknowledging this conception of divinity allows us to understand better an issue about imperial divine honors that has preoccupied many historians and New Testament scholars for much of the last century: did Greeks and Romans actually believe the Julio-Claudians to whom they gave divine honors were gods? Older scholars tended to answer this question skeptically. The leading early-twentieth-century interpreter of imperial divine honors, A. D. Nock, who worked with an understanding of worship (what is given to the gods) and homage (what is offered to humans) concluded that "ruler worship" was "an expression of gratitude which did not involve any theological implications . . . [because acts of devotion to rulers] are all of the nature of homage and not of worship in the full sense, for worship implies the expectation of blessing to be mediated in a supernatural way."[24] Today most historians point out that Nock's line of inquiry is flawed because it stems from a modern, Western, and Christianized conception of religion and worldview where politics and religion are (supposedly) separate entities.[25] Therefore, some scholars distance themselves from this question all together.[26] While I do not wish to return to such modernizing interpretations of imperial divine honors reminiscent of Nock's, I consider it possible to grasp what some Greeks and Romans thought about the Julio-Claudians to whom they granted

---

[*communis*] practice undertake to prove that people voluntarily lift up men to renown in heaven by their surpassing benefactions [*beneficiis excellentis*]."

23. Friedrich Bilabel, "Fragmente aus der Heidelberger Papyrussammlung," *Phil* 80 (1925): 339–40.

24. A. D. Nock, "Religious Developments from the Close of the Republic to the Death of Nero," in *The Augustan Empire 44 B.C.–A.D. 69*, vol. 10 of *Cambridge Ancient History*, ed. S. A. Cook, F. E. Adcock, and M. P. Charlesworth (Cambridge: Cambridge University Press, 1934), 481.

25. Price, *Rituals and Power*, 11–19, 235–48; Gradel, *Emperor Worship*, 27–32.

26. Gradel, *Emperor Worship*, 1–18.

divine honors, provided that we focus on the core of divine honors in the Greco-Roman world, sacrifice.[27]

Given that sacrifice was one of the main avenues to communicate with the divine, to propitiate the gods, and to entice them to provide benefactions needed to live, examining these rituals provides a window into conceptions of divinity that many Greeks and Romans held or in the words of one historian of ancient Rome, John Scheid, "belief in action."[28] Examining what ancients did to determine what they believed is not a modern method of inquiry but one that the second-century AD Greek biographer Plutarch used. In a now lost work entitled *On the Festival of Images of Plataea*, he notes that when he wishes to understand what Greeks and barbarians who lived before him believed, he examined their sacrificial rites because "the celebrations of the rites of initiation and those acts performed symbolically in religious services display more than anything the thought of the ancients."[29] Thus, for Plutarch, the "thought" (*dianoia*) of past peoples is evident in their rituals. Following this line of inquiry, I interpret imperial divine honors as "belief in action," which means that I determine what the inhabitants of Philippi, Thessalonica, and Corinth thought about certain Julio-Claudians by examining what divine honors and above all what sacrifices they granted them. To this end, I take seriously the claims of our ancient sources. When a coin or inscription from one of these cities hails a Julio-Claudian as a *theos*, *isotheos*, or a *divus*, I contend that for most people in that city, the Julio-Claudian in question was a *theos*, *isotheos*, or a *divus*. This does not mean that there were not dissenters in Philippi, Thessalonica, and Corinth, for example, Paul and his converts (!), because how Greeks and Romans viewed the Julio-Claudians was diverse, and there was such a thing as a god for a particular person or a particular people.[30] What I am saying is that Philippian, Thessalonian, and Corinthian inscriptions, coins, and archaeological data attesting to imperial divine honors provide us with the best evidence for what the individuals of those communities believed about the

---

27. For the essential place of sacrifice in traditional Greek and Roman divine honors, see Price, *Religion of the Greeks*, 30–39; Scheid, *Introduction to Roman Religion*, 79–110.

28. Scheid, *Introduction to Roman Religion*, 95–96, notes of "belief in action": "The kernel of the rite of sacrifice may be seen as a 'credo' expressed in action rather than words. This 'credo' was neither explicit nor prior to the ritual action itself: it was rather inherent in the ritual and proclaimed solely through a sequence of actions."

29. μάλιστα δ᾽ οἱ περὶ τὰς τελετὰς ὀργιασμοὶ καὶ τὰ δρώμενα συμβολικῶς ἐν ταῖς ἱερουργίαις τὴν τῶν παλαιῶν ἐμφαίνει διάνοιαν (Plutarch, *Fragments* 157).

30. For example, when Helen interprets an eagle snatching up a goose in its talons as the eventual destruction of Penelope's suitors in the *Odyssey*, Telemachus, Odysseus's son, exclaims, "May Zeus, the thunder-making husband of Hera, bring it to pass in this way! Then, I will pray to you even as to a god [θεῷ ὥς]" (Homer, *Odyssey* 15.180–181).

Julio-Claudians to whom they granted such honors—honors that local aristocrats promoted in these cities and encouraged the inhabitants of their communities to accept, to participate in, and thus to believe.

FINDING IMPERIAL DIVINE HONORS

Now that we have defined imperial divine honors, I must address where one finds evidence for them. The first and sometimes only place that New Testament scholars look for data attesting to such honors is Greco-Roman literature, especially ancient biographies and histories. These sources do attest to some grants of imperial divine honors, but they are focused on Rome, the capital of the empire. Some of these data are helpful for reconstructing the honors in question for Julio-Claudians in the Roman colonies of Corinth and Philippi, but not so much the Greek city of Thessalonica. There are one literary reference to divine honors for someone connected to the Julio-Claudians in Corinth and evidence that one Thessalonian considered some Julio-Claudians as godlike, but no mention of such honors in Philippi in surviving Greco-Roman literature.[31] If such is the case, you may be thinking, then how could I have written this book? More importantly, why have you spent your hard-earned money on it, or why are you wasting your valuable time reading it? The answer to that question is that there is a veritable abundance of evidence for imperial divine honors in Philippi, Thessalonica, and Corinth, which is not found in Greco-Roman literature. Virtually all the evidence in question comes from archaeology, inscriptions, and coins.[32] French archaeologists have been excavating in Philippi since 1914, American archaeologists in Corinth since 1896, and Greek archaeologists in Thessalonica since the mid-twentieth century. Given that Philippi and Corinth are not currently occupied, excavations in them have been more extensive and systematic than those in Thessalonica, which remains a bustling city to this day.[33] The archaeological records of these cities preserve evidence for Julio-Claudian temples, shrines, altars, and cultic images. Inscriptions and coins from Corinth, Philippi, and Thessalonica that archaeologists, antiquarians, and epigraphers have been cataloguing since the Middle Ages make up the bulk of the data sets for imperial divine honors in

31. Pausanias, *Description of Greece* 2.3.1; *Greek Anthology* 9.59, 297. I am not claiming that such references did not exist. They may have. If so, those ancient works have not survived.

32. For a short discussion of these sources, see pp. 17–18.

33. This means that we do not know as much as we would like about Thessalonian archaeology, but if we are honest, we do not know as much as we would like about Philippian or Corinthian archaeology either!

these cities.[34] These sources are valuable because they represent the actual words, customs, rituals, and conceptualizations of the inhabitants of Philippi, Corinth, and Thessalonica. Therefore, they are inestimable for reconstructing the "belief in action" of the citizens of these cities as it relates to the Julio-Claudians.

APPROACHING IMPERIAL DIVINE HONORS

Approaching Imperial Divine Honors in New Testament Studies

New Testament scholars have long noted the importance of imperial divine honors for interpreting Paul's letters.[35] One of the earliest interpreters to do so was the renowned, erudite, and groundbreaking German scholar Adolf Deissmann (1866–1937).[36] He marshaled a formidable array of evidence for what he calls "the imperial cult" (*Kaiserkult*) from inscriptions and papyri from the Greek East that recently had been discovered in the nineteenth century. His evidence consists mostly of titles that early Christians used for Jesus that resembled or mirrored those that provincials in the empire used for emperors, especially "son of a god" (*huios theou*) and "lord" (*kyrios*). Deissmann argues that the earliest Christians were aware of these imperial titles and their similarity to their burgeoning Christology. He contends that no genealogical relationship exists between the two because the Christian titles derive from the Greek Old Testament, not from the Greco-Roman pagan environment.[37] However, Deissmann concludes that Chris-

---

34. The so-called father of epigraphy, Cyriacus of Ancona (1391–1452), traveled to Philippi and recorded several inscriptions at the site. See Charles Mitchell, Edward W. Bodnar, and Clive Ross, eds., *Cyriac of Ancona Life and Early Travels*, The I Tatti Renaissance Library (Cambridge: Harvard University Press, 2015), 71–73.

35. One of the main exceptions is the study by Colin Miller, "The Imperial Cult in the Pauline Cities of Asia Minor and Greece," *CBQ* 72 (2010): 314–32, who fails to investigate the archaeology, inscriptions, and coins from cities associated with Paul and thus incorrectly concludes that "the imperial cult was marginal in the cities of Paul." Those who rely on Miller are equally problematic, for example, Judith A. Diehl, "Anti-imperial Rhetoric in the New Testament," in *Jesus Is Lord, Caesar Is Not: Evaluating Empire in New Testament Studies*, ed. Scot McKnight and Joseph B. Modica (Downers Grove, IL: InterVarsity Press, 2013), 38–81, esp. 53–55. For a critique of Miller's work, see Christoph Heilig, *Hidden Criticism? The Methodology and Plausibility of the Search for a Counter-cultural Subtext in Paul* (Tübingen: Mohr Siebeck, 2015), 93–98.

36. Adolf Deissmann, *Light from the Ancient East: The New Testament Illustrated by Recently Discovered Texts of the Graeco-Roman World*, trans. Lionel R. M. Strachan, 4th ed. (New York: Hodder & Stoughton, 1910; repr. Grand Rapids: Baker Books, 1978), 338–78.

37. Deissmann, *Light from the Ancient East*, 343.

tian use of *huios theou* and *kyrios* for Jesus, while not a direct assault on the emperor's divinity, was a silent protest against imperial divine honors.[38]

Deissmann's approach to imperial divine honors is generalized. His stated method is to use some ancient evidence for the "imperial cult," namely, inscriptions and papyri, to make broad conjectures about the practice in the Greek East: "It cannot be my task to collect together the whole gigantic mass of material in even approximate completeness; I can only offer a selection of characteristic parallelisms [to the New Testament]."[39] Thus, Deissmann was uninterested in specific contexts for imperial divine honors, how they were granted, for what purposes, and who received them. By overlooking these critical aspects, he fails to highlight the diversity and, as I explain below, the contextuality of grants of imperial divine honors. This may be traced to Deissmann's conceptualization of the honors in question, which his use of the term "imperial cult" highlights. He contends that this cult was part of "state law," which leaves the impression, however unintended, that he considered "the imperial cult" to be uniform and centrally controlled.[40]

Interest in imperial divine honors in New Testament studies declined in the period after World War II, mainly because of the important and epoch-making discoveries of the Nag Hammadi Gnostic texts (1945) and Dead Sea Scrolls (beginning in 1947). It was not until the late 1980s and early 1990s that scholars rediscovered imperial divine honors and began to use them as an interpretive backdrop for Paul's letters.[41] The impetus for this renewed interest was the publication of a seminal study on imperial divine honors in Asia Minor by Simon Price, *Rituals*

---

38. Deissmann, *Light from the Ancient East*, 342, 346–57, esp. 355. One reason for Deissmann's, *Light from the Ancient East*, 7–9, 339–40, conclusion is that he believed that Paul (and most early Christians) was from the lower classes of Roman society and thus indifferent to politics. Most scholars today reject this portion of Deissmann's conclusion; see Wayne Meeks, *The First Urban Christians: The Social World of the Apostle Paul*, 2nd ed. (New Haven: Yale University Press, 2003), 51–73.

39. Deissmann, *Light from the Ancient East*, 343.

40. Adolf Deissmann, *Licht vom Osten: Das Neue Testament und die neuentdeckten Texte der hellenistisch-römischen Welt*, 4th ed. (Tübingen: Mohr Siebeck, 1923), 291, concludes, "But the imperial cult itself was a portion of national law [*ist doch der Kaiserkult selbst ein Stück Staatsrecht gewesen*]." The official English translation of Deissmann, *Light from the Ancient East*, 343, reads, "the Imperial cult was in fact a portion of the law of the constitution."

41. Some of the earliest New Testament interpreters to highlight imperial divine honors and their connection to Paul and his churches were Klaus Wengst, Pax Romana *and the Peace of Jesus Christ*, trans. John Bowden (London: SCM, 1987), esp. 47–50, 72–89; Dieter Georgi, *Theocracy in Paul's Praxis and Theology*, trans. David E. Green (Minneapolis: Fortress, 1991), esp. 62–63, 67–71, 81, 87.

and Power. For most of the twentieth century, many Greco-Roman historians and New Testament scholars had followed Nock's interpretation of imperial divine honors and concluded that they were political tools devoid of religiosity. Price, however, points out that Nock's interpretation of imperial divine honors stems from a modern, Western, and Christian worldview read anachronistically into antiquity. He notes that religion and politics were inseparable in the Greco-Roman world, and he demonstrates that the inhabitants of Asia worked the emperor into their religious system for the purpose of legitimating his rule and authority. In the process, Price proposes that imperial divine honors stabilized the world for the Asian Greeks, which allowed them to conceptualize and accept Roman domination within their own cultural frame of reference. Finally and particularly important for New Testament studies, Price provided a catalogue of known evidence (up to 1984) for imperial divine honors in Roman Asia.[42]

Today many interpreters of Paul approach imperial divine honors with a combination of Price's reconstruction of them and his data set, the catalogue for imperial divine honors, and Deissmann's generalizing method. In the process, they take the evidence that Price has amassed from Asia Minor and use it to interpret Paul's epistles to his churches in Philippi, Thessalonica, and Corinth. This is done to varying degrees, which the works of N. T. Wright and Bruce W. Winter in particular highlight. I have chosen these two scholars because of their importance in the study of Paul and imperial divine honors and their outspokenness on these issues in numerous publications throughout the years. However, both interpreters differ in their approach to the honors in question and their conclusions about the relationship of imperial divine honors to early Christians. Wright's earlier work displays extreme generalizations about imperial divine honors and Paul. He assumes that a single, centrally controlled "imperial" cult existed in the Roman world in which the emperor demanded his subjects participate: "already by the time of Paul's missionary activity [the cult of Caesar had] become . . . the dominant cult in a large part of the empire . . . [and] Caesar demanded worship."[43] In his later two-volume tome on Paul, Wright tones down his generalizing and argues for a more contextual approach to imperial divine honors. He acknowledges their diversity, the need to speak of "imperial cults" rather than "the imperial cult," and the necessity of contextualization, which for him consists of an emperor-

---

42. Price, *Rituals and Power*, 1–22, 234–74.

43. N. T. Wright, "Paul's Gospel and Caesar's Empire," in *Paul and Politics: Ekklesia, Israel, Imperium, Interpretation: Essays in Honor of Krister Stendahl*, ed. Richard A. Horsley (Harrisburg, PA: Trinity Press International, 2000), 161, 168. For similar comments, see N. T. Wright, *Paul in Fresh Perspective* (Minneapolis: Fortress, 2005), 62–65.

by-emperor survey of imperial divine honors "proving" that each Julio-Claudian emperor received them.[44]

To date, Winter has produced the most comprehensive and sophisticated treatment of imperial divine honors and early Christianity associated (mostly) with Paul.[45] His work reveals less generalization than Wright's not only because Winter acknowledges the diversity of imperial divine honors but also because he works with inscriptions, coins, and papyri—the bulk of contextual evidence for imperial divine honors—far more than Wright.[46] Winter's main thesis is that early Christians clashed with imperial divine honors because the latter had "a powerful, all-pervasive and competing messianic-like ideology" that began with Augustus and was "propagated" across the empire. This conflict produced various Christian responses from compromise and evasion to imprisonment and even death.[47] Winter's work is divided into two parts. In the first, he attempts to establish the all-pervasiveness of imperial divine honors, and in the second, he brings his findings to bear on certain New Testament texts; the ones that most concern me are from the Corinthian and Thessalonian correspondences. Winter argues that some of Paul's Corinthian converts participated in imperial divine honors. In his discussion of the numerous gods and lords on earth and in heaven (1 Cor 8:5–6), Paul challenges this participation, for the gods and lords in heaven are deceased Julio-Claudians who are *divi*, while the gods and lords on earth are living ones. Winter supports his proposal by pointing to an obscure epigraph from Corinth that is a dedication to "Caesars Augusti" (for more on this inscription, see pp. 192–93), inscriptions from Athens, Cyprus, and Ephesus, and a papyrus from Oxyrhynchus (Egypt) that refer to certain Julio-Claudians as gods. For 1–2 Thessalonians, he contends that the social harassment that Paul's Thessalonian converts experienced was due to their failure to participate in imperial divine honors in their city.[48]

While Wright and Winter contend that a contextualizing approach to imperial divine honors is appropriate, in practice they fall short of their desired method, for

---

44. N. T. Wright, *Paul and the Faithfulness of God*, 2 vols. (Minneapolis: Fortress, 2013), 1:311–15. I assume that contextualization is what Wright means when he notes that one must "access what was actually happening on the ground" in Philippi, Corinth, and other cities.

45. Bruce W. Winter, *Divine Honours for the Caesars: The First Christians' Responses* (Grand Rapids: Eerdmans, 2015).

46. To provide a metric, Wright, *Paul and the Faithfulness of God*, 2:1593–1636, esp. 1633, 1635, lists only two inscriptions in his ancient-source index for a two-volume book that contains 1,519 pages of text, while Winter's, *Divine Honours*, 337–38, index lists approximately 137 inscriptions, 22 papyri, and approximately 40 coins for a book containing 306 pages of text.

47. Winter, *Divine Honours*, 5.

48. Winter, *Divine Honours*, 166–225, 250–65.

some of their conclusions are not based on contextual evidence. For example, to argue that the Julio-Claudians are gods in heaven and on earth in Corinth, Wright and Winter rely on evidence outside Corinth. Wright contends that Paul's references to the so-called gods and lords on earth "can only in his [Paul's] day refer to the Caesars."[49] As I show in chapter 4, direct evidence from Corinth refutes this conclusion.[50] In actuality, Wright's notion of contextualization, his emperor-by-emperor survey for the purpose of establishing that each one received imperial divine honors, is enough evidence for him to warrant the conclusion that imperial divine honors were the most important divine honors in the Roman Empire. In his latest work on Paul, a biography for a more generalized audience, Wright regresses to his earlier extreme generalizations about imperial divine honors and that provincials had to participate in them.[51] Despite the fact that Winter has amassed an impressive array of inscriptions, papyri, and coins to support his various arguments, his interpretation and treatment of these material objects presupposes incorrectly that a single "imperial cult" existed in the Roman world. This much is clear when Winter uses sources that attest to imperial divine honors in one city to contend that similar divine honors were given to an emperor in another city. For example, much of his evidence for imperial divine honors in Thessalonica and Corinth does not come from these cities but from Greek-speaking communities of Egypt, Galatia, and Roman Asia.[52]

Moreover, Wright and Winter move beyond Deissmann's conclusion that Paul's rhetoric evinces a silent protest against imperial divine honors. Both interpreters insist that such honors were the biggest opponent of Paul and earliest Christianity. For Wright, these honors are the "religion of empire," the only divine honors in the Roman world that mattered, and Paul's goal in preaching the gospel was to subvert, sometimes quite openly, the gospel of Caesar.[53] Similarly, Winter traces problems with Pauline congregations to imperial divine honors; the ones that

49. Wright, *Paul and the Faithfulness of God*, 2:1285.

50. Corinthian inscriptions provide us with the exact titles that the people of Corinth used for Julio-Claudians, and neither "god" nor "lord" is among them.

51. For example, N. T. Wright, *Paul: A Biography* (San Francisco: HarperCollins, 2018), 11, concludes, "Everybody else in Saul's day, in regions from Spain to Syria, had to worship the goddess Roma and *Kyrios Caesar*, 'Lord Caesar.'"

52. Winter, *Divine Honours*, 250–65. I am negatively criticizing not his comparative use of evidence but his failure to use such evidence soundly and within reason, which I elaborate on below.

53. Wright, *Paul and the Faithfulness of God*, 1:311–47, quotation from 332, notes, "Thus, though for the most part it was true that imperial cults took their place alongside, and sometimes blended with, local and traditional customs, there was always at least the veiled threat: whatever else you do, this one matters." Wright, *Paul and the Faithfulness of God*, 2:1306, con-

most concern me are the controversy in Corinth around dining in an idol's temple and the mistreatment of the Thessalonian Christians.[54] In the process, Winter leaves the impression, however unintended, that imperial divine honors were the main challenge that Paul and his converts faced, at least in the cities in question.[55] Finally, aside from Wright and Winter, there are a growing number of New Testament scholars, especially those from a neo-Marxist perspective or those who have adopted what is called postcolonial theory, who contend that Paul, his converts, and the gospel opposed, either covertly or overtly, not only imperial divine honors but also the Roman imperial government that enabled and encouraged them.[56] These discussions tend to be influenced by the twentieth-century philosopher Paul-Michel Foucault and focus on imperial divine honors (and the Roman Empire) in terms of power, thereby underscoring the political aspect of these honors and the use of them for political ends. Unfortunately, most of these treatments share the same flawed generalizing method of interpreting divine honors for Julio-Claudians that Wright and Winter use.[57]

The Contextual Approach to Imperial Divine Honors

In contrast to this generalizing approach, the most appropriate method for interpreting imperial divine honors and the only way to answer the more pressing question of what relationship, if any, these particular honors had with nascent

---

cludes that Paul's gospel was "upstaging, outflanking, delegitimizing and generally subverting the 'gospel' of Caesar and Rome."

54. Winter, *Divine Honours*, 196–225, 250–65.

55. Unlike Wright, Winter, *Divine Honours*, 18–19, acknowledges that nascent Christians were to honor the emperor without worshiping him as or like a god.

56. Richard Horsley, ed., *Paul and Empire: Religion and Power in Roman Imperial Society* (Harrisburg, PA: Trinity Press International, 1997); Horsley, *Paul and Politics*; Horsley, *Paul and the Roman Imperial Order* (Harrisburg, PA: Trinity Press International, 2004); John Dominic Crossan and Jonathan L. Reed, *In Search of Paul: How Jesus's Apostle Opposed Rome's Empire with God's Kingdom* (San Francisco: HarperCollins, 2004); Davina Lopez, *The Apostle to the Conquered: Reimagining Paul's Mission*, Paul in Critical Context (Minneapolis: Fortress, 2008). For a recent, sympathetic overview, see Warren Carter, "Paul and the Roman Empire: Recent Perspectives," in *Paul Unbound: Other Perspectives on the Apostle*, ed. Mark D. Given (Atlanta: SBL Press, 2022), 9–40.

57. For a thoughtful critique of anti-imperial readings of Paul from two differing perspectives, see J. Albert Harrill, "Paul and Empire: Studying Roman Identity after the Cultural Turn," *EC* 2 (2011): 281–311; Harrill, *Paul the Apostle: His Life and Legacy in Their Roman Context* (Cambridge: Cambridge University Press, 2012), 76–94; Christoph Heilig, *The Apostle and the Empire: Paul's Implicit and Explicit Criticism of Rome* (Grand Rapids: Eerdmans, 2022).

Christianity is what I term the "contextual approach."[58] This means acknowledging that there was no such thing as "the imperial cult" or "the emperor cult" and that every grant of them, whether in Rome, in a province, in a city, or by a group or an individual, occurred in a particular location, at a particular time, for a particular purpose, and was instituted by a particular legislative body, group, or person. To this end, I interpret imperial divine honors as I do Paul's letters, contextually. Every Pauline letter, regardless of whether scholars dispute its authorship (e.g., 2 Thessalonians, Colossians, Ephesians, and the Pastoral Epistles), has a particular historical and theological context in which it was composed. The task of Pauline interpreters is to do the hard work of reconstructing that context so that we can be faithful readers of Paul and interpret him, as best we can, as the apostle intended.[59]

The Roman Empire was much more diverse than the canonical letters of Paul. In the apostle's day, it stretched from modern-day England to Syria and was the only empire in history to control all the Mediterranean coastline at one time. The Romans governed their empire with a skeleton force. It placed its legions on the borders and ruled the provinces by partnering with local aristocrats, allowing them to oversee their cities as they always had done. As long as the taxes were paid and the peace was kept, Rome allowed its subjects to live by their own traditions, laws, and customs, at least those that did not conflict with Roman law, such as the right to administer capital punishment.[60] For this reason, for most inhabitants of the eastern Roman Empire, life resembled what it had looked like during the Hellenistic period.[61] This matters for imperial divine honors because many cities in the Greek East had particular customs

58. My narrow focus on imperial divine honors means that I do not address the larger question of Paul's relationship to the Roman Empire and Roman ideology. For a thoughtful treatment of issues surrounding this question, with which I am sympathetic, see Heilig, *Apostle and the Empire.*

59. For an excellent theological survey of the Pauline corpus, see Michael J. Gorman, *Apostle of the Crucified Lord: A Theological Introduction to Paul and His Letters*, 2nd ed. (Grand Rapids: Eerdmans, 2017).

60. For a balanced treatment on Roman governance, see Adrian Goldsworthy, Pax Romana: *War, Peace, and Conquest in the Roman World* (New Haven: Yale University Press, 2016).

61. John Scheid, *The Gods, the State, and the Individual: Reflections on Civic Religion in Rome*, trans. Clifford Ando (Philadelphia: University of Pennsylvania Press, 2016), 33, posits, "One cannot situate Rome in hermeneutic relation to the rest of the world. At the provincial level, where Rome controlled only the upper echelon of power and justice, daily life resembled life in the past. Only in capital cases was jurisdiction reserved to the governor and, in certain cases, it could come about that even this power was delegated. For the rest, power was local, which means that the life of individuals did not change much compared with earlier eras."

Fig. 1.1 The Egyptian Temple of Dendur | *Courtesy of the Metropolitan Museum of Art*

of honoring, sometimes divinely, their rulers, and when the Julio-Claudians appeared on the scene, these communities incorporated the latter into such already existing frameworks.[62]

One striking example of this practice is the temple of Dendur, which once stood in Egypt south of the Aswan Dam but is now in the New York Metropolitan Museum of Art in New York, New York (see fig. 1.1). It is dedicated to Isis and Osiris, native Egyptian deities, and its architecture and decoration resemble Egyptian temples. However, this temple does not date to the time of the great pharaohs but to 10 BC. Reliefs carved on it depict Augustus as an Egyptian pharaoh (see fig. 1.2), and two sets of cartouches—rectangular shapes with rounded edges that functioned as a good luck charm—with hieroglyphics even call the emperor "pharaoh" and "Caesar victorious general" (see figs. 1.3, 4)!

While this temple does not bespeak imperial divine honors per se, it provides an object lesson. It would be irresponsible and incorrect to conclude from this temple that all people living in the Roman Empire considered Augustus a pharaoh and carved reliefs and hieroglyphics on temples depicting him as such. However, when New Testament interpreters take an inscription, a coin, or a temple attesting to imperial divine honors from one Greek city, say Ephesus, and use it as evidence

62. Lily Ross Taylor, *Divinity of the Roman Emperor*, Philological Monographs 1 (Middletown, CT: American Philological Association, 1931), 244.

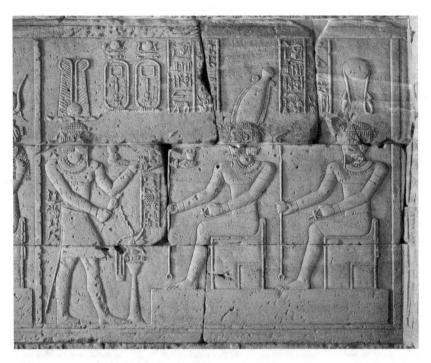

Fig. 1.2 Relief of Augustus as a pharaoh burning incense to the Egyptian gods from the Egyptian Temple of Dendur | *Courtesy of the Metropolitan Museum of Art*

for imperial divine honors in another city, especially a Roman one like Philippi, their interpretive move is similarly irresponsible, unless they have a good reason. All this means that we must be careful when approaching imperial divine honors and, above all, interpret them contextually.[63]

As we saw in this book's introduction, grants of imperial divine honors are rooted in specific historical and local contexts, which express themselves according to local customs. Thus, after Augustus's death, Gythium's sacred law legislated divine honors for him and four other living Julio-Claudians, while the Roman Senate divinized Augustus only. Because of similarities associated with who, that is, what legislative body, group, or individual, granted divine honors, on which spe-

63. Even in his own treatment of imperial divine honors in Asia, Price, *Rituals and Power*, 20, warns against making generalizations about these honors because of the diversity of the Roman Empire. Instead, he advocates localized studies that allow for "proper attention to be given to the historical, social, and cultural contexts."

Fig. 1.3 Cartouche from the Temple of Dendur calling Augustus "pharaoh" in hieroglyphics |
Courtesy of the Metropolitan Museum of Art

cific Julio-Claudians they were bestowed, and the ways that Greco-Roman sources
describe such honors, classicists have developed a fourfold typology for interpreting imperial divine honors: Roman, provincial, civic/municipal, and private.[64]
This taxonomy is useful for identifying the type of imperial divine honors that one
is examining, which in turn recommends what comparative evidence one must
use to fill out the almost certain fragmentary evidence attesting to such honors. In
what follows, I introduce each type of imperial divine honors describing whether
and how it relates to such honors in Philippi, Thessalonica, and Corinth.

64. For a concise discussion of these types in English, see Ittai Gradel, "Roman Apotheosis,"
in *Thesaurus Cultus et Rituum Antiquorum* (*ThesCRA*) (Los Angeles: The J. Paul Getty Museum,
2004), 2:186–99. For the best discussion to date, even though it is not in English, see Christian
Habicht, "Die augusteische Zeit und das erste Jahrhundert nach Christi Geburt," in *Le culte des
souverains dans l'Empire romain*, ed. Willem den Boer (Geneva: Fondation Hardt, 1973), 41–88.

Roman Imperial Divine Honors

Roman imperial divine honors are postmortem state-sponsored grants of divine honors that consisted of temples, altars, cultic images, priests/priestesses, processions, hymns, festivals, games, and sacrifices for deceased Julio-Claudians whom the Roman Senate divinized. In official Roman terminology, these were "public" divine honors, which means that the state paid for them and the sacrifices offered to these divinized

Fig. 1.4 Cartouche from the Temple of Dendur hailing Augustus "Caesar victorious general" in hieroglyphics | *Courtesy of the Metropolitan Museum of Art*

Julio-Claudians were made on behalf of the Roman Senate and the Roman people.[65] Divinized Julio-Claudians were known in Latin as *divi*, *divus* for a male Julio-Claudian and *diva* for a female Julio-Claudian.[66] It is important to note that there was no equivalent Greek term or concept for *divus*, and most often Greeks translated *divus* with *theos*.[67] In official Roman policy, however, there was a difference between a *divus* and a *deus*: the former was not full equation with the latter, despite what some court poets may have claimed.[68] Therefore, a fourth-century AD commentator on Virgil's *Aeneid* notes that while the great poet uses *divus* and *deus* or "god" indifferently (*indifferenter*), there is a "distinction" (*discretio*)

65. According to a second-century AD epitome, Wallace M. Lindsay, ed., *Sexti Pompei Festi De verborum significatu quae supersunt cum Pauli epitome* (Leipzig: Teubner, 1913), p. 284 lines 18–21, of a now lost Latin philological work by the renowned Roman grammarian Verrius Flaccus (55 BC–AD 20), "Public sacred rites are those that are made on behalf of the people [of Rome] at public expense . . . but private [sacred rites] are those made on behalf of singular persons, families, and clans" (*Publica sacra ,quae publico sumptu pro populo fiunt, quaeque pro montibus, pagis, curis sacellis: at privata, quae pro singulis hominibus, familiis, gentibus fiunt*).

66. After the divinization of a Julio-Claudian, the official Roman perspective was that the Julio-Claudian in question had been made divine by decree of the Roman Senate and people. See Appian, *Civil Wars* 2.148.

67. Simon R. F. Price, "God and Emperors: The Greek Language of the Roman Imperial Cult," *JHS* 104 (1984): 79–95.

68. In their works, Latin poets called select Julio-Claudians, especially Augustus, gods. See Kenneth Scott, "Emperor Worship in Ovid," *Transactions and Proceedings of the American Philological Association* 61 (1930): 43–69. Such is not the case with official Roman documents.

between the two: "we say that *dei* are perpetual, while *divi* are made by humans, as they have died."[69]

Roman public sacrifices underscored this distinction. The only surviving description of sacrifices in Rome to Julio-Claudians who became *divi* are the records of the Arval Brothers, a college of twelve priests in Rome who belonged to the senate and who were devoted to Dea Dia, a Roman fertility goddess whose temple was located in a sacred grove of trees about five miles outside Rome. These records consist of a collection of sacrifices that the Arval Brothers offered between 21 BC and AD 304 known as the *Acts of the Arval Brothers* that the annually elected president of this college oversaw, recorded in a book, and then had inscribed on marble plaques that were displayed in the goddess's temple complex.[70] These documents witness that on important days throughout the year, such as the reigning emperor's birthday and the anniversary of his accession to the imperial throne, sacrifices were offered to the gods and *divi* at the same time. In almost all cases, offerings were made to the gods first and *divi* second.[71]

Becoming a *divus* was neither assured nor dynastic. The Roman Senate made an emperor a *divus* only after his death and only if he ruled the empire well. That is, if his reign benefited the state by bringing peace, stability, and prosperity.[72] For this reason, the senate divinized only half the Julio-Claudians emperors, Julius Caesar, Augustus, and Claudius. In Caligula's reign, the senate extended divinization for the first time to female Julio-Claudians, and the most important female Julio-Claudian to receive this honor was Augustus's wife, Livia, in AD 42, even though she died in AD 29.[73] For a list of Julio-Claudian *divi*, see table 1.1.[74]

69. Servius, *Commentary on Vergil* 5.45.

70. For more on the Arval Brothers, see Mary Beard, "Writing and Ritual: A Study of Diversity and Expansion in the Arval Acta," *Papers of the British School at Rome* 53 (1985): 114–62; John Scheid, *Commentarii fratrum Arvalium qui supersunt: Les copies épigraphiques des protocoles annuels de la confrérie arvale (21 av.–304 ap. J.-C.)* (Rome: École Française de Rome, 1998), iii–xxii.

71. Gradel, *Emperor Worship*, 179–80, 275–76, notes, "The Arval records contain only one instance where sacrifices of the college included only the *Divi* and the emperor's *Genius*. . . . This rite is found in the *Acta* from the year 66 and took place" at *Divus* Augustus's temple in Rome and "the *Arval Acta* clearly show that the *Divi* ranked last among all gods worshipped by the Brothers."

72. Appian, *Civil Wars* 2.148; Dio Cassius, *Roman History* 51.20.8; Tacitus, *Annals* 15.74.

73. Livia died in AD 29, but her son, the emperor Tiberius, refused to allow her divinization. However, when Claudius became emperor in AD 41, he saw to it that Livia was divinized, an event that occurred in AD 42.

74. All dates are taken from Dietmar Kienast, *Römische Kaisertabelle: Grundzüge einer römischen Kaiserchronologie*, 2nd ed. (Darmstadt: Wissenschaftliche Buchgesellschaft, 1996).

TABLE 1.1 JULIO-CLAUDIAN *DIVI*

Divus/Diva	Date of Death	Date of Divinization
Divus Julius	March 15, 44 BC	January 42, 1 BC
Divus Augustus	August 19, AD 14	September 17, AD 14
Diva Drusilla (Caligula's sister)	June 10, AD 38	September 23, AD 38 (?) (divine honors for her appear to have ceased after Caligula's death on January 24, AD 41)
Diva Augusta (Augustus's wife)	AD 29	January 17, AD 42
Divus Claudius	October 13, AD 54	October 13, AD 54
Diva Claudia Augusta (Nero's four-month-old daughter who passed away)	April/May AD 63	April/May AD 63
Diva Poppaea Augusta (Nero's second wife)	Early summer AD 65	Early summer AD 65

This focus on *divi* in Roman imperial divine honors does not mean that living Julio-Claudians were not granted some divine honors in Rome during their lifetimes. They certainly were. However, these honors were private, not public, in nature and thus were not state funded and offered on behalf of Rome and her people. One such private imperial divine honor that eventually became part of public honors for the emperor is the honoring of his *genius*, which is difficult to define and translate into English. All Romans, places, bodies politic, and even things possessed a *genius* (see figs. 4.11, 12).[75] Sacrifices to the *genius* of a household's *paterfamilias* was a regular part of Roman domestic divine honors. One's *genius*, however, was distinct from a Roman's person and may be best described as a procreational and protective power. Thus, the most appropriate way to render *genius* into English is probably "life force."[76] To provide an example, an inscription on an imperial altar dating to AD 18 from a city in central Italy known as Forum Clodii notes that on the birthdays of Augustus and Tiberius, local aristocrats used incense and wine to invite "their *genii* to a banquet at the altar" (*genii eorum ad epulandum ara*).[77] In 30 BC, af-

75. Gradel, *Emperor Worship*, 36–44, 99–101, 162–97, 372–75.
76. Gradel, *Emperor Worship*, 36–38.
77. *CIL* 11.3303 = *ILS* 154, line 11. It is important to note that this epigraph presumes that Augustus's *genius* has remained alive, even after his death in AD 14.

ter Caesar Octavian returned to Rome in triumph as the sole ruler of the empire, the senate decreed that prayers were to be made on his behalf and that libations were to be poured to his *genius* at banquets.[78] Between 12 and 7 BC, Augustus reorganized Rome into fourteen regions with 265 districts. At the crossroads of each district, there was a shrine to the *Lares* or "divine beings" of that crossroads. After Augustus's reorganization, the inhabitants of these districts introduced divine honors for Augustus's *genius* and Augustus's own *Lares* into the *Lares* of their crossroads, which created the *Lares Augusti* (*Augusti* meaning "of Augustus" in Latin).[79]

The earliest evidence for public sacrifices to an emperor's *genius* in Rome dates to AD 55 and concerns Nero.[80] Thus, between 30 BC and this year, sacrifices for the reigning emperor's *genius* probably occurred in Rome, but not officially and at public expense. The reason for this change in AD 55 is unclear. One final note about sacrifices to an emperor's *genius*. While cultic activity is not unique to Roman imperial divine honors, the senate's decree of prayers and libations to Augustus's *genius* in 30 BC, the wedding of the emperor's *genius* and *Lares* with the *Lares* at the crossroads between 12 and 7 BC, and, beginning in AD 55, public sacrifices being offered to the emperor's *genius* were unheard of in Rome's history and meant that in some way, the emperor was viewed and functioned as the Roman people's *paterfamilias*.

Roman colonies, like Corinth and Philippi, were beacons for Roman language (Latin), ideology, governance, and customs, including Roman imperial divine honors.[81] According to the second-century AD Roman author Aulus Gellius, colonies are transplanted from the citizen body of the Romans and "possess all laws and institutions of the Roman people . . . [and] appear to be small like-

---

78. Dio Cassius, *Roman History* 51.19.7, records that the senate decreed that just as prayers were made "on behalf of" (ὑπέρ) the people and senate of Rome, they should be made "on behalf of him" (ὑπὲρ ἐκείνου) and that at public and private banquets, all were to "pour a libation of wine to him" (αὐτῷ σπένδειν). Even though Dio does not say that these prayers and libations were to Caesar Octavian's *genius*, most historians conclude that these offerings were made to his *genius*.

79. Mary Beard, John North, and Simon Price, *Religions of Rome*, 2 vols. (Cambridge: Cambridge University Press, 1998), 1:184–85; John Scheid, "To Honour the *Princeps* and Venerate the Gods: Public Cult, Neighbourhood Cults, and Imperial Cult in Rome," in *Augustus*, ed. Jonathan Edmondson (Edinburgh: Edinburgh University Press, 2009), 275–99. Gradel, *Emperor Worship*, 99–100, 374–75, notes that only clients of the emperor in Italy, slaves and freedmen, made dedications to his *genius*.

80. *Acts of the Arval Brothers* 24, lines 6–13.

81. For more information on Roman colonies and their divine honors, see Edward Togo Salmon, *Roman Colonization under the Republic* (London: Thames & Hudson, 1969), 13–28; Beard, North, and Price, *Religions of Rome*, 1:328–34.

nesses and copies" of Rome and her people.[82] As we shall see, Philippian and Corinthian archaeological, inscriptional, and numismatic evidences corroborate Aulus Gellius's claim. With few exceptions, Corinth and Philippi followed the lead of Rome and bestowed divine honors on Julio-Claudians whom the Roman Senate had divinized, *Divus* Julius, *Divus* Augustus, *Diva* (Livia) Augusta, and *Divus* Claudius. Roman colonies, however, were not carbon copies of Rome. Rather, they imitated Roman practices, including imperial divine honors, insofar as they aped their interpretation of them.[83] This situation accounts for divine honors for Julio-Claudians whom the Roman Senate did not divinize in Philippi and Corinth: Tiberius in the former and Octavia (Augustus's sister, who was not a Julio-Claudian), Gaius Caesar, and Lucius Caesar in the latter. Despite such deviation from the mother city, these grants of divine honors followed the Roman custom of waiting until the Julio-Claudian's death before bestowing such honors on him or her.

Provincial Imperial Divine Honors

The second type of imperial divine honors that occurred in the Roman Empire is provincial, which are divine honors that provinces established most often for living Julio-Claudians and often in conjunction with a cultic partner. The main context for these grants was imperial benefaction by which such honors showed a province's appreciation (see table 1.2). The provincial government of Greek provinces consisted of leading representatives of the province's cities often known as a *koinon*, best translated into English as "league," or of leading representatives of cities near each other that formed smaller, more local *koina* (the Greek plural of *koinon*). Cities in these *koina* pooled their resources to fund and promote imperial divine honors for their respective *koina*, which included temples, altars, cultic images, priests and priestesses, sacrifices, festivals, and imperial games held at regular intervals. Little evidence survives for provincial imperial sacrifices, but presumably, like civic/municipal imperial sacrifices (discussed below), provincials made offerings to the Julio-Claudians, to the gods on their behalf, or to both the Julio-Claudians and to the gods, at the same time. It appears that in some parts

82. *Sunt et iura institutaque omnia populi Romani . . . ceffigies parvae simulacraque esse quaedam videntur* (Aulus Gellius, *Attic Nights* 16.13.8–9).

83. Beard, North, and Price, *Religions of Rome*, 1:331. Gwynaeth McIntyre, *A Family of Gods: The Worship of the Imperial Family in the Latin West* (Ann Arbor: University of Michigan Press, 2016), 79, has shown that no canonical lists of *divi* in the Latin West and Roman colonies and municipalities offered divine honors to imperials as *divi* who had not been officially deemed as such in Rome.

of the Greek East such as Asia Minor, the granting of provincial imperial divine honors was the result of a negotiation among the *koinon*, the Roman provincial governor, the reigning emperor, and the Roman Senate. Because of the involvement of Roman officials, especially the reigning emperor, official documents such as inscriptions and coins associated with these grants tend to reflect the theological conservatism of Roman imperial divine honors. Thus, with few exceptions (namely, Caligula's grant of provincial imperial divine honors at the temple of Apollo in Didyma/Miletus in modern-day Turkey), official surviving documents, coins, and inscriptions associated with provincial imperial divine honors do not call the reigning emperor a *theos*.[84]

TABLE 1.2 KNOWN PROVINCIAL DIVINE HONORS FOR JULIO-CLAUDIANS IN THE GREEK EAST

Province, City	Julio-Claudian	Partner	Date
Asia, Ephesus	*Divus* Julius	Roma	29 BC (postmortem)
Bithynia, Nicaea	*Divus* Julius	Roma	29 BC (postmortem)
Asia, Pergamum	Augustus	Roma	29 BC
Bithynia, Nicomedia	Augustus	Roma	29 BC
Galatia, Ancyra	Augustus	Roma	AD 19/20
Asia, Smyrna	Tiberius, Livia	Roman Senate	AD 20s
Asia, Didyma	Caligula	Apollo	AD 37–41[85]

The provincial imperial divine honors about which we know the most are those of the *koinon* of Asia. Such divine honors were first created in 29 BC when Caesar Octavian allowed the province of Asia (and also Bithynia) to build a temple to him and Roma in Pergamum at which Greeks could offer divine honors to show the province's gratitude for Caesar Octavian's victory in the civil war with Marc Antony and the economic boom that Asia experienced after the former won.[86] Archaeologists have yet to discover this temple, but it must have been spectacular,

84. Habicht, "Augusteische Zeit," 45–46.
85. It is possible that two other grants of provincial divine honors to Julio-Claudians existed in the Greek-speaking East: one for Augustus or Tiberius in Galatia at Pessinus and the other for Claudius or Nero in Sardis in Asia. However, definitive proof that these two grants were provincial is lacking, though it is highly likely that the former temple was indeed provincial.
86. Dio Cassius, *Roman History* 51.20.6–9. For a discussion of this grant of provincial imperial divine honors, see Barbara Burrell, *Neokoroi: Greek Cities and Roman Emperors* (Leiden: Brill, 2004), 17–22.

Fig. 1.5 Silver coin known as a *cistophorus* minted in Pergamum in the early AD 40s depicting a bust of Claudius on the obverse (*left*) and the provincial imperial temple of Roma and Augustus in Pergamum along with its cultic images on the reverse (*right*) | *Courtesy of Yale University Art Gallery*

because one ancient author composed an entire work, now lost, dedicated to it.[87] We get a glimpse of how the temple looked from coins that the *koinon* of Asia minted picturing it (see fig. 1.5).[88]

The right for a city to host provincial imperial divine honors in Asia was coveted and caused fierce competition. In the mid-20s AD, the *koinon* desired to build a provincial temple for the emperor Tiberius, his mother Livia, and the Roman Senate to show appreciation for their aid in the Asian *koinon*'s successful prosecution of two unscrupulous imperial officials who had governed the province in AD 22 and 23, respectively.[89] Eleven cities vied to have the temple built in them with the result that the *koinon* was deadlocked. Representatives from the cities journeyed to Rome so that the senate and Tiberius could adjudicate the matter. Each city made its case before the body politic and the emperor. In the end, they

87. The author of this now lost work was the second-century AD author Telephus of Pergamum. See Felix Jacoby, ed., *Die Fragmente der griechischen Historiker: Geschichte von Staedten und Voelkern (Horographie und Ethnographie), B, Autoren ueber einzelne Staedte (Laender) Nr. 297–607* (Leiden: Brill, 1964), §505.

88. *RPC* 1:2221.

89. One of these officials extorted money, and the other overstepped his authority by using unlawful force (Tacitus, *Annals* 3.66–69; 4.15). Tacitus, *Annals* 4.15, notes the context for Asia bestowing this temple and its cult on Tiberius, Livia, and the senate was beneficence when he records that it was "in return for such retribution" (*ob quam ultionem*) that the Asian *koinon* decreed (*decrevere*) the temple (*templum*).

chose Smyrna to host this provincial imperial temple.[90] Like the temple of Roma and Augustus in Pergamum, archaeologists have yet to find this temple, mainly because the modern city of Izmir, Turkey lies atop it.

The types of provincial imperial divine honors and the intensity with which the provinces of Roman Asia adopted them differ markedly from the provincial imperial divine honors for Julio-Claudians found in Macedonia and Achaia, the two provinces in which Philippi, Thessalonica, and Corinth were located. The earliest known provincial imperial temple in Macedonia dates between AD 96 and 98 and thus was dedicated not to any Julio-Claudian but to the emperor Nerva.[91] It is probable that Macedonian provincial divine honors occurred in the mid-first century AD. However, the status of Philippi, a Roman colony, and Thessalonica, a "free city" in the Roman Empire, meant that neither city was required to participate in them, and the lack of evidence for any reference to provincial imperial divine honors in Philippi and Thessalonica suggests that these cities did not partake in provincial imperial festivities.[92] Therefore, my treatment of imperial divine honors in Philippi and Thessalonica will omit any discussion of Macedonian provincial imperial divine honors.

In a recent work on Achaian imperial divine honors, Francesco Camia and Maria Kantiréa note that Achaia did not have one provincial *koinon* as Asia and Galatia did but several local *koina* that appear to have kept to themselves. Thus, provincial imperial divine honors did not cover the geographical area of the province.[93] In the mid-50s AD, however, some *koina* united to form a single grant of provincial

---

90. Tacitus, *Annals* 4.55–56.

91. Burrell, *Neokoroi*, 191–92.

92. Victoria Allamani-Souri, "The Imperial Cult," in *Roman Thessaloniki*, ed. D. V. Grammenos, trans. David Hardy, Thessaloniki Archaeological Museum Publication 1 (Thessaloniki: Archaeological Museum, 2003), 100, notes, "Thessaloniki, as a *civitas liberta*, was not, in effect, an essential part of the province of Macedonia, and this may have been a factor in its non-participation in the Macedonian *koinon*, at least for the first two centuries after Christ." Contra Nijay K. Gupta, *1 and 2 Thessalonians* (Grand Rapids: Zondervan, 2019), 52, who attempts to use third-century AD evidence for a grant of provincial imperial divine honors in Thessalonica to describe Julio-Claudian imperial divine honors in the city: "Indeed, so enamored was Thessalonica with Rome that it was granted the title *tetrakis neokoros* (allowing it to dedicate *four* temples to the emperor)." This datum has no bearing on the imperial divine honors that I consider in this book.

93. Francesco Camia and Maria Kantiréa, "The Imperial Cult in the Peloponnese," in *Society, Economy and Culture under the Roman Empire: Continuity and Innovation*, vol. 3 of *Roman Peloponnese*, ed. A. Rizakis and C. Lepenioti, Meletemata 63 (Athens: Diffusion de Boccard, 2010), 398, note of Achaian provincial divine honors that they "cannot therefore be considered to be a provincial *koinon* like those of the eastern provinces of the Empire (*e. g.* Asia)."

divine honors for the Julio-Claudian family during Nero's reign (AD 54–68), which was based in Corinth, the provincial capital of Achaia.[94] This grant consisted only of a priesthood and the offering of imperial sacrifices. Thus, there was no grand temple, which would have been costly, and it is unclear whether there were any games or festivities associated with this grant of provincial imperial divine honors, as occurred with the same honors in Asia and Galatia.[95] For this reason, my discussion of provincial imperial divine honors for Achaia will be limited.

Civic/Municipal Imperial Divine Honors

The third type of imperial divine honors that flourished in the Roman Empire, civic/municipal, consists of grants of divine honors most often for living Julio-Claudians that local governments of cities and municipalities in the empire bestowed, such as Gythium's sacred law that opened this book. Given that there were more cities and municipalities in the Roman Empire than provinces, civic/municipal imperial divine honors were the commonest type and make up the abundance of our ancient evidence for imperial divine honors. These sources consist mostly of inscriptions, coins, and archaeological materials with an occasional reference to civic imperial divine honors in a surviving literary work. Because each Greco-Roman community had its own unique customs for honoring its rulers, civic/municipal imperial divine honors were diverse and consisted of any of the following divine honors: priests/priestesses, prayers, sacrifices, hymns, altars, processions, festivals, games, cultic images, divine titles, shrines, and temples. This variegation notwithstanding, such honors tended to share a common denominator: they were tokens of appreciation to living Julio-Claudians for their benefaction, which served to store up goodwill from which cities and municipalities could draw for future munificence.

For example, in 26 BC an earthquake struck the Greek city of Mytilene, a city on the western coast of Asia Minor in modern-day Turkey.[96] The emperor Augustus aided the city by providing some type of benefaction for it. Thereafter, the

---

94. These *koina* were named: Boeotian, Euboian, Phocidian, Locrian, and Dorian. See Camia and Kantiréa, "Imperial Cult," 398.

95. Francesco Camia, "Between Tradition and Innovation: Cults for Roman Emperors in the Province of Achaia," in *Kaiserkult in den Provinzen des Römischen Reiches: Organisation, Kommunikation, und Repräsentation*, ed. Anne Kolb and Marco Vitale (Berlin: de Gruyter, 2016), 255–83, esp. 274–75. To date, we know of no provincial temples that any *koinon* in Achaia erected. See the lack of discussion of such temples in Burrell, *Neokoroi*.

96. Christopher P. Jones, "The Earthquake of 26 BCE in Decrees of Mytilene and Chios," *Chiron* 45 (2015): 101–22, esp. 103–5.

leaders of Mytilene met to decide how best to show its gratitude to him. After some deliberation, they decided to create and to celebrate an imperial festival for Augustus and his family every five years, patterned after its games for Zeus; to offer yearly sacrifices of oxen—matching those that the city gave to Zeus—to Augustus on his birthday at a temple dedicated to him; and that certain citizens of the city take an annual oath of allegiance to the emperor. These civic officials made the further decision to engrave their decree on several stelae and to set them up in various cities across the empire, Pergamum, Actium in modern-day mainland Greece, Brundisium in modern-day Italy, Tarraco in modern-day Spain, Massalia in modern-day France, Antioch in modern-day Syria, and Mytilene itself, the last of which is our only surviving copy. After the decree lists the numerous honors that Mytilene bestowed on Augustus, it indicates that if the civic government discovers a new way to make the emperor even more of a god, it will do so:

> Of the benefactions [*euergesiōn*] . . . as a thanksgiving [*eucharistan*]. Now that it conforms to the greatness of mind to consider that those who have profited from heavenly glory and those who have the supremacy and power of the gods can never be made equal with things that are by fortune and by nature humbler. But if thereafter in the future anything more distinguished than these [i.e., the imperial festival, sacrifices, and oath to Augustus] will be found, the eagerness and piety [*eusebeian*] of the city will not fall short of anything of the possibilities to make him a god [*theopoiein*] even more.[97]

Because civic/municipal imperial divine honors focused on living Julio-Claudians, when the Julio-Claudians to whom these honors were given died, cities and municipalities either lumped in that Julio-Claudian into the ever-growing group of Julio-Claudians known as "Augustan gods" (*theoi Sebastoi*) or disbanded the divine honors in question altogether.[98] This latter option tended to be the case for either Julio-Claudians who fell out of favor with the reigning emperor, such as Caligula's sister, Julia Livilla, who was involved in an attempted coup d'état against the emperor, or emperors whose memories were damned and their identities erased from the collective memory of the Roman Empire, such as Nero.[99]

97. "Appendix 1: Inscriptions" §1.1, Column B, lines 1–15. The infinitive θεοποιεῖν is a combination of the Greek term θεός and the verb ποιέω.

98. Price, *Rituals and Power*, 40. For a discussion of the "Augustan gods," see Fernando Lozano, "*Divi Augusti* and *Theoi Sebastoi*: Roman Initiatives and Greek Answers," *CIQ* 57 (2007): 139–52.

99. There is evidence that some Greek cities in the Hellenistic period, which often sided with one Hellenistic king and then another, made official declarations ending grants of di-

The one exception for the lumping together or disbanding of civic/municipal imperial divine honors is Augustus, whose grants of such honors continued into the second and third centuries AD in some places, such as Thessalonica.[100] Unlike in Roman and provincial imperial divine honors, decrees and official communications associated with civic/municipal imperial divine honors had no qualms about hailing living Julio-Claudians as gods or goddesses during their lifetimes. Finally, the object of sacrifice in civic/municipal imperial divine honors differed from place to place. For example, sometimes cities and municipalities sacrificed to Julio-Claudians. At other times, like in Gythium's sacred law, they sacrificed to the gods on behalf of the Julio-Claudians. And still at other times, they sacrificed to the gods and the Julio-Claudians simultaneously.

As we shall see, the Greek city of Thessalonica established civic imperial divine honors for Julio-Claudians in Augustus's reign. In total, the city's government decided to divinely honor Julius Caesar, Augustus, and Livia, and probably Claudius and Nero. Thessalonica established imperial temples, set up altars and cultic images of these Julio-Claudians (some of which survive, see figs. 3.6, 9), appointed priests to make sacrifices probably to the Julio-Claudians in question, and hosted a set of imperial games that occurred at regular intervals. Because Thessalonica was the seat of provincial government in Macedonia, there was a large Roman presence in it, which in turn influenced the city's imperial divine honors in one respect: while Thessalonica granted divine honors to the aforementioned Julio-Claudians while they were alive (except for Julius Caesar), the city waited until these died before it hailed them as gods, with the exception of Livia.

Private Imperial Divine Honors

The final type of imperial divine honors that occurred in the Roman Empire is private, which is the least studied of all such honors.[101] These grants resembled in kind

---

vine honors for rulers. Livy, *History of Rome* 31.44.1–9, records that in the late third to second century BC once Philip V no longer served Athens's best interests, the city voted to destroy all images of and inscriptions relating to the king and his family, to proscribe any and all "sacred rites" (*sacra*) associated with Philip, and to curse the king and his family once a year. See Price, *Rituals and Power*, 40.

100. Given the length of his reign and the numerous benefits that Augustus provided the Roman Empire (it must be remembered that he came to power at the end of what had been almost forty years of civil war in which battles were fought in Greece and Asia Minor), imperial divine honors for Augustus are more attested than for any other Julio-Claudian, and they continued long after his death. See Price, "Gods and Emperors," 85.

101. For more information on individual imperial divine honors, see Gradel, *Emperor Worship*, 198–212.

their civic/municipal counterparts, with the exception that associations, groups, and individuals, not civic and municipal governments, bestowed them. The objects to whom the honors in question were given were most often living Julio-Claudians, and grants of these imperial divine honors functioned as tokens of appreciation for imperial benefaction. Private imperial divine honors are attested in inscriptions, archaeological remains, and some Greco-Roman literary sources. They are diverse and consist of offering libations and incense to the reigning emperor's *genius* before a meal, as the Roman Senate decreed for the people of Rome in 30 BC, or the assimilation of Julio-Claudians into a domestic shrine, such as when the Augustan poet Ovid was exiled to the Black Sea and had a friend send him statues of Augustus, Livia, and Tiberius to set up in his domestic shrine so that he could pray to these "gods" (*dei*) daily.[102] Archaeologists in Ephesus discovered a domestic shrine in an elite apartment (*insula*) known as Unit 7 in a block of such apartments (*insulae*) called Terrace House 2.[103] It dates between AD 14 and 37 and consists of a marble table and a stone altar with an eagle carved on it set up in front of a niche in a wall, in which marble busts of Tiberius and Livia and a statuette of Athena were found in situ or in their original location.[104] The second-century AD biographer of emperors Suetonius testifies that he owned a bronze statuette of Augustus depicted as a boy that he gave to the emperor Hadrian who "cares for it among the *Lares* of his bedroom."[105] In the early second century AD in Pergamum, an association of about forty male hymn singers of Roma and Augustus met in their own sacred space called a *hymnodeion* to provide divine honors for the long deceased Augustus, his divine consort Roma, and other emperors on their birthdays. During these celebrations, busts of the honored emperors were set up, and the hymn singers honored them with incense, bread, pastries, and wine as well as some form of imperial mysteries.[106]

102. Ovid, *Ex Ponto* 2.8.

103. For more information in English on Terrace House 2, see Sabine Ladstätter with Barbara Beck-Brandt, Martin Steskal, and Norbert Zimmermann, *Terrace House 2 in Ephesos: An Archaeological Guide*, trans. Nicole M. High with Emma Sachs (Istanbul: Homer Kitabevi, 2013), 75–83.

104. It is probable that the inclusion of Tiberius and Livia into this domestic shrine relates to his aid after a terrible earthquake that struck Ephesus in AD 26. See Elisabeth Rathmayr, "New Evidence for Imperial Cult in Dwelling Unit 7 in Terrace House 2 in Ephesos," in *Ephesos as a Religious Center under the Principate*, ed. Allen Black, Christine M. Thomas, and Trevor W. Thompson, WUNT 488 (Tübingen: Mohr Siebeck, 2022), 9–35. Often, scholarly works reference a bronze snake that was found with Tiberius's and Livia's busts. However, Rathmayr demonstrates that this is not the case and that the snake was placed in front of the niche much later.

105. *Inter cubiculi Lares colitur* (Suetonius, *Deified Augustus* 7).

106. *IPergamon* 2.374 = *IGR* 4.353 = PH302029. This inscription is inscribed on four sides of an imperial altar that was dedicated to the emperor Hadrian (AD 117–138). For more information on imperial mysteries, see H. W. Pleket, "An Aspect of Emperor Cult: Imperial Mysteries," *HTR* 58 (1965): 331–47.

Unfortunately, there is no evidence for private imperial divine honors in Philippi, Thessalonica, and Corinth, because almost all data that archaeologists have gathered in these cities are from public, not private, spaces. The reason for this is that excavations in Philippi and Corinth have concentrated largely on public buildings, especially those in the forums of both cities, and modern-day Thessaloniki sits atop ancient Thessalonica. There is one inscription from Thessalonica that indicates that a local benefactress and private citizen set up a temple near the city dedicated to Augustus, Hercules, and the divine personification of Thessalonica.[107] This temple, while paid for by this benefactress, seems to have been not private but public, however. The lack of evidence for private imperial divine honors in these cities notwithstanding, we know that such honors were celebrated in Rome and in domestic hearths of aristocratic Romans. This suggests that they were practiced in Philippi and Corinth, but no hard evidence corroborates it. Similarly, private imperial divine honors have been found in a Greek house in Ephesus, for example, which bespeaks that they could have been present in Thessalonica. However, we must be careful here. As we have seen in the above discussion of provincial imperial divine honors, divine honors for Julio-Claudians in Ephesus and Roman Asia were more intense than in Thessalonica and Macedonia. For example, and as noted above, the earliest attested provincial imperial temple in Macedonia dates to the end of the first century AD, while the earliest such temple in Roman Asia dates to 29 BC, roughly 167 years before its Macedonian counterpart. Therefore, use of comparative material from Greek cities in Asia may be inappropriate. Nonetheless, we must keep open the possibility that the inhabitants of Thessalonica practiced private imperial divine honors in some capacity.

Association of Imperial with Traditional Divine Honors and Aristocratic Brokerage

Before this introduction to imperial divine honors ends, we must address two more aspects of these honors that many New Testament scholars have underappreciated, which has resulted in the misinterpretation of the relationship among such honors, Paul, and his converts. The first is that imperial divine honors were often wedded to traditional divine honors. In Roman imperial divine honors, the *Acts of the Arval Brothers* attest that throughout the year, public sacrifices were made to the gods and *divi* on the same day for the same purpose. For example, on September 21, AD 38, the Arval Brothers sacrificed oxen and cows to Jupiter, Juno, Minerva, and *Divus* Augustus to show appreciation for the senate bestowing the title "father of

107. "Appendix 1: Inscriptions" §3.5.

the fatherland" on Caligula.[108] The provinces of Asia and Bithynia erected provincial temples to Roma and Augustus in Pergamum and Nicomedia, respectively, to show their gratitude for the end of the Roman civil wars and the economic boom that occurred thereafter, albeit with the inclusion of Roma being at the emperor's request. The inscription attesting to the grant of civic imperial divine honors in Mytilene—in which the city promised that if it found new ways to make Augustus even more of a god, it would put them into effect—indicates that certain citizens swore an oath to him and "to the ancestral gods" at the same time and that at the imperial festival, the emperor received the same sacrifices as Zeus.[109] Finally, Ovid, the emperor Hadrian, and the owner of Unit 7 in Terrace House 2 in Ephesus included Julio-Claudians into their domestic hearths, which consisted of their own household gods. In the case of the former, the two Romans placed imperial family members among their *Lares*, and in the latter, an unknown Ephesian Greek set up Tiberius's and Livia's busts beside a statuette of Athena, and the altar on which he sacrificed contained a symbol of Zeus, an eagle.[110] Such a melding of imperial with traditional divine honors was intentional and articulated various theological points that the inhabitants of the empire wanted to make. In Rome, that point was that the gods and *divi* worked together to support and ensure the prosperity of the reigning emperor, his family, the city, and the empire. For provinces, cities and municipalities, and private individuals, it was that their gods had in various ways and for various purposes appointed the Julio-Claudians to rule over and benefit them. Therefore, the gods supported the Julio-Claudians and worked their will through the latter. The inscription from Mytilene underscores this rationale well, for the city's government acknowledges that Augustus welds the "power of the gods."[111]

Due to this association of traditional and imperial divine honors, it is too difficult to separate the two from each other, especially in Philippi, Thessalonica, and Corinth. Francesco Camia, who focuses on imperial divine honors in mainland Greece, points out that one of the characteristics of such honors in this location is that they were "modeled on" and often combined with traditional divine honors.[112]

---

108. "Appendix 1: Inscriptions" §1.2.

109. [. . . ὀμνυ]ομένων σὺν τοῖς πατρίοις θεοῖς καὶ τὸν Σεβασ[τόν] . . . τῶν] αὐτῶν θυσιῶν ὡς καὶ τῷ Διῒ παρίσταται ("Appendix 1: Inscriptions" §1.1, Column A, lines 16–17, 21).

110. See Rathmayr, "New Evidence," 24–26, for a discussion of the possible owner of House 7 in the terrace houses.

111. θεῶν ὑπεροχὴν καὶ κράτος ἔχουσιν ("Appendix 1: Inscriptions" §1.1, Column B, lines 5–6). For more information, see D. Clint Burnett, "The Interplay between Indigenous Cults and Imperial Cults in the New Testament World," in *Inscriptions, Graffiti, Documentary Papyri*, ed. James R. Harrison and E. Randolph Richards (Grand Rapids: Zondervan, forthcoming).

112. Francesco Camia, "The *THEOI SEBASTOI* in the Sacred Landscape of the *Polis*: Cult

For this reason, it is incorrect to claim that the former competed with the latter or that imperial divine honors were the most important divine honors in the Roman Empire. To the contrary, the gods did not compete with the Julio-Claudians, and most inhabitants of the empire interpreted the continued success of the Julio-Claudians and the peace and prosperity that they brought as a testimony that their gods approved of, and supported the Julio-Claudians. The wedding of imperial with traditional divine honors was the surest confirmation that Greeks and Romans considered this the case. As we shall see, Paul and his converts in Philippi, Thessalonica, and Corinth knew well this fact, and for this reason, Paul never singles out imperial divine honors in his extant letters but "lumps together" all pagan cultic activity as idolatry.[113]

The second aspect of imperial divine honors that New Testament scholars have underappreciated is that local aristocrats brokered and promoted them to their communities. According to Plutarch, local aristocrats played key roles in the promotion of all divine honors within their cities. He says that they have an obligation to spend their money for public displays of honors for the gods because "[whenever the masses] see whom they honor and consider great so lavishly and eagerly competing with each other to honor the deity, a strong disposition is born in them and a notion that divine power is great and reverend."[114] Plutarch's observation applies equally to imperial divine honors. Fernando Lozano, a specialist focusing on such honors, has shown local aristocrats instigated the establishment of such divine honors in their cities.[115] In Rome, aristocrats known as senators and even the reigning emperor were responsible for the divinization of Julio-Claudians, deciding who after their deaths were worthy to be numbered among the gods. Some of these individuals even became priests of Julio-Claudian *divi*, or, at the very least, they offered sacrifice to them (see fig. I.1). The aristocrats of the leading cities of Greek provinces, sometimes along with the reigning emperor and the Roman Senate, created and promoted imperial divine honors for their

---

Places for the Emperors in the Cities of Mainland Greece," in *Im Schatten der Alten? Ideal und Lebenswirklichkeit im römischen Griechenland*, ed. Johannes Fouquet and Lydia Gaitanou, Studien zur Archäologie und Geschichte Griechenlands und Zyperns 71 (Mainz: Franz Philipp Rutzen, 2016), 10–11.

113. John M. G. Barclay, "Paul, Roman Religion and the Emperor," in *Pauline Communities and Diaspora Jews* (Grand Rapids: Eerdmans, 2016), 355.

114. οὓς αὐτοὶ τιμῶσι καὶ μεγάλους νομίζουσιν, οὕτως ἀφειδῶς καὶ προθύμως περὶ τὸ θεῖον ὁρῶσι φιλοτιμουμένους (Plutarch, *Precepts of Statecraft* 822B).

115. Fernando Lozano, "The Creation of Imperial Gods: Not Only Imposition versus Spontaneity," in *More Than Men, Less Than Gods: Studies on Royal Cult and Imperial Worship*, ed. Panagiotis P. Iossif, Andrezj Chankowski, and Catharine Lorber (Leuven: Peeters, 2011), 483–87.

provinces. Similarly, in Greek cities, the leaders of local governments decided and endorsed which Julio-Claudians to honor divinely. In provincial and civic imperial divine honors, many of the individuals responsible for the creation of such honors in their respective communities served as imperial priests and organizers of imperial festivals and games. Finally, almost all our surviving evidence, mainly literary and archaeological, for private imperial divine honors relates to the households of Roman and Greek aristocrats. This point must be kept in mind as we move through this book and especially to its conclusion where I address Paul's positive comments about the Roman Empire in Rom 13:1–7.

CONCLUSION

To summarize, imperial divine honors are diverse honors that resembled in kind but differed in degree from those given to the gods. Such honors were grants in keeping with local customs that can be divided into four types: Roman, provincial, civic/municipal, and private, most of which were given to Julio-Claudians to show appreciation for benefaction. Roman imperial divine honors were found in Rome and its colonies, such as Philippi and Corinth, and were bestowed on deceased Julio-Claudians whom the Roman Senate divinized and made *divi*. However, there were exceptions in some Roman colonies, as they divinely honored deceased but not divinized Julio-Claudians. Provincial imperial divine honors were granted by the *koinon* of a province or a *koinon* within a province most often on living Julio-Claudians and sometimes with a cultic partner. Such honors could be part of a negotiation process among the representatives of the *koinon* in question, the provincial governor, the Roman Senate, and the reigning emperor to determine the objects of worship and where these divine honors occurred. Civic and municipal as well as private imperial divine honors were granted by cities/municipalities, associations, and individuals, respectively, most frequently to living Julio-Claudians. All these types of imperial divine honors were often wedded to traditional divine honors and brokered to communities (or households and meeting places of associations in the case of private imperial divine honors) through the patronage and support of local aristocrats. For these reasons, it is impossible to isolate the former from the latter or to ignore the key role that aristocrats played in facilitating, promoting, and administering imperial divine honors in Greco-Roman communities.

This portrait and method of interpreting divine honors for Julio-Claudians is not one found often among many New Testament scholars and their works, especially commentaries on the letters that Paul and his apostolic colleagues composed to Philippi, Thessalonica, and Corinth. Many Pauline interpreters fail to define imperial divine honors and to approach them as local cultic phenomena. Instead, they opt for a generalizing method of interpretation that obfuscates the honors in question and in the end serves their interpretive agenda more so than the quest for accurate historical reconstructions. Interpreting imperial divine honors in Philippi, Thessalonica, and Corinth with the contextual method that I advocate and laid out above means reconstructing these honors in these cities in light of the evidence from them first and foremost and bringing in comparative material if and when appropriate. For this book's remainder, my aim is to present such contextual reconstructions and demonstrate how they help us to appreciate and to understand better the relationship among such honors, Paul, and his converts.

CHAPTER 2

Imperial Divine Honors, Paul, and the Philippian Church

The last chapter introduced imperial divine honors and the more appropriate and accurate method of interpreting them, the contextual approach. This chapter brings this contextualized method of interpreting such honors to bear on the ancient Roman colony of Philippi, the first place that Paul established early Christianity in mainland Greece after his arrival on the continent, to reconstruct what relationship, if any, these honors had with nascent Christianity in the city. To this end, this chapter has two main goals. The first is to lay out all the ancient evidence for imperial divine honors in Philippi to date and to build a contextualized portrait of them (see "Imperial Divine Honors in Philippi"). In the process, we shall see that such honors fall into the category of Roman imperial divine honors and that they were wedded to the colony's public life—what today we would call the political, religious, social, and economic fabric of the city. This chapter's second goal is to use this contextualized portrait to offer a fresh reading of Paul's letter to the Philippians and a nuanced interpretation of the relationship between the suffering that some Philippian Christians experienced and imperial divine honors in Philippi (see "Imperial Divine Honors and Early Christianity in Philippi"). Accordingly, we will see that while such honors contributed somewhat to the harassment and even imprisonment of some Philippian Christians, they were not the sole source of their woes. Before we arrive at these two goals, however, I must describe the state of imperial divine honors in Philippi in New Testament scholarship and how exegetes interpret the relationship between the honors in question and early Christianity in the colony (see "New Testament Scholars on Imperial Divine Honors, Paul, and the Philippian Church").

New Testament Scholars on Imperial Divine Honors, Paul, and the Philippian Church

Most New Testament scholarly discussions of imperial divine honors in Philippi tend to be generalized, not based on evidence or the latest evidence from the Roman colony, and focused on the relationship among these honors, the so-called Philippian hymn (Phil 2:6–11), especially the acclamation of Jesus as "Lord" (*kyrios*) (Phil 2:9–11), and Paul's later reference to the Messiah as "Savior" (*sōtēr*) (Phil 3:20–21).[1] Several interpreters contend that the inhabitants of Philippi hailed the reigning emperor by these titles and that the Christian use of them conflicted directly with what they call "the imperial cult." One of the earliest exegetes to hold this position was Adolf Deissmann. His main evidence for *kyrios* being an imperial title in mainland Greece is a Greek epigraph from Acraephia, a city in Greece's Boeotian region, that dates to AD 67 and refers to the emperor Nero as "*kyrios* of the entire world" (*ho tou pantos kosmou kyrios*).[2] He acknowledges that this is the earliest evidence for the hailing of a Julio-Claudian with this epithet in mainland Greece, but because other Julio-Claudians were called *kyrioi* in Egypt and Palestine, he concludes that this lack of evidence is due to chance.[3] For the use of *sōtēr* for Julio-Claudians, Deissmann points to inscriptions from the "Hellenistic East" that acclaim Julius Caesar, Augustus, Claudius, and Nero by that title.[4]

Today most scholars follow Deissmann's conclusion about *kyrios* and *sōtēr* without qualification, even if they do not cite him directly.[5] N. T. Wright, who

---

1. The main exception to date is Lukas Bormann, *Philippi: Stadt und Christengemeinde zur Zeit des Paulus* (Leiden: Brill, 1995), 11–67, esp. 37–54, 222–23, who approaches imperial divine honors in Philippi in this manner. He examines almost all evidence available to him (up till 1995) and concludes that such honors were Roman in nature and that Paul does not directly oppose imperial divine honors, but that the acclamation of Jesus as *kyrios* relativizes the emperor's power. Besides being in German and thus inaccessible for many English-speaking clergy, the limitation of Bormann's work is that some newer discoveries nuance some of his conclusions.

2. *IG* 7.2713 = *SIG* 814 = PH146221, line 31.

3. Adolf Deissmann, *Light from the Ancient East: The New Testament Illustrated by Recently Discovered Texts of the Graeco-Roman World*, trans. Lionel R. M. Strachan, 4th ed. (New York: Hodder & Stoughton, 1910; repr. Grand Rapids: Baker Books, 1978), 349–59.

4. Deissmann, *Light from the Ancient East*, 363–65.

5. Joseph A Fantin, *The Lord of the Entire World: Lord Jesus, a Challenge to Lord Caesar?*, New Testament Monographs 31 (Sheffield: Sheffield Phoenix, 2011), 191–266, follows Deissmann and provides more evidence to support this proposal. His data, the appearance of *kyrios* in 109 Egyptian papyri and ostraca hailing Nero as lord, as well as his reading of the inscription from Acraephia are unconvincing. The papyri and ostraca testify to the influence of the Levantine cul-

assumes that imperial rule was despotic and that "Romans" were coerced to believe that they lived in a world of peace and prosperity that the Julio-Claudians had secured, contends that these "Romans" hailed their emperors as "savior" and "lord."[6] Gordon Fee proposes that *kyrios* and *sōtēr* were common titles for the emperor and that the Roman citizens of Philippi offered divine honors to many lords, including Caesar.[7] John Reumann notes that the reference to Jesus as *kyrios* in Phil 2:11 reflects a setting in which Caesar was known as *dominus* ("lord" in Latin) and that although *sōtēr* was not an official Roman title, it was "increasing" in use in "Roman Imperial cult."[8] Even scholars who attempt to contextualize the letter to the Philippians through Philippian archaeological remains follow Deissmann on this point. Peter Oakes appears to argue that the reigning emperor was acclaimed as *kyrios* and *sōtēr* in Philippi, even though the former was not an official epithet. The Philippian Christians, however, would have interpreted Paul's message as the relativizing of the emperor and his power, because his lordship and saviorship extended beyond "Emperor-cult" to "society and politics."[9]

These scholars differ about how the use of *kyrios* and *sōtēr* in early Christianity and the supposed use in imperial divine honors in Philippi affected Paul and his Philippian converts. Deissmann's main goal was not to address this issue, but he characterizes Christian use of *kyrios* and *sōtēr* as a "polemical parallelism" against imperial divine honors and *kyrios* in particular as "a silent protest" against the

---

tural practice of hailing ancient Near Eastern monarchs as lords, which spread westward toward the end of Nero's reign. See D. Clint Burnett, *Studying the New Testament through Inscriptions: An Introduction* (Peabody, MA: Hendrickson, 2020), 58–76. Moreover, Fantin misinterprets the epigraph from Acraephia, arguing that it was probably set up in cities in mainland Greece, and thus he contends that other communities knew of its contents. There is no evidence that the inscription was set up elsewhere, and when such is the case, the text of an epigraph tends to acknowledge it. See "Appendix 1: Inscriptions" §1.1, Column A, lines 11–14.

6. N. T. Wright, "Paul and Empire," in *The Blackwell Companion to Paul*, ed. Stephen Westerholm (Malden, MA: Wiley-Blackwell, 2011), 285–86, chides, "Romans as a whole, wisely, went along with this convenient fiction [that Augustus's reign brought a new era of peace and prosperity], hailing Augustus and then his successors as 'savior' and 'lord.'"

7. Gordon D. Fee, *Paul's Letter to the Philippians*, NICNT (Grand Rapids: Eerdmans, 1995), 31, 222, 380–81

8. John Reumann, *Philippians: A New Translation with Introduction and Commentary*, AYB 33B (New Haven: Yale University Press, 2008), 372, 577–78, 597–98.

9. Peter Oakes, *Philippians: From Letter to People*, SNTSMS 110 (Cambridge: Cambridge University Press, 2001), 130, 138–45, 171–74. Eduard Verhoef, *Philippi: How Christianity Began in Europe; The Epistle to the Philippians and the Excavations at Philippi* (London: Bloomsbury T&T Clark, 2013), 37, 45–46, incorrectly equates *dominus* with *divus* and asserts that the people of Philippi called emperors "savior" and "lord."

reigning emperor. This "polemical parallelism" and "silent protest" appear not to have attracted the attention of Roman authorities, for, as Deissmann posits, Paul probably "more often experienced the blessings than the burdensome constraint of State organisation," including imperial divine honors.[10] Reumann concludes that the Christian use of *kyrios* and *sōtēr* probably contributed to the suffering of Paul's Philippian converts, but these were not the sole source of their harassment. Instead, the withdrawal of Christians from traditional and imperial divine honors contributed to their ill-treatment.[11] Wright, Fee, and others appear to contend that use of *kyrios* and *sōtēr* for the reigning emperor in imperial divine honors in Philippi was one of the main sources for the suffering of Christians in the colony. Wright proposes that in Phil 3:20–21, Paul encourages these believers not to participate in "cultic and other activities" but to imitate Christ and take the path of suffering. These "cultic and other activities" seem to be imperial divine honors, for immediately after using this phrase, he notes that "the time will come when Caesar and all who follow and worship him will be humbled before the throne of the true Lord of the World."[12] Fee seems to single out divine honors for the living emperor as one reason, possibly the reason (he is unclear), for the harassment of Philippian Christians.[13] Finally, Walter Hansen concludes, "Paul's gospel that Jesus Christ is now the exalted Lord who will come as the Savior from heaven to bring everything under his control directly confronted the Roman imperial gospel that Caesar is Lord and Savior."[14]

10. Deissmann, *Light from the Ancient East*, 339, 342, 355. This conclusion may stem from his view that imperial divine honors concerned only Greco-Roman aristocrats and that early Christians, including Paul, were from lower social classes. See pp. 31–32.

11. Reumann, *Philippians*, 278–79, following the conclusion of Craig Steven de Vos, *Church and Community Conflicts: The Relationship of the Thessalonian, Corinthian, and Philippian Churches with Their Wider Civic Communities*, SBLDS 168 (Atlanta: Scholars Press, 1999), 264.

12. N. T. Wright, "Paul's Gospel and Caesar's Empire," in *Paul and Politics: Ekklesia, Israel, Imperium, Interpretation; Essays in Honor of Krister Stendahl*, ed. Richard A. Horsley (Harrisburg, PA: Trinity Press International, 2000), 179–80.

13. Fee, *Philippians*, 197, proposes that the use of *kyrios* for Jesus was "in bold contrast to 'lord Nero,' whose 'lordship' they refused to acknowledge." This was even more serious because, according to Fee, this occurred "in a city where the cult of the emperor undoubtedly played a significant role."

14. G. Walter Hansen, *The Letter to the Philippians*, PNTC (Grand Rapids: Eerdmans, 2009), 103, following Richard A. Horsley, "Paul's Counter-Imperial Gospel: Introduction," in *Paul and Empire: Religion and Power in Roman Imperial Society*, ed. Richard A. Horsley (Harrisburg, PA: Trinity Press International, 1997), 140.

Excursus: Imperial Divine Honors
and Jesus's "Equality with God" (*isa theō*)

Recently, some scholars point to the use of the phrase "equality with God" (*isa theō*) in the so-called Philippian hymn (Phil 2:6) as evidence for a polemic, even a "hidden transcript" (the use of a state's official terminology and propaganda for dissenting and antistate purposes), against imperial divine honors that local aristocrats promoted in Philippi. The evidence for this position is the use of the cognate *isotheos* in Greco-Roman literature and inscriptions attesting to imperial divine honors. In an influential essay, Erik M. Heen contends that "godlike honors" was a technical term for such honors for human rulers in the Greek East and that during Paul's day, only Julio-Claudians received such honors.[15] While Greco-Roman sources clearly use *isotheos* to refer to imperial divine honors, Heen has overstated his case. Greek sources evince that the term is not technical, and epigraphs attest that cities bestowed such honors on non-Julio-Claudians. The island city Cnidus honored one of its late-first-century BC benefactors with *isotheoi timai*, which included erecting a statue of him in a temple of Artemis on the island.[16] The people of Lycia in southern Asia Minor honored divinely one of their mid-first-century AD benefactresses, a woman who lived in Corinth named Junia Theodora. They even sent their decision to the Corinthian government informing them of Junia's munificence and their decision to apotheosize (*apotheōsis*) her.[17] Closer to the apostle Paul, the first-century Jewish philosopher Philo uses *isotheos* four times in his extant works, none of which refers explicitly to divine honors for human

15. Erik M. Heen, "Phil 2:6–11 and Resistance to Local Timocratic Rule: *Isa theō* and the Cult of the Emperor in the East," in *Paul and the Roman Imperial Order*, ed. Richard A. Horsley (Harrisburg, PA: Trinity Press International, 2004), 125–53, esp. 142, "The term *isotheoi timai* was virtually a *terminus technicus* for the highest honors a city might bestow on an individual. As noted above, beginning with the reign of Augustus such honors were restricted to the emperor and his family."

16. See *IKnidos* 1.59 = PH258452 and the discussion by D. Clint Burnett, *Christ's Enthronement at God's Right Hand and Its Greco-Roman Cultural Context*, BZNW 242 (Berlin: de Gruyter, 2021), 42–45.

17. Jacques Vénencie, Séraphin Charitonidis, and Demetrios Pallas, "Inscriptions trouvées à Solômos, près de Corinthe," *BCH* 83 (1959): 498–508 = Przemyslaw Siekierka, Krystyna Stebnicka, and Aleksander Wolicki, eds., *Women and the Polis: Public Honorific Inscriptions for Women in the Greek Cities from the Late Classical to the Roman Period*, 2 vols. (Berlin: de Gruyter, 2021), 241–46, no. 85, line 2.44.

rulers.[18] In one of these occurrences, Philo says that Abraham allegorically represents the noble person casting off polytheism with its strange laws and monstrous customs for the worship of the one God. He then defines pagan sacrifices as "godlike honors to stones, wood, and lifeless items altogether."[19] In the end, context determines the meaning of a word. Paul (or the material that he quotes in Phil 2:6–11, which may or may not be a hymn) uses *isa theō* in a distinctive way.[20] Most uses of *isotheos* in Greco-Roman literature and inscriptions refer to specific divine honors given to a benefactor, ruler, or emperor. Greeks did not use *isotheos* to describe the preincarnate state of any of the aforementioned individuals, nor did they as a synonym for "in the form of God" (*en morphē theou*) (Phil 2:6), as is the case in Paul's letter to the Philippians.[21] Finally, it is evident that Phil 2:6–11 contains allusions to the Jewish Scriptures (what became the church's Old Testament), most notably, Isa 53:3, 11 (Old Greek) in Phil 2:7 and Isa 45:23 (Old Greek) in Phil 2:10.[22] For these reasons, I cannot follow Heen's proposal that the so-called Christ hymn functions anti-imperially, because his conclusion's premises are flawed.

While we shall explore the relationship of imperial divine honors and early Christianity in Philippi below, it is important to note that the premises on which the above scholars have constructed their various arguments are problematic. Evidence from the colony does not support the contention that *kyrios* and *sōtēr* were imperial titles in the city. Surviving Philippian inscriptions and coins provide the exact titles that the colonists used for Julio-Claudians, and to date, *kyrios* and

18. Philo, *On the Life of Moses* 2.194; *On the Decalogue* 7; *On the Special Laws* 1.25; *On the Virtues* 219. Heen, "Phil 2:6–11," 147–48, acknowledges Philo's use of ἰσόθεος in *On the Decalogue* 7 and yet concludes, "All the examples reflect the honorific tradition of Greek cities, which granted heroes and rulers *isotheoi timai* . . . , although some are critical of it or make a metaphorical application."

19. λίθοις καὶ ξύλοις καὶ συνόλως ἀψύχοις ἰσοθέους ἀπένειμε τιμάς (Philo, *On the Virtues* 212–219).

20. For my interpretation of Phil 2:6–11 as early Christian confessional material, see Burnett, *Christ's Enthronement*, 113–18.

21. A. D. Nock, "Notes on Ruler-Cult I–IV," *JHS* 48 (1928): 35, notes, "There is not, therefore, in general a definite popular belief that a particular ruler is in a strict sense the reincarnation of a particular deity."

22. For a discussion of the scriptural allusions in Phil 2:6–11, see Richard Bauckham, *Jesus and the God of Israel: God Crucified and Other Studies on the New Testament's Christology of Divine Identity* (Grand Rapids: Eerdmans, 2008), 197–210. That Phil 2:6–11 contains such allusions does not mean that the passage does not depict Jesus as an exalted ruler. See Burnett, *Christ's Enthronement*, 111–56.

sōtēr and their Latin counterparts *dominus* and *salvator* are not among them. The earliest attestation that the colony acclaimed an emperor as lord dates between AD 326 and 331 and hails Constantine the Great as *dominus*, one to six years after he convened the First Council of Nicaea in AD 325.[23] To date, the only evidence for anyone being called *sōtēr* in Philippi is a fifth-century AD Christian inscription that acclaims Jesus as such.[24] While *salvator* has not been found in any Latin epigraphs from the colony that have been published, six inscriptions attest to the use of a cognate Latin term, *salus*, meaning "health, safety, well-being." These inscriptions, however, were erected and directed to traditional gods "on behalf of" (*pro salute*) Julio-Claudians, certain Philippians, or the body politic of the city.[25] It is probable that the Philippians considered Augustus a *sōtēr/salvator* while he was alive, because the Roman Senate had hailed him as such in 27 BC, after he emerged victorious in the Roman civil war with Marc Antony (see pp. 68–69).[26] However, by the time Christianity arrived in Philippi, Augustus had been acknowledged as a divine being who had ascended to heaven to rule with the gods—he was *Divus Augustus*—which trumped his former status as *sōtēr/salvator*, one who had saved the Roman state from disorder and reestablished it.

The reason scholars have failed to notice that *kyrios* and *sōtēr* are not imperial titles in Philippi is their underlying assumption about imperial divine honors that I noted in the last chapter. Their method of interpreting such honors is generalized and presupposes that a monolithic "imperial cult" existed in the Roman Empire. Consequently, one need not reconstruct "the imperial cult" in Philippi, because Greco-Roman cities treated emperors equally, and if one city honored a certain Julio-Claudian divinely, then all cities did.[27] As I demonstrated in the last

---

23. *CIPh* 2.1.30.

24. Pilhofer 2.131. This epigraph contains the legendary correspondence between Abgar and Jesus.

25. *CIPh* 2.1.6, 23 (= Pilhofer 2.132), 158; Pilhofer 2.588, 621. *CIPh* 2.1.4 (= Pilhofer 2.699) is an epitaph that contains the Latin noun *salus* only.

26. Dio Cassius, *Roman History* 53.16.4–5, notes that in 27 BC the senate voted to plant laurel trees (the symbol of victory) in front of Augustus's house and to place an oak crown above them, which symbolized that with his military victories "he [had] saved the citizens [of Rome]" (τοὺς πολίτας σώζοντι). During Augustus's reign, the Roman government minted coin series with Augustus's bust on the observe and the legend "because he saved the citizens" (*ob cives servatos*). See C. H. V. Sutherland and R. A. G. Carson, eds., *From 31 BC to AD 69*, vol. 1 of *The Roman Imperial Coinage* (London: Spink & Son, 1984), 47, nos. 75A–78. I am indebted to Cédric Brélaz for the reference to this coin series.

27. Scores of the phrase "imperial cult" appear in scholarly works on Philippi: Joseph H. Hellerman, *Reconstructing Honor in Roman Philippi: Carmen Christi as Cursus Pudorum*, SNTSMS 132 (Cambridge: Cambridge University Press, 2005), 80–87; Colin Miller, "The Imperial Cult in the

chapter, this approach is inappropriate, and, in its place, I presented the more appropriate contextual method of interpreting imperial divine honors. Following this approach means, first and foremost, creating a localized, contextual profile of such honors by amassing all evidence for such honors in Philippi: inscriptions, coins, archaeological, and literary sources (if applicable). When this occurs, the Roman nature of these honors becomes clear, for all evidence consists of Latin inscriptions and coins attesting to postmortem divine honors for certain Julio-Claudians that local aristocrats with Roman citizenship administered, promoted, and patronized. The Roman character of these honors means that the only appropriate comparative material to fill in our fragmentary Philippian sources must be from places where Roman imperial divine honors were practiced—Rome and other sister colonies of Philippi, like Corinth. It is to this contextual reconstruction that we now turn.

DIVINE HONORS FOR HUMANS IN PHILIPPI

History of Philippi

To reconstruct imperial divine honors in Philippi, we must begin with a history of the city, because normally a city's customs as well as its status in the Roman Empire impacted the types of imperial divine honors that it decreed, financially supported, and practiced. The founding of Philippi as a Roman colony in 42 BC, however, renders much of its Greek past obsolete. Nevertheless, the city's Greek history provides a notable contrast with the later Roman colony. Thus, the history of Philippi is indeed a tale of two cities, a Greek city and a Roman colony. The origins of the Greek city go back to 360 BC when Greeks from an island in the north Aegean Sea known as Thasos, thus Thasians, colonized a narrow strip of land between mountains and a marsh (now mostly drained) and called it Krenides.[28] Soon these colonists came into conflict with a tribal people who lived on the

---

Pauline Cities of Asia Minor and Greece," *CBQ* 72 (2010): 314–32; Lynn H. Cohick, "Philippians and Empire," in *Jesus Is Lord, Caesar Is Not: Evaluating Empire in New Testament Studies*, ed. Scot McKnight and Joseph B. Modica (Downers Grove, IL: InterVarsity Press, 2013), 166–82.

28. Diodorus Siculus, *Library of History* 16.3.7; 16.8.6–7; Strabo, *Geography* 7, fragments 34, 36, 41–42; Appian, *Civil Wars* 4.105. For discussions of the history of Philippi in English, see Chaido Koukouli-Chrysantaki, "Colonia Iulia Augusta Philippensis," in *Philippi at the Time of Paul and after His Death*, ed. Charalambos Bakirtzis and Helmut Koester (Harrisburg, PA: Trinity Press International, 1998), 5–35. For a concise discussion of the ancient sources of Philippi, see James R. Harrison, "Excavating the Urban and Country Life of Roman Philippi and Its Territory,"

plains near them, the Thracians. In their fight against the Thracians, whom the Thasians perceived as marauding barbarians, they asked a growing superpower, Macedon, and its king, Philip II (reigned 359–336 BC), Alexander the Great's father, for military aid. Philip appears to have gladly obliged. He marched his army to Krenides and defeated the Thracians. Instead of withdrawing from his spear-won territory, Philip annexed Krenides in 356 BC and founded a new Greek city with a Greek constitution on the spot, which he named after himself, "Philippi." From its founding until the mid-second century BC, the city remained under Macedonian control and appears to have prospered. The Romans took control of Philippi in 168 BC after a Roman army defeated the last reigning Macedonian king, Perseus, in open battle. In the aftermath of this defeat, Rome turned the kingdom of Macedon into the Roman province of Macedonia.[29] The main change in Philippi's fortunes during this period was that it now paid allegiance and taxes to Rome, not the kings of Macedon.

The only evidence for divine honors for a ruler in Greek Philippi is a fragmentary marble inscription found reused in a window of a Byzantine church known as Basilica A (see fig. 2.1, no. 4). The epigraph dates between 350 and 300 BC and refers to "the other sacred precinct of Philip" (*allou temenous Philippou*).[30] The Greek word *temenos* has a wide range of meaning—from a temple complex containing a temple, treasuries, other sacred buildings, and an altar to a small enclosed and consecrated area in which divine honors occurred.[31] Given that the epigraph was not found in situ or in its original location, we will probably never know for certain of what Philip's "other *temenos*" consisted. This structure might have been a small shrine, because in the Hellenistic period, cities rarely constructed large temple complexes for rulers on whom they bestowed divine honors, as they sometimes did for emperors in the Roman period.[32] This grant of such honors for Philip is fitting, for Greek cities (as well as Rome) commonly bestowed these types of honors on their founders. What is interesting about this *temenos* is that Philippi evidently dedicated more than one shrine to Philip. Notice that the inscription

---

in *Roman Philippi*, vol. 4 of *The First Urban Churches*, ed. James R. Harrison and L. L. Welborn, WGRWSup 13 (Atlanta: SBL Press, 2018), 1–61, esp. 3–11.

29. This occurred during the Third Macedonian War (171–168 BC). For a concise history of Macedonia, see Burnett, *Studying the New Testament*, 109–15.

30. "Appendix 1: Inscriptions" §2.1, line 6.

31. LSJ 1774.

32. Christian Habicht, *Divine Honors for Mortal Men in Greek Cities: The Early Cases*, trans. John Noël Dillon (Ann Arbor: Michigan Classical Press, 2017), 100, notes that τεμένη associated with divine honors for rulers in Greek and Hellenistic sources are typically an "entire enclosed area designated as the cult site."

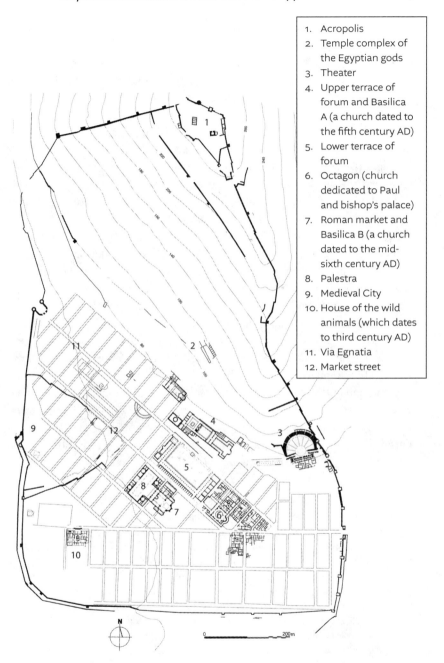

1. Acropolis
2. Temple complex of the Egyptian gods
3. Theater
4. Upper terrace of forum and Basilica A (a church dated to the fifth century AD)
5. Lower terrace of forum
6. Octagon (church dedicated to Paul and bishop's palace)
7. Roman market and Basilica B (a church dated to the mid-sixth century AD)
8. Palestra
9. Medieval City
10. House of the wild animals (which dates to third century AD)
11. Via Egnatia
12. Market street

Fig. 2.1 Site map of Roman Philippi | *Drawing by P. Weber and S. Provost, École française d'Athènes, used with permission*

refers to the "other *temenos*" (*allou temenous*), meaning that at least one more existed in the city.[33] The epigraph's broad possible date (350–300 BC) and Philip's death in 336 BC make it unclear whether these *temenē* date to during or after his lifetime. Either is possible. In the end this matters little, for the Philippi to which Paul brought the gospel was not a Greek city but a Roman colony.

This reference to Roman Philippi brings us to the second city in our tale of two cities. The origins of the Roman colony go back to 44 BC when Brutus and Cassius (and other Roman senators) assassinated Julius Caesar on March 15 of that year (see fig. 2.1).[34] Soon after, a bloody civil war erupted in Rome between these two murderers of Caesar and two of the deceased dictator's allies, Marc Antony and his adopted son Caesar Octavian (known after 27 BC as Augustus). Brutus and Cassius fled with their armies to mainland Greece, and Antony and Caesar Octavian and their forces pursued them. The generals and their troops met each other outside Philippi's walls on a plain known as the Drama plain. For two days in late October 42 BC, the opposing armies clashed. When the dust settled, (mostly) Antony and Caesar Octavian and their forces emerged victorious.[35] Having avenged Caesar's murder, these two generals divided up most of the Roman Empire between them and parted under an alliance that was shaky at best. Caesar Octavian returned to Rome and the western portion of the empire, his sphere of influence, while Antony remained in the Greek East, the territory under his authority.[36] After the victory at Philippi, Antony demobilized some of his troops, settled them in the city, and refounded Philippi as a Roman colony, naming it after himself and the victory over Caesar's murderers: "the Victorious Colony of the Philippians by Antony's Command."[37] In the process, Antony confiscated the land inside and outside the city. He had a priest with his toga pulled atop the back and top of his head, a posture known as *capite velato*, plow the sacred boundary of the city, the *pomerium*, with two oxen, which is a ritual that mimicked the supposed founding

---

33. Archaeologists have uncovered a tomb inside the walls of Philippi, which has been identified as a ἡρῷον or tomb-like shrine for Philip. However, the latest archaeological evidence suggests that the tomb dates to the Roman period, which means that the ἡρῷον cannot be Philip's. See Michel Sève and Patrick Weber, "Le côté Nord du forum de Philippes," *BCH* 110 (1986): 531–81. For a recent discussion see Habicht, *Divine Honors*, 182–83.

34. Appian, *Civil Wars* 2.117–149.

35. Velleius Paterculus, *Roman History* 2.70–71; Appian, *Civil Wars* 4.105–132. In the *Res gestae divi Augusti* 2, Augustus claims that only he, and not Antony, won the battle of Philippi. For a description of the battle, see Adrian Goldsworthy, *Augustus: First Emperor of Rome* (New Haven: Yale University Press, 2014), 134–43.

36. Goldsworthy, *Augustus*, 143.

37. *Antoni iussu colonia Victrix Philippensis* (*RPC* 1:1646–49).

of Rome in 753 BC.[38] Afterward, Antony or one of his associates had the confiscated land distributed among the new colonists for them to live on and to farm.[39]

The alliance between Antony and Caesar Octavian remained intact for almost ten years, but in 32 BC, each man's desire to be the sole ruler of the empire forced the eruption of open hostility between the two. In 31 BC, Antony and Caesar Octavian met in a decisive naval

Fig. 2.2 Coin (probably from Philippi) (AD 14–37) (*RPC* 1:1658) depicting the busts of Drusus and Tiberius on the obverse (*left*) and two priests plowing Philippi's *pomerium* with oxen on the reverse (*right*) | *With permission of wildwinds.com, ex CNG, 2008*

battle off the coast of Greece near a city called Actium. The latter won the day, and Antony fled with Cleopatra to Egypt where he committed suicide, thereby leaving Caesar Octavian the only real power in Rome's empire.[40] Almost immediately, the victor of Actium began to wipe out Antony's memory and sever any allegiances that anyone had with his old enemy. One of the ways that Caesar Octavian accomplished this was by refounding Roman colonies, like Philippi, that Antony had founded. Thus, in 30 BC, Rome's emperor sent more discharged soldiers and Italians, who had sided with Antony and as a result had their Italian lands confiscated, to Philippi. The foundation rituals of the colony were repeated, and somehow the land inside and outside the city was divided among the old and new colonists for them to live on and to farm (see fig. 2.2).[41]

38. The reverse of a coin minted between 42 and 31 BC pictures this scene (*RPC* 1:1646). According to ancient Roman tradition, Romulus plowed Rome's boundary when he founded the city (Plutarch, *Romulus* 11).

39. Cédric Brélaz, *Philippes, colonie romaine d'Orient: Recherches d'histoire institutionelle et sociale*, Bulletin de correspondance hellénique Supplément 59 (Athens: École française d'Athènes, 2018), 19–22. Pilhofer 2.397a is a marble boundary marker found near Philippi that attests to this land division. The sources tell us nothing about what happened to the disenfranchised Greeks, but inscriptions indicate that some of them as well as some Thracians maintained their homes and land outside the city's boundary that was part of the colony's rural territory.

40. Goldsworthy, *Augustus*, 170–94, esp. 180–94.

41. Dio Cassius, *Roman History* 51.4.5–6; Brélaz, *Philippes*, 23–30. The names of the colonists evince that they came from Italy. See Cédric Brélaz, "Philippi: A Roman Colony within Its Regional Context," in *Les communautés du Nord égéen au temps de l'hégémonie romaine: Entre ruptures et continuités*, ed. Julien Fournier and Marie-Gabrielle G. Parissaki, Melethmata 77 (Athens: Institute of Historical Research, 2018), 163–82, esp. 169–71; Brélaz, "First-Century Philippi,"

Like Philip II and Antony, Caesar Octavian named his refounded colony after himself. Unlike these two former founders of the city, he included someone else's name in the colony's title, that of his (adopted) father: "the Julian Augustan Colony of the Philippians by Augustus's Command."[42] Finally, he provided them with "the right of Italians" (*ius Italicum*), which meant that Philippi was considered Italian soil, its colonists were tax exempt, and governors of Macedonia could not interfere in the city's affairs.[43]

This double founding of Philippi as a Roman colony erased the city's Greek history and identity. In the words of one of Philippi's epigraphers, Cédric Brélaz, "the Hellenistic city of Philippi ceased to exist."[44] To this end, a Roman constitution, which has not survived, replaced the city's old Greek one.[45] However, we can reconstruct aspects of this constitution from inscriptions from Roman Philippi and surviving charters of other Roman colonies.[46] This document established a Roman form of government with Roman institutions in Philippi. Latin replaced Greek as the city's official language.[47] The inhabitants of Philippi were divided into two main groups: *coloni* or "colonists" with full legal rights, who made up the *populus* or "legal assembly" of the Philippian people, and *incolae* or noncitizen "resident aliens" with no civic rights. This second group consisted of those Greeks

---

in *Roman Philippi*, vol. 4 of *The First Urban Churches*, ed. James R. Harrison and L. L. Welborn, WGRWSup 13 (Atlanta: SBL Press, 2018), 159.

42. *colonia Iulia Augusta Philippensis iussu Augusti* (*RPC* 1:1650). For the title *colonia Iulia Augusta Philippensis*, see *RPC* 1:1653–55. The Roman Senate bestowed the title Augustus on Caesar Octavian in January 27 BC, which means that the final name of Philippi dates after that. Thus, from 30 BC until 27 BC, Philippi's official name was probably "the Julian Colony of the Philippians" (*colonia Iulia Philippensis*).

43. Brélaz, *Philippes*, 36–37. Antony may have enrolled the Philippian colonists into the Voltinia tribe, and Caesar Octavian may have affirmed it. Either way, the latter is ultimately responsible for the voting tribe of the colonists.

44. Brélaz, "First-Century Philippi," 155.

45. Brélaz, *Philippes*, 34–37; Brélaz, "First-Century Philippi," 155, 166–73.

46. One such constitution is the "Law of the Julian Colony of Urso," in modern-day Spain, which dates between 59 and 44 BC and was found engraved on bronze tablets that date to the end of the first century AD. See Michael Crawford, ed., "*Lex Coloniae Genetivae*," in *Roman Statutes*, 2 vols. (London: Institute of Classical Studies, 1996), 1:393–454.

47. Brélaz, *Philippes*, 73–85; Brélaz, "First-Century Philippi," 160. The distinction between Greek and Roman Philippi is evident in the city's use of Latin for official inscriptions and its coinage. After Philip II founded the city, the coins were gold, silver, and bronze, and the images and their legends are Greek: Barclay V. Head, *A Catalogue of the Greek Coins in the British Museum: Macedonia, Etc.* (London: Trustees of the British Museum, 1879), 96–98, nos. 1–22. When Roman Philippi was founded, the coins were minted only in bronze, the images are Roman, and the legends are in Latin (*RPC* 1:1646–55, and possibly 1656–60).

and Thracians who lived in the city after its conversion to a Roman colony, some of whom had probably been disenfranchised of some or all of their land in the creation and re-creation of Philippi as a colony of Rome.[48] The first group were enrolled into a single Roman voting tribe, the Voltinia, and only a small portion of these men, between seventy and one hundred, attained the *ordo* or "rank" of *decurio* (*decuriones* in the Latin plural) or member of the *curia* or Philippi's "local senate." Thus, *decuriones* were local senators who administered and oversaw colonial public affairs.[49] The wives and daughters of all colonists were considered *cives* or "citizens," and they possessed some limited rights. However, Roman custom precluded women from voting or holding public office.

Each year, the colony's *populus* elected aristocratic men to several local magistracies, the two most important of which were *duovir* and *aedile*. The colonists selected only two men to serve as *aediles*. Their main tasks were to oversee the colony's roads, public buildings, food supply, and commerce in the forum. After their year of office ended, these *aediles* attained the *ordo* of *decurio* and took a seat on the colony's *curia*.[50] Philippi elected two *decuriones* annually to serve as *duoviri*, literally a "board of two men," and to be the ultimate local authority in the colony, resembling the two consuls of Rome that the Roman *populus* selected each year. The task of the *duoviri* was to oversee Philippi's legal system, finances, and public cults, including imperial divine honors.[51] Every fifth year, Philippi's *populus* elected two special *duoviri*, *duoviri quinquennales* or *duoviri* every fifth year, who performed a census of Philippi's citizens, especially of the *decuriones*. In the process, the *duoviri quinquennales* purged dead citizens from the colony's official list and added new ones.[52] One aspect of Philippi's local government that is of import in its relationship with nascent Christianity is its socially Roman conservative character. Unlike other Roman colonies such as Corinth, Philippi's *decuriones* strove to ensure that the colony maintained its distinctive Roman culture and cus-

---

48. Brélaz, *Philippes*, 119–28; Brélaz, "First-Century Philippi," 159–66. Epaphroditus (Phil 2:25–30; 4:18), Euodia (Phil 4:2), Syntyche (Phil 4:2), and maybe Lydia (Acts 16:14–15, 40) probably belonged to the class of *incolae* in the city, while Clement (Phil 4:3) may have been a *colonus*, although Brélaz, "First-Century Philippi," 163, is certain that Clement was an *incola* (the Latin singular of *incolae*).

49. Brélaz, *Philippes*, 128–44; *Lex Coloniae Genetivae* 64, 69, 75, 80, 96–100, 103–31, 134.

50. Brélaz, *Philippes*, 144–47; *Lex Coloniae Genetivae* 62, 77, 98, 128–30, 134.

51. Brélaz, *Philippes*, 185–86; *Lex Coloniae Genetivae* 62–64, 67–71, 81, 93–105, 130–31, 134. According to Acts 16:16–40, the owners of the slave from whom Paul cast out the prophetic spirit hauled Paul and Silas before the *duoviri* (whom Luke calls the στρατηγοί) (Acts 16:20, 22, 35, 38). These *duoviri* stripped Paul and Silas of their cloths, had them beaten, and then threw them into prison (Acts 16:22–24). See Brélaz, *Philippes*, 231–44; Brélaz, "First-Century Philippi," 170.

52. Brélaz, *Philippes*, 148–58, esp. 154–58.

toms. To this end, they tended to shun non-Roman traditions and embrace Roman ones. For example, Philippi's *decuriones* kept Latin as the colony's official language for three hundred years, they laid out their forum and filled it with Roman-style buildings (see figs. 2.1, nos. 4–5, 7), and most importantly, they did not integrate Greeks and other outsiders into their governing class, as other colonies, such as Corinth, did.[53] The reason that Philippi held on to its Roman identity so effectively is that, as Brélaz observes, the same Roman families "retained power in Philippi" from its founding until the mid-third century AD.[54]

Imperial Divine Honors in Philippi

Philippian inscriptions, coins, and archaeological remains allow us to reconstruct imperial divine honors in the colony. These sources evince that such honors in Philippi mirrored Roman imperial divine honors almost perfectly, with one exception. However, this exception proves the rule. That is, it demonstrates the Roman character of these honors in the colony. In what follows, I reconstruct the honors in question in Philippi. I begin by presenting the sources for these honors in chronological order of the Julio-Claudians on whom they were bestowed. Then, I explore the identity of the imperial cultic officials in the colony, parsing out who they were and the other public offices that they held in the city. Finally, I address the location whence these cultic officials offered imperial sacrifices to the Julio-Claudians, as well as how and when these offerings were made.

Divus Julius

Despite Julius Caesar's assassination on March 15, 44 BC, the Roman Senate did not officially divinize him until January 1, 42 BC, almost a year before Antony founded Philippi as a Roman colony and twelve years before Caesar Octavian refounded it. The city may have established divine honors for *Divus* Julius after

---

53. All of this differed markedly from Corinth where that colony began to use Greek as one of its official languages in the second century AD, the city preserved some of the Greek city's monuments, and freedmen and Roman businessmen known as *negotiatores* who had lived in the Greek East were able to hold public offices. See Brélaz, "First-Century Philippi," 157, 159–60, and chapter 4. Even though Paul traveled to other Roman colonies such as Corinth or Antioch of Pisidia, Luke singularly identifies Philippi as a κολωνία of Rome, which is a transliteration of the Latin *colonia* (Acts 16:12). The charge brought against Paul and Silas (also known as Silvanus) in the city is that they were "proclaiming customs illegal for us Roman citizens to accept or practice" (Acts 16:21).

54. Brélaz, "First-Century Philippi," 160.

Fig. 2.3 Coin minted in Philippi between 27 BC and AD 14 (*RPC* 1:1650) depicting the head of Augustus on the obverse (*left*) and a statue base with Augustus in military garb, on the left, with a half-naked *Divus* Julius wearing a toga and crowning him with the *corona civica* on the reverse (*right*). The legend above the statue group reads *Aug(ustus) divi f(ilius)* | *With permission of wildwinds.com*

its initial Antonian founding. No evidence, however, substantiates this claim. All Philippian sources for divine honors for the divinized dictator postdate the Augustan refounding of the colony. Three Philippian coin series minted between 27 BC and AD 68 attest to divine honors for *Divus* Julius, and one inscription acknowledges his divinization in Rome.[55] The three coin series are almost identical, and the earliest dates between January 27 BC and August AD 14. This latter coin pictures, on the obverse, Augustus's bust and, on the reverse, a statue base on top of which stand the images of Augustus and *Divus* Julius. Two altars flank the statues (see fig. 2.3).

The statue group on the coin probably depicts an actual monument that was set up in Philippi's lower forum during Augustus's reign (31 BC–AD 14) (see figs. 2.1, no. 5; 7). The image of Augustus shows him bedecked in military garb with a sword girded on his left side. The Latin legend above the emperor's image reads, "Augustus son of the *divus*" (*Aug(ustus) divi f(ilius)*). The statue of *Divus* Julius depicts him half naked and thus in a divine, Jupiter-like posture. *Divus* Julius extends his right hand over Augustus's head crowning him with the *corona civica* or civic crown, which was a Roman honor given to a soldier who saved the life of a fellow citizen in battle.[56] The Latin legend above *Divus* Julius identifies him as

---

55. *RPC* 1:1650, 1653, 1655; "Appendix 1: Inscriptions" §2.2.

56. Adrian Goldsworthy, *The Complete Roman Army* (London: Thames & Hudson, 2003), 96.

such, "(dedicated) to *Divus* Julius" (*divo Iul(io)*).[57] Provided that these coins picture a Philippian monument, one or both the altars flanking the statue base were probably used for sacrifices to *Divus* Julius (for a description of these sacrifices, see pp. 91–94). The inscription acknowledging *Divus* Julius's divinization is engraved on a broken marble stele that was found reused in Basilica B (see fig. 2.1, no. 7). Originally, the epigraph was part of a monument in Philippi's forum that held statues of certain Julio-Claudians, possibly different from the one depicted on the above Philippian coins, that was set up between AD 16 and 37. Its text identifies the emperor Tiberius (AD 14–37) as *Divus* Julius's grandson, and Tiberius's son, Drusus, as *Divus* Julius's great-grandson (*Ti(berius) · C[aesa]r . . . divi [Iuli] n(epos) . . . Dru[sus] Caesar . . . divi · Iuli pro[n(epos)]*).[58]

Divus Augustus

Although Augustus refounded Philippi as a Roman colony in 30 BC, the city followed Rome and did not provide him with divine honors during his lifetime.[59] Instead, it waited until Augustus's death (August 19, AD 14) and the Roman Senate's divinization of him (September 17, AD 14) to establish divine honors for the deceased emperor. Two coin series and six inscriptions attest to these honors, and two epigraphs postdating Augustus's death acknowledge the deceased emperor's divine status.[60] The two coin series date between AD 41 and 68 and contain the image of the statue base of *Divus* Julius and Augustus in between the two altars described above. There is, however, one key difference in these two coin series.[61] Those minted after Augustus's divinization in Rome reflect his new divine status. Instead of calling the deceased emperor "Augustus son of the *divus*" (see fig. 2.3), they acclaim him as *Divus Augustus* (see fig. 2.4). This critical difference in Augustus's name underscores that divine honors for Julio-Claudians in Philippi, even for the colony's founder, were postmortem.

The six inscriptions attesting to heavenly honors for *Divus* Augustus are part of epigraphs connected to aristocratic Philippian men who served as his priests

---

57. *RPC* 1:1650.

58. "Appendix 1: Inscriptions" §2.2, lines 1–5. This monument was erected by a freedman of the emperor Gaius Caligula and consisted of a long base, and the Julio-Claudians whose images were displayed on it were those who held tribunician power from Augustus onward. Brélaz, "First-Century Philippi," 158.

59. This provides a notable contrast with the Greek city and the divine honors that it bestowed on Philip II (see pp. 66–68).

60. *RPC* 1:1653, 1655; "Appendix 1: Inscriptions" §2.2, 3, 4, 5, 6, 7, 8, and 9.

61. *RPC* 1:1653, 1655.

Fig. 2.4 Coin minted in Philippi between AD 41 and 54 (*RPC* 1:1654) depicting a bust of Claudius on the obverse (*left*) and *Divus* Augustus, on the left, and *Divus* Julius, on the right, on a statue base on the reverse (*right*), with the legend *Divus Aug*(*ustus*) on the statue base | *With permission of wildwinds.com, ex Fritz Rudolf Künker GmbH*

(for more on these priests, see pp. 78–80).[62] Two of these are from statue bases of these priests,[63] one may be from an Augustan priest's funerary monument,[64] one is from a monument honoring such an official,[65] and two are from inscriptions commemorating benefactions to Philippi that two different priests of *Divus* Augustus provided.[66] This priesthood must have been of great importance in the colony, for it is the longest attested imperial cultic office in Philippi's history. The earliest record of it dates soon after Augustus's divinization in AD 14, and the latest to the second century.[67] For more on these priests, see my discussion below.

The first of the two inscriptions that acknowledge this deceased emperor's divinization is from the monument in the forum that once held statues of certain Julio-Claudians that was set up between AD 16 and 37, as noted above. It identifies Tiberius as *Divus* Augustus's son and Drusus, Tiberius's son, as *Divus* Augustus's grandson (*Ti*(*berius*) · *C*[*aesa*]*r* · *divi* · *Augusti* · *f*(*ilius*) . . . *Dru*[*sus*] *Caesar* . . . *divi* · *A*[*ug*(*usti*) *n*(*epos*)]).[68] The second epigraph served as a dedication engraved on marble probably for a building in the forum that had been dedicated to Tiberius,

62. "Appendix 1: Inscriptions" §2.3, 4, 5, 6, 7, 8.
63. "Appendix 1: Inscriptions" §2.3, 8.
64. "Appendix 1: Inscriptions" §2.7.
65. "Appendix 1: Inscriptions" §2.5.
66. "Appendix 1: Inscriptions" §2.4, 6.
67. "Appendix 1: Inscriptions" §2.3, 5, 8.
68. "Appendix 1: Inscriptions" §2.2, lines 1–5.

which calls that emperor *Divus* Augustus's son ([. . . *Ti(berius) Cae]sar · div(i) · Aug(usti) · [f(ilius) Aug(ustus)* ---]).[69]

Tiberius

Toward the end of his life, Tiberius was not a popular emperor. He retired to the island of Capri in AD 26, where he spent his time chasing pleasures of the flesh, orchestrating the deaths of certain Roman aristocrats, and neglecting matters of the state.[70] His actions appear to have been so widely known that, according to the second-century AD biographer of emperors Suetonius, the king of Rome's bitter enemy Parthia, Artabanus, sent Tiberius a letter charging him with parricide, murder, laziness, and extravagance. The Parthian king went so far as to urge the emperor to do the Romans a favor and to kill himself.[71] Therefore, it is unsurprising that after his death (March 16, AD 37), the Roman Senate did not divinize Tiberius. Despite this fact, Philippi deviated from its mother city and established a postmortem priesthood for him. This deviation, however, acknowledged the senate's refusal to divinize the emperor, for the colony did not hail Tiberius as *divus*. One fragmentary inscription from the city, engraved on marble and found in the Octagon or church dedicated to Paul (see fig. 2.1, no. 6), is the total evidence for the honors in question. It was set up in the Philippian bath between AD 41 and 54 and was probably part of a dedication to the gods on behalf of the emperor Claudius. The individual responsible for this dedication notes that among the public offices in which he served, he was Tiberius's priest (for more on this priest, see pp. 79, 86).[72]

Diva Augusta

The only female Julio-Claudian for whom Philippi established divine honors is Livia, Augustus's wife. After her husband's death in AD 14, she was adopted into his family, and her name was changed to Augusta.[73] She died in AD 29 and was buried with Augustus in his mausoleum in Rome. Many people in Rome wanted the Roman Senate to divinize Augusta, but her son, Tiberius, refused. Therefore, she was not made a *diva*.[74] That changed, however, when Augusta's grandson Claudius

---

69. "Appendix 1: Inscriptions" §2.9.
70. Suetonius, *Tiberius* 41, 43–44, 62, 69.
71. Suetonius, *Tiberius* 66.
72. "Appendix 1: Inscriptions" §2.4, line 3.
73. Suetonius, *Deified Augustus* 101.2; Tacitus, *Annals* 1.8.
74. Tacitus, *Annals* 5.1–2; Dio Cassius, *Roman History* 58.1.1–6.

became emperor in AD 41. The newly crowned emperor oversaw her divinization on January 17, AD 42.[75] Soon after this event, Philippi established divine honors for the newly minted *Diva* Augusta, to which two inscriptions attest. The first is part of the largest known surviving honorary monument from Philippi: a statue base that once held the images of at least four, but probably seven, Roman priestesses of *Diva* Augusta (see figs. 2.5, 6; for more on these priestesses, see pp. 81–82, and for more on this monument, see pp. 81–82, 89). This monument was constructed in the last quarter of the first century AD in the northeastern part of the forum's lower terrace (see fig. 2.1, no. 5) next to the colony's imperial temple and was found there in situ.[76] The second epigraph is a funerary inscription engraved on a white limestone sarcophagus that was found in the nearby port city of Kavala and that dates between AD 80 and 90. According to the epitaph's text, the interred was a priestess of *Diva* Augusta.[77]

Divus Claudius

The last Julio-Claudian granted divine honors in Philippi is the emperor Claudius. When he died (October 13, AD 54), the Roman Senate divinized him the same day. When news reached Philippi, it bestowed divine honors on the freshly consecrated *Divus* Claudius.[78] The evidence for these honors is a single funerary inscription that postdates AD 54. Like the above epigraph attesting to *Diva* Augusta's priestess, this inscription is inscribed on a marble sarcophagus that was found in Kavala. The epigraph's text notes that the person laid to rest in it was *Divus* Claudius's priest.[79]

Imperial Cultic Officials

Now that we know on whom Philippi bestowed divine honors, the next issue we must address is who offered such honors on behalf of the colony. As we have seen, much of the evidence for imperial divine honors consists of inscriptions attesting to priests and priestesses who oversaw them. From the titles of these imperial cultic priesthoods, the names of the officials who filled them, and other informa-

---

75. Suetonius, *Deified Claudius* 11.2; Dio Cassius, *Roman History* 60.5.1–5.

76. "Appendix 1: Inscriptions" §2.10.

77. "Appendix 1: Inscriptions" §2.11.

78. Seneca, *Apocolocyntosis*; Tacitus, *Annals* 12.69; Suetonius, *Nero* 9; Dio Cassius, *Roman History* 61.35.2.

79. "Appendix 1: Inscriptions" §2.12, line 3.

tion that we can cull from these epigraphs, we can reconstruct some information about these imperial priests and priestesses, their careers and that of their family members, and their social status in the colony. Inscriptions attest to two types of imperial priestly offices in Philippi, both of which were Roman in nature, *flamines* (*flamen* in the singular) for male Julio-Claudians and *sacerdotes* (*sacerdos* in the singular) for the one female Julio-Claudian.

Flamines

In Philippi, *flamines* were exclusively imperial priests. The office of a *flamen* or *flaminia* was a traditional Roman priesthood dating back to the time when kings ruled Rome (753–509 BC). Most *flamines* were appointed to serve a particular deity such as the *flamen Dialis* or *flamen* of Jupiter.[80] When the Roman Senate began to divinize deceased Julio-Claudians, individual *flamines* were chosen to serve specific *divi*. Philippi followed its mother city in this practice, appointing *flamines* to administer divine honors for *Divus* Julius, *Divus* Augustus, Tiberius, and *Divus* Claudius.[81] The colony probably held annual elections for these priesthoods, and the individuals who filled them were aristocratic, indeed some of the most aristocratic, men in Philippi (see table 2.1). This much is clear, in that these priests held other public offices in the colony, including the highest ones: that of *duovir* or *duovir quinquennalis*. It is unclear whether these men served as imperial priests before, during, or after they reached the apex of their public careers. Despite this uncertainty, at the time of their service as *flamines*, these individuals were or were on their way to becoming the most powerful men of their day in the colony.[82]

---

80. Livy, *History of Rome* 1.20.1–4; Varro, *On the Latin Language* 5.84.

81. Brélaz, *Philippes*, 191–93. Unlike Rome, Philippian *flamines* oversaw imperial divine honors exclusively, and priests of traditional deities were known as *pontifices* (the plural of *pontifex*: *CIPh* 2.1.53 (= Pilhofer 2.1 = *CIL* 3.650), 60 (= Pilhofer 2.235a), 152 (= Pilhofer 2.241). For more on the *flamines* of Rome, see John Scheid, *An Introduction to Roman Religion*, trans. Janet Lloyd (Bloomington: University of Indiana Press, 2003), 133.

82. Along with my own primary research, I am grateful for Brélaz, *Philippes*, 191–93, a superb discussion of imperial *flamines* in Philippi and his table containing information about them.

TABLE 2.1 PHILIPPIAN *FLAMINES*

Name	Imperial Priestly Office	Other Philippian Offices	Status
Gaius Antonius Rufus ("Appendix 1: Inscriptions" §2.3)	*flamen* of *Divus* Augustus	*princeps* or first citizen of Philippi, which means that he was *aedile*, *duovir*, and *duovir quinquennalis*	Equestrian (second highest rank in the Roman Empire)
Lucius Atiarius Schoenias ("Appendix 1: Inscriptions" §2.4)	*flamen* of *Divus* Augustus, *flamen* of Tiberius		Equestrian
Gaius Oppius Montanus ("Appendix 1: Inscriptions" §2.5, 7)	*flamen* of *Divus* Augustus	Son of the colony; given honors of the ornaments belonging to the *decuriones*, the *duoviri*, and the *duoviri quinquennales*; peace officer; *duovir*; *munerarius* or overseer of gladiatorial games; *princeps* and *patronus* of the colony; priest (*pontifex*) (of nonimperial divine honors)	Equestrian
Name lost ("Appendix 1: Inscriptions" §2.6)	*flamen* of *Divus* Augustus	Military tribune	
Name lost ("Appendix 1: Inscriptions" §2.8)	*flamen* of Augustus (but *divus* should most probably be restored before Augustus)	*duovir*; *duovir quinquennalis*; priest (*pontifex*) (of nonimperial divine honors)	

Name	Imperial Priestly Office	Other Philippian Offices	Status
Publius Cornelius Asper Atiarius Montanus ("Appendix 1: Inscriptions" §2.12)	*flamen* of *Divus* Claudius	given the ornaments belonging to the *decuriones* and *duoviri*; priest (*pontifex*) (of nonimperial divine honors)	Equestrian

One of the most interesting *flamines* of *Divus* Augustus and the one about whom we know the most is Gaius Antonius Rufus. The reason we are so informed about Rufus is that four *vici* (*vicus* in the singular) or "neighborhoods" of the Roman colony of Alexandria Troas, which is about 218 miles east of Philippi, set up four statues of Rufus and inscribed his career on marble bases that held these images.[83] Rufus was born in the early first century AD to a Roman family who probably lived in Philippi.[84] As a young man, he quitted the colony and joined the Roman army. There, he rose to the rank of tribune (a commander of a Roman legion) of two different cohorts and prefect (or commander) of a cavalry division. At some point, he attained the *ordo* or "rank" of equestrian, the second highest in the Roman Empire. Upon discharge, Rufus returned to live either in Philippi or in Apri, another Roman colony about 170 miles east of Philippi.[85] Once settled, he began to serve in public offices in four Roman colonies that were relatively close to each other: Philippi, Apri, Alexandria Troas, and Parium. In particular, Rufus was a priest of *Divus* Julius in Alexandria Troas and a priest of *Divus* Augustus both in Apri and Philippi. However, he must have held every major public office in the Roman colonies in question, including Philippi, because the epigraph on the statue bases calls him *princeps coloniae* or "first citizen of the colony." This Latin title was one that *curiae* or local senates of Roman colonies tended to bestow on individuals who were *decuriones* who had held all major public colonial offices.[86] Therefore, it is probable that, alongside being a *decurio*, Rufus was *aedile* and *duovir* in Philippi (as well as Apri, Alexandria Troas, and Parium).

83. "Appendix 1: Inscriptions" §2.3.

84. Because the epigraph mentions Rufus's voting tribe, the Voltinia, we know that he was a member of a wealthy family from Philippi.

85. The reason it is difficult to know whether Rufus lived in Philippi or Apri is that when the emperor Claudius (AD 41–54) founded the latter, he enrolled its citizens in the Voltinia tribe, the same tribe into which Philippi's citizens were enrolled.

86. Marijana Rici, *The Inscriptions of Alexandreia Troas*, Inschriften griechischer Städte aus Kleinasien 53 (Bonn: Habelt, 1997), p. 70.

Fig. 2.5 Remains of the monument of *sacerdotes* of *Diva* Augusta in Philippi | *Photo by Carole Raddato; photographed with the permission of Hellenic Republic, Ministry of Culture and Sports, General Directorate of Antiquities and Cultural Heritage, Ephorate of Antiquities of Kavala*

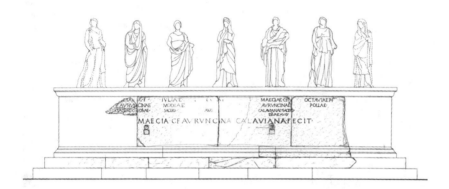

Fig. 2.6 Reconstruction of the monument of *sacerdotes* of *Diva* Augusta in Philippi | *Drawing by P. Weber and M. Sève, École française d'Athènes, used with permission*

Sacerdotes

Sacerdotes derives from the Latin noun *sacra* meaning "sacred things" and is a generic term that Romans used for priesthoods in general.[87] Like their male Philippian counterparts, *sacerdotes* in the colony were exclusively imperial priestesses serving the only divinized female Julio-Claudian, *Diva* Augusta. These women were from the wealthiest and most aristocratic Philippian families. Their male relatives tended to hold high public offices in the city, such as *pontifex* or priest of traditional divine honors, and to set up monuments to the Julio-Claudians.

87. *Res gestae divi Augusti* 9.1; Varro, *On the Latin Language* 5.83.

Some *sacerdotes* were from indigenous families who received their Roman citizenship directly from Augustus (see table 2.2).[88] Occasionally, administering imperial divine honors was a family affair, even though such priesthoods were not hereditary, as aristocratic men and women from the same family served as *flamines* and *sacerdotes*.[89] These imperial priestesses held prominent places in the colony in their own right, although they were women. As noted above, in the late first century AD, a priestess of *Diva* Augusta paid for the construction of one of the largest known monuments in Philippi: a statue base that was set up in the northeastern corner of the forum's lower terrace (see fig. 2.1, no. 5) that once held between four and seven statues of Philippian women, most of whom inscriptions identify as *sacerdotes* of *Diva* Augusta (see figs. 2.5, 6).[90] The process by which a Philippian woman became a *sacerdos* is unclear. She may have been elected or appointed to this post.

TABLE 2.2 PHILIPPIAN *SACERDOTES* OF *DIVA* AUGUSTA

Name	Male Relatives
Cornelia Asprilla ("Appendix 1: Inscriptions" §2.11)	Publius Cornelius Asper Atiarius Montanus ("Appendix 1: Inscriptions" §2.12)
Julia Auruncina ("Appendix 1: Inscriptions" §2.10)	Gaius Julius (*CIPh* 2.1.5 = Pilhofer 2.232a) who set up a monument in Philippi's forum to Drusus the Elder, father of the emperor Claudius
Julia Modia ("Appendix 1: Inscriptions" §2.10)	Gaius Julius (see above)
Name lost ("Appendix 1: Inscriptions" §2.10)	Relatives lost
Maecia Auruncina Calaviana ("Appendix 1: Inscriptions" §2.10)	Crispus son of Gaius (Pilhofer 2.222), who was probably prominent in the colony

88. Brélaz, *Philippes*, 193–96.

89. "Appendix 1: Inscriptions" §2.10, 11.

90. Michel Sève and Patrick Weber, *Guide du forum de Philippes*, Sites et Monuments 18 (Athens: École française d'Athènes, 2012), 76–77. Contra N. T. Wright, *Paul and the Faithfulness of God*, 2 vols. (Minneapolis: Fortress, 2013), 1:329, who incorrectly concludes that "Claudius caused a large monument to be placed there in the forum as part of the cult of Livia, Augustus's wife, whom Claudius deified," because he misinterprets the work of Peter Oakes, "Re-mapping the Universe: Paul and the Emperor in 1 Thessalonians and Philippians," *JSNT* 27 (2005): 301–22, esp. 307–8. Claudius had nothing to do with the erection of the monument, for he died, at the earliest, twelve years before it was erected, and technically the senate, not Claudius, divinized Livia. Moreover, the local Philippian *decuriones*, not the emperor, made the ultimate decision to set up the monument in question.

Augustales

In the late first century BC, Latin-speaking communities began to bestow a title on certain wealthy outsiders, freedmen or emancipated slaves, and rich non-aristocrats who were unable to become *decuriones* in their respective Roman and Latin communities, that of *Augustalis* (*Augustales* in the plural) or some variation of that title.[91] These *Augustales* used their riches to promote the honor, not necessarily divine, of Julio-Claudians by setting up public monuments and buildings, underwriting the cost of imperial festivals, and by patronizing and facilitating imperial divine honors.[92] Philippian inscriptions attest to the presence of this group in the colony, or, as its members preferred to call themselves, *seviri Augustales* or "members of the *Augustales*" (see table 2.3). Because many of these epigraphs are terse funerary inscriptions, some of which are fragmentary, we cannot extract as much information about the activities of group members in the city as we are able to for Philippi's *flamines* and *sacerdotes*. Provided that they functioned as they did elsewhere in the empire, they facilitated benefactions for Philippi. As we shall see in chapter 4, the Corinthian *Augustales* erected a monumental bronze statue of *Divus* Augustus atop an eight-foot base in the Corinthian forum (see figs. 4.6–8). Philippi's *seviri Augustales* may even have had their own building in which they met, as was the case for *Augustales* elsewhere in the Latin West. At the very least, it is evident from an inscription from the city's theater that they had their own assigned seating there (see fig. 2.1, no. 3).[93] Epigraphy testifies that four Philippian *seviri Augustales* were freedmen (*liberti, libertus* in the singular) and the names of

91. I am indebted to Margaret L. Laird, "The Emperor in a Roman Town: The Base of the *Augustales* in the Forum at Corinth," in *Corinth in Context: Comparative Studies on Religion and Society*, ed. Steven J. Friesen, Dan N. Showalter, and James C. Walters (Leiden: Brill, 2010), 67–116, for the notion that *Augustales* were "wealthy outsiders." The three commonest names of *Augustales* in the Latin West are *Augustales, seviri Augustales*, and *seviri*. For a recent, informed discussion of *Augustales*, including their various names, see Gwynaeth McIntyre, *A Family of Gods: The Worship of the Imperial Family in the Latin West* (Ann Arbor: University of Michigan Press, 2016), 111–29.

92. Gwynaeth McIntyre, *Imperial Cult* (Leiden: Brill, 2019), 27–28. Contrary to the claims of some New Testament scholars, such as Hellerman, *Reconstructing Honor in Roman Philippi*, 81–84, *Augustales* were probably not imperial priests. Mary Beard, John North, and Simon Price, *Religions of Rome*, 2 vols. (Cambridge: Cambridge University Press, 1998), 1:358, note, "There is no real case for seeing *Augustales* of this kind as priests, but *Augustales*, like other public figures, certainly carried out religious functions in their public role . . . and there is no reason to think of them as particularly connected by definition with 'the imperial cult.' Their name '*Augustales*' may in fact not derive from their presumed cult function, but mark the creation of the status by Augustus."

93. "Appendix 1: Inscriptions" §2.13. See McIntyre's, *Family of Gods*, 111–29, survey of *Augustales* in the Roman Empire, despite her conclusion that these individuals were priests.

other *seviri Augustales* indicate that they were not from the ruling class of Italians but were from local Greek and Thracian families.[94] As far as we can tell, there is no direct evidence that any *sevir Augustalis* in Philippi was involved in imperial divine honors. If they offered divine honors to certain Julio-Claudians, this probably occurred on the private, not public, level. That is, Philippi neither officially sanctioned their actions nor paid for their offerings. They may have offered such sacrifices at altars in the various *vici* or neighborhoods of Philippi, as was the case in Rome (see p. 44).

TABLE 2.3 PHILIPPIAN *AUGUSTALES*

Name	Title	Servile Origin (if known)
Titus Cottius Viriles (*CIPh* 2.1.197 = Pilhofer 2.074B)	*sevir Augustalis*	*libertus*
Gaius Galgestius . . . tus (*CIPh* 2.1.198 = Pilhofer 2.505)	*sevir*	
Lucius Licinius Euhemer (*CIPh* 2.1.199 = Pilhofer 2.721)	*sevir Augustalis*	*libertus*
Publius Naevius Symphorus (*CIPh* 2.1.200 = Pilhofer 2.463 = *CIL* 3.14206[7])	*sevir Augustalis*	
Gaius Postumius Januarius (*CIPh* 2.1.201 = Pilhofer 2.037 = *CIL* 3.657)	*sevir Augustalis*	
Gaius Sallustius Viator (*CIPh* 2.1.202)	*sevir Augustalis*	
Valerius Euhelpistus (*CIPh* 2.1.203 = Pilhofer 2.289)	*sevir Augustalis*	
Marcus Velleius Symphorus (*CIPh* 2.1.204 = Pilhofer 2.321)	*Augustalis*	*libertus*
. . . Myrus (*CIPh* 2.1.205)	*sevir Augustalis*	
? (*CIPh* 2.1.206 = Pilhofer 2.639)	*sevir Augustalis*	
? (*CIPh* 2.1.207 = Pilhofer 2.455 = *CIL* 3.14206[16])	*sevir Augustalis*	
? (*CIPh* 2.1.208 = Pilhofer 2.412)	*sevir Augustalis*	

94. Known Greek names of *seviri Augustales* are Euhemerus and Symphorus (*CIPh* 2.1.199 [= Pilhofer 2.721], 200 [= Pilhofer 2.463 = *CIL* 3.14206[7]], 204 [= Pilhofer 2.321]). Known Greek names of wives of *seviri Augustales* are Nice, Cleopatra, and Damalis (*CIPh* 2.1.200 [= Pilhofer 2.463 = *CIL* 3.14206[7]], 203 [= Pilhofer 2.289], 207 [= Pilhofer 2.455 = *CIL* 3.655]). For more on *seviri Augustales* in Philippi, see Brélaz, *Philippes*, 202–9.

Name	Title	Servile Origin (if known)
? (*CIPh* 2.1.209 = Pilhofer 2.276)	*sevir Augustalis*	
? (*CIPh* 2.1.211 = Pilhofer 2.256)	*sevir Augustalis*	
? (*CIPh* 2.1.212 = Pilhofer 2.043 = *CIL* 3.7344)	*sevir Augustalis*	
? (*CIPh* 2.1.213)	*sevir Augustalis*	
? (*CIPh* 2.1.214)	*Augustalis*	
? (*CIPh* 2.1.215)	*sevir Augustalis*	
? (*CIPh* 2.1.216)	*sevir Augustalis*	
? (*CIPh* 2.1.217)	*sevir Augustalis*	*libertus*
? (*CIPh* 2.1.218)	*sevir Augustalis*	
? (*CIPh* 2.1.219)	*sevir Augustalis*	

Imperial Cultic Officials as Benefactors

In addition to overseeing imperial divine honors, Philippi's *flamines* and *sacerdotes* used their wealth to benefit their fellow colonists. Because of the greatness of the munificence of two *flamines*, Gaius Antonius Rufus and Gaius Oppius Montanus, Philippi bestowed the honorific title *princeps coloniae* or "first citizen of the colony" on them (see table 2.1).[95] This epithet meant that both men were the most respected and preeminent of the colonists of their day, literally first among equals. Thus, Rufus and Montanus possessed the most authority, influence, and power in Philippi, which the Romans called *auctoritas*. The latter's benefactions were so great that Philippi erected an equestrian statue of him—an image of him seated on a horse—and granted him the official title *patronus coloniae* or "patron of the colony." By bestowing this title, the Philippians acknowledged that they were in some way Montanus's clients and that he sought their well-being.[96]

Philippian inscriptions allow us to reconstruct specific benefactions that *flamines* and *sacerdotes* provided. Another epigraph from the colony that mentions Montanus notes that he served a term as its *munerarius* or the person who oversaw, including to the point of funding, gladiatorial combats and wild-beast fights for the denizens of the city in Philippi's theater (see fig. 2.1, no. 3).[97] Such activities were a regular part of colonial life and may have been connected to

---

95. "Appendix 1: Inscriptions" §2.3, 5.

96. "Appendix 1: Inscriptions" §2.7. For the inscription that was connected to this statue, see "Appendix 1: Inscriptions" §2.5.

97. "Appendix 1: Inscriptions" §2.5. For more on gladiatorial games and beast fights, see Christopher Epplett, *Gladiators: Deadly Arena Sports of Ancient Rome* (New York: Skyhorse, 2017).

imperial divine honors, although no Philippian evidence corroborates this.[98] The second-largest known Latin inscription from the entirety of the Roman world (!), measuring sixty-five feet with letters nearly two feet tall, is located in the Philippian forum and commemorates its paving with marble by a *flamen* of *Divus* Augustus, whose name has been lost.[99] The epigraph attesting to the *flamen* of Tiberius lists a number of benefactions that the priest, Lucius Atiarius Schoenias, who also served as *flamen* of *Divus* Augustus, provided. He set up bronze statues of the gods on a marble base in the Philippian bath between AD 41 and 54, which he dedicated to Claudius; he distributed money or food to Philippi's citizen body (*viritim populo*), noncitizen residents (*paganis*), soldiers (*militaribus*), and *Augustales*; he funded a Roman banquet (*triclinium*) for the *decuriones*; he renovated the city's bath, which included the construction of a stone staircase; and he underwrote the costs (*gratuitum*) of the bath for the colony. It is probable that other *flamines* and *sacerdotes* as well as *Augustales* provided similar munificent acts for Philippi, which have not survived.

Location of Imperial Divine Honors

So far, we have focused on which Julio-Claudians received divine honors in Philippi and who oversaw and administered sacrifices to them. The question remains, Where did the colony's *flamines* and, in some cases, *sacerdotes* make imperial offerings? Philippian coins and archaeological evidence suggest that such sacrifices occurred in the most public and central part of the colony, the forum. The forum of Philippi that one visits today is not the forum that Paul saw when he first entered the colony in AD 49. The colonists appear to have established their forum soon after they settled, but the archaeological record attests to no

---

98. According to *Lex Coloniae Genetivae* 70, there were an annual "show of gladiators" (*munus*) and a "public set of games" (*ludus*) for Jupiter, Juno, Minerva, and all the gods and goddesses for four days in the *colonia Julia Genetiva*. Granted, these were put on by the *duoviri* and not by a *munerarius*. Louis Robert, *Les gladiateurs dans L'orient grec* (Limoges: Bontemps, 1940; repr., Amsterdam: Hakkert, 1970), 270, observes that we do not know the occasion of the gladiatorial combats and wild-beast fights in Philippi. However, "in all other cases, gladiatorial combats are expressly linked to the imperial cult" (*Dans tous les autres cas, les combats de gladiateurs sont liés au culte impérial de façon expresse*).

99. This occurred between AD 14 and 67. See "Appendix 1: Inscriptions" §2.6. Brélaz, "First-Century Philippi," 157–58, observes that the epigraph was carved into the forum's marble in its "whole central portion" and filled with bronze. The inscription's size and the fact that its bronze shone in the Mediterranean sun mean that it "must have looked very impressive to anyone visiting the city center of Philippi."

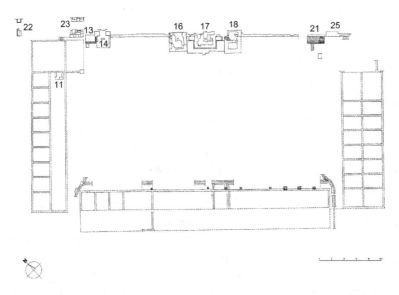

Fig. 2.7 Site map of the lower terrace of Philippi's forum | *Drawing by M. Sève, École française d'Athènes, used with permission*

significant building projects in Philippi's public spaces for almost fifty years.[100] Provided that the coin series picturing the statue base of *Divus* Julius and (after his death) *Divus* Augustus flanked by two altars reflects an actual monument (see figs. 2.3, 4), it was probably erected in the Philippian forum.[101] If this is correct,

100. The evidence that the forum dates to Augustus's reign is the reuse of late first-century BC and early first-century AD statue bases in construction projects there, a small monument built into the foundation of the Via Egnatia that passes through the forum, and an early first-century AD sewer found along a building in the forum. See Sève and Weber, *Guide du forum*, 11–12. For a more concise treatment in English, see Michel Sève, "The Forum at Philippi: The Transformation of Public Space from the Establishment of the Colony to the Early Byzantine Period," in *Philippi, from* Colonia Augusta *to* Communitas Christiana: *Religion and Society in Transition*, ed. Steven J. Friesen, Michalis Lychounas, and Daniel N. Schowalter, NovTSup 186 (Leiden: Brill, 2022), 13–35.

101. We know from "Appendix 1: Inscriptions" §2.2 and the remains of a statue dating to Augustus's reign (a marble head depicting his adopted son Gaius Caesar) that monuments containing images of Julio-Claudians were in the forum, which lends credence to the proposal that the statue group and altars on the coins were actually erected in the forum. See Sève and Weber, *Guide de forum*, 12–13. This head is not direct evidence of imperial divine honors, as some New Testament scholars claim. Furthermore, there is no way to know whether this was part of a cultic statue.

then sacrifices to *Divus* Julius, *Divus* Augustus, the deceased Tiberius, and *Diva* Augusta were probably offered on these altars for two reasons. The first is that an altar was the most important and only essential component of ancient sacrifice.[102] The second reason is that there is no evidence of an imperial temple in Philippi predating Claudius's reign (AD 41–54). During his reign, however, the forum experienced a construction boom (see fig. 2.7).[103]

We do not know as much about this explosion of building activity as we would like, because the Philippian forum was dismantled and rebuilt in another construction boom that occurred in the mid-second century AD. Despite this lack of evidence, traces of foundations of buildings and inscriptions dating between AD 41 and 54 allow for a partial reconstruction of the forum during the time that Paul visited the colony. The forum consisted of one large rectangle divided into two parts, an upper and a lower terrace. The upper terrace is on the slope of the Philippian acropolis, and its southern boundary is the Via Egnatia, which passed through the heart of Philippi (see fig. 2.1, nos. 4, 11). It is not entirely clear what the upper terrace looked like in Claudius's reign, but in keeping with Roman colonies elsewhere, it was probably a sacred area with temples and shrines and most certainly a temple to Jupiter, the king of the Roman pantheon.[104] The lower terrace was bounded by the Via Egnatia to the north and streets to the south, east, and west and measured about 474 feet by 256 feet (see figs. 2.1, nos. 5, 11, 12; 7).[105] There were three buildings on the south, east, and west sides of the lower terrace forming a U-like shape, and the open area between these buildings was paved with marble by the *flamen* of *Divus* Augustus, as noted above.[106] The western and eastern buildings resemble each other in shape, and at their northernmost ends—the ends closest to the Via Egnatia—there were two similar structures (see fig. 2.7).[107]

102. Valerie M. Warrior, *Roman Religion* (Cambridge: Cambridge University Press, 2006), 8, notes, "The altar, not the temple, was the focal point of the gods' worship."

103. The construction techniques used in the forum were Greek, which means that Greek architects and craftsmen were used, but the look was Roman. See Sève and Weber, *Guide de forum*, 29–31; Brélaz, "First-Century Philippi," 157.

104. Sève and Weber, *Guide de forum*, 15; Sève, "Forum at Philippi," 19; Brélaz, "First-Century Philippi," 157. This proposal is supported by the prominent place of temples of Jupiter in Roman cities and colonies throughout the Roman Empire. See Ian M. Burton, "Capitoline Temples in Italy and the Provinces (Especially Africa)," *ANRW* 12.1:259–342, esp. 259–70.

105. The Via Egnatia at this point was bounded by two monumental arches. Two ramps provided access from the Via Egnatia to the lower terrace, which was about six and a half feet lower than the level of the Via Egnatia. Sève and Weber, *Guide de forum*, 14–15; Sève, "Forum at Philippi," 18–21.

106. "Appendix 1: Inscriptions" §2.6.

107. These buildings contained various rooms: the eastern building, a double row of nine rooms; the southern building, a double row of seventeen rooms with one row opening into the

The identity of the structure in the western building is not entirely clear, but it was not an imperial temple, despite what some New Testament scholars claim.[108] This conclusion is outdated and archaeologists now identify this building as most likely the colony's *curia* or meeting place of the *decuriones*, as it definitely was in the mid-second century AD.[109] The northernmost structure on the eastern building was probably an imperial temple dedicated to the Julio-Claudians who had become *divi* and the deceased Tiberius, even though no archaeological evidence confirms it.[110] There are, however, three strong reasons supporting this identification. First, it is clear that an imperial temple existed in the forum on the same site in the mid-second century AD. This temple was a renovation of an earlier one, because the Latin inscription that was engraved on its architrave, a horizontal stone piece resting atop the columns on the front of the temple, notes that a certain second-century AD benefactor "restored" (*restituit*) the temple via a bequest in his will.[111] The Latin verb *restituo*, "restore," means that a similar structure with a similar purpose existed on the site of the second-century AD temple, most probably an older imperial temple.[112] Second, the monument of *sacerdotes* of *Diva Augusta* was set up in that northeastern corner of the forum in the latter portion of the first century AD, next to the building that in the mid-second century AD was an imperial temple (see figs. 2.1, no. 5; 5, 6).[113] This supports the identification of this area of the forum as devoted to imperial divine honors. This is especially the case because when the second-century AD imperial temple was renovated, the colonists took the time-consuming and painstaking option of working around the monument of the *sacerdotes* instead of dismantling it.[114] Finally, other Roman col-

---

paved area of the forum; and the western building, a single row of nine rooms. See Sève and Weber, *Guide de forum*, 13–15, 55–59; Sève, "Forum at Philippi," 18–19.

108. Hansen, *Philippians*, 3; Hellerman, *Reconstructing Honor in Roman Philippi*, 80; Cohick, "Philippians and Empire," 169. Heen, "Phil 2:6–11," 135–36, concludes that there was an imperial temple on the east end of the forum's lower terrace and "perhaps" on its western end, too.

109. This was the case in the forum in the mid-second century AD. See Sève and Weber, *Guide de forum*, 66–67; Sève, "Forum at Philippi," 19; "Appendix 1: Inscriptions" §2.14.

110. Brélaz, "First-Century Philippi," 156; Sève, "Forum at Philippi," 19.

111. "Appendix 1: Inscriptions" §2.15, line 2.

112. Most Latin epigraphs commemorating the initial construction of a building omit the verb *fecit*, "built," and the verb *restituo* is added in cases where a patron pays for work to an already existing building. See Burnett, *Studying the New Testament*, 30.

113. Peter Pilhofer, *Die erste christliche Gemeinde Europas*, vol. 1 of *Philippi*, WUNT 87 (Tübingen: Mohr Siebeck, 1995), 118–20, a limited discussion of Philippian imperial divine honors, leaves the impression that Paul would have seen this monument upon his arrival in Philippi, which he most certainly could not have. See Brélaz, "First-Century Philippi," 158.

114. Bormann, *Philippi*, 41–42, contends that the reason that Philippi did not dismantle the monument of these priestesses is the colonists' penchant for "Caesar worship" (*Caesarenvereh-rung*) in Philippi. This may be correct, but the reputation of the women and their families is an-

onies like Corinth (see pp. 204–7) and Pisidian Antioch in the Roman province of Galatia in modern-day Turkey had imperial temples during the Julio-Claudian period.[115] Taken together, the cumulative evidence suggests that an imperial temple dedicated to the Julio-Claudian *divi* and the deceased Tiberius existed in Philippi during Claudius's reign and was either being built or completed in time for Paul to see it on one of his three known visits to the colony.[116]

There would have been at least one imperial altar in front of this temple, possibly more if the Philippians dedicated one or both of the altars that flanked the monument devoted to *Divus* Julius and (after his death) *Divus* Augustus in the forum to imperial cultic activity (see figs. 2.3, 4). This (or these) altar(s) would have been the focus of imperial sacrifice, which was the defining and most important component of all forms of ancient divine honors, because it encapsulated "belief in action" (for more on imperial sacrifices, see pp. 91–96).[117] There were probably statues of the Julio-Claudians who had become *divi* and of Tiberius inside this temple, in the largest part of it known as the cella, which is where Romans tended to display cultic statues. This portion of the second-century temple measures approximately fifty-eight feet by thirty-seven feet.[118] Provided that the mid-first-century temple's cella had similar dimensions, it could have held five imperial statues without any difficulty. One final note about the location of imperial sacrifices is in order. Imperial sacrifices were confined neither to the forum nor to the imperial temple. Because Philippi probably offered imperial sacrifices in conjunction with sacrifices to the traditional gods (see pp. 94–95), *flamines* and *sacerdotes* probably made offerings to the colony's gods and the above Julio-Claudians on altars of the former. Moreover, if any divine honors were given to the Julio-Claudians in question during gladiatorial combats and wild-beast shows in Philippi's theater, they were offered on altars and before imperial images that were set up there. Finally, it is possible, even probable, that certain Philippians offered private imperial sacrifices to Julio-Claudian *divi* and Tiberius and to the gods for

---

other probable reason why the city left the monument standing during the mid-second-century renovation of its forum. See Burnett, *Studying the New Testament*, 121–39.

115. For the imperial temple in Pisidian Antioch, see Benjamin Rubin, "Ruler Cult and Colonial Identity: The Imperial Sanctuary at Pisidian Antioch," in *Building a New Rome: The Roman Colony of Pisidian Antioch (25 BC–300 AD)*, ed. Elaine K. Gazda and Diana Ng (Ann Arbor: Kelsey Museum, 2011), 33–60.

116. It is clear from Acts and Paul's letters that the apostle made three visits to Philippi probably between AD 49 and 57: Acts 16:11–40; 19:21; 20:1–3, 6; 2 Cor 1:15–17; 2:13; 7:5.

117. For more on sacrifice as "belief in action," see Scheid, *Introduction to Roman Religion*, 95–96, and my discussion on pp. 28–30.

118. Sève and Weber, *Guide de forum*, 39–43.

the safety of the living imperial family on their domestic shrines, as some Romans did, and at shrines within Philippian neighborhoods, as was the case in Rome (see pp. 43–44). Such offerings were not public but private and thus not made on behalf of the colony. The difficulty with this contention is that to date there is no archaeological evidence from Philippi attesting to such honors. However, we must be open to the possibility that such sacrifices occurred.

Aspects of Imperial Divine Honors

Now that we know where imperial sacrifices for Julio-Claudian *divi* and Tiberius occurred, we must explore the particular aspects of such honors, mainly, of what they consisted and when and how *flamines* and in some cases *sacerdotes* in Philippi made them. Unfortunately, we cannot reconstruct these aspects of imperial divine honors from Philippian evidence alone, but we must draw on comparative material from Rome and official documents associated with Roman imperial administration. The best evidence to address these questions is the *Acts of the Arval Brothers*, which I discussed in chapter 1 (see p. 42), and an official calendar for Roman soldiers discovered in Syria known as the *Feriale Duranum*. To recap, the former is a collection of sacrifices inscribed in Latin on marble plaques that the Arval Brothers, a group of Roman priests from the senatorial class, offered in Rome between 21 BC and AD 304. The *Feriale Duranum* is a list of Roman festivals that a group of Roman soldiers stationed in Dura Europos, Syria celebrated each year.[119] The text is written in Latin on a papyrus that was part of the garrison's archives, and it probably dates between AD 225 and 227 (see fig. 2.8).[120] Despite this text's late date, some festivals mentioned in the *Feriale Duranum* go back to the time of Augustus and his immediate successors, the period that we are considering.[121]

The *Acts of the Arval Brothers* and the *Feriale Duranum* indicate that state-sponsored sacrifices of bulls, male cows, and female cows were made to Julio-Claudians who had been made *divi* in Rome, and the former testifies that beginning in the same city in AD 55, a bull was offered to the reigning emperor's *genius*.

---

119. These soldiers were known as Cohort XX of the Palmyrenians (*cohors XX Palmyrenorum* in Latin).

120. The *Feriale Duranum* was discovered in 1931–1932 with other documents that date between AD 200 and 250 and that were found in a temple of Artemis in Dura Europos. See Austin M. Harmon et al., "The *Feriale Duranum*," in *Yale Classical Studies* 7 (New Haven: Yale University Press, 1940): 11–210.

121. The *Acts of the Arval Brothers* and the *Feriale Duranum* display striking similarities, despite the fact that they are separated by nearly two hundred years and more than eighteen hundred miles.

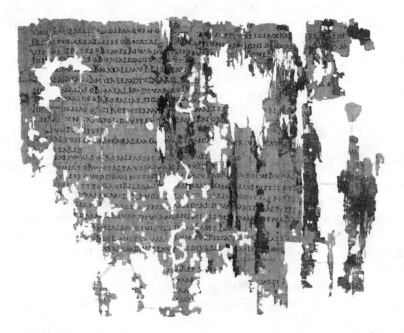

Fig. 2.8 One of the eight papyrus pages that make up the extant *Feriale Duranum* | *Courtesy of Yale University Library*

In Philippi, *flamines*—not *sacerdotes*, for Roman custom prohibited women from offering blood sacrifices—probably offered these animals to *Divus* Julius, *Divus* Augustus, the deceased Tiberius, *Diva* Augusta, *Divus* Claudius, and, beginning in AD 55, to Nero's *genius* on imperial altars that were set up in the forum (see pp. 86–91).[122] Once the colony's imperial temple was completed during Claudius's reign, such sacrifices were probably made regularly on an (or the) altar(s) erected in front of that temple, though there is no archaeological evidence to corroborate this. In addition to animal sacrifices, the *Feriale Duranum* attests that another type of sacrifice, one of wine and incense known as a *supplicatio*, was offered probably before the images of *divi* and certain imperial family members. Philippian *flamines* and *sacerdotes*, for Roman custom allowed women to make such offerings, probably offered the sacrifices in question to the Julio-Claudian

122. John Scheid, "The Religious Roles of Roman Women," in *From Ancient Goddesses to Christian Saints*, vol. 1 of *A History of Women in the West*, ed. Pauline Schmitt Pantel (Cambridge: Harvard University Press, 1992), 377–408, esp. 378–80.

divi, the deceased Tiberius, and, beginning in AD 55, Nero's *genius*.[123] It is likely that the *seviri Augustales* made offerings to Julio-Claudian *divi*, the deceased Tiberius, and even the emperor's *genius* before AD 55, be they blood sacrifices or *supplicationes* (the plural of *supplicatio*). Such offerings, however, were conducted on the private, not public, level and thus were not regulated by the colony. Similarly, it is possible that some Romans made offerings of wine and incense on their domestic hearths to these same divine beings, for which there is no Philippian evidence to date.

Given that imperial sacrifices mentioned in the *Acts of the Arval Brothers* and the *Feriale Duranum* were the same as those offered to the Roman gods, bulls, bovines, wine, and incense, we can reconstruct the particulars of how such sacrifices were carried out in Philippi. These offerings would have been offered in public view in the forum for the sake of the community. Offerings of wine and incense would have been carried out without many trappings and need not have occurred on the imperial altars in the forum or, during and after Claudius's reign, on the imperial altar(s) in front of the imperial temple, but they could have been offered before images, painted or statues, of the Julio-Claudian *divi*, the deceased Tiberius, and, beginning in AD 55, the emperor's *genius* in various locations in Philippi such as the theater. Blood sacrifices would have occurred at the end of sacred processions similar to the one in Gythium, as discussed in the opening of this book, but in the Roman custom. This means that imperial priests would have led in procession other aristocrats, musicians, and *victimarii*, the slaves responsible for killing the animal, winding their way through the city to Philippi's forum.

Once the procession arrived at its destination, the *flamen* on duty would have washed his hands with water, burned incense, and poured a libation of wine to his object of sacrifice, the Julio-Claudian *divi*, the deceased Tiberius, or, beginning in AD 55, to Nero's *genius*.[124] Having completed these sacred rites, the *flamen* would have poured wine and some special flour atop the sacrificial animal's head as well as run his knife down the beast's back.[125] These acts functioned to transfer ownership of the bull or cow from the *flamen* and thus the citizens of Philippi to the object of sacrifice, the Julio-Claudian *divi*, the deceased Tiberius, or, beginning in AD 55, Nero's *genius*. At this point, the animal was supposed to nod its

123. See "Appendix 2: Reconstructed Julio-Claudian Imperial Calendar in Philippi and Corinth."

124. Warrior, *Roman Religion*, 21–22.

125. In Rome, the Vestal Virgins made this flour, which was mixed with other ingredients and called *mola salsa*. There is no evidence, however, that *mola salsa* was used in Roman sacrifices outside Rome. Thus, the people of Philippi may have used something else. See Scheid, *Roman Religion*, 81, 83.

head, thereby giving consent to be slaughtered.[126] Whereupon, the *victimarius* would have struck the animal on its head to stun it, cut its throat, and drained its blood.

The beast dead, a *haruspex* or ritualistic specialist would have inspected its entrails (liver, lungs, gall bladder, the peritoneum, and heart) to ensure that the Julio-Claudian *divi*, the deceased Tiberius, or, beginning in AD 55, the emperor's *genius* had accepted the offering. If no abnormalities were found, the object was believed to have been acceptable to the divine being to whom it was offered.[127] After the confirmation was received, the animal's entrails would have been boiled in a pot. Once finished, the priest would have dumped them, along with more wine and special flour, onto the fire(s) of the altar(s) where they would have been consumed. Finally, the remainder of the animal would normally have been divided among the priest and the aristocratic participants to consume near the imperial altars. Thus, not every citizen or denizen of Philippi would have eaten meat or drunk wine from imperial sacrifices, which explains why Schoenias, the Philippian *flamen* of Tiberius and of *Divus* Augustus, boasts in an inscription that he provided distributions of such foodstuffs for every person in Philippi: the citizens (*populus*), noncitizen residents (*paganes*), soldiers (*militares*), and the *Augustales*, alike.[128]

The *Acts of the Arval Brothers* provide us with another way that imperial sacrifices would have been offered in Philippi, in conjunction with those offered to traditional Roman gods. According to Ittai Gradel, a specialist of Roman imperial divine honors, the *Acts of the Arval Brothers* that date to the Julio-Claudian period testify that sacrifices were almost always offered to the gods, the Julio-Claudian *divi*, and, beginning in AD 55, the reigning emperor's *genius*, in that order.[129] To provide an example, on January 3, AD 38, the president of the Arval Brothers vowed to sacrifice cows and to donate a certain weight of gold and silver to Jupiter, Queen Juno, Minerva, Dea Dia, *Salus* (the personification of public

126. Scheid, *Roman Religion*, 83.

127. No *haruspices* (the plural of *haruspex*) are attested (yet?) in Philippi, but given that they were active in other Roman colonies, they probably were in Philippi, too. *Lex Coloniae Genetivae* 62 stipulates that every *duovir* has the right to have a *haruspex*, among several other attendants.

128. "Appendix 1: Inscriptions" §2.4, lines 5–6.

129. Ittai Gradel, *Emperor Worship and Roman Religion* (Oxford: Clarendon, 2002), 179–80, notes that the exception is in AD 66 and the commemoration of the day on which the temple of *Divus* Augustus in Rome was founded, at which time sacrifices to the gods were omitted: "The Arval records contain only one instance where the sacrifices of the college included only the *Divi* and the emperor's *Genius*. . . . The rite is found in the *Acta* from the year 66 and took place 'in the new temple of *Divus* Augustus.'"

health, security, and well-being), and *Divus* Augustus, provided that these divine beings preserved Caligula, supported his well-being, and kept him safe from any assassination plots.[130] What this means for sacrifices to Julio-Claudian *divi*, the deceased Tiberius, and, beginning in AD 55, the emperor's *genius* in Philippi is that they would have been wedded to offerings to the traditional gods. Therefore, the relationship between imperial and traditional divine honors in Philippi was not one where the aforementioned Julio-Claudians competed with the traditional gods for the populace's attention and devotion, as some New Testament scholars contend.[131] Rather, the gods worked together with the Julio-Claudian *divi*, the deceased Tiberius, and, after AD 55, the emperor's *genius* to rule Philippi, Rome, and the empire.[132]

The final aspect of imperial sacrifices that we must reconstruct is when they were offered. Once again, the *Acts of the Arval Brothers* and *Feriale Duranum* are most helpful, for they provide the exact days when the Arval Brothers and the Roman soldiers stationed at Dura Europos offered imperial sacrifices.[133] Both texts evince that imperial offerings were made to imperial *divi* on their birthdays and anniversaries of special occasions throughout the year, especially for the reigning emperor. To provide an idea of what such offerings looked like, appendix 2 lists the imperial sacrifices that the Arval Brothers offered in Rome for the year AD 59, the most complete year among the *Acts of the Arval Brothers* dating to the Julio-Claudian period, alongside the days throughout the year that the soldiers in Dura Europos made offerings to Julio-Claudian *divi*. Given that Paul visited Philippi for the first time in AD 49, the second in the mid-50s AD, the third in the late 50s AD, and that he probably composed Philippians around AD 56/57, the list of birthdays of Julio-Claudian *divi*, the deceased Tiberius, and the reigning emperor that would have been celebrated in Philippi were the following: *Divus* Julius's (July 12), *Divus* Augustus's (September 23), (maybe) *Diva* Augusta's (January 30), *Divus* Claudius's (August 1), the deceased Tiberius (November 16), and Nero's (December 15) (this latter sacrifice would have been to his *genius*).

130. "Appendix 1: Inscriptions" §2.16.

131. Wright, *Paul and the Faithfulness of God*, 1:311–47, esp. 332, posits, "though for the most part it was true that imperial cults took their place alongside, and sometimes blended with, local and traditional customs, there was always at least the veiled threat: whatever you do, this one [i.e., imperial divine honors] matters."

132. Gradel, *Roman Religion*, 275–76, notes, "There was evidently no question of rivalry, and the old [Roman] gods had nothing to fear from the newcomer [i.e., the Julio-Claudian *divi*]."

133. See "Appendix 2: Reconstructed Julio-Claudian Imperial Calendar in Philippi and Corinth."

Fig. 2.9 Bronze coin, minted in Philippi during Claudius's reign (AD 41–54) (*RPC* 1.1651), depicting the goddess Victory with a wreath and a palm branch and the Latin legend *Vic(toria) Aug(usta)* on the obverse (*left*) and three Roman military standards with the legend *Cohor(s) Prae(toria) Phil(ippensis)* on the reverse (*right*) | *Courtesy of Yale University Art Gallery*

Besides birthdays, imperial sacrifices in Philippi would have commemorated important milestones associated with Julio-Claudian *divi*, the deceased Tiberius, and the reigning emperor, such as anniversaries of their ascensions to the imperial throne; military victories; granting of offices, like consul of Rome, or titles, like "father of the fatherland"; and their safe return to Rome after traveling.[134] Some important anniversaries for Philippi would have been the celebration of Augustus's victory at the battle of Philippi in October 42 BC, the battle of Actium in 31 BC, and Augustus's refounding of it as a Roman colony in 30 BC.[135] The minting of a coin series, during Claudius's reign, focused on Augustus's military victories strengthens this suggestion. The coin depicts a statue of the goddess Victory holding a wreath and a palm branch—both symbols of victory—with the Latin legend "Augustan Victory" (*Vic(toria) Aug(usta)*) on the observe and three Roman military standards with the legend "Cohort of the Praetorium of the Philippians" (*Cohor(s) Prae(toria) Phil(ippensis)*) on the coin's reverse (see fig. 2.9). Thus, on these days, there were probably imperial festivals during which *flamines* and *sacerdotes* processed through the city to offer sacrifices to Julio-Claudian *divi*, the deceased Tiberius, beginning in AD 55, Nero's *genius*, and to the Roman gods who worked with the former to ensure the peace and prosperity of Philippi, Rome, and the empire.

134. Bormann, *Philippi*, 48–50, contends that a loyalty oath to the reigning emperor would have been part of imperial divine honors in Philippi. I find no evidence to suggest this. For a discussion of these loyalty oaths and the contextual interpretation of them, see Burnett, *Studying the New Testament*, 97–120.

135. Bormann, *Philippi*, 47.

Synthesis and Conclusion

To conclude our discussion of imperial divine honors in Philippi, I will synthesize and summarize our findings. The colony established postmortem divine honors for five Julio-Claudians, four whom the Roman Senate divinized—*Divus* Julius, *Divus* Augustus, *Diva* Augusta, and *Divus* Claudius—and one whom it did not, Tiberius. This exception, however, showcases that Philippi followed the practice of Roman imperial divine honors. Thus, it awarded them to Tiberius after his death. However, the colony did not acknowledge him as a *divus*. Philippian evidence indicates that the city elected or appointed special Roman imperial cultic officials each year: *flamines* (always male) to serve the male Julio-Claudian *divi* and the deceased Tiberius and *sacerdotes* (always female) for *Diva* Augusta. The only Julio-Claudian *divus* for whom a *flamen* is unattested is *Divus* Julius, but one most certainly existed. How long these *flaminia* lasted we do not know. *Flamines* of *Divus* Augustus are attested into the second century AD, while those of Tiberius and *Divus* Claudius are found once in the epigraphic record. *Sacerdotes* of *Diva* Augusta appear in inscriptions in the late first century AD, but this office must have continued into the late second century AD, because when the forum was renovated in the mid-second century AD, the monument of *sacerdotes* of *Diva* Augusta was left in place, even though it would have been easier for the colonists to remove it (see figs. 2.5, 6).

These *flamines* and *sacerdotes* were from local aristocratic Philippian families who were prominent in the colony. Most *flamines* either held, had held, or would go on to hold the most prestigious public offices in Philippi, that of *duovir* and *duovir quinquennalis*, and some *sacerdotes* were related to men who filled these offices. Occasionally, overseeing divine honors for Julio-Claudian *divi* was a family affair, as parents and children were *flamines* and *sacerdotes*. The former offered oxen, male cows, female cows, bulls, incense, and wine to Julio-Claudian *divi*, the deceased Tiberius, and, beginning in AD 55, the reigning emperor's *genius*. Since Roman custom prohibited women from making blood sacrifices, *sacerdotes* probably offered incense and wine to *Diva* Augusta. These latter offerings, even those that *flamines* made, were small and could have been carried out anywhere in the colony, not just the forum. The larger, more expensive blood sacrifices occurred at the end of processions that *flamines* led on special days connected to Julio-Claudians that were celebrated throughout the year or spontaneously upon hearing important events related to them. These processions ended at the imperial altar(s) in the colony's forum, probably in its northeastern corner, where in Claudius's reign Philippi's imperial temple was located. The actual sacrifices that the colony offered were probably made in conjunction with those of the city's gods and goddesses, symbolizing that Rome's gods worked alongside the Julio-Claudian *divi*, the deceased Tiberius, and, beginning in AD 55, Nero's *genius* to ensure the peace and prosperity of Philippi, Rome, and the empire. Therefore, imperial sacrifices need not have occurred only on the colony's imperial altar(s) but on the altar of any deity. In addition to these public divine honors, the Philippian *Augustales* may have offered private imperial sacrifices to Julio-Claudian *divi*, the deceased Tiberius, and, beginning in AD 55, Nero's *genius* at various locations. Furthermore, citizens of the colony and even some resident aliens may have incorporated these Julio-Claudians into their domestic hearths and made imperial offerings to them and to their *Lares*. If such was the case, these cultic acts have left no trace in Philippi's archaeological record.

Not only did *flamines* and *sacerdotes* oversee the aforementioned imperial public offerings, but also they used their wealth to provide benefactions for Philippi, such as renovating the colony's bathhouse, underwriting its admission cost, paving the forum with marble, and other beneficent acts for which there is no surviving evidence. Such munificence, as we have seen, was connected with imperial divine honors in some capacity, and these acts increased their own reputations and that of their families and ultimately served to promote their public careers in the colony and, if they were lucky, in the province and in the imperial bureaucracy.

Imperial Divine Honors and Early Christianity in Philippi

We have reached the point that we can bring our contextual reconstruction of imperial divine honors in Philippi to bear upon what relationship, if any, these honors had with early Christianity in the colony. It is evident that such honors had a prominent place in the city and that early Philippian Christians would have been aware of them.[136] When Paul made his first, second, or third visit between AD 49 and 57 (Acts 16:11–40; 19:21; 20:1–3, 6; 2 Cor 1:15–17; 2:13; 7:5), he would have seen the imperial altar(s) in Philippi's forum and the imperial temple in the northeastern corner of it, either in the midst of construction or already finished. The Philippian Christians and possibly Paul would have seen, heard, and smelled imperial processions and sacrifices as they winded their way through the colony during imperial celebrations throughout the year. Christians in Philippi who could read would have noticed the imperial titles of *divus* and *diva* on inscriptions attached to monuments, such as the statue base of *Divus* Julius and *Divus* Augustus between two altars in the forum (see figs. 2.3, 4), the massive bronze inscription cut into the

---

136. Contra Miller, "Imperial Cult," 314–32.

marble surface of the forum indicating that it was laid by a *flamen* of *Divus* Augustus, and on statue bases and tombs and sarcophagi honoring imperial priests and priestesses. These latter epigraphs would have been on funerary monuments outside Philippi lining the Via Egnatia. Paul's converts would have seen the Latin legends and images on the Philippian coins depicting the monument dedicated to *Divus* Julius and *Divus* Augustus that was probably set up in the forum—coins that these Christians used to buy their daily bread and wine (see figs. 2.3, 4), including for their eucharistic meals, that they sent to support Paul in Thessalonica more than once (Phil 4:15–16), and that they contributed to the collection for the saints in Jerusalem (Rom 15:26; 2 Cor 8:1–5). In short, early Christians in Philippi could not have escaped imperial divine honors. Thus, the scholarly use of them to interpret Paul's letter to the Philippians is accurate and indeed appropriate.[137] Moreover, there is no doubt that these Christians for whom Paul composed the missive in question were suffering at the hands of local opponents (Phil 1:28, 29) and that some believers had even been imprisoned.[138] Aside from prison, exactly what else this suffering consisted of remains a point of scholarly contention.[139] This raises the possibility that there is a connection between the woes of Philippian Christians and imperial divine honors in the colony. The question is, What is that connection?

As noted above, many New Testament scholars provide a Christ-versus-Caesar answer to this question, contending that the titles that early Christians used for Jesus—*kyrios* and *sōtēr*—and the term that they used to describe the early Christian message, *euangelion*, conflicted directly with the *euangelion* of the Julio-Claudian *kyrioi* and *sōtēres* whom the Philippians granted divine honors. For this reason, the Philippian Christians were suffering, with some even being imprisoned. However, as we have seen, there is no evidence that Greek- or Latin-speaking Philippians referred to any Julio-Claudian, alive or dead, divinized or not, as *kyrios* and *sōtēr* or as, their Latin counterparts, *dominus* and *salvator*.[140] Instead, the Philippians

137. To quote Deissmann, *Light from the Ancient East*, 340, on this point, "It must not be supposed that St. Paul and his fellow-believers went through the world blindfolded, unaffected by what was then moving through the world of men in great cities."

138. This much is clear from Phil 1:30, which indicates that the Philippian Christians had "*the same fight*" (τὸν αὐτὸν ἀγῶνα) that they had witnessed Paul had and, at the time of the letter's composition, they heard that the apostle was experiencing in Ephesus. This is a point that Fee, *Philippians*, 172–73, rightly stresses, although he places Paul's imprisonment in Rome, not in Ephesus, as I do. However, Reumann, *Philippians*, 282, disagrees: "No evidence any Philippian was in prison [*sic*]."

139. For a recent informed discussion of this suffering and its possible economic connections, see Oakes, *Philippians*, 77–102, esp. 96–99.

140. It is likely that Augustus was known as σωτήρ during his lifetime, because the third-

followed the decrees of the Roman Senate and acclaimed four of the five Julio-Claudians whom they divinely honored with the official Latin title and Roman concept of *divus*. As noted in chapter 1, there was no equivalent Greek concept or term for *divus*, and Greeks most often rendered it as *theos*, not *kyrios*. This means that it is improbable that when the Philippians, both pagan and Christian, heard the proclamation of Jesus with the specific titles of Lord (Phil 2:9–11) and Savior (Phil 3:20), they would have thought that Christians were singling out the Julio-Claudians, including the reigning emperor.[141] To this end, strikingly absent from Philippi (and, as we shall see, from Thessalonica and Corinth) is any reference to anything associated with the Julio-Claudian governance and administration of the empire, including imperial divine honors, as *euangelion* or its Latin counterpart *evangelium*.[142] Furthermore, Acts of the Apostles does not trace the arrest, beating, and imprisonment that Paul and Silas experienced when they brought early Christianity to the city to the honors in question. Rather, Luke connects this mistreatment to Paul's exorcism of a prophetic spirit from a slave girl, the fury of her owners at the loss of income, and the charges of fomenting civic unrest by advocating deviant non-Roman, Jewish customs to the populace (Acts 16:16–22). All this suggests that the suffering that the Philippian Christians were experiencing and to which Paul references in his missive to them was not because the gospel of the Lord and Savior Jesus conflicted directly with the gospel of the Lord and Savior Caesar, either living or dead.[143]

In place of this proposal, the above contextual reconstruction provides a more nuanced and complex answer to the question of what connection, if any, existed between imperial divine honors and the suffering of Philippian Christians: the latter experienced mistreatment because of the conservative Roman nature of Philippi's public life, which included but was not limited to imperial divine honors. As the above data collected from Philippi showcase, the colony was a

century AD Roman historian Dio Cassius, *Roman History* 53.16.4–5, testifies that the Roman Senate acknowledged in 27 BC that by becoming emperor, Augustus had "saved the citizens" of Rome (τοὺς πολίτας σώζοντι). By the time Paul introduced Christianity into Philippi, however, Augustus had graduated from being a σωτήρ to a *divus*.

141. Contra Deissmann, *Light from the Ancient East*, 349–59, 363–65; Wright, "Paul and Empire," 285–86; Fee, *Philippians*, 31, 197, 222, 380–81; Reumann, *Philippians*, 372, 577–78, 597–98; Hansen, *Philippians*, 103; Oakes, *Philippians*, 130, 138–45, 171–74.

142. Given that the Latin *evangelium* is a Christianized transliteration of the Greek, we would not expect to find it in Philippi. In the mid-first century BC, Cicero wrote a letter to his friend Atticus giving good news. Cicero, *To Atticus* 23.1 (2.3.1), or rather his scribe used not a Latin noun for this term but the Greek εὐαγγέλια, because a Latin term probably did not exist.

143. Wright, "Paul and Empire," 285–86; Fee, *Philippians*, 31, 197, 222, 380–81; Hansen, *Philippians*, 103.

bastion of traditional Roman values. After Philippi's founding, Latin became and remained the colony's official language for three centuries. The early aristocrats laid out their forum and constructed buildings in the Roman, not Greek, architectural style. The reason for the Roman character of the city is that from Philippi's founding until the mid-third century AD, its leaders consisted of a small group of aristocratic men, almost all of whom were related to the disenfranchised Italians who had been the first colonists.[144] The colony's leaders worked hard to maintain Philippi's Roman culture and were suspicious of non-Roman values, a fact that Luke's account of Paul and Silas's first visit to the city notes. The author of Acts records the singular charge leveled against Paul and Silas in the city that they were "proclaiming [Jewish] customs that are unlawful for us Romans to receive and to practice" (Acts 16:20–21). The unlawful customs that these Romans had in mind probably centered on two things. First, Paul and Silas advocated the abandonment of Philippi's public divine honors, both imperial and traditional, as well as other overtly pagan practices.[145] Second, they championed the acceptance of the God of Israel as the one true and only God (Phil 1:5–6), to whom every being in the universe would give glory (Phil 2:11), and his crucified and resurrected Son, Jesus the Messiah, as the world's rightful ruler through whom God would receive that glory (Phil 2:6–11).

Because imperial and traditional divine honors were embedded into the life of the colony, the practice of them was part of what it meant to be a good *colonus* of Philippi and thus *civis* or "citizen" of Rome.[146] To this end, Oakes is certainly correct that imperial divine honors, to which I would add traditional divine honors, extended beyond the bounds of what today we would call religion to "society and politics."[147] This much is clear from the Philippian evidence. The colonial treasury or the benefaction of (a) wealthy Philippian(s) paid for the construction and upkeep of the city's imperial temple located in the colony's heart, the forum, directly across from the meeting place of Philippi's *decuriones*, the *curia*. Men who held or would go on to hold the highest public Philippian offices, including some

144. Thus, non-Romans had little to no chance of advancement up the social ladder in Philippi.

145. The Philippian Christians could not have escaped imperial and traditional divine honors, because such honors surrounded them. Paul did not wish for his converts to withdraw from their cities (1 Cor 5:10), and he made accommodations for them, but he drew the line at participating in a pagan sacrifice (1 Cor 8–10).

146. Thus, a portion of Reumann's, *Philippians*, 278–79, conclusion—that of Philippians harassing their Christian counterparts in Philippi for their withdrawal from traditional and imperial divine honors—is correct.

147. Oakes, *Philippians*, 130.

traditional cultic priesthoods such as *pontifex*, served as *flamines*, and women who served as *sacerdotes* were related to such men. Moreover, Philippi, these *flamines* and *sacerdotes*, or in some cases both the colony and these individuals paid for and promoted imperial divine honors, some of which were embedded within gladiatorial combats and wild-beast fights, and in particular, the core of Greco-Roman divine honors, sacrifice. As the *Acts of the Arval Brothers* demonstrate, the objects of these sacrifices were probably not only Julio-Claudian *divi* and, beginning in AD 55, the emperor's *genius* but also Philippi's gods.[148] Consequently, the practice of traditional and imperial divine honors in the colony was one way that the city displayed and promoted its Roman cultural identity.[149]

Provided that Paul's converts advocated the abandonment of Philippi's public divine honors and the acceptance of the God of Israel and his Son Jesus the Messiah, the Philippians and in particular the leaders of the colony would have viewed this group with suspicion and contempt.[150] For them, their divine citizens, their *dei*, their *divi*, the deceased Tiberius, and, beginning in AD 55, Nero's *genius*, controlled their city and empire. These divine beings worked together to ensure

---

148. The Arval Brothers made yearly vows to the gods and the Julio-Claudian *divi*, asking them to keep and to maintain Rome's boundaries and the well-being and safety of the reigning emperor. This does not mean that some syncretism of local deities with Roman ones did not occur. However, Philippian inscriptions indicate that most public divine honors were devoted to Roman or Romanized gods: Jupiter (*CIPh* 2.1.225 [= Pilhofer 2.177]), Augustan Mercury (*CIPh* 2.1.132 [= Pilhofer 2.250]), Augustan Equity (*CIPh* 2.1.117 [= Pilhofer 2.249]), Cupid (*CIPh* 2.1.223 [= Pilhofer 2.350]), Diana Gazoria (*CIPh* 2.1.135 [= Pilhofer 2.177 = CIL 3.14206^{13}]), the Hero Aulonites (*CIPh* 2.1.76 [= Pilhofer 2.620], 158), Isis (*CIPh* 2.1.23 [= Pilhofer 2.132], 134 [= Pilhofer 2.252], 193), Augustan Quietude (*CIPh* 2.1.84 [= Pilhofer 2.203]), Augustan Victory (*CIPh* 2.1.17), Serapis (*CIPh* 2.1.134 [= Pilhofer 2.252]), the colony's *genius* (*CIPh* 2.1.43 [= Pilhofer 2.232]), and the deceased spirits (*CIPh* 2.1.72, 79, 80 [= Pilhofer 2.429 = CIL 3.645], 86 [= Pilhofer 2.080], 91 [= Pilhofer 2.136], 100, 123 [= Pilhofer 2.502]).

149. The worship of gods and divinities in the Roman Empire was tied to specific ethnic groups and even cities. The fifth-century BC historian Herodotus, *Histories*, 8.144, defined what it meant to be Greek (Ἑλληνικός), "being of the same blood, the same language, the temples of the gods and common sacrifices, and the same habits and customs" (ὅμαιμόν τε καὶ ὁμόγλωσσον καὶ θεῶν ἱδρύματά τε κοινὰ καὶ θυσίαι ἤθεά τε ὁμότροπα). As Julius Caesar refused the kingship of the Romans in 44 BC, he pointed out that Jupiter was "king *of the Romans*" (τῶν Ῥωμαίων βασιλεύς [Dio Cassius, *Roman History* 44.11.2–3]). To be a Roman in Philippi meant to worship Roman gods and divinities, including Julio-Claudians.

150. Two second-century AD Roman authors, Tacitus, *Annals* 15.44, and Pliny the Younger, *Letters* 96.8, called Christianity a "superstition" (*superstitio*), by which they meant improper, unreasonable divine honors. The former referred to Christianity as a "destructive superstition" (*exitiabilis superstitio*), while the latter "a distorted and unrestrained superstition" (*superstitionem pravam et immodicam*). See Robert Louis Wilken, *The Christians as the Romans Saw Them*, 2nd ed. (New Haven: Yale University Press, 2003), 1–30, 48–67.

its maintenance, peace, and prosperity.[151] This means that the universal obeisance that the earliest Christians in Philippi proclaimed—that of every being, both divine and human, bowing down and acknowledging Jesus's *kyrios*-ship to God the Father's glory at the second coming (Phil 2:9–11)—would have offended the pagan Philippians. If every deity, divine being, and human in the universe would give obeisance to someone or something, the pagan Philippians conceived, it would be to their gods in general and to Jupiter in particular, whose temple stood in the upper terrace of Philippi's forum (see fig. 2.1, no. 4). The eventual submission of the entire world to the God of Israel through Jesus the Messiah would have been particularly outrageous to the Philippian aristocrats, especially the *decuriones*. It was through their governance of the colony and oversight of its public divine honors, both imperial and traditional, that the city's gods, the *divi*, the deceased Tiberius, and, beginning in AD 55, the emperor's *genius* were pleased. These divinities demonstrated this fact by blessing the city with peace and prosperity, including the construction boom that occurred in the colony during Claudius's reign and resulted in the beautification of Philippi and the building of the city's imperial temple.[152] Some Philippian aristocrats had even gone so far as to pay for these sacrifices as well as other benefactions connected to imperial divine honors from their own pocketbooks. Thus, in their eyes, the notion that a foreign god, the God of Israel, and this God's Son, Jesus the Messiah, a crucified criminal from the political backwater of Judea, would soon strip them of their *auctoritas* and force them to bow their knees in homage would have struck these aristocrats as odious.[153]

Therefore, these leaders and probably some concerned colonists attempted to stamp out the early Christian movement, what they considered to be a deviant strain of Judaism, before it gained a foothold in their city.[154] The method that they

151. In a passage resembling Phil 2:9–11, the first-century BC and AD poet Ovid, *Metamorphoses* 15.858–859, notes that "Jupiter controls the heights of heaven and the kingdoms of the trifold universe" (*Iuppiter arces temperat aetherias et mundi regna triformis*), and according to the first-century BC poet Virgil, *Aeneid* 1.279, Jupiter had given the Romans "empire without end" (*imperium sine fine*). Ovid, *Metamorphoses* 15.860, compares Jupiter's sovereignty over the universe with that of Augustus's over the earth, contending that both, Jupiter and Augustus, are both "father" (*pater*) and "master" (*rector*). For more on the aristocratic Roman attitude to Christianity, see Wilken, *Christians*, 1–30, 48–67.

152. Warrior, *Roman Religion*, 6, observes, "The assumption was that the gods would protect an individual or the state if their worship was properly maintained."

153. For the way that most Romans thought of Christianity and Jesus's crucifixion, see Tacitus, *Annals* 15.44.

154. Romans had a practice of suppressing divine honors they considered antithetical to traditional Roman values. See the Roman Senate's suppression of the Bacchanalia in 186 BC

chose to accomplish this task was the mistreatment of some Christians (exactly of what this consisted remains unknown) and the imprisonment of others, probably leaders in the early Christian house-church (Phil 1:28–30). Such confinement, however, was not the means by which to rehabilitate Christians but the place where they waited until Philippi's *duoviri* could hear their case (as happened to Paul and Silas in Acts 16:11–40).[155] All that said, there is no indication from Paul's letter to the Philippians that this mistreatment included the death penalty. Besides imprisonment, whatever methods of persuasion that the Philippian authorities tried to use on Christians in the colony, their purpose would have been to return what they considered to be wayward pagans back to the polytheistic fold, which would have included the imperial and traditional divine honors that the local authorities had deemed appropriate for those living in the colony.[156] In short, I contend that it was the Jewish countercultural or better non-Roman nature of the gospel—with its call for the abandonment of all forms of traditional and imperial divine honors and acceptance of the God of Israel and his Son Jesus the Messiah—and not its suffusion of supposed anti-imperial rhetoric that caused the suffering of Paul's converts in the colony.

Conclusion

To summarize, imperial divine honors in the Roman colony of Philippi were Roman in nature and consisted of postmortem cultic acts that the Philippians gave to *Divus* Julius, *Divus* Augustus, *Diva* Augusta, *Divus* Claudius, the deceased Tiberius, and, beginning in AD 55, the emperor's *genius*. These divine honors consisted of divine titles, an (or the) imperial altar(s) in the forum, an imperial temple (built during Claudius's reign, AD 41–54) in the northeastern corner of the forum, cultic statues, processions, festivals, and sacrifices that local Roman *flamines* and *sacerdotes* offered to Julio-Claudian *divi*, the deceased Tiberius, beginning in AD 55, Nero's *genius*, and to the gods during various imperial celebrations throughout the year, all of which Philippi funded from its colonial coffers. Alongside these impe-

---

(Livy, *History of Rome* 39.8–19). In the early second century AD, Pliny the Younger investigated and tried to suppress Christianity in his province of Bithynia. He wrote a letter to the emperor Trajan in which he called Christianity a contagion (*contagio*) that had spread not only in towns but also in villages in the countryside (*Letters* 96.9–10).

155. See Brian Rapske, *The Book of Acts and Paul in Roman Custody*, vol. 3 of *The Book of Acts in Its First Century Setting* (Grand Rapids: Eerdmans, 1994).

156. Sacrifice to the gods and to the living emperor was part of Pliny the Younger's, *Letters* 96.5–6, trial of Christians. See Wilkin, *Christians*, 25–30.

rial cultic officials, Philippi had a group of rich freedmen and wealthy outsiders known as *seviri Augustales* who promoted Julio-Claudian rule in the colony and may have offered private, not public, imperial divine honors. *Flamines* in particular not only administered imperial divine honors, but also they filled the highest public offices in the colony either before, during, or after their tenure as priests. Thus, imperial divine honors in the city were embedded into Philippi's public life and were part of what it meant to be a good *colonus* of the colony and *civis* of Rome. This reconstruction demonstrates that while Paul's converts were aware of imperial divine honors in their city, these honors only contributed somewhat to but were not the sole reason for suffering that they experienced (Phil 1:28–30). Rather, pagan Philippians mistreated their Christian counterparts because, by accepting and proclaiming the Jewish gospel, the latter were advocating non-Roman customs that the socially conservative Roman aristocrats, and probably some other leading colonists, found preposterous, dangerous, and worthy to be stamped out of existence.

CHAPTER 3

Imperial Divine Honors, Paul,
and the Thessalonian Church

This chapter brings the contextual approach to imperial divine honors to bear on the second city in mainland Greece in which Paul established nascent Christianity and to which he composed letters, the Greek city of Thessalonica. Its purpose is to reconstruct mid-first-century AD Thessalonian imperial divine honors and to explore what relationship, if any, these honors had with early Christianity in the city. To this end, this chapter has two main goals. The first is to lay out all the known ancient evidence for imperial divine honors dating to the Julio-Claudian period in Thessalonica to build a contextualized portrait of them (see "Imperial Divine Honors in Thessalonica"). In the process, we will see that the honors in question fall into the category of Greek civic imperial divine honors with some influence from Roman imperial divine honors and that such Thessalonian honors were wedded to the city's public life. This chapter's second goal is to use this contextualized portrait to offer a fresh reading of 1–2 Thessalonians and Acts 17:1–9 and thus a nuanced interpretation of the persecution that the first Thessalonian Christians faced (see "Imperial Divine Honors and Early Christianity in Thessalonica"). In this regard, we will see that because of the embeddedness of imperial divine honors into Thessalonica's public life, they contributed to but were not the sole source for the harassment of Christians in the city. Before we arrive at these two goals, however, I must describe the state of Thessalonian imperial divine honors in New Testament scholarship and how historians interpret the relationship between these honors and early Christianity in the city (see "New Testament Scholars on Imperial Divine Honors, Paul, and the Thessalonian Church").

New Testament Scholars on Imperial Divine Honors, Paul, and the Thessalonian Church

Unlike imperial divine honors in Philippi, the work of one New Testament scholar, Holland Hendrix, has dominated all discussions of such honors in Thessalonica.[1] In his doctoral dissertation, which was never published, Hendrix reconstructs divine honors for Romans in the city from almost all archaeological, epigraphic, numismatic, and literary evidence available to him (up to 1984). He traces imperial divine honors back to the second century BC and the divine honors that Thessalonica bestowed on a group of Romans who benefited the city. Hendrix concludes that Julius Caesar is the only Julio-Claudian whom the city hailed as a god and that there was only one imperial temple in Thessalonica dedicated to the cultic honor of Julius Caesar and the noncultic honor of Augustus.[2] Unfortunately for us, Hendrix did not extrapolate about what relationship, if any, imperial divine honors had with early Christianity in Thessalonica in his dissertation or any further publications. With few exceptions, today most scholars rely on Hendrix's reconstruction and have accepted it without reservation. Many conclude that imperial divine honors are an important interpretive backdrop for nascent Christianity in the city.[3]

Some interpreters use Hendrix's work to establish the presence of imperial divine honors in Thessalonica, but they interpret such honors in a more generalizing manner. These scholars tend to point to Greek terms found in 1 and 2 Thessalonians,

1. Holland Lee Hendrix, "Thessalonicans Honor Romans" (ThD diss., Harvard University, 1984), esp. 257–338; Hendrix, "Thessalonica," *ABD* 6:523–27.

2. For a more substantial critique of Hendrix's work, see D. Clint Burnett, "Imperial Divine Honors in Julio-Claudian Thessalonica and the Thessalonian Correspondence," *JBL* 139 (2020): 567–89; Burnett, "Imperial Divine Honors in Julio-Claudian Thessalonica and the Thessalonian Correspondence," in *Thessalonica*, vol. 7 of *The First Urban Churches*, ed. James R. Harrison and L. L. Welborn, WGRWSup 21 (Atlanta: SBL Press, 2022), 63–92. Besides Hendrix, another notable contextual approach to Thessalonian imperial divine honors is Christoph vom Brocke, *Thessaloniki—Stadt des Kassander und Gemeinde des Paulus*, WUNT 2/125 (Tübingen: Mohr Siebeck, 2001), 59–60, 138–41. However, newer discoveries associated with the honors in question made since publication nuance some of his conclusions. Moreover, the fact that this work is in German hinders most English-speaking clergy from accessing it.

3. Robert Jewett, *The Thessalonian Correspondence* (Philadelphia: Fortress, 1986), 124–25; Todd D. Still, *Conflict at Thessalonica: A Pauline Church and Its Neighbours*, JSNTSup 183 (Sheffield: Sheffield Academic, 1999), 262–66; Gene J. Green, *The Letters to the Thessalonians*, PNTC (Grand Rapids: Eerdmans, 2002), 38–42; Nijay K. Gupta, *1 and 2 Thessalonians* (Grand Rapids: Zondervan, 2019), 50–53. The exception is Colin Miller's "The Imperial Cult in the Pauline Cities of Asia Minor and Greece," *CBQ* 72 (2010): 319, 322, an article that claims incorrectly that Thessalonica is "without evidence for the [imperial] cult."

specifically *euangelion* and *kyrios*, that also appear in some Greek inscriptions associated with imperial divine honors in cities in the Greek East. However, the epigraphs
connecting *euangelion* to the Julio-Claudian dynasty are not from Thessalonica, and
the one inscription hailing a Julio-Claudian as *kyrios* postdates the Thessalonian
letters by almost twenty years. For the use of *euangelion* as an imperial cultic term,
scholars reference an inscription from the Greek city of Priene in modern-day Turkey near Ephesus that dates to 9 BC and refers to Augustus's birth as "the beginning
of good news for the world."[4] For Greeks hailing Julio-Claudians as *kyrioi*, exegetes
point to an epigraph from the Greek city of Acraephia in the Boeotian region of the
Roman province of Achaia that dates to AD 67 and calls Nero "*kyrios* of the entire
world."[5] In addition to these terms, interpreters note other words in the Thessalonian
correspondence that have a political connotation, such as *basileia* and two supposed
technical terms for a royal or imperial visit, *parousia* and *apantēsis*, the latter often
being translated as "meeting." Then these scholars point out that the Thessalonian
correspondence evidences that Christians in the city were experiencing suffering of some kind at the hands of pagan Thessalonians (1 Thess 1:6; 2:14–16; 3:1–5;
2 Thess 1:4–9). Most propose that this mistreatment consisted of social harassment
and possibly violence, with some scholars contending that a few Christians suffered
martyrdom.[6] The root cause of this harassment and, for some scholars, even death
of Thessalonian believers was the proclamation of the *euangelion* of *kyrios* Jesus and
God's *basileia*, which directly attacked *kyrios* Caesar and the *euangelia* of his *basileia*.[7]

---

4. ἦρξεν δὲ τῶι κόσμωι τῶν δι᾿ αὐτὸν εὐαγγελί[ων . . .] (*OGIS* 458 = *IPriene* 105 = PH253018 and
PH252886, line 40). The inscription indicates that a copy of the decree in Greek and Latin was
set up in the temple complex of Roma and Augustus in Pergamum, but epigraphs containing
copies of the decree have been found in five other Asian cities: Metropolis, Maoionia, Apameia,
Eumeneia, and Dorylaion. See Peter Thonemann, "The Calendar of the Roman Province of Asia,"
ZPE 196 (2015): 123–41.

5. ὁ τοῦ παντὸς κόσμου κύριος Νέρων (*IG* 7.2713 = *SIG* 814 = PH146221, line 31).

6. For an excellent discussion of the nature of the persecution of the Thessalonian Christians, see Still, *Conflict at Thessalonica*, 208–27.

7. Karl Paul Donfried, "The Cults of Thessalonica and the Thessalonian Correspondence,"
NTS 31 (1985): 336–56, esp. 342–52; James R. Harrison, *Paul and Imperial Authorities at Thessalonica and Rome: A Study in the Conflict of Ideology*, WUNT 273 (Tübingen: Mohr Siebeck, 2011),
47–95; Edward Pillar, *Resurrection as Anti-imperial Gospel: 1 Thessalonians 1:9b–10 in Context*
(Minneapolis: Fortress, 2013). Donfried, "Cults of Thessalonica," 349–50, and Michael J. Gorman, *Apostle of the Crucified Lord: A Theological Introduction to Paul and His Letters*, 2nd ed.
(Grand Rapids: Eerdmans, 2017), 191, 194, 196, 203, contend that some Thessalonian Christians
were executed. Gorman, *Apostle of the Crucified Lord*, 194, suggests, "Paul's strong emphasis
on apocalyptic hope in this letter may well derive from the Thessalonians' own experience of
persecution and even death because of their faithful life and witness. If that situation was a
reaction to their explicit or implicit rejection of the imperial cult, as part of forsaking idolatry,

Thus, in the words of Gene Green, "the proclamation of Christ was the counterpoint to imperial claims."[8]

While I appreciate the attempt to take imperial divine honors as a serious background for the interpretation and reconstruction of early Christianity in Thessalonica, such a generalizing approach to these honors is inadequate and problematic because the premises on which the above scholars have constructed their various arguments are flawed. As we shall see, Thessalonian evidence does not support the notion that *euangelion* and *kyrios* are "imperial" terms in first-century Thessalonica. Nor does the ancient data, including Paul's letters, lend credence to the idea that *parousia* and *apantēsis* are "technical" terms for a royal or an imperial visit. The reason scholars have failed to notice that *euangelion* and *kyrios* are not imperial titles in Thessalonica is their underlying assumption about imperial divine honors that I noted in chapter 1. Their method of interpreting such honors presupposes that a monolithic "imperial cult" existed in the Roman Empire. For such interpreters, one need not reconstruct "the imperial cult" in Thessalonica because Greco-Roman cities treated emperors equally, and if one city honored a certain Julio-Claudian divinely, then all cities did.

In place of this generalized method of interpreting imperial divine honors, I advocate the approach of Hendrix and the creation of a localized, contextual profile of such honors by amassing all evidence from Thessalonica: inscriptions, coins, archaeological remains, and literary sources (if applicable). However, some of Hendrix's conclusion are incorrect for two reasons: (1) he did not consider all the evidence available to him, and (2) newer discoveries have undermined some of his conclusions.[9] These difficulties with Hendrix's work notwithstanding, when we follow the contextual method of interpreting Thessalonian imperial divine honors that he and I espouse, their Greek civic nature becomes clear, for most evidence attesting to them consists of public Greek inscriptions and legends on coins that Thessalonica set up or minted, respectively. The Greek civic character of these honors and their location in the province of Macedonia mean that the most appropriate comparative material to fill in our fragmentary Thessalonica sources should be evidence from places where Greek and particularly Macedonian civic imperial divine honors were practiced, Greek cities close to Thessalonica. With this in mind, we now turn to our contextual reconstruction.

---

it may also explain why Paul uses a significant number of theopolitical metaphors to describe the present reign and future return of Jesus the Lord."

8. Green, *Letters to the Thessalonians*, 41.

9. Hendrix, "Thessalonicans Honor Romans," 256–338. As I show below, Thessalonica hailed more Julio-Claudians than Julius Caesar as a god, and there was more than one Julio-Claudian imperial temple in the city.

DIVINE HONORS FOR HUMANS IN THESSALONICA

History of Thessalonica

Thessalonica differed from the two other cities we are considering in this book, because, unlike Philippi and Corinth, it remained a Greek city throughout antiquity. The Hellenistic king, Cassander (reigned 317–297 BC)—one of Alexander the Great's subordinates who seized control of part of his kingdom after his death in 323 BC—founded Thessalonica around 316/315 BC, naming it after his wife, Thessalonica, Alexander's half sister.[10] He chose the site of the new city carefully. Cassander placed it at the junction of a well-traveled east-west trade route, linking the Adriatic Sea, to Thessalonica's west, and Byzantium (later known as Constantinople and what today is known as Istanbul), to Thessalonica's east. Moreover, the king situated Thessalonica at the deepest part of the Thermaic Gulf to the city's south—a location that also meant mountains were to Thessalonica's east and north.[11] This strategic placement ensured not only Thessalonica's economic prosperity but also its security from invading armies. In creating Thessalonica, Cassander combined several nearby Greek townships and formed a new Greek political entity, a *polis*, with a Greek constitution.[12] This constitution, which has not survived, divided the population of Thessalonica into two main groups, *politai* or "citizens" and noncitizen "resident aliens," who were probably called *metoikoi* (literally, "dwelling," *oikos*, "with," *meta*). The collective body of *politai* were known as Thessalonica's *dēmos* or "citizen body." These individuals elected certain aristocrats to serve on the city's *boulē* or "civic council," which oversaw Thessalonian public affairs.[13] Each year, the city's *dēmos* selected a number of men to serve in

10. Diodorus Siculus, *Library of History* 19.52.1; Strabo, *Geography* 7 fragments 10, 21, 24; Dionysius of Halicarnassus, *Roman Antiquities* 1.49. Our current, incomplete archaeological evidence from Thessalonica and its environs contradicts the testimony of Dionysius of Halicarnassus, *Roman Antiquities* 1.49, and Strabo, *Geography* 7 fragment 21, that Cassander demolished a number of these Greek towns in the founding of Thessalonica. See Polyxeni Adam-Veleni, "Thessaloniki: History and Town Planning," in *Roman Thessaloniki*, ed. D. V. Grammenos, trans. David Hardy, Thessaloniki Archaeological Museum Publication 1 (Thessaloniki: Thessaloniki Archaeological Museum, 2003), 121–27, esp. 122.

11. This trade route eventually became part of the Roman Via Egnatia.

12. Of the 1,673 published inscriptions, approximately fifty-one are in Latin, about fourteen are in Latin and Greek, and the rest are in Greek. See *IG* 10.2.1; *IG* 10.2.1s.

13. For the Thessalonian *boulē*, see *IG* 10.2.1.200, 202. For the *dēmos*, see *IG* 10.2.1.136. For a concise and excellent discussion of these offices in a Greek city, see B. H. McLean, *An Introduction to Greek Epigraphy of the Hellenistic and Roman Periods from Alexander the Great down to the Reign of Constantine (323 B.C.–A.D. 337)* (Ann Arbor: University of Michigan Press, 2002), 303–9.

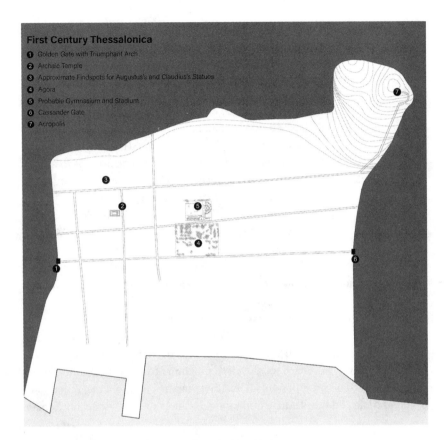

First Century Thessalonica
1. Golden Gate with Triumphant Arch
2. Archaic Temple
3. Approximate Findspots for Augustus's and Claudius's Statues
4. Agora
5. Probable Gymnasium and Stadium
6. Cassander Gate
7. Acropolis

Fig. 3.1 Site map of Thessalonica | *Map prepared by Chloe Dyar*

various public offices, the highest of which was its politarchy, which consisted of between two and five of Thessalonica's most prominent aristocratic men.[14]

The early history of Thessalonica down to the Roman period is difficult to reconstruct, because the city has been inhabited since its foundation (see fig. 3.1). Therefore, unlike Corinth and Philippi, modern Thessaloniki sits atop ancient Thessalonica, which makes systematic archaeological investigation of the ancient Greek city impossible. This problem of historical reconstruction is compounded by the fact that no ancient Greek or Latin sources recounting the city's history

14. For the politarchs, see G. H. R. Horsley, "The Politarchs," in *The Book of Acts in Its Graeco-Roman Setting*, ed. David W. J. Gill and Conrad Gempf, vol. 2 of *The Book of Acts in Its First Century Setting* (Grand Rapids: Eerdmans, 1994), 419–31.

survive. Thus, we are forced to piece together the city's history from information gleaned from inscriptions (many of which are fragmentary), coins, excavated Thessalonian sites scattered throughout the modern city, and passing references to the city in surviving Greco-Roman literature.

From these sources, it appears that Thessalonica experienced growth after its founding and became a commercial center and military base for the kings of Macedon.[15] The city passed into Roman hands at the end of a war between Macedon and Rome, known as the Third Macedonian War (171–168 BC), in which the latter was victorious. The general in charge of the Roman army at that time, Aemilius Paulus, divided the territory of Macedon's kingdom into four administrative districts known as *merides* in Greek (cf. Acts 16:12) and made Thessalonica the second district's capital.[16] Within twenty years of this territorial division, Macedon attempted to throw off the yoke of Rome in what is known as the Fourth Macedonian War (150–148 BC). This war, too, ended in Roman victory.[17] The general commanding Rome's forces during that war, Quintus Caecilius Metellus, reorganized the province and consolidated Macedonia's four administrative districts into one. In the process, he made Thessalonica the provincial capital.[18]

To expedite the movement of troops across the newly organized province, the Romans built a great road, the Via Egnatia, in the mid-second century BC.[19] Unlike at Philippi (see fig. 2.1, no. 11), the Via Egnatia did not run through Thessalonica but only past it.[20] Nevertheless, the city's proximity to the Via Egnatia allowed Thessalonica to become not only a bustling seaport but also a major center of overland trade and travel. Many traders and businesspersons, especially Roman,

15. From this period to the first century AD, Thessalonica's walls did not extend to its extreme west and to the city's port: Adam-Veleni, "Thessaloniki," 121–34.

16. Diodorus Siculus, *Library of History* 31.8.6–9.

17. The cause of the Fourth Macedonian War was a man named Andriscus claiming to be the rightful king of Macedon and attempting to revive the Macedonian kingdom (Diodorus Siculus, *Library of History* 31.40a).

18. For a more thorough description of Rome's involvement with Macedonia, see D. Clint Burnett, *Studying the New Testament through Inscriptions: An Introduction* (Peabody, MA: Hendrickson, 2020), 110–14.

19. Strabo, *Geography* 7.7.4. In the mid-first century BC, the Roman senator and orator Cicero, *On Consular Provinces* 2.4, called the Via Egnatia "that military road of ours" (*via illa nostra . . . militaris*) that runs through Macedonia all the way to the Hellespont.

20. Adam-Veleni, "Thessaloniki," 135–36, notes, "The Via Egnatia, which was originally intended for the movement of troops, exploited and improved earlier roads. For this reason, it did not pass through . . . Thessaloniki, and is certainly not to be identified with the modern Egnatia Street that crosses it."

moved to the city.[21] From available evidence, the people of Thessalonica knew that they owed their prominence and prosperity to Rome, and they were loyal to her throughout the first centuries BC and AD, despite the fact that the province and the city became embroiled in three Roman civil wars.[22]

In 49 BC, the Roman senator and general Pompey the Great and his partisans declared war on Julius Caesar. He, along with the Roman senator, orator, and philosopher Cicero, and about two hundred other senators, left Rome and chose Thessalonica as his strategic military base. Pompey and these senators claimed to be the legitimate Roman Senate, and they even made a portion of the city into a mini-Rome by consecrating a piece of land on which they could practice their distinctive form of Roman augury and meet to make decisions for the Roman people.[23] In 48 BC, Caesar crossed the Adriatic Sea and eventually met Pompey in a pitched battle about one hundred twenty-five miles south of Thessalonica in a place known as Pharsalus, modern-day Farsala. When the dust settled, Caesar emerged the victor and the most powerful man in Rome and thus the Mediterranean world.[24] In the aftermath of this battle, there is no evidence that Caesar showed any ill will toward Thessalonica for harboring Pompey and his other enemies. Thus, he must have shown his renowned clemency to the Greek city.

Four years later, Thessalonica was caught up in another martial conflict. After Julius Caesar's assassination (March 15, 44 BC), two of his main assassins, Brutus and Cassius, and their armies fled from Caesar's partisans—Marc Antony and Caesar's adopted son, Caesar Octavian (the future emperor Augustus)—to Macedonia. As Brutus and Cassius passed along the Via Egnatia, they and their troops attempted to take refuge in Thessalonica. The city, however, refused to admit them. Incensed, and in stark contrast to the merciful Caesar whom he had

21. The Roman businessmen in particular were involved in commerce, banking, and finance and gained prominence in Thessalonica. See Victoria Allamani-Souri, "Brief History of Imperial Thessaloniki," in *Roman Thessaloniki*, ed. D. V. Grammenos, trans. David Hardy, Thessaloniki Archaeological Museum Publication 1 (Thessaloniki: Thessaloniki Archaeological Museum, 2003), 92–93.

22. In 58 BC, Cicero, *On Behalf of Fonteius* 20 (44), spent seven months of his exile from Rome in Thessalonica, which left him with the impression of Macedonia's fidelity to Rome and that the province was "firmly committed to and a friend toward the Roman people" (*fidelis et amica populo Romano*). Cicero made this comment in a speech before the senate in 56 BC after he returned to Rome. Because of his correspondence with his friend Atticus, we know that Cicero, *To Atticus* 53–67, was in Thessalonica from May 29 to November 25, 58 BC.

23. Dio Cassius, *Roman History* 41.18.5–6; 41.43.1–5.

24. For a description of the battle of Pharsalus and its outcome, see Adrian Goldsworthy, *Caesar: Life of a Colossus* (New Haven: Yale University Press, 2006), 405–47, esp. 422–31.

Fig. 3.2 Thessalonica's triumphant arch at the city's Golden Gate that was demolished in 1874 | *Drawing from Léon Heuzey and H. Daumet,* Mission archéologique de Macédoine (*Paris: Librairie de Firmin-Didot, 1876), plate 22; Wikimedia Commons*

murdered, Brutus promised his army that after he defeated Antony and Caesar Octavian, his troops could return to Thessalonica to rape and pillage.[25] Brutus and his men were never afforded that opportunity, because when he and Cassius met Antony and Caesar Octavian on the Drama plain before the walls of Philippi in October 42 BC, the latter won the day (see pp. 68–69).[26] Following this victory, Antony, who by agreement with Caesar Octavian was given control of the Greek East, rewarded Thessalonica for its loyalty to the Caesarian cause. He made it a "free city," which meant that Thessalonica no longer had to pay tribute to Rome or billet troops. To show appreciation for such munificence, the city's government commemorated its new "free" status in inscriptions and on coins, it established public divine honors for the Greek goddess *Eleutheria* or "Freedom" (see fig. 3.3), and Thessalonica may have set up a triumphant arch in an ancient gateway on the western side of the city, known as the Golden Gate, which stood in the city until

25. Plutarch, *Brutus* 46.
26. For a discussion of the battle of Philippi, see Adrian Goldsworthy, *Augustus: First Emperor of Rome* (New Haven: Yale University Press, 2014), 134–43.

its demolition in 1874 (see figs. 3.1, no. 1; 2).[27] It is entirely possible, however, that Thessalonica erected this arch during Augustus's reign.[28]

After about a decade, the alliance between Caesar Octavian and Antony broke, and another Roman civil war spilled into mainland Greece. In 31 BC, Caesar Octavian, with the help of his distinguished general and close friend Marcus Agrippa, defeated Antony in a naval battle off the western coast of mainland Greece near the city of Actium. Antony fled to Egypt with his lover Cleopatra, where both committed suicide. This act left Caesar Octavian sole general of (almost) all Rome's armies and thus the most powerful man in the Roman Empire. As he began to consolidate his power, Caesar Octavian's treatment of Thessalonica followed in the footsteps of his adopted father Julius Caesar. He allowed the city to retain its "free" status in the empire, despite its support of Antony. At this point, the city entered into an age of unprecedented peace and prosperity that lasted for three hundred years. Thus, Paul, Silvanus, and Timothy were certainly correct to characterize mid-first-century Thessalonica as living in an age of "peace and security" (*eirēnē kai asphaleia* [1 Thess 5:3]). This is evidenced by the construction boom that began in Thessalonica in Augustus's reign (31 BC–AD 14) and continued throughout the rest of the Julio-Claudian period, which may have included the triumphant arch at the city's Golden Gate (see fig. 3.2), that is, unless Thessalonica erected the arch in 42 BC.[29] The result was that the first-century AD Thessalonian poet Antipater was able to boast that his city was "the mother of all Macedonia."[30]

Divine Honors for Romans in Thessalonica

Long before the Julio-Claudian period, Thessalonica granted divine honors to certain of its beneficent rulers and inhabitants. The earliest case dates right after the Fourth Macedonian War in 148 BC. When that war erupted in 150 BC, Thessalonica remained loyal to Rome. The city celebrated Metellus's victory and the subsequent reorganization of Macedonia that made it the provincial capital by adopting a new system of dating. The first year of this system, which historians call the provincial dating method, began in 148 BC, which was "year 1." Macedonians

27. *IG* 10.2.1.6; *RPC* 1.1151.

28. Victoria Allamani-Souri, "The Province of Macedonia in the Roman Imperium," in *Roman Thessaloniki*, ed. D. V. Grammenos, trans. David Hardy, Thessaloniki Archaeological Museum Publication 1 (Thessaloniki: Thessaloniki Archaeological Museum, 2003), 77–78.

29. Adam-Veleni, "Thessaloniki," 143.

30. *Greek Anthology* 9.428, Θεσσαλονίκη μήτηρ ἡ πάσης πέμψε Μακηδονίης. By the late first century BC, the geographer Strabo, *Geography* 7.7.4, notes that Thessalonica "had more inhabitants than any of the other cities" (ἡ νῦν μάλιστα τῶν ἄλλων εὐανδρεῖ) of Macedonia.

in general and Thessalonians in particular continued to use this dating method into the third century AD.[31] In addition to the way that the city calculated time, Thessalonica granted divine honors to Metellus, setting up a statue of him on a base with an inscription hailing the general as its *sōtēr* or "savior" and *euergetēs* or "benefactor."[32] That Thessalonica acclaimed Metellus as a benefactor does not necessarily translate to divine honors. However, as one specialist in divine honors for Greek rulers, Christian Habicht, has shown, such honors "always" accompanied the recognition of someone as *sōtēr*.[33]

Sometime between 148 and 95 BC, Thessalonica established divine honors for a group of Roman citizens whom it called *Rōmanoi euergetoi* or "Roman benefactors." The identity of these individuals is unknown, but they probably consisted of certain Roman governors and wealthy Romans who had moved to Thessalonica to conduct business and subsequently provided benefactions to the city during their time there.[34] Some of these munificent acts probably relate to invasions of barbarian tribes from the north of Macedonia. One consequence of the creation of Macedonia as a province and the dissolution of Macedon's kingdom was that from the second century BC to the late first century BC, Macedonia was the northern border of Rome's territory in mainland Greece. In between these years, barbarian tribes from the Balkan peninsula made incursions into Macedonia frequently to raid for booty and slaves, as such tribes in antiquity were wont to do.[35] It is probable that the *Rōmanoi euergetoi* defeated or in some way deflected these barbarian hordes from raiding Thessalonica.[36] In response, the city granted such honors to these individuals to show appreciation. The earliest evidence for these

31. Adam-Veleni, "Thessaloniki," 135.

32. "Appendix 1: Inscriptions" §3.1, line 3. A certain Thessalonian set up a statue of Metellus at Olympia in Greece and dedicated it to Olympian Zeus (*IG* 10.2.1.1031 = *IvO* 325).

33. Christian Habicht, *Divine Honors for Mortal Men in Greek Cities: The Early Cases*, trans. John Noël Dillon (Ann Arbor: Michigan Classical Press, 2017), 113, concludes, "the epithets *Theos* and *Soter*, originally reserved for gods and heroes, always indicate a cult for the person who receives them."

34. *IG* 10.2.1.32, 33. For more information, see Allamani-Souri, "Brief History," 92–93.

35. In speeches delivered before the Roman Senate, Cicero, *On Consular Provinces* 2.4 and *Against Piso* 34 (84), notes the large number of barbarian tribes on Macedonia's norther border and that the senate had awarded many governors of the province Roman triumphs because of their campaigns against them. For more information on Macedonia and barbarian invasions, see Fanoula Papazoglou, "Macedonia under the Romans," in *Macedonia: 4,000 Years of Greek History and Civilization*, ed. M. B. Sakellariou (Athens: Ekdotike Athenon, 1983), 192–207, esp. 193–96.

36. Cicero, *On Consular Provinces* 2.4, complained that a barbarian raid on Thessalonica forced the Thessalonians to abandon their city and fortify their citadel. See also Cicero, *Against Piso* 34 (84).

Fig. 3.3 Bronze coin, minted in Thessalonica in 37 BC (*RPC* 1.1551), depicting the goddess Freedom, on the obverse (*left*), and the goddess Victory with a palm branch and wreath in her hand, on the reverse (*right*) | *Courtesy of Yale University Art Gallery*

honors is a decree of the *neoi* or "young men" of Thessalonica's gymnasium dating to 95 BC that is engraved on a marble stele, which was once displayed in the city's gymnasium but was found in a Byzantine Thessalonian church. The epigraph's text lauds a certain leader of the gymnasium known as a gymnasiarch. According to the decree, this gymnasiarch performed many noble feats for the gymnasium, but the one that most concerns me is the increasing of "the customary honors" that the *neoi* offered to the "gods (of the gymnasium) and the Roman benefactors."[37] It is unclear whether some, any, or all these Roman benefactors were alive in 95 BC. Any of these options are possible, because divine honors for this group continued long after the lifetimes of the Roman benefactors in question and are attested in the second and third centuries AD where they were embedded into imperial divine honors.[38] This uncertainty notwithstanding, these sacrifices were wedded to those for the gods of gymnasium, Hermes and Hercules, in a symbiotic, not competitive, relationship.

After the Roman benefactors, Thessalonica probably bestowed divine honors on one last first-century BC Roman, Antony. This grant is uncertain, because no evidence remains for it. However, given that Antony made Thessalonica a "free city" after the battle of Philippi, divine honors for him are probable for three reasons. First, the city boasted of its new "free" status in inscriptions and on coins.

37. τὰς ἠθισμένας τειμὰς . . . τοῖς τε θεοῖς καὶ Ῥωμαίοις εὐεργέταις ("Appendix 1: Inscriptions" §3.2, lines 10–11).

38. "Appendix 1: Inscriptions" §3.4, 10, 11; *IG* 10.2.1.128, 226.

A fragmentary marble inscription from the city that probably dates to 42/41 BC contains a decree of Thessalonica's *dēmos*. One part of this epigraph mentions "the free Thessalonians" (*Thessalonikeis eleutheroi*) and emphasizes they are "free persons" (*eleutheroi*).[39] A coin that the city minted in 37 BC bears an image of *Eleutheria* with the Greek legend *Thessalonikeōn Eleutherias* or "*Eleutheria* of the Thessalonians" on the obverse and a picture of *Nikē*, the goddess of victory, carrying a palm branch and a wreath on the reverse (see fig. 3.3).[40]

Second, the city altered and supplemented its dating system, making the year that Antony gave Thessalonica its "free" status "year 1."[41] One epigraph from the city commemorates the dedication of a temple complex of Osiris and its peristyle—a court enclosed by columns—to Osiris and the other gods of the temple by two Roman citizens during "year three of Antony" ([*etous*] *g'* [[*Antōniou*]]). The reason that *Antōniou* is in double brackets is that after the battle of Actium in 31 BC, Antony's name was effaced from the epigraph.[42] Recall that Thessalonica had adopted the provincial dating system in conjunction with the divine honors that it bestowed on Metellus after his victory. Hence, it is probable that the city did likewise to Antony. Third, if Thessalonica's triumphant arch was dedicated after the battle of Philippi (42 BC) (see figs. 3.1, no. 1; 2), then this lends credence to the probability that the city established divine honors for Antony. Given that the city destroyed Antony's name and reputation from its collective memory after Actium, which would have included the destruction of any sources mentioning divine honors for him, we will never know for certain, the extent to which, and exactly how the city divinely honored him.[43]

Imperial Divine Honors in Thessalonica

The above divine honors for Romans pale in comparison to those that Thessalonica offered certain Julio-Claudians. Beginning with the reign of Caesar Octavian/Augustus (31 BC–AD 14), there is a veritable explosion of sources attesting to divine honors both in quantity and quality. For the first time in Thessalonica's historical record, the number of inscriptions referring to or mentioning divine honors for rulers increases dramatically, the divine status of certain rulers is advertised on coins, and temples and cultic images of rulers are attested. These sources

39. *IG* 10.2.1 6.
40. *RPC* 1.1551.
41. *IG* 10.2.1.83, 109, 124.
42. "Appendix 1: Inscriptions" §3.3, line 1.
43. For the magnitude of the bestowal of free status on Thessalonica, see below and Burnett, *Studying the New Testament*, 97–120.

allow us to reconstruct which Julio-Claudians the city divinely honored. They testify that with one exception (the case of Julius Caesar) Thessalonica followed the custom of Greek civic imperial divine honors, bestowing such honors most often on living Julio-Claudians for the purpose of showing appreciation for their benefaction. However, the city deviated from Greek civic imperial divine honors in one area: it tended to wait until these Julio-Claudians died before Thessalonica hailed them as gods. In what follows, I reconstruct the Thessalonian honors in question. I begin by presenting the sources for these honors in chronological order of the Julio-Claudians on whom they were bestowed. Then, I explore the identity of the imperial cultic officials in the city, parsing out who they were and the other public offices that they held. Finally, I address the location whence these cultic officials offered imperial sacrifices to the Julio-Claudians as well as how and when these offerings were made. To fill out the fragmentary nature of these sources, I use comparative material mostly from Greek cities of Macedonia, with the occasional reference to imperial divine honors from Greek cities outside Macedonia and mainland Greece.

Theos Julius Caesar

The evidence for divine honors for Julius Caesar is two coin series that Thessalonica minted during Caesar Octavian's, or Augustus's, reign. These coins differ in quality, but both show Julius Caesar's bust on the obverse, with the Greek legend *theos*, and Caesar Octavian's, or Augustus's, bust on the reverse, with the Greek legend *Thessalonikeōn* or "of the Thessalonians" (see fig. 3.4).[44] These coins demonstrate that the city bestowed divine honors on Julius Caesar after his assassination (March 15, 44 BC) and divinization in Rome (January 1, 42 BC), which is a rare occurrence in Greek cities.[45] This means that Thessalonica followed the public affairs of Rome and chose to mimic the capital of the empire in establishing divine honors for *Divus* Julius. If this is the case, then the Greek title *theos* on these coins translates Julius Caesar's official posthumous title in Rome, *Divus* Julius.[46]

The context for this grant of divine honors is Caesar Octavian's victory at Actium in 31 BC and Thessalonica's desire to demonstrate its allegiance to the new leader of Rome's armies, Julius Caesar's adopted son Caesar Octavian. After Ac-

---

44. *RPC* 1.1554, 1555.

45. The cities that engraved Julius Caesar's image on their coins and established postmortem divine honors for him tended to be more Romanized communities of the empire, such as Roman colonies like Philippi and Corinth (see chapters 2 and 4).

46. As noted in chapter 1, *theos* is the commonest Greek translation of *divus*.

tium, Thessalonica effaced inscriptions related to or that mentioned Antony, in its quest to erase him from the city's collective memory. Moreover, Thessalonica minted coins depicting iconography associated with Caesar Octavian's victory at Actium, such as those with the prow of a ship—a clear reference to the naval battle at Actium—and one coin series in particular depicts the goddess Victory standing on the prow of a ship with her right hand outstretched.[47] Finally, it is important to note that the coins picturing *theos* Julius Caesar date to Augustus's reign, not to the time when Antony, whom the Roman Senate had appointed as *Divus* Julius's priest, ruled over Thessalonica.[48] This, along with the fact that these coins have Augustus's face on the opposite side, suggests that the city was attempting to stress Augustus's connection to Julius Caesar, not Antony's. However, that the deceased dictator held no ill will toward the city for harboring his enemies, Pompey and the other Roman senators who opposed him in 49–48 BC, probably encouraged the Thessalonian government to grant divine honors to Julius Caesar.

Fig. 3.4 Bronze coin from Thessalonica (*RPC* 1:1555) with the head of Julius Caesar with the Greek legend *theos*, on the obverse (*left*), and the head of Augustus with the Greek legend *Thessalonikeōn*, on the reverse (*right*) | *With permission of wildwinds.com, ex CNG, 2001*

(*Theos*) *Augustus*

The bulk of evidence for imperial divine honors in Thessalonica relates to Augustus, most of which dates to his lifetime. To date, two inscriptions, one coin series, and one statue attest to such honors for the emperor, and two epigraphs evidence that Thessalonica hailed Augustus as *theos* after his death and divinization in Rome. The first inscription attesting to divine honors for Augustus during his lifetime was found in AD 1874 built into a Roman era gate known as the Cassander Gate, on the eastern side of Thessalonica (see fig. 3.1, no. 6), not, as I mistakenly noted in earlier publications, from the Golden Gate, which is on the western side

47. *RPC* 1.1560, 1556. See Roman Provincial Coinage Online, https://rpc.ashmus.ox.ac.uk/coins/1/1556A.

48. See pp. 168–72 for the discussion of divine honors for *Divus* Julius in Corinth.

of Thessalonica. At that time, workers were in the process of demolishing the Cassander Gate with pickaxes when two French antiquarians who happened to be in the city discovered a badly damaged stone stele with a Greek inscription among the rubble. They sketched a picture of it, copied the remaining text, and in 1876 published the epigraph in a work detailing the antiquities that they encountered on their travels (see fig. 3.5).

The inscription, which is now lost, dates to Augustus's reign (27 BC–AD 14) and testifies to an imperial temple dedicated to the emperor.[49] Though badly damaged, the epigraph commemorates the temple's construction. It names the project's patron, a Roman governor of the province of Macedonia whose name is lost, who paid for the building material of the temple—quarried stone. The inscription notes that several Greek Thessalonians played a role in the building of the temple, serving as architect of the project, supervisor of the work, and treasurer of the city. The completion of the temple is dated to a particular year when certain Greeks served as politarchs and priests of two important public Thessalonian priesthoods.

```
                    I.

                 ΒΟΣΑ
          Α.ΘΥΠΑΤΟΣ
         ΛΑΤΟΜΙΑΣΕΠΟΗΣ
           ΚΑΙΣΑΡΟΣΝΑ
    5  ΕΠΙΙΕΡΕΩΣΚΑΙΑΓΩΝ
       ΤΟΚΡΑΤΟΡΟΣ·ΚΑΙΣΑ
       ΥΙΟΥΣΕΒΑΣΒΑΣΤΟ
       ΩΣΤΟΥΝΕΙΚΟΠΟΛ
       ΔΕΤΩΝΘΕΩΝ·ΔΩ
   10  ΠΟΥ·ΡΩΜΗΣΔΕΚ
       ΕΥΕΡΓΕΤΩΝ·ΝΕΙΚ
       ΠΑΡΑΜΟΝΟΥ·
            ΠΟΛΕΙΤΑ
       ΔΙΟΓΕΝΟΥΣΤΟ
   15  ΚΛΕΩΝΟΣΤΟΥΠ
       ΖΩΠΑΤΟΥΚΑΛ
       ΕΥΛΑΝΔΡΟΥΤΟΥ
       ΠΡΩΤΟΓΕΝΟΥΣ
       ΤΟΥΚΑΙΠΡΟΣΤΑΤ
   20  ΤΟΥΕΡΓΟΥ·ΤΑΜ
       ΣΩΣΩΝΟΣΤ
            ΑΡΧΙΤΕΚ
       ΔΙΟΝΥΣΙΟ
```

Fig. 3.5 Inscription attesting to the temple of Caesar Augustus | *Drawing from Louis Duchesne and Charles Bayet,* Mémoire sur une mission au Mont Athos *(Paris: Ernest Thorin, 1876), 11–12, no. 1*

The priesthood that most concerns me is that of "priest and president of games for the victorious general Caesar Augustus son of a god" (for more on this priesthood see pp. 129–32).[50]

For many years, New Testament scholars thought that this was the only imperial temple in the city. However, the recent discovery of an inscription, which forms the second epigraph attesting to divine honors for Augustus, engraved on marble and found about nine miles southeast of Thessalonica attests to a second temple dedicated to Augustus, and two other divine beings, that a Thessalonian benefactress set up with her own money. The inscription is in Greek and Latin

---

49. Since the official publication of this inscription in 1972 and Hendrix's work, "Thessalonicans Honor Romans," 106–9, 174–76, 292–99, historians have misidentified the temple as belonging to Julius Caesar. For more, see Burnett, "Imperial Divine Honors," 575–77.

50. ἱερεὺς καὶ ἀγωνοθέτης Αὐτοκράτορος Καίσαρος Θεοῦ υἱοῦ Σεβαστοῦ ("Appendix 1: Inscriptions" §3.4, 10, 11, 12).

and dates between 12 BC and AD 14. Its text indicates that this benefactress, Avia Posilla, had a temple, a bath, a pool, and a portico surrounding the latter built and dedicated "to the victorious general Augustus Caesar son of a god, Hercules, and the (divine personification of) the city (of Thessalonica)."[51] Unfortunately, archaeologists have yet to find and excavate this temple, so not much else is known about it. However, it is clear from the epigraph that Avia Posilla interweaved the fortunes of her city with a demigod, Hercules, and a Julio-Claudian, Augustus.

In 1939, archaeologists discovered a marble statue of Augustus on the western side of the city that probably dates to Caligula's reign (AD 37–41) and that makes up the only statuary evidence from Thessalonica for divine honors for this emperor (see figs. 3.1, no. 3; 6).[52] The image depicts Augustus in the guise of Zeus. He is naked from the waist up and extends his right hand, which now is empty but once held a spear. The emperor holds the excess of the mantle covering his lower body with his left hand and arm. The statue stresses Augustus's godlikeness and Zeusness, and thus it is cultic. It may be a or the cultic statue that was housed in the temple of Caesar Augustus (not the temple of Augustus, Hercules, and the divine personification of Thessalonica). However, because much about the temple of Caesar Augustus remains uncertain, this suggestion must remain tentative.

Although there were two Thessalonian temples dedicated to Augustus while he was alive, Thessalonica did not hail him as *theos* during Augustus's lifetime. Instead, the city waited until the emperor passed on August 19, AD 14, and the Roman Senate divinized him on September 17 of the same year to acclaim him as divine. This much is clear, in that the Thessalonian epigraphs mentioning divine honors for him that predate his death never call him a god, but one coin series and two inscriptions that postdate his death do. The Thessalonian coin was minted in Claudius's reign (AD 41–54) and pictures Claudius's bust on the observe, with a Greek legend identifying him as the emperor. The coin's reverse depicts Augustus's

---

51. Αὐτοκράτορι Καίσαρι θεοῦ υἱῶι Σεβαστῶι καὶ Ἡρακλεῖ καὶ τῆι πόλει ("Appendix 1: Inscriptions" §3.5, lines 1–2). The Latin text deviates from the Greek text; see "Appendix 1: Inscriptions" §3.5, lines 6–7.

52. Paul Lemerle, "Chronique des fouilles et découvertes archéologiques en Grèce en 1939," *BCH* 63 (1939): 315; G. Despinis, T. Stefanidou-Tiveriou, and E. Voutyras, eds., *Κατάλογος γλυπτών του Αρχαιολογικού Μουσείου Θεσσαλονίκης* (Thessaloniki: Morphotiko Hidryma Ethnikes Trapezes, 2003), no. 244; Theodosia Stefanidou-Tiveriou, "Art in the Roman Period, 168 BC–337 AD," in *Brill's Companion to Ancient Macedon: Studies in the Archaeology and History of Macedon, 650 BC–300 AD*, ed. Robert J. Lane Fox (Leiden: Brill, 2011), 570. Though Allamani-Souri, "Imperial Cult," 115, dates the statue to the time of Tiberius (AD 14–37).

bust with the Greek legend *theos Sebastos Thessaloneikeōn* or "god Augustus of the Thessalonians" (see fig. 3.7).[53]

The two epigraphs that call Augustus a *theos* may not be direct evidence for divine honors for the emperor in Thessalonica, but they indicate that the city knew of his postmortem Roman divinization. The first is an inscription inscribed on a marble plaque that was found reused in a Byzantine church. Its text commemorates the dedication of a building or part of one to Augustus's wife Livia that calls her the wife of *theou Sebastou Kaisa[ros]* or the "god Caesar Augustus."[54] The second is an epigraph on a fragmentary marble block that dates to Nero's reign (AD 54–68), which may contain a reference to that emperor as the great-grandson of the god Augustus, for the inscription's latest editor, *IG* 10.2.1s, has restored the following: "Nero . . . great-grandson of the god Augustus."[55]

The context for these divine honors for Augustus is the munificence that the emperor or his reign brought Thessalonica. As noted, when Augustus defeated Antony at the battle of Actium, he allowed the city to retain its "free" status,

Fig. 3.6 Statue of Octavian Augustus, AD 14–37, Thessaloniki, Archaeological Museum of Thessaloniki, Inv. No. MΘ 1065 | *Photo by O. Kourakis; photographed with the permission of the Archaeological Museum of Thessaloniki, Hellenic Ministry of Culture & Sports—Hellenic Organization of Cultural Resources Development*

---

53. *RPC* 1.1578, 1579, 1580.

54. "Appendix 1: Inscriptions" §3.6, line 2.

55. [[Νέρωνος]] . . . [. . . θεου Σεβαστοῦ] υἱων[ου] υἱωνοῦ ("Appendix 1: Inscriptions" §3.7, lines 1, 6).

which Antony had bestowed in 42 BC. This act was not one that the emperor granted lightly. A letter that Augustus composed in the late first century BC to the island of Samos that has been inscribed on the wall of a theater in the city of Aphrodisias in western Asia Minor, modern-day Turkey, in the second to third century AD provides his thoughts on the status of freedom for a Greek city. Samos has petitioned Augustus's wife Livia to intercede on its behalf and ask the emperor to bestow "free" status upon it, as Augustus had done for Aphrodisias. He declined their request, stating that the granting of such a status is "the greatest benefaction of all," and he does not give it without due consideration. The only reason, the emperor says, that he granted it to Aphrodisias was that the city had "considered my affairs in the war [with Antony]."[56]

Fig. 3.7 Bronze coin, minted in Thessalonica between AD 41 and 54 (*RPC* 1:1578), depicting the bust of Claudius with the Greek legend, on the obverse (*left*), and a bust of Augustus with the Greek legend *theos Sebastos Thessaloneikeōn*, on the reverse (*right*) | *Courtesy of Yale University Art Gallery*

Therefore, this Augustan benefaction for Thessalonica is enough to warrant divine honors for him in the city.

Moreover, Thessalonica experienced physical and economic growth during Augustus's lifetime, for his reign was the beginning of an era of peace and prosperity heretofore unknown to the city (cf. 1 Thess 5:3). Inscriptional and archaeological evidence from nearby Macedonian cities demonstrates the connection between Augustus's munificence and the granting of divine honors for him. In a city that Paul and his apostolic colleagues passed through on their way to Thessalonica, Amphipolis (Acts 17:1), Augustus probably paid for the construction of a new gymnasium and temple of the Egyptian gods and gave the city "free" status in the empire just like Thessalonica.[57] To show appreciation, Amphipolis erected a statue of Augustus on a base with an accompanying inscription outside its city gates. The statue no longer remains, but the base with the epigraph does. The text of this

---

56. ὃς ἐν τῷ πολέμῳ τὰ ἐμὰ φρονήσας . . . τὸ πάντων μέγιστον φιλάνθρωπον (*IAph* 8.32 = PH256915, lines 3–4). This inscription and an English translation can be found on the online corpus of inscriptions from Aphrodisias: Joyce Reynolds, Charlotte Roueché, and Gabriel Bodard, *Inscriptions of Aphrodisias*, 2007, https://insaph.kcl.ac.uk/insaph/iaph2007/iApho80032.html.

57. Ch. Koukouli-Chrysanthanki, "Amphipolis," in *Brill's Companion to Ancient Macedon: Studies in the Archaeology and History of Macedon, 650 BC–300 AD*, ed. Robert J. Lane Fox (Leiden: Brill, 2011), 433–34.

inscription calls Augustus Amphipolis's *sōtēr* and *ktistēs* or "founder"—titles that imply that the city bestowed divine honors on him.[58] One of the most appropriate comparative data for Thessalonian civic imperial divine honors is from the Macedonian city Calindoia, about twenty-five miles east of Thessalonica. There, archaeologists have uncovered several inscriptions, statues, and a multifunctional building that included a shrine to Zeus, Roma, and Augustus. I discuss this evidence in more detail below, but for the current discussion, I wish to emphasize that Calindoia established a priesthood to serve Zeus, Roma, and Augustus. One Calindoian aristocrat who held this office set up a statue of Augustus (which archaeologists may have found; see fig. 3.10) on a base in the city and had an inscription placed on it. In the epigraph, this priest notes that the emperor's image functions as "an everlasting memorial of Augustus's benefactions for all humanity" and that by setting up this statue, "he dispensed the proper honor and gratitude for the god (Augustus)."[59] Consequently, the creation of divine honors for Augustus in Thessalonica functioned similarly: as a token of appreciation for the emperor's munificence, especially for the maintenance of the city's "free" status.

Thea Livia

One inscription and one coin evince that Thessalonica granted divine honors to Livia, Augustus's wife, during her lifetime. The latter evidence was minted in Augustus's reign. The coin in question depicts Livia's bust on the obverse, with the Greek legend *thea* or *theou Libia*, while a bucking horse is on the reverse, with the Greek legend *Thessalonik[eōn]* or "of the Thessalonians" (see fig. 3.8). The epigraph in question was found reused in a Byzantine church in Thessalonica and dates between AD 14 and 29, after the death of Augustus but before Livia's passing. Its text, which also calls Augustus a god (see p. 123), commemorates a dedication of a building or a portion of one to Livia Augusta, calling her *thea*. It is important to note that *thea* along with other parts of her name are restored in the inscription.[60] However, given that Thessalonica acclaimed her as a goddess on coinage, this restoration is probable.

This coin and probably the inscription make Livia the only Julio-Claudian to date whom Thessalonica hailed as divine during her lifetime. This fact suggests that Livia must have provided a magnificent beneficent act for the city. Unfortu-

---

58. Unfortunately, this inscription has not been officially published. See Frank Daubner, "Macedonian Small Towns and Their Use of Augustus," *RRE* 2 (2016): 399; Koukouli-Chrysanthanki, "Amphipolis," 429.

59. αἰώνιον ὑπόμνημα τῆς εἰς πάντας ἀνθρώπους εὐεργεσίας τοῦ Σεβαστοῦ . . . τῶι θεῶι τὴν καθήκουσαν τειμὴν καὶ χάριν ἔνειμεν ("Appendix 1: Inscriptions" §3.8, lines 36–39).

60. [θεᾷ Ἰουλίᾳ Σεβαστῇ] ("Appendix 1: Inscriptions" §3.6, line 1).

Fig. 3.8 Coin minted in Thessalonica during Augustus's reign (*RPC* 1:1563) hailing Livia as *theou Libia* | *With permission of wildwinds.com, ex CNG, 2021*

nately, no Thessalonian evidence provides a clue about what this munificence might have been. However, inscriptions across the Roman Empire testify to Livia's habit of bestowing such beneficence on cities. According to a decree engraved on bronze dated to Tiberius's reign (AD 14–37), the Roman Senate acknowledged and praised Livia for her philanthropy of birthing the reigning emperor Tiberius and for providing "many great benefits for people of every *ordo*" or social class.[61] Closer to Thessalonica, the Greek city of Thasos in the Roman province of Thrace, just north of Macedonia, honored Livia for an unknown beneficent act. An inscription dated between 19 and 12 BC notes that Thasos's citizen body acclaimed the empress as a *thean euergetin* or "benefactor goddess."[62] While there is no Thessalonian evidence linking divine honors for Livia to her beneficence, it is most probable that this was the case. This is especially true when we consider that the city hailed her as a goddess during her lifetime—an honor it withheld from the emperor who bestowed (or rather maintained its) "free" status and whose reign was the beginning of an age of Thessalonian peace and prosperity.

61. *multis magnisq(ue) erga cuiusq(ue) ordinis homines beneficis* (Alison E. Cooley, *The* Senatus Consultum de Cn. Pisone Patre: *Text, Translation, and Commentary* [Cambridge: Cambridge University Press, 2023] lines 116–17).

62. θεὰν εὐεργέτιν ("Appendix 1: Inscriptions" §3.9, line 7). For more on Livia's benefactions, see Anthony Barrett, *Livia: First Lady of Imperial Rome* (New Haven: Yale University Press, 2002), 186–214.

(*Theos*) *Claudius*

A marble statue probably attests that Thessalonica bestowed divine honors on the emperor Claudius during his lifetime, and one inscription acknowledges the deceased emperor's divine status in Rome. The statue in question was discovered in 1957 close to Augustus's image (see p. 122) (see figs. 3.1, no. 3; 9).[63] How close, however, is unclear, because its exact findspot, as well as that of the statue of Augustus, was unrecorded.[64] This detail notwithstanding, the image depicts a Julio-Claudian in the same posture as the statue of Augustus: naked from the waist up with a cloak wrapped around the statue's lower half, the excess of which is draped over the left arm. The image's right arm is missing, so it is unclear whether it was raised as the right arm of Augustus's statue is. However, the most crucial piece for identifying the image, the head, is missing. While we cannot be certain about the identification, it seems probable that the statue was of Claudius.[65] If this identification is correct, it attests to divine honors for him in Thessalonica while he was alive. The context for this grant, however, remains unknown. It was probably in keeping with the establishment of divine honors for Augustus in the city and thus to show gratitude for some benefaction that Claudius provided. This epigraph that refers to Claudius's divinization in Rome is from an inscription that we have already seen: the fragmentary marble block dating to Nero's reign that may refer to Augustus's divinization in the capital of the empire (see p. 123). This same epigraph, which was effaced after the Roman Senate damned Nero's memory, contains a reference to the disgraced emperor as the "son of the god Augustus Claudius."[66]

Nero

Thessalonica probably bestowed divine honors on one final Julio-Claudian while he was alive, the emperor Nero who reigned from AD 54 to 68. The evidence for this grant is another marble statue. This one, however, was found in a temple on the western side of the city, known as the Archaic Temple (fig. 3.1, no. 2; for

63. George Daux, "Chronique des fouilles et découvertes archéologiques en Grèce en 1957," *BCH* 82 (1958): 759; Despinis, Stefanidou-Tiveriou, and Voutyras, Κατάλογος, no. 245; Stefanidou-Tiveriou, "Art in the Roman Period," 570; Allamani-Souri, "Imperial Cult," 116.

64. Burnett, "Imperial Divine Honors," 580–82.

65. Stefanidou-Tiveriou, "Art in the Roman Period," 570, suggests that this statue once depicted Caligula, but after his ignominious death and Claudius's elevation to the imperial throne, the latter's head replaced the former's.

66. θεοῦ [Σ]εβα[στοῦ] [Κλα]υδίου υἱοῦ ("Appendix 1: Inscriptions" §3.7, lines 2–3).

Fig. 3.9 Statue thought to represent the emperor Claudius, AD 50, Thessaloniki, Archaeological Museum of Thessaloniki, Inv. No. MΘ 2467+2468 | *Photo by M. Skiadaresis; photographed with the permission of Archaeological Museum of Thessaloniki, Hellenic Ministry of Culture & Sports—Hellenic Organization of Cultural Resources Development*

more on this temple, see pp. 135–37). This image depicts a Julio-Claudian in the guise of a military general, which suggests that it is of an emperor or high-ranking Julio-Claudian family member. On balance, it is the former. Which emperor is difficult to answer, because the main source for identifying the statue, its head, is missing. One specialist on Thessalonian statuary, Theodosia Stefanidou-Tiveriou, has identified this image as Nero.[67] If she is correct, and given that the statue was found in a temple, it is probably cultic and associated with divine honors for that emperor. Like the contexts for Livia's and Claudius's Thessalonian divine honors, the circumstances surrounding the city's establishment of such honors for Nero remains uncertain but probably relates to some benefaction.

A Romanized Form of Greek Civic Imperial Divine Honors

One final note about imperial divine honors in Thessalonica relates to the use of *theos* in inscriptions and coins from the city. The fact that Thessalonica divinely honored Augustus, Livia, and probably Claudius and Nero during their lifetimes indicates that it followed the

67. Stefanidou-Tiveriou, "Art in the Roman Period," 570. Unfortunately, the Archaeological Museum of Thessaloniki and the Hellenic Ministry of Culture and Sports—Hellenic Organization of Cultural Resources Development could not allow me to include a picture of this statue, because it has not been officially published. However, the image is on display at the museum. Stefanidou-Tiveriou, "Art in the Roman Period," 570, notes that along with the statue probably of Claudius, archaeologists found part of a third marble image on the western side of Thessalonica, a right hand. She surmises that this hand belonged to a now-lost statue of Tiberius.

tradition of Greek civic imperial divine honors of bestowing such honors on living rulers. However, that the city established divine honors for the deceased *theos* Julius Caesar and, besides the case of Livia, that it waited until the deaths of Augustus and Claudius to hail them as *theoi* suggest that Thessalonica followed the Roman Senate's divinization of Julio-Claudians. This much is clear from the inscriptions related to Augustus. None of the epigraphs predating his death refer to him as *theos*. It is only after his death and official divinization in Rome that Thessalonian inscriptions acclaim him as a god. Therefore, when used of Julio-Claudians in Thessalonica, *theos* functioned as the Greek translation of *divus*. When we consider the Thessalonian sources for imperial divine honors, there is one probable explanation for this Roman influence. To date, the only known benefactors of these honors were Roman: the unknown Roman governor of Macedonia who underwrote the cost of building the temple of Caesar Augustus, and Avia Possila, a Thessalonian benefactress with Roman citizenship who paid for the construction of the temple of Augustus, Hercules, and the personification of Thessalonica.

Imperial Cultic Officials

Now that we know on whom Thessalonica bestowed imperial divine honors, the next issue we must address is who offered such honors on behalf of the city. The evidence for these Thessalonian cultic officials pales in comparison to what has survived from Philippi and, as we shall see, Corinth. Inscriptions from the city record only one type of imperial cultic official whose office was a combination of two Greek public ones, "the priest and president of games for the victorious general Caesar Augustus son of a god."[68] This office was created during Augustus's reign and continued into the second and third centuries AD, up to two hundred years after his death. Thessalonica's *dēmos* probably elected one aristocratic male to fill it each year. As *hiereus* or "priest," this individual oversaw imperial sacrifices and matters associated with them, especially at the temple of Caesar Augustus. As *agōnothetēs* or "president," this person administered and superintended these games in honor of Augustus (how often is unknown), which consisted of any one or combination of the following: athletics, music, poetry, and possibly even chariot-racing.[69] If need be, the *agōnothetēs* underwrote the cost of these contests

68. ἱερεὺς καὶ ἀγωνοθέτης Αὐτοκράτορος Καίσαρος Θεοῦ υἱοῦ Σεβαστοῦ ("Appendix 1: Inscriptions" §3.4, 10, 11, 12); *IG* 10.2.1.132. The original editor of "Appendix 1: Inscriptions" §3.7 restored [ἐπὶ ἱερέως καὶ ἀγωνοθέτου Αὐτοκράτορος Καίσαρος θεοῦ υἱ]οῦ θεοῦ [Σ]εβα[στοῦ] in the inscription but the latest edition of the epigraph, *IG* 10.2.1s.131, rejects this restoration.

69. The duties of an ἀγωνοθέτης were to oversee the administration and operation of the games. In the process, this person superintended any monies earmarked for the games; regis-

from his own coffers.[70] To date, the priest and *agōnothetēs* of Caesar Augustus is the most attested public priestly office in Thessalonian sources, and events in the life of Thessalonica were dated during the tenure of the aristocratic men who filled this post. Thus, this priesthood must have been one of the most coveted public offices in the city.[71]

From Thessalonian inscriptions, we know the names or partial names of three men who held this office. The earliest known *hiereus kai agōnothetēs* of the imperial games was not from the Thessalonian aristocracy but of Thracian royalty.[72] His name is Gaius Julius Rhoemetalces, also known as Rhoemetalces II, who reigned as king of Thrace, a region northeast of Thessalonica that consisted of parts of modern-day Greece, Bulgaria, and Turkey, from AD 19 to 36.[73] Rhoemetalces's family received its Roman citizenship from Augustus, and the king owed his kingdom to Tiberius, who had placed him on the throne.[74] In return, the monarch showed his appreciation to Tiberius for this benefaction by refusing to side with some Thracians who revolted against Rome, backing the city of seven hills rather than his own countrymen.[75] The evidence for Rhoemetalces's service as *hiereus kai agōnothetēs* of the imperial games in Thessalonica is a fragmentary early first-century AD inscription that was engraved on a marble plaque that appears to be an official dedication, possibly of a building, by the gymnasium's *neoi* and the Thessalonian *boulē* to an individual who made a large bequest to the city.[76] This

---

tration of participants; judgment of the games; awarding prizes to victors; adjudication of any related disputes; and proper execution of any divine honors associated with the games. For Greek ἀγῶνες, see A. H. M. Jones, *The Greek City from Alexander to Justinian* (Oxford: Clarendon, 1940), 227–35.

70. Emil Reisch, "*Agonothetes*," PW 1:870–77.

71. "Appendix 1: Inscriptions" §3.4, 10, 11, 12; *IG* 10.2.1.132. In Calindoia, events in the life of the city were dated by the tenure of priests of "Zeus, Roma, and the victorious general Caesar Augustus son of a god" (ἐπὶ ἱερέως Διὸς καὶ Ῥώμης καὶ Αὐτοκράτορος Καίσαρος θεοῦ υἱοῦ Σεβαστοῦ). See Sebastian Prignitz, "Ein Augustuspriester des Jahres 27 v. Chr.," *ZPE* 178 (2011): 210–14.

72. The Thracians are the same tribal group who harassed the Thasians who originally settled Krenides in 360 BC. In response, the latter appealed to Philip II, Alexander the Great's father, for help. After ridding the Thracian problem in Krenides, Philip refused to leave and founded the community as the Greek city of Philippi. For more information, see pp. 65–66.

73. "Appendix 1: Inscriptions" §3.10.

74. Tiberius exiled Rhoemetalces's father, Rhescuporis, for killing Rhoemetalces's uncle and Rhescuporis's brother, Cotys, the king of Thrace (Tacitus, *Annals* 2.67).

75. Tacitus, *Annals* 4.47.

76. The end of the epigraph contains the names of the politarchs, the gymnasiarch, the ephebarch, and the city treasurer of that year as well as an architect and treasurer of the gymnasium's νέοι.

epigraph predates Rhoemetalces's kingship in AD 19, because its calls him a *dynastos* or "prince," not a *basileus* or "king."[77] Consequently, when he served in this public Thessalonian office remains unknown, but it was before he ascended to the Thracian throne. Finally, it is probable that Rhoemetalces's tenure as *hiereus kai agōnothetēs* of the imperial games was honorary, because the inscription notes that during his time in office, a Greek, probably from Thessalonica, who did not possess Roman citizenship, served as *antagōnothetēs* or "vice president of the games," Heliodorus son of Heliodorus.

The second known *hiereus kai agōnothetēs* of the imperial games is mentioned in a fragmentary inscription on a marble plaque that was found among the ruins of a Byzantine church and that dates to the end of the first century BC. In this epigraph, Thessalonica (*hē polis*) and a group of Roman bankers, moneylenders, traders, and commercial farmers who had lived in Thessalonica, known in Latin as *negotiatores*, honored a local benefactor.[78] The inscription is dated to the year when a certain Gaius Julius, whose last name or *cognomen* is unknown, served in the office in question. It is clear this individual is a Roman citizen who received his citizenship from Julius Caesar or Augustus, for their names are Gaius Julius Caesar and, after 27 BC, Gaius Julius victorious general Caesar Augustus, respectively. It is possible that this Gaius Julius is Gaius Julius Rhoemetalces, the king of Thrace, just discussed.[79] However, because Julius Caesar and Augustus bestowed Roman citizenship on many Greeks, the first and middle names or the Latin *praenomen* and *nomen*, Gaius Julius, were common. In fact, they appear thirty-one times in Thessalonian inscriptions, in almost 2 percent of epigraphs from the city, and refer to at least twenty-eight different men bearing that name.[80] Now all these men were not alive at the same time, but the high number of male Thessalonians who bore the name Gaius Julius should give us pause before one identifies the Gaius Julius, whose last name or *cognomen* is lost, as Gaius Julius Rhoemetalces.

---

77. Louis Robert, "Les inscriptions de Thessalonique," *RevPhil* 48 (1974): 212–15. The only known coin series that Rhoemetalces minted calls him "King Rhoemetalces" (βασιλέως Ῥοιμητάλκου [*RPC* 1.1721]). A Roman citizen of Philippi set up a monument to Rhoemetalces during Tiberius's reign (AD 19–37), calling the former "King Gaius Julius Rhoemetalces" (*C(aio)* · *Iulio* · *Roeme[talci] regi*) (*CIPh* 2.1.3 [= Pilhofer 2.199, lines 1–2]).

78. "Appendix 1: Inscriptions" §3.11.

79. As argued by Hendrix, "Thessalonicans Honor Romans," 119–23, 366–85.

80. *IG* 10.2.1.32, 67, 68, 127, 129, 136, 195, 196, 204, 206, 226, 241, 243, 245, 251, 259, 290, 473, 534, 538, 621, 661, 883, 1033, 1036, 1086, 1368, 1406. Hendrix, "Thessalonicans Honor Romans," 377–79, uses these same data to argue for the probability that the Gaius Julius in "Appendix 1: Inscriptions" §3.11 is Gaius Julius Rhoemetalces.

The final known Thessalonian who served in this public office is found in an honorary inscription engraved on a marble statue base found in Thessalonica's

agora (fig. 3.1, no. 4) that once held the image of a civic benefactor. The epigraph dates between 27 BC and AD 14 and testifies that *hē polis* and the Roman *negotiatores* honored a munificent aristocrat during the time when a certain Nicolaus son of Demetrius known also as Clitomachus served as *hiereus kai agōnothetēs* of the imperial games.[81] Unfortunately, we cannot cull much more information about Nicolaus from this inscription other than, unlike the former two priests and presidents but like the only known *antagōnothetēs*, he was not a Roman citizen.

Imperial Cultic Officials as Benefactors

Besides overseeing and offering imperial sacrifices, the *hiereis kai agōnothetes* of the imperial games probably used their wealth to defray the costs of the games, which Thessalonica would have hosted on a regular schedule. Exactly when, however, is unknown. It may have been every year, which seems to be the case in Calindoia (see pp. 137–38), or every two or four years.[82] The point is that the person serving as *hiereus kai agōnothetēs* of the imperial games would have had regular opportunities to provide benefits connected to these contests for his community. In addition to the games, these public officials probably

Fig. 3.10 Cuirassed statue, possibly of Octavian Augustus, late 1st century BC, Thessaloniki, Archaeological Museum of Thessaloniki, Inv. No. MΘ 2663 | *Photo by O. Kourakis; photographed with the permission of Archaeological Museum of Thessaloniki, Hellenic Ministry of Culture & Sports—Hellenic Organization of Cultural Resources Development*

made significant munificent acts to the city, although to date, no evidence attests to them. However, imperial priests in other Macedonian Greek cities provided

---

81. "Appendix 1: Inscriptions" §3.12.

82. For a discussion of the time frame for Greek imperial games, see Simon R. F. Price, *Rituals and Power: The Roman Imperial Cult in Asia Minor* (Cambridge: Cambridge University Press, 1984), 104–5.

benefactions for their communities. The city of Calindoia (see p. 125) had an imperial priesthood resembling the one in Thessalonica, "the priesthood of Zeus, Roma, and Augustus son of a god."[83] According to a first-century AD inscription that the city engraved on a marble stele and set up, Calindoia honored one of these priests, Apollonius, for his munificence, which consisted of a long list of beneficent acts. Apollonius personally paid for monthly sacrifices that the city made to Zeus and Augustus. He offered "expensive honors to the gods" and paid for "sumptuous feasting and entertainment for the citizens" of Calindoia.[84] Apollonius underwrote the cost of a civic festival for Zeus, Augustus, and the other benefactors that included a *pompē* like the one in Gythium that opened this book and "expensive contests for Zeus and Caesar Augustus."[85] Apollonius even paid for the creation and erection of "a statue of Caesar [Augustus]" (*Kaisaros agalma*) that archaeologists may have found (see fig. 3.10).[86]

The inscription goes on to note that "whatever [the tribes of Calindoia] wished to take delight in, they were entertained by his benefaction."[87] Similarly, another priest of Zeus, Roma, and Augustus from Calindoia, along with two other Greeks, paid for the renovation of a building in Calindoia that included the place where the city's *boulē* met, the *bouleutērion*, an exedra or recess in a wall that is semicircular, and a stoa.[88] Consequently, it is probable that the *hiereis kai agōnothetes* of the imperial games in Thessalonica provided similar benefactions for their city.

In addition to the munificence of imperial cultic officials, some wealthy individ-

---

83. ἱερατήαν [*sic*] Διὸς καὶ Ῥώμης καὶ Καίσαρος θεοῦ υἱοῦ Σεβαστοῦ ("Appendix 1: Inscriptions" §3.8, lines 10–11).

84. τοῖς θεοῖς τὰς τειμὰς πολυτελεῖς προσηνέγκατο καὶ τοῖς πολείταις τὴν ἑστίασιν καὶ εὐωχίαν μεγαλομερῆ παρέσχετο ("Appendix 1: Inscriptions" §3.8, lines 17–19).

85. τοὺς ἀγῶνας Διὶ καὶ Καίσαρ[ι τῶ]ι Σεβ[αστῶι] πολυτελεῖς θέμενος ("Appendix 1: Inscriptions" §3.8, line 22).

86. ("Appendix 1: Inscriptions" §3.8, lines 34–35); Polyxeni Adam-Veleni, "Institutions . . . Inscribed on Marble," in *Kalindoia: An Ancient City in Macedonia*, ed. Polyxeni Adam-Veleni (Thessaloniki: Archaeological Museum of Thessaloniki, 2008), 109–10; Allamani-Souri, "Imperial Cult," 116.

87. ὅποι ποτ' ἂν ἥδεσθαι βούλωνται, τὴν αὐτοῦ χάριν ἑστιῶνται ("Appendix 1: Inscriptions" §3.8, lines 33–34).

88. Prignitz, "Augustuspriester," 210–14. During the reign of the emperor Nerva (AD 96–98), the *archiereis kai agōnothetes* of the Macedonian provincial imperial divine honors in Berea (in which Thessalonica did not participate in the first century AD), Quintus Popillius Python, provided a number of benefactions for Berea and Macedonia. He went on a successful embassy to the "god Nerva" (θεὸν Νέρουαν) to ask that Berea be granted a certain civic status in the Roman Empire. He contributed to the province's poll tax, repaired Macedonian roads with his own funds, held games and paid for the prizes with his own money, staged wild-beast hunts and gladiatorial combats, and subsidized the cost of grain when food prices rose (*IBeroia* 117 = *SEG* 17.315 = PH149594).

uals living in Thessalonica patronized imperial divine honors. As we have seen, an unknown provincial governor of Macedonia paid for the building material of the temple of Caesar Augustus in the city, and a Thessalonian woman with Roman citizenship, Avia Posilla, had a temple complex consisting of a temple, a bath, a pool, and a portico surrounding the latter, built and dedicated to Augustus, Hercules, and the divine personification of Thessalonica.[89] It is clear from her name that Avia Posilla's family had influence in Thessalonica, for one of her male family members became a politarch, the highest and most prestigious public office in the city.[90] While no evidence exists, it is likely and even probable that other rich Thessalonians provided similar munificence associated with imperial divine honors for their city.

Location of Imperial Divine Honors

Up to this point, we have reconstructed which Julio-Claudians received divine honors in Thessalonica and who oversaw and administered them. The question remains, Where did the city's *hiereis kai agōnothetes* of the imperial games make offerings connected to these divine honors? Thessalonian sources, two inscriptions and one archaeological site, attest to two, perhaps three, imperial temples at which such honors were housed.[91] The first inscription is one we have already seen, the epigraph attesting to the temple of Caesar Augustus (see fig. 3.5). To date, scholars disagree on where this temple was located in ancient Thessalonica. Because the inscription attesting to it was found on the eastern side of the city in the rubble of the Cassander Gate (see fig. 3.1, no. 6), some historians propose that it was located there.[92] This proposal presumes that the epigraph in question is a

---

89. "Appendix 1: Inscriptions" §3.5. This temple was not the only site at which she demonstrated her wealth and generosity to her city. *IG* 10.2.1s.1052, another Greek and Latin inscription, evinces that Avia Posilla also restored Thessalonica's temple of Isis and built its front porch.

90. *IG* 10.2.1.126.

91. Contra N. T. Wright, *Paul and the Faithfulness of God*, 2 vols. (Minneapolis: Fortress, 2013), 1:329, who concludes that excavations in Thessalonica "have not been sufficiently extensive to establish whether there was an imperial temple there." Contra Green, *Letters to the Thessalonians*, 40, who takes a reference to "Caesar's altar" (Καίσαρος ἐκ βωμοῦ) from the first-century AD poet Philippus of Thessalonica, *Greek Anthology* 9.307, as evidence for an imperial altar in Thessalonica: "The altar in Thessalonica was one of the many dedicated to the imperial cult throughout the eastern empire." Nowhere in Philippus's text does he state where the altar in question is located, and some historians conclude that he is referring to an altar of Augustus in Tarraco, a Roman city in Spain. See Duncan Fishwick, *The Imperial Cult in the Latin West: Studies on the Ruler Cult of the Western Provinces of the Roman Empire* (Leiden: Brill, 1987–2002), 1:1.171.

92. As I noted above, almost all historians incorrectly identify this temple as belonging to Julius Caesar.

dedication associated with the temple and in some way attached to or connected with it. This is unclear, because the inscription's beginning is lost. Thus, the type of epigraph in question is unknown, which means that its findspot may have no bearing on the temple's location.

It seems probable that the temple of Caesar Augustus was located on Thessalonica's western side, because almost all archaeological evidence associated with imperial divine honors in the city—the statues of Augustus and probably Claudius and Nero (see figs. 3.1, no. 3; 6; 9)—has been discovered there.[93] These large marble images are probably cultic and may be connected to a temple, as the statue identified as Nero certainly was. The images of Augustus and probably of Claudius are very heavy, and thus it is likely that they were found near the place in which they were originally housed, probably in a temple. The temple in which the image identified as Nero was found was first discovered in 1936 on Thessalonica's western side (see fig. 3.1, no. 2). Archaeologists dubbed it the Archaic Temple because it had been constructed with repurposed building material known as *spolia* in Latin (*spolium* in the singular). At this time, excavators discovered among the temple's ruins a marble statue of the emperor Hadrian and another of the goddess Roma, suggesting that divine honors for these two occurred there.[94] The temple was recovered, and its location was lost! In 2000, the Archaic Temple was rediscovered, and excavations resumed. It was at this time that the marble statue identified as Nero was found. Moreover, through further study of the temple, archaeologists discovered that while it had been made of older building material, some construction occurred on it during the Julio-Claudian period. For this reason, it is possible that the Archaic Temple is the temple of Caesar Augustus and that the statues of Augustus and probably Claudius were set up there alongside the image that may be of Nero.[95] I must stress, however, that this proposal is tentative until further, more conclusive evidence is found.[96]

The second epigraph that mentions an imperial temple was in the temple complex—the temple, pool, bath, and portico—that the Thessalonian benefactress Avia Posilla dedicated to Augustus, Hercules, and to the divine personification of the city between 12 BC and AD 14. Given that this inscription is a dedication (hence Augus-

---

93. The triumphant arch that was erected after either the battle of Philippi (42 BC) or the battle of Actium (31 BC) was also on the western side of the city. See fig. 3.1, no. 1; pp. 113–15.

94. For the statue, see Despinis, Stefanidou-Tiveriou, and Voutyras, Κατάλογος, nos. 212, 261; Stefanidou-Tiveriou, "Art in the Roman World," 571.

95. However, most historians would identify this temple as belonging to Julius Caesar and possibly Augustus. See Burnett, "Imperial Divine Honors," 575–79.

96. Stefanidou-Tiveriou, "Art in the Roman World," 570, notes of the statues of Augustus and Claudius as well as a third image that may have depicted Tiberius, "we know almost nothing of the location where they were set up in the western sector of the city."

tus's, Hercules's, and Thessalonica's names are in the dative case),[97] it was almost certainly attached to the temple itself, which was located near the inscription's find-spot, in the environs of Thessalonica. We know next to nothing about this temple, because archaeologists have yet to locate and excavate it. Presumably, the temple was fully functional. Thus, cultic images of Augustus, Hercules, and Thessalonica were standing in its cella, and an altar or altars were set up in front of the temple, at which cultic officials, whose identity remains unknown, offered sacrifices.

Therefore, Thessalonica had only two imperial temples, if the temple of Caesar Augustus is identified with the Archaic Temple, but three if it is not: (1) the temple of Caesar Augustus, (2) the Archaic Temple, and (3) the temple of Augustus, Hercules, and Thessalonica. The discovery of the above statues near the Archaic Temple and the two inscriptions attesting to imperial temples dedicated to Augustus evinces that divine honors occurred at these temples for Augustus and probably for Claudius and Nero, too. This means that we do not know where divine honors for Julius Caesar and Livia were located. Given the cost of building and maintaining a temple, it was commonplace for Greco-Roman communities to have a single imperial temple in which multiple Julio-Claudians were divinely honored, as was the case at Philippi and, as we shall see, at Corinth, although this latter city had two other Julio-Claudian-era imperial shrines, too.[98] For this reason, it is probable that divine honors for Julius Caesar and Livia occurred at the temple of Caesar Augustus, the Archaic Temple, and possibly even the temple of Augustus, Hercules, and Thessalonica. However, this does not mean that divine honors for Julius Caesar and Livia, as well as for Augustus and probably for Claudius and Nero, occurred only at imperial temples. As we have seen and I shall discuss below, the Thessalonians wedded imperial divine honors to their traditional divine honors. This means that the former could have been celebrated at any temple of any deity or on any altar, including domestic hearths of Thessalonians. Unfortunately, no evidence survives for such private imperial divine honors in the city.

Moreover, the games dedicated to Augustus had an imperial cultic element to them, and they were celebrated somewhere in the city; exactly where is unclear. In the second century AD, when Thessalonica participated in the provincial imperial divine honors of Macedonia, imperial games were conducted in the city's theater/stadium, which was built in the late first century AD and modified to house Roman gladiatorial combats and wild-beast fights.[99] Several second-century AD

97. Αὐτοκράτορι Καίσαρι θεοῦ υἱῶι Σεβαστῶι καὶ Ἡρακλεῖ καὶ τῆι πόλει ("Appendix 1: Inscriptions" §3.5, lines 1–2).

98. vom Brocke, *Thessaloniki*, 59, makes a similar conclusion, although he contends that the temple of Caesar Augustus belonged to "*Divus*" Julius. See also vom Brocke, *Thessaloniki*, 139.

99. For a description of provincial imperial divine honors, see pp. 45–49. For Thessalonica's theater/stadium, see Adam-Veleni, "Thessaloniki," 157–59. For a discussion of gladiatorial

gravestones of gladiators from Thessalonica with inscriptions and reliefs carved on them attest to the popularity of such spectacles in the city.[100] The problem is that this evidence postdates the Julio-Claudian period. Most probably, there was a Hellenistic-era theater in Thessalonica, which has yet to be discovered and excavated.[101] If this is the case, then it may have been the site of gladiatorial combats, wild-beast fights, and imperial divine honors associated with the Julio-Claudian contests that the *hiereus kai agōnothetēs* of imperial games oversaw. However, no hard evidence supports this claim. Thus, where these imperial games were conducted during the mid-first century AD currently remains a mystery.

Aspects of Imperial Divine Honors

Now that we know the most probable locations of divine honors for Julius Caesar, Augustus, Livia, and probably Claudius and Nero, we must explore aspects of these honors, mainly, of what they consisted and when and how the *hiereis kai agōnothetes* of the imperial games celebrated them. Unfortunately, we cannot reconstruct these aspects of imperial divine honors from Thessalonian evidence alone, but we must draw on comparative material from other Macedonian Greek cities and Calindoia in particular, where there was an imperial priesthood resembling the one in Thessalonica. Even with this information, we cannot arrive at a full picture of what we desire to know about Thessalonian imperial divine honors. Therefore, we are forced to look further afield, outside Macedonia. When such comparative material is used, I will highlight it, because it is always possible that these sources are inapplicable to Thessalonica.

We can arrive at a portrait of the specifics of imperial sacrifices in Thessalonica, and when they were offered, from the inscription from Calindoia that we have already seen, the decree honoring Apollonius, one of that city's priests of Zeus, Roma, and Augustus. As noted above, this epigraph records that one of the benefactions that Apollonius provided was paying for the monthly "public sacrifices" (*dēmoteleis thysias*) that Calindoia offered to Zeus and Augustus. The Greek term *thysia* often refers to animal sacrifices to the traditional gods that were burned on their altars that participants in the ritual then consumed.[102] In

---

combats and wild-beast fights that occurred in second- and third-century AD Thessalonica and Macedonia, see Allamani-Souri, "Imperial Cult," 100–103.

100. Allamani-Souri, "Imperial Cult," 102.

101. Polyxeni Adam-Veleni, "Entertainment and Arts in Thessaloniki," in *Roman Thessaloniki*, ed. D. V. Grammenos, trans. David Hardy, Thessaloniki Archaeological Museum Publication 1 (Thessaloniki: Thessaloniki Archaeological Museum, 2003), 263–64.

102. LSJ 812; BDAG 462–63; Johannes Behm, "θύω, θυσία, θυσιαστήριον," *TDNT* 3:180–90. In his attempt to convince the Corinthians not to partake of pagan sacrificial meat and the Lord's

addition to monthly sacrifices, Apollonius underwrote the cost of Calindoia's "festival" (*panēgyris*) dedicated to Zeus and Augustus, which seems to have occurred every year, but Apollonius probably covered the cost for only one year. At this cultic celebration, there was a "procession" (*pompē*), "games" (*agōnes*) dedicated to Zeus and Augustus, and *dēmoteleis thysias* offered to Zeus, Augustus, and to the rest of the city's benefactors. On top of the *panēgyris*, Apollonius paid for the erection of a "cultic statue" (*agalma*) of Augustus, the purpose of which was to be a permanent memorial of the emperor's munificence (see fig. 3.10).[103]

Calindoia's connection of the cultic terms *panēgyris, pompē, agōn, thysia,* and *agalma* with divine honors for Augustus without any nuance or qualifier means that we can assume that they resembled those that the city provided for its gods, especially for Zeus.[104] If this is correct, we can reconstruct the *panēgyris, pompē, agōnes, thysiai,* and *agalma,* because they are general terms associated with traditional divine honors and because, as one specialist in Greek religion, Walter Burkert, notes, rituals associated with sacrifices to the gods, while varying according to local customs, shared the same "fundamental structure."[105] The *panēgyris* would have been a time when the citizens of Calindoia ceased from their labors and gathered as a group to celebrate the munificence of Zeus, Augustus, and other benefactors of the city. During this *panēgyris* and in preparation of the *agōnes,* there would have been a *pompē,* like the one from Gythium that opened this book, with participants, including musicians, dressed in white clothes, winding its way through Calindoia and escorting sacrificial victims to the altar of Zeus, Roma, and Augustus. From the inscription praising Apollonius, we know that these victims were oxen, but they need not have been oxen all the time.[106] The altar in question was probably located in the city's *agora* near what in the mid-first century AD was a five-room building containing shrines to Zeus, Roma, and Augustus, in which their "cultic statues" (*agalmata*) were set up.[107]

Banquet, Paul asks, "are not those who eat of τὰς θυσίας partners of the altar [θυσιαστήριον]?" (1 Cor 10:18)

103. "Appendix 1: Inscriptions" §3.8, lines 34–35.

104. It is unfortunate that, as Price, *Rituals and Power*, 208, notes, we do not possess "the full details of the slaughtering of the animal and the division of the parts between emperor, priests and others."

105. Walter Burkert, *Greek Religion,* trans. John Raffan (Cambridge: Harvard University Press, 1985), 57, concludes, "The ritual of animal sacrifice varies in detail according to the local ancestral custom, but the fundamental structure is identical and clear: animal sacrifice is ritualized slaughter followed by a meat meal."

106. "Appendix 1: Inscriptions" §3.8.

107. Three of these rooms date to the late first century BC and two to the mid-first century AD. See Kostas Sismanides, "The Sevasteion Building Complex (Rooms A–E)," in *Kalindoia: An Ancient City in Macedonia,* ed. Polyxeni Adam-Veleni (Thessaloniki: Archaeological Museum of Thessaloniki, 2008), 124–31.

Some of the *pompē*'s participants would have carried various objects needed for the oxen's slaughter: a knife, barley grains, and a jug of water. Once they had reached the altar, someone would have poured water on the hands of those involved in the sacrifice and sprinkled some on the heads of the oxen. The participants would have grabbed handfuls of barley, recited a prayer, and tossed the barley grains on the fire of the altar as well as on the oxen about to be sacrificed. The person offering the sacrifice or the sacrificer would have taken the knife, cut some of the hair on the animals' foreheads, and cast it on the fire. One of the participants would have stunned the animals by striking them on the head with the blunt end of an axe, after which he would have cut their throats. Then the sacrificer would have taken some blood from the oxen and sprinkled it on the lit altar. A slave or group of slaves would have butchered the animals, removed their skin, and gathered the internal organs (*splanchna* in Greek) of the beasts. These vitals, along with bones, would have been roasted on the altar's fire, and wine would have been poured over them as a libation to Zeus, Roma, and Augustus. Once these had received their portion, the edible parts of the oxen would have been either roasted or boiled for the participants to consume.[108]

Given the similarity between the public office of *hiereus kai agōnothetēs* of the games for Augustus in Calindoia and Thessalonica and the proximity of the cities—they were twenty-five miles apart—we may presume that a similar imperial *panēgyris* with a *pompē* in preparation for the *agōnes* occurred in Thessalonica. When and how often this occurred remains unknown. It seems that the imperial festival in Calindoia occurred every year, which lends credence to the notion that the same occurred in Thessalonica. Exactly how long these possible annual imperial celebrations occurred is unclear. In AD 252, when Thessalonica was part of provincial imperial divine honors for Macedonia, the *agōnes* that the Macedonian *koinon* celebrated in the city lasted three days.[109] However, it is possible that these yearly festivals in Thessalonica during the Julio-Claudian period lasted longer. As we have seen, the imperial festival in Gythium lasted six days, with two more days being added for two of the city's local benefactors. Consequently, any of these options for the length of imperial celebrations in mid-first-century AD Thessalonica is possible, and it is likely that the number of days was not the same from year to year, with different *hiereis kai agōnothetes* vying to outdo each other in the scale of their beneficence for their fellow pagan Thessalonians.[110]

---

108. For the best descriptions of Greek sacrifice, see Homer, *Odyssey* 3.447–463; *Iliad* 1.457–468; Burkert, *Greek Religion*, 55–57.

109. *SEG* 49.815; Allamani-Souri, "Imperial Cult," 102.

110. It is also possible that the games lasted for different periods of time based on the benefactions and how much money the ἱερεὺς καὶ ἀγωνοθέτης of the imperial games wished to spend.

Imperial sacrifices need not have occurred during imperial festivals, however. The inscription from Calindoia attesting to Apollonius's benefactions records that that city offered monthly sacrifices to Zeus and Augustus. Thus, Thessalonica may have done the same and offered monthly sacrifices to the Julio-Claudians whom it granted divine honors. In addition to regular sacrifices, Thessalonica probably put on spontaneous festivals or offered spontaneous sacrifices to celebrate major events in the lives of the Julio-Claudians. For example, when Gaius Caesar, Augustus's eldest adopted son, reached manhood, the Greek city of Sardis in modern-day Turkey placed a statue of the young man in Augustus's temple in that city. It celebrated the event with the city's citizens dressing in white and the magistrates sacrificing to the gods; Sardis consecrated the day on which the city received the "good news" (*euangelisthē polis*) as holy, and it decreed to celebrate its anniversary every year.[111] I am not suggesting that Thessalonica did the same when it heard of Gaius Caesar's transition into manhood. However, that the city kept up with affairs in Rome, to the point that it most often waited until the Roman Senate divinized a Julio-Claudian before Thessalonica hailed him or her as a *theos/thea* (the commonest Greek translations of the Latin concept of *divus/diva*), supports the notion that it probably held impromptu festivals and offered spontaneous sacrifices celebrating milestones in the lives of Julio-Claudians.

The aforementioned public animal sacrifices were not the only imperial sacrifices that probably occurred in Thessalonica. Some offerings would have been much simpler and consisted of incense or a libation before images of Julio-Claudians either publicly in locations around the city, such as the theater (provided that one existed in the mid-first century AD), or privately in the domestic hearths of pagan Thessalonians.[112] According to Gythium's sacred law, all the magistrates of that city offered incense and wine to the gods before the painted images of Augustus, Livia, and Tiberius that had been set up on tables in the city's theater.[113] The famous letter referencing Christians that the Roman governor of the province of Bithynia in modern-day Turkey, Pliny, wrote to the emperor Trajan (who reigned AD 98–117) indicates that Pliny had those suspected of being Christians take a certain oath and "supplicate with incense and wine" Trajan's image as well as "the images of the gods."[114] As I noted in chapter 1, archaeologists working in Ephesus have found a domestic imperial shrine in an elite apartment (*insula*)

---

111. "Appendix 1: Inscriptions" §3.13, line 14.

112. Libations (σπονδαί) were primarily of wine poured from a container that had a handle or a bowl called a phial so that the pourer could control the amount. Burkert, *Greek Religion*, 70–73.

113. "Appendix 1: Inscriptions" §I.1, lines 1–7.

114. *imagini tuae, quam propter hoc iusseram cum simulacris numinum adferri, ture ac vino supplicarent* (Pliny, *Letters* 10.96).

in Ephesus known as Unit 7 in a block of such apartments (*insulae*) known as Terrace House 2. The shrine dates between AD 14 and 37 and consists of an altar and a table in front of busts of Tiberius and Livia and a statuette of Athena in a niche in the wall (see pp. 51–53).

The object of these sacrifices associated with Julio-Claudians in Thessalonica is unclear from evidence from the city. As I noted in chapter 1, there was diversity in the object of sacrifices in Greek civic imperial divine honors. Some Greeks and cities sacrificed to Julio-Claudians directly, others sacrificed to the gods on behalf of the Julio-Claudians like the citizens of Gythium, and still others sacrificed to both.[115] The comparative evidence from Calindoia suggests that the public sacrifices in Thessalonica were directed to, not on behalf of, the Julio-Claudians whom the city divinely honored. The inscription from Calindoia cataloguing Apollonius's benefactions notes that the monthly *thysiai* were offered "to Zeus and Caesar Augustus," that the *agōnes* that the city conducted were dedicated "to Zeus and Caesar Augustus," and that public sacrifices were offered "to Zeus and Caesar Augustus" at the *panēgyris*.[116] In all three cases, Zeus's and Caesar Augustus's names are in the same dative case, thereby indicating that both were objects of the same sacrifices and set of civic contests. There is one piece of evidence for imperial divine honors in Thessalonica that suggests that sacrifices were made to, not on behalf of, them, the temple of Augustus that Avia Posilla dedicated. According to the inscription, this temple belonged to Augustus, Hercules, and the divine personification of Thessalonica.[117] There is no evidence from the epigraph's Greek or Latin text that Augustus is somehow distinct from Hercules or the personification of the city: all three objects of dedication are in the same dative case. Consequently, it is probable that the sacrifices that Thessalonian *hiereis kai agōnothetes* of the imperial games offered were directed to the Julio-Claudians.

This reference to the temple of Augustus, Hercules, and Thessalonica brings us to the final aspect of imperial divine honors in the city that we must address, their incorporation into the city's traditional divine honors. As noted above, Thessalonica had a history of wedding divine honors for humans with those of their gods, the earliest evidence for which is the cultic honors given to the Roman benefactors

---

115. Price, *Rituals and Power*, 207–33, considered sacrifices "on behalf of" emperors as normative for imperial divine honors. Steven J. Friesen, *Twice Neokoros: Ephesus, Asia and the Cult of the Flavian Imperial Family*, RGRW 116 (Leiden: Brill, 1993), 146–52, rightly critiques Price's conclusion, highlighting the diversity of objects of imperial divine honors.

116. Διὶ καὶ Καίσαρι τῶι Σεβαστῶι ("Appendix 1: Inscriptions" §3.8, lines 16–17, 22, 27–28).

117. Αὐτοκράτορι Καίσαρι θεοῦ υἱῶι Σεβαστῶι καὶ Ἡρακλεῖ καὶ τῆι πόλει . . . *Imp(eratori) · Caesari · divi · f(ilio) · Aug(usto) · pontif(ici) · max(imo) et · Herculi et civitati Thessalonicensium* ("Appendix 1: Inscriptions" §3.5, lines 1–2, 6–7).

and the gods of the gymnasium, Hermes and Hercules. This association of gods and beneficent human rulers continued with the Julio-Claudians, as is clearest from the temple complex that Avia Posilla had constructed. Provided that the statue from the Archaic Temple depicts Nero, divine honors for him were assimilated with Roma, whose statue was also found in the temple. The evidence from Calindoia corroborates that Macedonian Greek cities often combined imperial with traditional divine honors. One of the, if not the, most important priesthoods in Calindoia was the *hiereus kai agōnothetēs* of the games for Zeus, Roma, and Augustus. The city offered monthly sacrifices to Zeus and Augustus, there were games in honor of Zeus and Augustus, there was a festival at which Calindoia made offerings to Zeus, Augustus, and civic benefactors, and archaeologists have uncovered shrines dedicated to Zeus, Augustus, and Roma.[118] What this means for imperial divine honors in Thessalonica is that it is virtually impossible to separate them from traditional divine honors and thus to isolate the former as the main competitor against early Christianity in the city, as some New Testament scholars do. Instead of competing with the traditional gods, the combination of traditional and imperial divine honors articulates that a cooperative relationship exists between the gods and the Julio-Claudians. The former had chosen the latter to rule Thessalonica by welcoming them into their midst, which they demonstrated by blessing the reign of the Julio-Claudians and Thessalonica in particular with a healthy local economy, peace, and prosperity.

Synthesis and Conclusion

To conclude our discussion of imperial divine honors in Thessalonica, I will synthesize and summarize our findings. Thessalonica established divine honors for Julius Caesar, Augustus, Livia, and probably Claudius and Nero. All these grants, except for Julius Caesar's, were made while the Julio-Claudians in question were alive. When there is evidence, it is clear that the establishment of these divine honors was for the purpose of showing appreciation for imperial benefaction, such as the acknowledgment of Thessalonica's status as a "free city" in the empire and the economic prosperity that began with Augustus's reign and continued through that of the Julio-Claudian dynasty. Other Julio-Claudians, especially Livia, probably provided similar munificence to the city, but there is no concrete Thessalonian evidence for it. In granting such honors for this purpose, the city followed the practice of Greek civic imperial divine honors. However, because of

118. Sismanides, "Sevasteion Building Complex," 124–31. For the inscription, see "Appendix 1: Inscriptions" §3.14.

the influence of Roman patrons of imperial divine honors in the city, Thessalonica established said honors for the deceased Julius Caesar and, except in the case of Livia, waited until the deaths of Augustus and Claudius before hailing them as gods. To this end, in the city *theos* functioned as a translation of *divus*.

Evidence from Thessalonica attests to one imperial cultic office, that of *hiereus kai agōnothetēs* of the games for the victorious general Caesar Augustus, son of a god. This individual was always an aristocratic Thessalonian man or other notable elite, such as the prince of Thrace who became King Rhoemetalces II, whom the city's *dēmos* elected possibly every year. His main task was to oversee imperial offerings and all the aspects of the games for Augustus, which were held at regular intervals in the city. Much about these games remains unknown. We do not know how often Thessalonica put them on, but it seems likely that these games occurred every year. We are unsure about how long they lasted, whether just one day or more, or, as seems probable, the length of time fluctuated each year. There is uncertainty about where these games were housed, but they may have occurred in Thessalonica's Hellenistic-era theater, provided that such a structure existed. Moreover, we do not know whether the *hiereus kai agōnothetēs* of the games for Augustus oversaw divine honors for Julius Caesar, Livia, and Claudius and Nero (provided that the latter two were divinely honored in Thessalonica), but he may have. Alongside these priestly and presidential duties, the aristocratic men who became *hiereis kai agōnothetes* of the games for Augustus held this office and probably provided concrete benefactions to the city, for which Thessalonica honored them.

The main site at which the *hiereus kai agōnothetēs* of the games for Augustus executed his commission was the temple of Caesar Augustus. A Roman provincial governor paid for the building of it during Augustus's reign, and it is probably located on Thessalonica's western side. This temple has not been confidently identified, but it may be the Archaic Temple that archaeologists uncovered on that side of the city in which a statue probably of Nero was found. If the temple of Caesar Augustus is not the Archaic Temple, then Thessalonica had two Julio-Claudian-era imperial temples on its western side: (1) the temple of Caesar Augustus and (2) the Archaic Temple. In addition to this temple or possibly these temples, there was a second or perhaps third imperial temple dedicated to Augustus, Hercules, and the divine personification of the city in the environs of Thessalonica. These temples would have been richly decorated with imperial altars in front, and cultic statues, some of which have survived, inside (see figs. 3.6, 9). These surviving images are marble and finely crafted. There is, however, no reason to think that imperial offerings were confined to these temples. Sacrifices to Julio-Claudians probably occurred throughout Thessalonica, such as on altars before temples of other gods, in its *agora*, in its theater (as evident from Gythium's sacred law), or on domestic hearths of certain pagan Thessalonians.[119]

These sacrifices were the same types that Thessalonica offered to the gods and consisted of public offerings—that is, those that the city paid for itself and made for the benefit of its citizens—of animals, incense, and wine on a regular and spontaneous basis (the latter being when Thessalonica was informed of milestones in the life of the reigning emperor and his family). Provided that private offerings were made, these probably consisted mostly of incense and wine that various pagan Thessalonians may have offered on altars around their city, including in their own homes. When exactly the public regular sacrifices occurred is still unclear, but they may have been monthly, as in Calindoia. At the very least, the *hiereus kai agōnothetēs* of the games for Augustus offered them during the contests in his honor and probably that of other Julio-Claudians. Finally, imperial divine honors in Thessalonica were wedded to those of the city's gods. This much is clear, in that the Thessalonian benefactress Avia Posilla erected a temple dedicated to Augustus, Hercules, and the divine personification of Thessalonica, and the divine honors at the Archaic Temple for Nero included the goddess Roma. By combining these imperial and traditional divine honors, the city was articulating its celestial reality: the Julio-Claudians were the divinely chosen earthly viceregents of the gods and mediators of their blessings to the city. This perspective is clear from one of the only surviving literary sources composed by a Thessalonian who lived during the reign of the Julio-Claudians in general and Augustus in particular, Antipater of Thessalonica. In two of his epigrams, he prays that Hercules would make Gaius Caesar—Augustus's adopted son—invincible (*anikatos*), that Aphrodite would bless his marriage, that Athena would grant Gaius wisdom, and that Ares would make him fearless. Moreover, he goes so far as to call Gaius Zeus's child (*Zēnos tekos*).[120] For Antipater, the gods of his city work their will through the Julio-Claudians. Provided that other Thessalonians shared this perspective, it means that any attempt to overturn the rule of Augustus and his successors was a direct assault against the will of Thessalonica's gods and vice versa. The two, the city's divine citizens and the Julio-Claudian dynasty, were inseparable.

IMPERIAL DIVINE HONORS AND EARLY CHRISTIANITY IN THESSALONICA

We have now reached the point that we can bring our contextual reconstruction of divine honors for Julio-Claudians in Thessalonica to bear upon what relationship,

119. "Appendix 1: Inscriptions" §I.1, lines 1–7.
120. *Greek Anthology* 9.59, 297.

if any, these honors had with Paul and his converts in the city. It is evident that such honors had a prominent place in Thessalonica and that Thessalonian Christians would have been aware of them.[121] Early Christians, including Paul, saw the Archaic Temple in which imperial divine honors occurred, the temple of Caesar Augustus (provided that this temple was not the former), and they may have seen the temple of Augustus, Hercules, and the divine personification of Thessalonica just outside the city. Possibly Paul but definitely the Thessalonian Christians would have known of the *hiereus kai agōnothetēs* of the games for Augustus, as they would have seen, heard, and smelled imperial processions winding their way through the city and ending at altars in front of the above imperial temples, temples of the gods, or in other locations in their city. Probably Paul but certainly his converts knew of the games that this cultic official oversaw in Thessalonica at regular intervals for Augustus, which consisted of any one or combination of athletic, music, poetry, and chariot-racing contests. Paul and the Christians in the city who could read probably noted the Thessalonian coinage hailing Julius Caesar and Augustus as posthumous gods and Livia as a goddess during her lifetime. These believers and the apostle may have seen and (for those who could) read the above inscriptions attesting to imperial divine honors plus the many more that were certainly set up but have not survived. Thus, early Christians in Thessalonica could not escape such honors, and it is appropriate for scholars to use them to reconstruct nascent Christianity in the city.[122]

To this end, most scholars agree that the Thessalonian correspondence, or at least 1 Thessalonians, if they deny the authenticity of 2 Thessalonians, and Acts 17:1–9 attest that Christians in the city suffered mistreatment from their pagan counterparts. As noted, there is a consensus that this ill-treatment consisted of social ostracism and maybe violence, with only a minority of scholars suggesting martyrdom. Many interpreters trace the harassment of Christians to a direct conflict with imperial divine honors, arguing that Christian acceptance of and proclamation of the *euangelion* of the *basileia* of God and of *kyrios* Jesus opposed directly the *euangelion* of *kyrios* Caesar and his *basileia*. For these scholars, the fact that Thessalonian Christians were awaiting and acclaiming the royal/imperial *parousia* and *apantēsis* of Jesus, compounded the so-called political and anti-Roman Christian message, with the result that it increased the persecution of believers.

Our contextual reconstruction exposes two problems with this proposal. To date, there is no evidence that warrants the conclusion that *euangelion* and *kyrios*

---

121. Contra Miller, "Imperial Cult," 314–32, esp. 319, 320.

122. To quote Deissmann, *Light from the Ancient East*, 340, on this point, "it must not be supposed that St. Paul and his fellow-believers went through the world blindfolded, unaffected by what was then moving through the world of men in great cities."

were "technical imperial" terms in Thessalonica. *Euangelion* is a common word for "good news" in ancient sources and in fact appears in a fragmentary second-century AD Thessalonian inscription, where it refers to "good news" concerning Thessalonica that an ambassador brought back to the city from an embassy to the emperor Hadrian in AD 133.[123] According to the Packard Humanities Institute's digital database for Greek inscriptions (which currently contains over two hundred thousand inscriptions and counting!), *euangelion* is found in only three epigraphs related to Julio-Claudians, none of which are from Thessalonica, Macedonia, or mainland Greece.[124] The first epigraph is the inscription from Priene, noted above, that is the linchpin of the argument that *euangelion* was a "technical imperial" term.[125] The second is the epigraph from Sardis, referenced above, that dates between 5 and 1 BC, which calls the news that Augustus's adopted son Gaius put on the toga of manhood "good" for the city (*euangelisthē polis*) and notes that Sardis was to celebrate this event every year.[126] The final epigraph dates before AD 4 and is from the city of Eresus on the island of Lesbos, which is an island that, while being part of modern-day Greece, is not located on its mainland. The inscription in question is a civic decree honoring a local benefactor, whose name is unknown, and lists the munificent acts that he provided for Eresus, one of which occurred upon hearing "the good news" of an Augustan military victory, at which point he sacrificed to "all the good news gods and goddesses."[127] In my opinion, these three instances are not enough evidence to warrant the oft-stated conclusion that *euangelion* was a technical "imperial" term.[128]

---

123. *IG* 10.2.1.14.

124. εὐαγγέλιον appears in a variety of contexts in ancient inscriptions. Most often it is a proper name for Greeks, Εὐάγγελος. It can mean "good news" or "good news offerings," both of which are unassociated with the emperor. A curse table from Attica promises that if the deities invoked will adversely affect a particular person named Manes's business, then the person who created the curse tablet will "sacrifice good news offerings to you, goddesses of vengeance and Hermes the restrainer, provided that Manes's affairs are evil" (ὑμῖν ἐγὼ Πραξιδίκαι καὶ Ἑρμῇ κάτοχε Μανο[ῦς] κακῶς πράξαντος εὐαγγέλια θύσω; *IG* 3 App.109 = PH234462, lines 5–7).

125. *OGIS* 458 = *IPriene* 105 = PH253018 and PH252886, line 40.

126. "Appendix 1: Inscriptions" §3.13, line 14.

127. ἐβουθ[ύτη][σε]ν ἐπὶ τοῖς εὐαγγελίοις τοῖς θέοις πάντεσσι καὶ παίσαις ("Appendix 1: Inscriptions" §3.15, lines 12–13).

128. See the above discussion on pp. 107–9 and Wright, *Paul and the Faithfulness of God*, 1:325–28; 2:915, who contends, "The other obvious context for 'gospel' [the first being the term's use in Isa 52:7] in Paul was the world where Caesar reigned supreme. In that world, Caesar's birth, his accession and his rule itself were spoken of as 'good news'—as indeed they were, in a fairly limited sense, for those who had suffered the chaos of civil war and all that went with

Moreover, conspicuously absent from Thessalonian sources attesting to imperial divine and even nondivine honors is the title *kyrios*. There is no evidence that the city hailed any Julio-Claudian, dead or alive, by that epithet, even though Thessalonica called Julius Caesar, Augustus, and Claudius gods after their deaths, and Livia a goddess during her lifetime. Elsewhere, I have surveyed the use of *kyrios* for Julio-Claudians, pointing out that the one inscription on which scholars rely as evidence—the epigraph from Acraephia that dates to AD 67, referenced above—is the first attested use of the title for a Julio-Claudian outside Egypt or the ancient southern Levant (roughly the modern-day areas of Israel, Jordan, and southern Syria). In fact, the use of *kyrios* for an emperor was a practice concentrated in this area that, at the end of Nero's reign, began to spread westward in the Roman Empire.[129]

The second problem with the proposal that the early Christian message conflicted directly with imperial divine honors relates to the use of *parousia* and *apantēsis*. Adolf Deissmann was one of the first New Testament scholars to propose that *parousia* is a "technical term" for the visit of an emperor, king, or dignitary to a Greek city. Pointing to the use of the word in mainly papyri from Egypt from the Hellenistic period to the second century AD, he contends, "we are able to trace the word in the East as a technical expression for the arrival or visit of the king or the emperor."[130] Similarly, in an influential article in German, Erik Peterson examines the use of *apantēsis* and cognates in Greco-Roman literature (excluding the Greek Old Testament), papyri, and inscriptions and concludes that it was a "technical term" for an emperor's, king's, or dignitary's visit to a city that "followed a prescribed ceremony."[131] I do not question that *parousia* and *apantēsis* can have the meanings that Deissmann and Peterson ascribe to them. But a close reading of Paul's letters, the New Testament, and the Greek Old Testament demonstrates that these two terms are not "technical" words for royal/imperial visits.[132] *Parousia* appears fourteen times in Paul's letters, seven of which refer to Christ's *parousia*, three of which refer to Paul's, three of which to one of Paul's coworker's, and one of which refers to the coming of the man of lawlessness (see table 3.1).

---

it. By Paul's day that threat had receded for the moment; the notion of 'good news' was no doubt received with the usual measure of detachment and cynicism which accompanies the self-glorifying of empires."

129. Burnett, *Studying the New Testament*, 58–76.

130. Deissmann, *Light from the Ancient East*, 368–73, quotation 368.

131. Erik Peterson, "Die Einholung des *Kyrios*," *ZST* 7 (1930): 683, notes that the ἀπάντησις was "nach einem vorgeschriebenen Zeremoniell."

132. Michael R. Cosby, "Hellenistic Formal Receptions and Paul's Use of ΑΠΑΝΤΗΣΙΣ in 1 Thessalonians 4:17," *BBR* 4 (1994): 15–34.

TABLE 3.1 *PAROUSIA* IN PAUL'S LETTERS

Christ's *parousia*	Paul's *parousia*	Pauline coworker's *parousia*	Man of lawless-ness's *parousia*
1 Cor 15:23; 1 Thess 2:19; 3:13; 4:15; 5:23; 2 Thess 2:1, 8	2 Cor 10:10; Phil 1:26; 2:12	1 Cor 16:17; 2 Cor 7:6, 7	2 Thess 2:9

The varied use of *parousia* in Paul's letters is all the more interesting when one considers that in every other appearance in the New Testament documents, it refers specifically to Jesus's second coming.[133] This suggests that for the apostle, *parousia* did not have a technical meaning of the visitation or coming of a king, emperor, or even the Messiah Jesus. In the same vein, *apantēsis* occurs only once in the Pauline Epistles (1 Thess 4:17), where it is associated with Jesus's second coming. However, in the two other appearances in the New Testament documents, *apantēsis* does not refer to a royal/imperial meeting. In Matt 25:6, the wise virgins who have trimmed their lamps, go out "to meet" (*eis apantēsin*) the bridegroom, and in Acts 28:15, Italian Christians leave their cities "to meet" (*eis apantēsin*) Paul and Luke at Three Taverns on the Appian Way. When *apantēsis* is found in the Greek Old Testament, it most often is used for "meetings" of armies on the battlefield (1 Sam 4:1) or two persons with each other (Judg 4:18). To be clear, I am not suggesting that *apantēsis* and *parousia* are not used for royal/imperial visits and meetings. Rather, there is no evidence in the Greek Old and New Testaments that they are technical terms for royal/imperial visitations. Nor is there much evidence from the larger Greek-speaking Roman world that the words convey that particular technical meaning.[134] Consequently, the scholarly contention that the Thessalonian Christians suffered because the imminent *parousia* of Jesus and their *apantēsis* of him conflicted directly with the imperial *parousia* of Caesar, whose *apantēsis* may be expected at any time, must be nuanced.

To this end, I suggest that the above contextual reconstruction of imperial divine honors reveals that the Thessalonians mistreated their Christian counterparts for a more complex reason than a Christ-versus-Caesar paradigm. We have seen that it is almost impossible to separate imperial from traditional divine honors in the city. The leaders of the city's gymnasium wedded divine honors for Roman benefactors to those that its *neoi* offered to Hermes and Hercules in the gymnasium. Avia Posilla dedicated a temple, bath, pool, and portico to Augustus, Hercules, and the personification of Thessalonica. If the image found in the Archaic Temple identified as Nero is of him, then divine honors for the emperor

133. Matt 24:3, 27, 37, 39; Jas 5:7, 8; 2 Pet 1:16; 3:4, 12; 1 John 2:28.
134. LSJ 178, 1343; BDAG 97, 780–81.

were probably associated with those for Roma (whose statue was found also in the temple). Evidence from Calindoia underscores the incorporation of Julio-Claudians into the honors that Macedonian Greek cities gave to their gods. The city had shrines dedicated to Zeus, Roma, and Augustus; one of the most important public offices in that city was the priesthood of Zeus, Roma, and Augustus; Calindoia offered monthly sacrifices to Zeus and Augustus; and it celebrated a regular festival in honor of Zeus and Augustus.[135]

For the inhabitants of Thessalonica, the decision to embed imperial divine honors into traditional divine honors stemmed from local leaders articulating the relationship between the two groups. The gods chose the Julio-Claudians to be their earthly viceroys, worked through them for the peace and prosperity of Thessalonica, and upon the deaths of some Julio-Claudians (Julius Caesar, Augustus, and Claudius)—but in one instance during life (Livia)—the gods welcomed them among their number. Therefore, the granting of imperial divine honors was an earthly manifestation of the heavenly reality in which the Thessalonians lived. The perspective that the gods worked through the Julio-Claudians is evident in the work of Antipater of Thessalonica, who, when Gaius Caesar went to Armenia on a military campaign, prayed for Hercules to make Gaius invisible, Aphrodite to give him a happy marriage, Athena to grant him wisdom, and Ares to make Gaius fearless.[136] The message of this epigram is that the gods have power over the Julio-Claudians, and they are the ones who protect them, provide legitimate heirs to continue their dynasty, inspire their decrees and decisions, and instill courage in them so that they can fight battles, no doubt those that are divinely approved (at least in the minds of most first-century Thessalonians).

This cooperative relationship between Thessalonica's gods and Julio-Claudians, cemented by divine honors for the latter, means that from the perspective of the Thessalonians, the conversion of some of their compatriots to Christianity was akin to some form of treason against the divine rulers and their earthly viceroys.[137] Thus, early Christians in the city had rejected the symbiotic source of benefaction and blessing for Thessalonica, which threatened the future peace and prosperity of the city.[138] On top of this rejection, Paul's converts in the city were actively

135. Sismanides, "Sevasteion Building Complex," 124–31.

136. *Greek Anthology* 9.59.

137. This is why Paul and his coauthors Silvanus and Timothy do not isolate the former directly but condemn pagan religious activity in general (1 Thess 1:9–10).

138. The earliest inscription attesting to divine honors for the Roman benefactors acknowledges that when a certain Paramonus served as gymnasiarch, he underwrote the costs for the accustomed honors for the gods and the Roman benefactors. The epigraph states that it was erected in order that the *neoi* who trained at that gymnasium "might become zealous imitators of similar actions" (τῶν ὁμοίων ζηλωταὶ γίνωνται) ("Appendix 1: Inscriptions" §3.2, line 19). A de-

and, it appears, aggressively proselytizing.[139] In the process, these believers were claiming that Thessalonica's gods and the Julio-Claudians whom the former had welcomed into their ranks—namely, *theos* Julius Caesar, *theos* Augustus, and *thea* Livia (the city did not hail Claudius as a god until after his death in October AD 54 and thus a few years after the composition of 1–2 Thessalonians)—were not "real gods" but only dead and false "idols" (1 Thess 1:9).[140] In place of these false divinities, Christians in the city were advocating the necessity of devoting one's life to a foreign god, the God of Israel, and his Son Jesus the Messiah (1 Thess 1:1, 3, 9–10; 3:11; 4:5; 2 Thess 1:1; 2:8). Evidently, the Thessalonian Christians were heralding this message loudly and frequently, for Paul notes that they became an example to Christians in Macedonia and Achaia, as the gospel message and its impact on their lives spread centrifugally from Thessalonica throughout those two respective provinces (1 Thess 1:7–10). The Thessalonian believers probably took Jesus, Paul, his apostolic colleagues, and the Judean Christian Jews as examples and indeed became "imitators" (*mimētai*) of them (1 Thess 1:6; 2:14). Since Jesus's preaching of the gospel had resulted in his death, Paul's proclamation of the same gospel had caused his expulsion and banishment from the city (1 Thess 2:17–18; Acts 17:1–9),

---

cree from Thessalonica dated to 60 BC honors a certain Parnassus for his benefactions to the city, which Thessalonica interpreted as his "love of doing good" (φιλάγαθη) and "goodwill" (εὔνοια) toward it. The city crowned him with a laurel crown and erected a bronze statue of him in the most prominent place in its *agora*. One of the purposes of these actions is that when others "see the gratitude of the city, they might become eager for their ancestral city and their province" ([. . . προθυμότ]εροι γίνωνται πρὸς τὴν [πατρίδα καὶ τὴν ἐπαρχεί]αν ὁρῶντες τὴν εὐχα[ριστίαν τῆς πόλεως . . .]; *IG* 10.2.1.5). Thus, from an early age, Thessalonica's citizens were inculcated in the necessity of devoting themselves to the customs of the city, including traditional and imperial divine honors.

139. Still, *Conflict at Thessalonica*, 245–50, relying on John M. G. Barclay, "Conflict in Thessalonica," *CBQ* 55 (1993): 522–24.

140. Although not attested directly in the Thessalonian correspondence, it is probable that under the influence of Paul, the Thessalonian Christians considered these false, dead idols demons (cf. 1 Cor 10:19–21). The condemnation of pagan gods is a departure from Second Temple diaspora Judaism. Exodus 22:28 [ET; 22:27 in Hebrew] instructs Israelites not to curse or revile God (*Elohim*). In rendering this verse into Greek, the translator(s) took the plural Hebrew term for God (*Elohim*) as a reference to pagan gods: "you will not speak evil of the gods" (θεοὺς οὐ κακολογήσεις [Exod 22:27 LXX]). Two of the most prominent Second Temple Jews living in the diaspora, Philo and Josephus, follow the LXX translation over the Hebrew. Philo, *On the Special Laws* 1.53, says Moses commanded Jews not to blaspheme "those that others supposed to be gods" (βλασφημοῦντας οὓς ἕτεροι νομίζουσι θεούς). See also Philo, *Questions and Answers on Exodus* 2.5. Josephus, *Against Apion* 2.237; *Jewish Antiquities* 4.207, notes that Moses forbids Jews from "scoffing or blaspheming those supposed to be gods by others" (μήτε χλευάζειν μήτε βλασφημεῖν τοὺς νομιζομένους θεοὺς παρ᾽ ἑτέροις), and the Lawgiver commands, "let no one blaspheme gods whom other cities supposed (to be gods)" (Βλασφημείτω δὲ μηδεὶς θεοὺς οὓς πόλεις ἄλλαι νομίζουσι).

and the Thessalonian Christians' own acceptance of the Christian message had caused "much affliction" (*thlipsei pollē*) (1 Thess 1:6), the latter of those believers who were eagerly awaiting Jesus's second coming (1 Thess 5:14; 2 Thess 3:6–13) reasoned that their preaching should produce a similar outcome.[141] This situation drew the ire of the pagan Thessalonians and resulted in the harassment of Christians in the city (1 Thess 3:3, 4; 2 Thess 1:4, 6, 7). For this reason, Paul and his apostolic coworkers instruct their converts to tone down, not to cease, their aggressive evangelistic activity by reminding them "to strive to live a quiet life, to tend to your own affairs, and to work with your hands, as we commanded you" (1 Thess 4:11). The result is that these Christians might "walk honorably to those outside" the early Christian movement (1 Thess 4:12a).

In addition to loudly and vehemently denying the existence of Thessalonica's gods, the legitimacy of their chosen vice-regents, and advocating the devotion to one foreign god, the God of Israel and his Son Jesus the Messiah, the early Christians in Thessalonica claimed that the God of Israel had called them "into his own kingdom and glory" with his own divinely chosen ruler, Jesus the Messiah.[142] *Basileia* and its cognates, especially *basileus*, have a long history in Macedonia going back to the kingdom of Macedon that Rome dissolved in 168 BC. Surviving Thessalonian epigraphs attest that *basileia* and in particular one of its cognates, *basileus*, was a loaded term in the city and one with which Thessalonians were familiar. A decree that the city passed in 223 BC is dated by the year in which Antigonus "reigned as king" (*basileuō*).[143] Between 221 and 179 BC, Thessalonica set up an honorary statue of King Philip V hailing him as *basileus* and the son of a *basileus*.[144] The second and third centuries AD witnessed the revival of interest in the Macedonian kingdom, which included divine honors for the long-dead Alexander the Great, whom the city acclaimed *basileus* and Zeus, and for its namesake, Thessalonica, whom the city hailed as *basilissa*.[145] Finally, one of the only surviv-

---

141. It was Barclay, "Conflict in Thessalonica," 512–30, who first brought to my attention that the suffering of the Thessalonian Christians probably reinforced their belief in the imminent second coming of Jesus and thus strengthened their faith.

142. εἰς τὴν ἑαυτοῦ βασιλείαν καὶ δόξαν (1 Thess 1:10; 2:12; 4:13–18; 2 Thess 1:5).

143. βασιλεύοντος Ἀντιγόνου (*IG* 10.2.1.2, line 1).

144. βασιλεὺς Φίλιππος βασιλέως Δημητρίου (*IG* 10.2.1.25).

145. Διὸς Ἀλέξανδρον βασιλέα (*IG* 10.2.1.275); Θεσσαλονίκην Φιλίππου βασίλισσαν (*IG* 10.2.1.277). Despite claims of some New Testament scholars, vom Brocke, *Thessaloniki*, 138; Green, *Letters to the Thessalonians*, 39, divine honors for Alexander the Great appear not to date to the first century AD but seem to be a later revival of Hellenism in the second and third centuries AD. See Allamani-Souri, "Imperial Cult," 107–8. Saint John Chrysostom, *Homily on First Thessalonians* 8, interprets Jesus's παρουσία as a ruler visiting a city. However, he appears not to make the argument based solely on the terms παρουσία or ἀπάντησις, although the surviving Latin manuscript of his homily uses the same Latin term for ἀπάντησις as the Latin New Testament, *obviam*: "If He

ing literary sources connected to Thessalonica, the epigrams of Antipater from Thessalonica, connects the title *basileus* to the Julio-Claudians. In one epigram written during Augustus's reign, Antipater calls the emperor his "brave king."[146]

The pagan Thessalonians probably understood the early Christian proclamation of the *basileia* of God and of his Son, Jesus the Messiah, as the announcement of a kingdom and a divinely appointed ruler different from the *basileia* that and the *basileus* who had provided their city with its "free" status. Thus, the gospel threatened to undermine the peaceful and prosperous status quo of Thessalonica (1 Thess 5:3). In the words of Luke, by preaching the gospel, early Christians in the city were proclaiming another king, Jesus (Acts 17:7), and by implication, another God whose viceroy this new monarch was. Consequently, Paul's Thessalonian converts were turning the world, or less hyperbolically, the world of Thessalonica, upside down (Acts 17:6). One important element of this world-changing gospel was its opposition to Caesar's decrees (Acts 17:7). Elsewhere, I have argued that this enigmatic phrase refers to letters that emperors composed and sent to Thessalonica granting and maintaining the city's "free" status in the empire, which was a gift to a city that the emperor Augustus considered "the greatest benefaction of all" that he could provide.[147] Moreover, it is of import that freedom was an honor that an emperor could give and, just as easily, take away. For example, the city of Cyzicus in modern-day northwest Turkey had been a "free city" in the empire since 73 BC.[148] In 20 BC, Augustus stripped the city of this coveted status, because some inhabitants of Cyzicus had flogged and killed some Roman citizens during a riot.[149]

---

is about to descend, on what account shall we be caught up? For the sake of honour. For when a king (*rex*) enters a city (*civitas*), those who are in honour go out to meet him (*exeunt obviam*), but the condemned await the judge within" (translation by Members of the English Church).

146. τὸν ἐμὸν βασιλῆα τὸν ἄλκιμον (*Greek Anthology* 10.25).

147. τὸ πάντων μέγιστον φιλάνθρωπον (*IAph* 8.32 = PH256915, line 4). This inscription and an English translation can be found on the online corpus of inscriptions from Aphrodisias: Reynolds, Roueché, and Bodard, *Inscriptions of Aphrodisias*, https://insaph.kcl.ac.uk/insaph/iaph2007/iApho80032.html. See Burnett, *Studying the New Testament*, 97–120.

148. Strabo, *Geography* 12.8.11.

149. Dio Cassius, *Roman History* 54.7.6, refers to this removal of "free" status as Augustus "enslaving" (ἐδουλώσατο) the people of the city.

In 15 BC, Agrippa, Augustus's son-in-law, restored Cyzicus's freedom.[150] In AD 25, the emperor Tiberius revoked the city's "free" status once again, because of offenses committed against Roman citizens in Cyzicus and for the city neglecting aspects of divine honors for Augustus that evidently it had promised Augustus, Tiberius, or both.[151] In short, being a "free city" in the empire was an uncertain status that Thessalonica's leaders had to work to maintain by keeping peace and order in their city, which the aggressive evangelistic activity of Christians in the city appears to have threatened. Thus, Thessalonian authorities persecuted Christians to quell their behavior and to prevent any uprisings like the one that occurred when Paul and his apostolic colleagues initially brought the gospel to the city (Acts 17:1–9). Their ultimate goal was to retain their "free" status—and thus freedom from Roman taxes and the billeting of Roman soldiers—that their gods, working through their divinely chosen vice-regents, the Julio-Claudians, had given them.

CONCLUSION

To summarize, Thessalonica established divine honors to Julius Caesar, Augustus, Livia, and probably Claudius and Nero. All these grants, except for Julius Caesar's, were made while the Julio-Claudians in question were alive, and when evidence exists, it is clear that the purpose of such grants was to show Thessalonica's appreciation for imperial benefaction. However, because of the influence of Roman patrons on such honors, Thessalonica established postmortem divine honors for Julius Caesar and waited until the deaths of Julio-Claudians before hailing them as gods, except in the case of Livia. Thessalonian evidence attests to one imperial cultic office, that of the *hiereus kai agōnothetēs* of Augustus, to which the most aristocratic men from Thessalonica and sometimes from other cities and even kingdoms were elected, possibly every year. This individual oversaw sacrifices probably to the above Julio-Claudians and the games for Augustus that occurred on a regular schedule possibly every year. From the reign of Augustus onward, the main site(s) at which the *hiereus kai agōnothetēs* of Augustus executed his office was the temple of Caesar Augustus, which may or may be identical to the Archaic Temple on Thessalonica's western side. It is clear that from Nero's reign onward, this temple was a location of imperial divine honors, and such honors may date even earlier. In addition to this one or these two imperial temples, there was another temple dedicated to Augustus, Hercules, and the divine personification of

---

150. Dio Cassius, *Roman History* 54.23.7–8.
151. Tacitus, *Annals* 4.36; Suetonius, *Tiberius* 37.3.

the city in the environs of Thessalonica that was built during Augustus's reign. It is unclear, however, where the games that the *hiereus kai agōnothetēs* of Augustus oversaw were housed, because of the lack of direct Thessalonian evidence. They were probably located in Thessalonica's Hellenistic-era theater, which archaeologists have yet to locate. Finally, imperial divine honors in Thessalonica were embedded into the city's public life, which served to articulate Thessalonica's celestially informed geopolitical reality: the Julio-Claudians were the divinely chosen earthly vice-regents of the gods and mediators of their blessings to the city.

From the time that Christianity arrived in Thessalonica (Acts 17:1–9), the pagan Thessalonians resisted the spread of this new movement in their city. Their magistrates banished early Christian leaders such as Paul from their city, and these authorities, along with other pagan Thessalonians, socially harassed believers. While some scholars conclude that imperial divine honors were the main cause of this mistreatment, our contextualized reconstruction paints a different picture. These honors contributed to but were not the sole reason for the suffering of Thessalonian Christians. Rather, pagan Thessalonians mistreated their Christian counterparts because the latter denied the existence of the city's gods, including but not limited to certain Julio-Claudians, they refused to participate in traditional and imperial divine honors, and they aggressively proclaimed the imminent kingdom of God with its divinely chosen ruler Jesus. All of this would have amounted to treason in Thessalonica. For the pagan Thessalonians, this sedition threatened the safety and security of their city and the real possibility of divine and imperial retribution, especially the removal of Thessalonica's "free" status in the empire.

CHAPTER 4

Imperial Divine Honors, Paul,
and the Corinthian Church

This last chapter brings the contextual approach to imperial divine honors to bear on the last city in mainland Greece in which the apostle Paul established embryonic Christianity and to which he composed letters, the Roman colony of Corinth. Like the two previous chapters, this one has two main goals. The first is to lay out all the known ancient evidence for imperial divine honors in Corinth and to build a contextualized portrait of them (see "Imperial Divine Honors in Corinth"). In the process, we will see that such honors fall into the category of Roman imperial divine honors with a few outliers, which are probably due to the influence of Corinth's Greek past and the hellenized Roman identity of the colony's leaders. This chapter's second goal is to use this contextualized portrait to offer a fresh reading of the Corinthian correspondence but mostly 1 Corinthians (see "Imperial Divine Honors and Early Christianity in Corinth"). To this end, we will see that even though 1–2 Corinthians attests that there was frequent interaction between Christians and pagans in the city, there is no evidence from these documents, or Acts of the Apostles, of any conflict between the two groups related to imperial divine honors. Before we arrive at these two goals, however, I must describe the state of Corinthian imperial divine honors in New Testament scholarship and how exegetes interpret the relationship between these honors and early Christianity in the colony (see "New Testament Scholars on Imperial Divine Honors, Paul, and the Corinthian Church").

New Testament Scholars on Imperial Divine Honors, Paul, and the Corinthian Church

Many New Testament scholars acknowledge the importance of imperial divine honors in Corinth and that they form a background for interpreting the Corinthian correspondence, especially 1 Corinthians.[1] These interpreters tend not to delve into the content or context of such honors, because of their assumption that a monolithic "imperial cult" existed in the Roman Empire.[2] Those scholars who mention specifics of Corinthian imperial divine honors most often reference the largest temple in Corinth's forum, Temple E, which they identify as imperial.[3] This identification leads some of these interpreters to conclude that the honors in question were the most important divine honors in mid-first-century AD Corinth and the biggest competitor to early Christianity. To this end, Paul sought to counteract the influence of such honors upon his converts in 1 Corinthians.[4] For example, a growing number of scholars hold that Paul's Christianizing exposition of the Shema (Deut 6:4) in 1 Cor 8:5–6—that there is one God, the Father, and one Lord, Jesus the Messiah—is a polemic against the participation of Corinthian Christians in imperial divine honors. The apostle's reference to *theoi* and *kyrioi* "in heaven" and "on earth," the argument goes, refers to the emperor and other Julio-Claudians whom Corinth hailed as such.[5]

1. The main exception is the study by Colin Miller, "The Imperial Cult in the Pauline Cities of Asia Minor and Greece," *CBQ* 72 (2010): 329–31, whose failure to investigate Corinthian archaeology, inscriptions, and coins as well as his inaccurate interpretation of what he does cite led him to conclude incorrectly that there is a "lack of evidence [for imperial divine honors] in Corinth." Some scholars claim that divine honors for Julio-Claudians form a background for 2 Corinthians. See Fredrick J. Long, "'The God of This Age' (2 Cor 4:4) and Paul's Empire-Resisting Gospel at Corinth," in *Roman Corinth*, vol. 2 of *The First Urban Churches*, ed. James R. Harrison and L. L. Welborn, WGRWSup 8 (Atlanta: SBL Press, 2016), 219–69, who argues that the reference to "the god of this age" (2 Cor 4:4) refers to the emperor Nero, not to the devil/Satan, as most exegetes conclude.

2. The assumption of a monolithic "imperial cult" is evident in David E. Garland, *1 Corinthians*, BECNT (Grand Rapids: Baker Academic, 2003), 9–11, quotation 11, who comments, "S. Mitchell's . . . reflections about the imperial cult in Anatolia are applicable to Corinth." He goes on to cite Stephen Mitchell, *The Rise of the Church*, vol. 2 of *Anatolia: Land, Men, and Gods in Asia Minor* (Oxford: Clarendon, 1993), 10 as cited by Bruce W. Winter, "The Achaean Federal Imperial Cult II: The Corinthian Church," *TynBul* 46 (1995): 176.

3. Richard A. Horsley, *First Corinthians*, ANTC (Nashville: Abingdon, 1998), 27; Joseph A. Fitzmyer, *First Corinthians: A New Translation with Introduction and Commentary*, AYB 32 (New Haven: Yale University Press, 2008), 27; N. T. Wright, *Paul in Fresh Perspective* (Minneapolis: Fortress, 2009), 65; Wright, *Paul and the Faithfulness of God*, 2 vols. (Minneapolis: Fortress, 2013), 1:330, 332, 2:1275–76, 1285.

4. Garland, *1 Corinthians*, 10; Wright, *Paul and the Faithfulness of God*, 1:311–47, esp. 332; Mark Finney, "Christ Crucified and the Inversion of Roman Imperial Ideology in 1 Corinthians," *BTB* 35 (2005): 20–33.

5. For a discussion of the identity of the gods and lords "in heaven" and "on earth," see D. Clint Burnett, "Divine Titles for Julio-Claudian Imperials in Corinth," *CBQ* 82 (2020): 437–55. Some interpreters argue that Paul's intention in 1 Corinthians is to subvert the Roman Empire

The most detailed discussion of imperial divine honors in Corinth and their relationship to early Christianity to date is Bruce Winter's. For him, the former were a fount of difficulties for Paul and the struggling Corinthian Christians.[6] Winter marshals inscriptions, papyri, and archaeological evidence, some of which are from Corinth, to reconstruct the honors in question in the city. He concludes that Temple E was dedicated to the emperor Augustus's sister, Octavia, and that there was an imperial shrine in a building in the forum known as the Julian Basilica (for more on these buildings, see pp. 204–9). From an epigraphic dedication to the "Caesars Augusti" found in the Julian Basilica, Winter proposes that the inscription provides the interpretive key to 1 Cor 8:5–6. The "Caesars Augusti," Winter posits, is a general reference to deceased and living Julio-Claudians, some of whom are the *kyrioi* and *theoi* "in heaven" and "on earth." The former are Julio-Claudians whom the Roman Senate divinized—Julius Caesar, Augustus, and Claudius—and the latter are living Julio-Claudians.[7] He goes on to argue that the citizens of Corinth, including some of Paul's converts, were forced to celebrate imperial divine honors for these personages, which included the deceased and reigning emperor's *genii* (the plural of *genius*). It seems that Winter identifies these *genii* as the demons of which Paul speaks in 1 Cor 10:20–21.[8] Some celebrations of these honors occurred at sacred meals, according to Winter, in the boundary of Temple E, which is the idol's temple to which Paul refers in 1 Cor 8:10.[9] Thus, he concludes that for Paul, such imperial cultic activity was participation in "the cup . . . and table of demons" (1 Cor 10:21).[10]

---

by setting up an alternative society. For a recent and informed presentation of this perspective, see Neil Elliott, "Paul and Empire 1: Romans, 1 Corinthians, 2 Corinthians," in *An Introduction to Empire in the New Testament*, ed. Adam Winn (Atlanta: SBL Press, 2016), 143–63.

6. These works span the years 1990 to 2015 when Bruce Winter, *Divine Honours for the Caesars: The First Christians' Responses* (Grand Rapids: Eerdmans, 2015), published the culmination of his work on imperial divine honors and (mostly) Paul's letters.

7. To support the identification of Julio-Claudians as gods, Winter, *Divine Honours*, 209–12, appeals to inscriptions, coins, and the archaeological remains of Corinth. However, only one inscription—whose interpretation is debated—and one coin are from Corinth. The rest of his data are from Cyprus, Athens, Ephesus, and Thasos.

8. Winter, *Divine Honours*, 214–25. It is unclear to me from Winter's, *Divine Honours*, 217, discussion of the *genius* of Corinth if he includes this *genius* among the *genii* whom he identifies as demons.

9. Winter's, *Divine Honours*, 166–81, 184–92, 203–9, evidence for compulsory imperial sacrifices is an epigraph dated to AD 2 from the Greek city of Messene that details aspects of an imperial festival with sacrifices "to" (διά) Augustus that a certain Roman official in the province of Achaia instituted to celebrate Augustus's adopted son Gaius's military victory. See James E. G. Zetzel, "New Light on Gaius Caesar's Eastern Campaign," *GRBS* 11 (1970): 259–66.

10. Winter's, *Divine Honours*, 217–21, evidence for δαίμων referring to the emperor's *genius* in Corinth is the use of δαίμων in a Greek papyrus from Egypt for the deceased Claudius ("good

While the above reconstructions attempt to take imperial divine honors in Corinth seriously, they are problematic. Again, many scholars work with the assumption that a monolithic "imperial cult" existed in the Roman Empire. Thus, aside from Winter, these interpreters have not investigated such honors in Corinth contextually, thereby failing to note the peculiarities of the honors in question— that is, their Roman character, that archaeologists debate several aspects of these honors, such as the identity of Temple E, that there is no Corinthian evidence that Julio-Claudians, alive or dead, were hailed as *kyrioi*, and that while Greeks in the colony would have called the Julio-Claudian *divi* "*theoi*," *theoi* does not equal *divi*. The result is a misrepresentation of the honors in question in the colony. Winter's attempted contextualization of these Corinthian divine honors is laudable. His presentation of ancient inscriptions and papyri is impressive, and his research into the most recent archaeological discoveries in the city is commendable. Thus, he is correct to bring in Corinthian epigraphs to reconstruct imperial divine honors and their relationship to early Christianity, to identify the Julian Basilica as having an imperial shrine in it, and to note that scholars debate Temple E's identification, even though he sides with those who identify the temple as imperial.

On the other hand, there are difficulties with Winter's reconstruction, which in turn render his conclusions about the relationship of imperial divine honors and early Christianity problematic. One of the most prominent is his use of comparative material. Instead of looking to Rome and other Roman colonies such as Philippi to fill in the gaps that the evidence for Corinthian imperial divine honors leaves, Winter uses inscriptions and papyri from Greek cities, which are associated with Greek civic and provincial imperial divine honors, even though he acknowledges the Roman character of Corinth and that imperial divine honors in the colony differed from such honors in Greek cities.[11] The result is that Winter misrepresents the Corinthian honors in question.[12] Moreover, his interpretation of some Corinthian

---

δαίμων" [P.Oxy. 7.1021]), in a Greek inscription from Egypt for the living emperor Nero ("the good δαίμων of the civilized world" [*OGIS* 666]), and that ancient Greek authors tended to translate the Latin *genius* as δαίμων.

11. Winter, *Divine Honours*, 184, 190, quotation 190, notes, "Because it [Corinth] was a Roman colony, aspects of the cult in Corinth differed from those in Greek cities of the province." Throughout his work, Winter's comparative evidence, however, consists of inscriptions, papyri, and archaeological sites from the Greek cities of Acraephia, Aphrodisias, Athens, Cos, Ephesus, and Olympia; the Roman provinces of Cyprus and Egypt; and the Latin cities of Caesarea Maritima, Carthage, and Pompeii.

12. No Corinthian evidence exists for compulsory sacrifices to living or deceased Julio-Claudians in the city, much less in the confines of Temple E. Winter's, *Divine Honours*, 172–75, evidence for such sacrifices to the emperor is the inscription, noted above, from Messene that states that there were "(sacrifices) of thanksgiving on behalf of the sacrifice διά Augustus" (τᾶς

material is questionable. Winter's use of the dedication to the "Caesars Augusti" from the Julian Basilica to interpret the *theoi* and *kyrioi* "in heaven" and "on earth" (1 Cor 8:5–6) is not supported by the evidence. As we shall see, the official publication of this inscription argues convincingly against the identification of the "Caesars Augusti" as a "generic" dedication to living and deceased Julio-Claudians. Finally, Winter's identification of demons in 1 Cor 10:20–21 with imperial *genii* is eisegetical. There is no evidence from Corinth that the colony's citizens gave deceased *genii* of Julio-Claudians divine honors. It is probable that Paul considered the living emperor's *genius* as demonic, but he thought and identified all divine beings hostile to Israel's God, not just the imperial *genius*, as *daimonia*.[13]

In sum, because of the limitation of current discussions of imperial divine honors in Corinth in New Testament studies, this chapter offers a fresh contextual interpretation of them and their relationship to early Christianity in the Roman colony of Corinth. This means, first and foremost, creating a localized, contextual profile of such honors by amassing all known evidence for such honors in Corinth: inscriptions, coins, archaeology, and literary sources. When this occurs, the Roman nature of these honors becomes clear, for almost all the evidence consists of Latin inscriptions and legends on coins attesting to postmortem divine honors for certain Julio-Claudians that local aristocrats with Roman citizenship administered, promoted, and patronized. The Roman character of these honors means that the only appropriate comparative material to fill in our fragmentary Corinthian sources must be from places where Roman imperial divine honors were practiced, Rome and other sister colonies of Corinth, like Philippi. It is to this contextual reconstruction that we now turn.

DIVINE HONORS FOR HUMANS IN CORINTH

History of Corinth

Our contextual reevaluation of imperial divine honors in Corinth must begin with a reconstruction of the city's history, which, like its Macedonian counterpart

---

ὑπὲρ τὰν διὰ τοῦ Σεβαστοῦ θυςίαν εὐχαριστίας [Zetel, "New Light," 259–60, lines 8–9]). This translation of διά as "to" is not widely accepted, which Winter acknowledges, and some historians render it as "for." See Robert K. Sherk, ed., *The Roman Empire: Augustus to Hadrian*, Translated Documents of Greece and Rome 6 (Cambridge: Cambridge University Press, 1988), 33–34, no. 18; Fergus Millar, "Two Augustan Notes," *Classical Review* 18 (1968): 264–65.

13. See Paula Fredricksen, *Paul: The Pagans' Apostle* (New Haven: Yale University Press, 2017), 39–41.

Philippi, is a tale of two cities. The first city was Greek and dates from about the tenth century to 44 BC.[14] This Corinth was founded on a narrow strip of fertile land four miles long, called an isthmus—a tract of land between two seas, which in this case are the Corinthian and Saronic Gulfs—that connected central mainland Greece to its southern peninsula, the Peloponnesus.[15] By the eighth century BC, Corinth's control of the harbor at Lechaeum on the Corinthian Gulf and the harbor at Cenchreae on the Saronic allowed it to become a wealthy maritime trading power.[16] Between the seventh and early second century BC, Corinth and the city's aristocrats used their riches to beautify the city with a number of magnificent temples, fountains, stoas, a theater, and other civic structures.[17] Corinth's prosperity afforded it the ability to be an influential player on the Greek world stage. During the eighth century BC, Corinth founded several Greek colonies, the most notable of which are Corcyra (modern-day Corfu) and Syracuse.[18] From the sixth to the fifth century BC, Corinthian men fought in wars that determined the destiny of Greece's city-states or *poleis* (*polis* in the singular), such as the Persian (492–449 BC) and Peloponnesian Wars (431–404 BC).[19]

In the fourth century BC, Philip II, Alexander the Great's father, conquered Corinth (and most of mainland Greece). From then to the third century BC, the city was under the authority of Macedonian kings. However, around 281/280 BC, Corinth and other nearby Greek cities formed a confederation known as the Achaian League, whose main purpose was to secure political autonomy for *poleis*

---

14. It is the case, however, that beginning in the second century AD, there was a revival of Hellenism in Corinth, and the city became more Greek, which is evident in that Greek began to eclipse Latin as the official language of the city. See John H. Kent, *The Inscriptions 1926–1950*, vol. 8, part 3 of *Corinth: Results of Excavations Conducted by the American School of Classical Studies at Athens* (Princeton: American School of Classical Studies at Athens, 1966), 18–19 (abbreviated Kent, *Corinth* 8.3 hereafter).

15. Pliny, *Natural History* 4.9–10.

16. Corinth's wealth derived from its ability to levy taxes on imports and exports across the isthmus (Strabo, *Geography* 8.6.20, 22). By the end of the seventh century BC, a road of some kind had been constructed across the isthmus for the transportation of goods and people (not ships). For more on the isthmus, see David K. Pettegrew, *The Isthmus of Corinth: Crossroads of the Mediterranean World* (Ann Arbor: University of Michigan Press, 2016), 28–46, 59–68, 113–34, who demonstrates that the portaging of ships across the isthmus was infrequent and happened on few occasions.

17. Guy D. R. Sanders, Jennifer Palinkas, and Ioulia Tzonou-Herbst with James Herbst, *Ancient Corinth: Site Guide*, 7th ed. (Princeton: American School of Classical Studies at Athens, 2018), 16–18.

18. Fitzmyer, *First Corinthians*, 22.

19. Herodotus, *Persian Wars*; Thucydides, *History of the Peloponnesian War*.

in the league.[20] To achieve this end during the early second century BC, it allied with a growing superpower in the western Mediterranean, Rome. Thereafter, Roman armies marched into Greek territory and defeated the kingdom of Macedon in a war known as the Second Macedonian War (200–197 BC).[21] Corinth and the other cities of the Achaian League expected that the autonomy for which they had labored was forthcoming. However, Rome quickly disabused these cities of this notion when it began to exert direct influence on them, which culminated in ordering the Achaian League to dissolve itself.[22] Resenting such an incursion, the communities of the Achaian League went to war against Rome in 146 BC in a contest that became known as the Achaian War. During this short military campaign, the Roman consul Lucius Mummius besieged and captured the heart of the Achaian League's resistance, Corinth.[23] In the process, he destroyed much (but not all!) the Greek city and eradicated Greek Corinth as a political entity, tearing down its walls, looting its treasures, slaughtering its adult males, and selling Corinthian women and children into slavery. Finally, Rome made Corinth and its fertile environs *ager publicus* or "public Roman land."[24]

Ancient authors lamented Corinth's destruction and often describe it as complete.[25] Many New Testament scholars have accepted this testimony uncritically and concluded that from 146 BC to 44 BC (when the city was refounded as a Roman colony), Corinth was akin to an unoccupied barren wasteland.[26] However, a critical reading of these ancient authors and an examination of Corinthian archaeological evidence confirm that the city was neither completely destroyed

20. This founding of the Achaian League was actually a refounding of it, which is first attested in 453 BC. See R. M. Errington, "Achaean Confederacy," *OCD* 4–5.

21. The First Macedonian War was between 215 and 205 BC. See D. Clint Burnett, *Studying the New Testament through Inscriptions: An Introduction* (Peabody, MA: Hendrickson, 2020), 110.

22. Fitzmyer, *First Corinthians*, 24.

23. For a history of Corinth from the third century BC to the third century AD, see James Wiseman, "Corinth and Rome I: 228 B.C.–A.D. 267," *ANRW* 7.1:438–548, part 2, *Principat*, 7.1.

24. Charles K. Williams III, Nancy Bookidis, Kathleen W. Slane with Stephen Tracy, "From the Destruction of Corinth to Colonia Laus Iulia Corinthiensis," in *The Destruction of Cities in the Ancient Greek World: Integrating the Archaeological and Literary Evidence*, ed. Sylvian Fachard and Edward M. Harris (Cambridge: Cambridge University Press, 2021), 258–87.

25. *Greek Anthology* 7.297, 493; 9.151, 284; Diodorus Siculus, *Library of History* 32.27.1; Strabo, *Geography* 8.6.23; Cicero, *Tusculan Disputations* 3.22 (53–54); Pausanias, *Description of Greece* 2.2.1; 7.16.7–10.

26. Hans Conzelmann, *1 Corinthians: A Commentary on the First Epistle to the Corinthians*, trans. James W. Leitch, Hermeneia (Philadelphia: Fortress, 1975), 11–12; Richard B. Hays, *First Corinthians*, Interpretation (Louisville: Westminster John Knox, 1997), 3; Gordon D. Fee, *The First Epistle to the Corinthians*, rev. ed., NICNT (Grand Rapids: Eerdmans, 2014), 1–2.

nor abandoned. The literary works that describe Corinth's destruction as total are not contemporary to Mummius's sack of the city, and the main aim of the authors in question is not historical accuracy.[27] The Roman philosopher, orator, and senator Cicero personally visited Corinth between 79 and 77 BC. While sometimes he laments the city's destruction as total, he testifies to seeing "Corinthians" (*Corinthii*) living in Corinth among the ruins (*parietinae*) on his visit there.[28] The archaeological evidence is difficult to interpret and date with precision, but it suggests that the city was not a barren wasteland and that Greek Corinthians began to rebuild portions of their city between 146 and 44 BC.[29]

The nontotal destruction of Corinth notwithstanding, the devastation that Mummius wrought to the Greek city wiped it out as a political entity. This is evident in that the general must have called for the systematic destruction of Corinthian epigraphs containing any reference to Greek Corinth's political bodies.[30] Such destruction means that it is impossible to reconstruct its history and customs in a complete manner. Thus, it is unclear whether Greek Corinth granted divine honors to any ruler or human benefactor of the city. It is possible that the city did, because the earliest divine honors for a ruler in the Greek world date to the late fifth century BC.[31] However, on balance, it is improbable that Corinth divinely honored one of its leaders, because there is little pre–Roman era evidence in mainland Greece that its inhabitants bestowed such honors on human benefactors.[32] In the end, this matters little, for the Corinth in which Paul established nascent Christianity was not Greek but Roman Corinth.

27. Williams, Bookidis, and Slane with Tracy, "From the Destruction of Corinth," 258.

28. Cicero, *Tusculan Disputations* 3.22 (53–54). In another place, Cicero, *On Agrarian Laws* 2.32 (87); *On Duties* 2.22 (76), notes that a vestige (*vestigium*) of Corinth is scarcely "left behind" (*relictus*) and that Mummius "destroyed the richest city from its foundation" (*copiosissimam urbem funditus sustulisset*).

29. Williams, Bookidis, and Slane with Tracy, "From the Destruction of Corinth," 267–75. For example, Mummius and his army did not destroy the South Stoa (built around 300 BC), which became part of the Roman city's forum (see fig. 4.1).

30. Mary E. Hoskins Walbank, "The Foundation and Planning of Early Roman Corinth," *JRA* 10 (1997): 95–96, concludes, "Another curious aspect of the sack is the way in which the inscriptions, particularly those of a public nature, were treated. Their condition, I suggest, indicates that they were deliberately smashed into tiny fragments and scattered. . . . The intention must have been to destroy Corinth as a political entity but not to obliterate the city."

31. Christian Habicht, *Divine Honors for Mortal Men in Greek Cities: The Early Cases*, trans. John Noël Dillon (Ann Arbor: Michigan Classical Press, 2017), 1–5.

32. Francesco Camia and Maria Kantiréa, "The Imperial Cult in the Peloponnese," in *Society, Economy and Culture under the Roman Empire: Continuity and Innovation*, vol. 3 of *Roman Peloponnese*, ed. A. Rizakis and C. Lepenioti, Meletemata 63 (Athens: Diffusion de Boccard, 2010), 375–406, esp. 375–76 note 3.

This reference to Paul's visit to Corinth brings us to the second part of our tale of two cities, the founding of the city as a Roman colony. In 44 BC, Julius Caesar, the Roman dictator and adopted father of Caesar Octavian (later the emperor Augustus), decided to found Corinth as "the Renowned Julian Colony of the Corinthians."[33] He made this decision because of Corinth's strategic position on the isthmus—master of two harbors—and the fertility of the city's environs. This plan must have been well in place before Caesar's assassination on March 15, 44 BC, because his death neither halted nor prevented its execution. The first colonists who populated Roman Corinth were veterans of the Roman army, freedmen (enslaved Greeks whom their Roman masters had emancipated), and some of Italy's urban poor.[34] These men received plots of land inside and outside Corinth, the former for living and the latter mainly for farming.[35]

Either Caesar or one of his partisans after his death provided Corinth with a new Roman constitution, which, like Philippi's charter, has not survived.[36] However, we can reconstruct aspects of this constitution from inscriptions from Roman Corinth and surviving charters of other Roman colonies.[37] The Corinthian constitution established a Roman form of government with Roman institutions, including making Latin the city's official language (at least until the early second century AD).[38] Furthermore, it divided the inhabitants of the city into two main groups, *coloni* or "colonists" and *incolae* or noncitizen "resident aliens" who had no civic rights. The men in Corinth who were fortunate enough to be *coloni* made up Corinth's *populus* or "people," which was the totality of the city's voting pop-

---

33. *Colonia Laus Julia Corinthiensis* (*RPC* 1.1116). See Strabo, *Geography* 8.6.23; Pausanias, *Description of Greece* 5.1.2; Diodorus Siculus, *Library of History* 32.27.1; Dio Cassius, *Roman History* 43.50.3–5.

34. Strabo, *Geography* 8.6.23, testifies that the new colonists were mostly freedmen, Plutarch, *Caesar* 57, that they were mostly discharged soldiers, and Appian, *Roman History: The African Book* 8.136, that they were mostly the urban poor of Italy. The number of original colonists is unknown.

35. For a description of this process, see David Gilman Romano, "Urban and Rural Planning in Roman Corinth," in *Urban Religion in Roman Corinth: Interdisciplinary Approaches*, ed. Daniel N. Schowalter and Steven J. Friesen, HTS 53 (Cambridge: Harvard University Press, 2005), 25–59.

36. This would have been engraved on bronze and displayed either in Roman Corinth's forum or in one of the official governmental buildings in the forum. The reason that it has not survived is that at some point, the bronze was probably melted down to serve other purposes.

37. One such constitution is the "Law of the Julian Colony of Urso," in modern-day Spain, which dates between 59 and 44 BC and was found engraved on bronze tablets that date to the end of the first century AD. See Michael Crawford, ed., *"Lex Coloniae Genetivae,"* in *Roman Statutes*, 2 vols. (London: Institute of Classical Studies, 1996) 1:393–454.

38. Kent, *Corinth* 8.3:18–19.

ulation. The colony's *populus* was further divided into tribes, which by the first century AD numbered at least ten but possibly twelve. The names of these tribes demonstrate that Corinth, at least after 31 BC, cultivated connections with the Julio-Claudians (see table 4.1).[39]

TABLE 4.1 KNOWN CORINTHIAN TRIBES[40]

Voting Tribe	Connection to the Julio-Claudians
Agrippa	Augustus's closest friend and son-in-law
Atia	Julius Caesar's niece and Augustus's mother
Aurelia	Julius Caesar's mother
Calpurnia	Julius Caesar's third or fourth wife
Claudia	Named after the Claudian family line
Domitia	Possibly named after the son of Octavia and Marc Antony, Gnaeus Domitius Ahenobarbus
Hostilia	?
Livia	Augustus's wife
Maneia	?
Vatinia	Possibly a friend of Julius Caesar, Publius Vatinius
Vinicia	Possibly named after Marcus Vinicius, the father of Julia Livilla, Caligula's sister
Sae(lia) or Ae(lia)	?

The small fraction of the male *populus* who were the most aristocratic, probably around one hundred, attained the *ordo* or "rank" of *decurio* (*decuriones* in the Latin plural) or member of the *curia* or Corinth's "local senate." These *decuriones* were local senators who administered and oversaw colonial public affairs and had "wide-ranging powers."[41]

Each year, Corinth's *populus* elected aristocrats to several magistracies, the two most important of which were *aedile* and *duovir*.[42] The Corinthian colonists

39. Wiseman, "Corinth and Rome I," 497–98.
40. This table was made with data from Wiseman, "Corinth and Rome I," 497–98, who notes that one tribe, the Sae(lia) or Ae(lia) may date to Hadrian's reign (AD 117–138).
41. Donald Engels, *Roman Corinth: An Alternative Model for the Classical City* (Chicago: University of Chicago Press, 1990), 17–18. See *Lex Coloniae Genetivae* 64, 69, 75, 80, 96–100, 103–31, 134.
42. There were also other less prestigious public offices that the Corinthians voted to fill, such as *quaestor*, which was a position that one of Paul's converts, Erastus, held (Rom 16:23). See John K. Goodrich, "Erastus, *Quaestor* of Corinth: The Administrative Rank of ὁ οἰκονόμος τῆς

selected two *aediles* annually who were responsible for the maintenance of streets, public works, and the oversight of the city's marketplace.[43] After their year in office, these *aediles* were admitted to the *ordo* of *decurio* and took a seat on the colony's *curia*.[44] Every year, Corinth elected two of the most aristocratic men in the colony to be *duoviri* (the Latin plural of *duovir*), which literally means "board of two men." These two men were the ultimate local authority in the colony, resembling the two consuls of Rome that the Roman *populus* selected each year, as they oversaw Corinth's political, religious, social, and legal system.[45] Every fifth year, the Corinthian colonists selected two special *duoviri*, *duoviri quinquennales* or *duoviri* every fifth year, who performed a census of the colony—purging dead colonists from the list of *coloni* and adding new ones to the registry—and who chose new members to sit on the colony's *curia*.[46] The names of *duoviri* and *aediles* found in Corinthian epigraphs and on coins demonstrate that most who filled these magistracies in the Julio-Claudian period were a small group of Italian freedmen and Roman *negotiatores*—Romans who were bankers, moneylenders, traders, and commercial farmers who had lived in the Greek East for generations and moved to Corinth after its founding.[47] Finally, the wives and daughters of the Corinthian male colonists, even those who were the most aristocratic, possessed some rights but were not allowed to vote or hold public office in the city.

Not long after the decision to found Corinth as a colony, Rome was plunged into war when Brutus, Cassius, and a number of other senators assassinated Julius Caesar to end his monopoly on power in Rome.[48] Soon after, two loyal supporters of Caesar, Marc Antony and Caesar Octavian, and two of the main assassins, Brutus and Cassius, gathered armies to fight for control of Rome in a bitter civil war. The deciding battle of the conflict was on a plain of Philippi before that city's walls in October 42 BC, where Antony's and Caesar Octavian's forces emerged

---

πόλεως (Rom 16:23) in an Achaean Colony," *NTS* 56 (2010): 90–115. For the other public offices in the colony see Wiseman, "Corinth and Rome I," 499–502.

43. Wiseman, "Corinth and Rome I," 499; *Lex Coloniae Genetivae* 62, 77, 98, 128–30, 134.

44. Engels, *Roman Corinth*, 17–18.

45. Wiseman, "Corinth and Rome I," 498–99; Engels, *Roman Corinth*, 18; *Lex Coloniae Genetivae* 62–64, 67–71, 81, 93–105, 130–31, 134.

46. Wiseman, "Corinth and Rome I," 498–99; Engels, *Roman Corinth*, 18.

47. Antony J. S. Spawforth, "Roman Corinth: The Formation of a Colonial Elite," in *Roman Onomastics in the Greek East*, ed. A. D. Rizikis (Athens: de Boccard, 1996), 167–82, notes that from Augustus onward the colonial aristocrats were *negotiatores* and freedmen but that, during Nero's reign, aristocrats from Greece became some of the leading families in Roman Corinth.

48. For a description of Julius Caesar's assassination and the events that unfolded directly after, see Adrian Goldsworthy, *Caesar: Life of a Colossus* (New Haven: Yale University Press, 2006), 490–511.

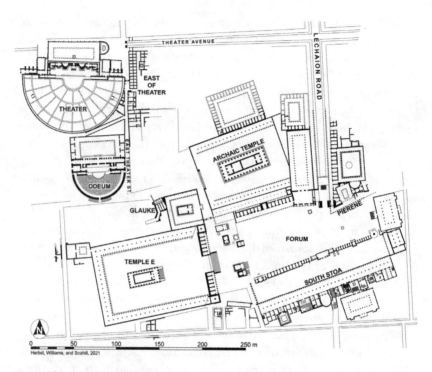

Fig. 4.1 This site map is of second-, not first-, century AD Corinth. Thus, some of the buildings on this site map had not been built in the first century AD and others, like Temple E, looked different. The reader should pay close attention to my discussion of these buildings so that they gain the most accurate picture of the mid-first-century forum. | *Courtesy of the artists, C. K. Williams II and F. Hemans, American School of Classical Studies at Athens, Corinth Excavations; used with permission.*

victorious (see pp. 68–69). Thereupon, the latter divided up most of the Roman Empire between them in spheres of influence. Antony was given the Greek East and Caesar Octavian (most of) the Latin West. Thus, from 42 to 31 BC, Corinth was under Antony's authority.[49] He probably visited the city between 39 and 36 BC, because the colony minted coins featuring his bust on them (a point that may be of relevance for divine honors for Julius Caesar and Octavia in Corinth; see pp. 168–74).[50] In 32 BC, Antony's alliance with Caesar Octavian broke, and another Roman civil war ensued. Caesar Octavian's closest friend, Marcus Agrippa, captured Corinth soon thereafter, and the conflict with Antony ended in 31 BC

49. Wiseman, "Corinth and Rome I," 502.
50. *RPC* 1.1124; Wiseman, "Corinth and Rome I," 502.

when Caesar Octavian defeated Antony at the naval battle of Actium. This made Caesar Octavian sole ruler of Rome's empire.[51]

The new commander of all Rome's forces appears to have shown no ill will toward Corinth for its connection to Antony, and the city prospered after Actium. In 27 BC, Caesar Octavian, now known as Augustus, formed the province of Achaia around Corinth, and he appears to have made the city the provincial capital.[52] Sometime during Augustus's reign, the Corinthian colonists began massive building projects in their colony and in particular in the public, religious, and political center of their city, the forum (see fig. 4.1). The Corinthian forum was bounded by buildings on four sides. By the time that Paul arrived there in AD 50/51, the two-story South Stoa (built around 300 BC) formed the forum's southern border, the Archaic Temple (built around the mid-sixth century BC) and the two-story Northwest Stoa (built between 27 BC and AD 14) the northern border, Temple E, the highest point in the forum (built between AD 14 and 37), the western border, and the Julian Basilica (built between 2 BC and AD 4/5) the eastern border (see fig. 4.1). Most of these buildings were constructed of limestone and decorated elegantly, some with marble revetment, thin pieces of marble attached to walls as decoration.[53]

This forum is an excellent object lesson of Roman Corinth's cultural life, a new Roman city constructed alongside the older, more historic Greek one. Thus, elements of Greek Corinth remained in the Roman city and influenced aspects of the Roman colony.[54] For example, Corinth's connection to Bellerophon, the Corinthian hero whose father was Poseidon and who battled the Chimera, and Pegasus, the flying horse that Bellerophon tamed, remained important for Roman Corinth's

51. Valleius Paterculus, *Compendium of Roman History* 2.84.

52. To date, no ancient source, literary or nonliterary, confirms the testimony of Acts 18:11–12 that Corinth was the capital of Achaia: Wiseman, "Corinth and Rome I," 501–2. Between AD 15 and 44, Achaia's status as a senatorial province changed, and the emperors Tiberius, Caligula, and, for a time, Claudius oversaw it as an imperial province. However, in AD 44, Claudius granted Achaia the status of a senatorial province once again (Suetonius, *Deified Claudius* 25; Dio Cassius, *Roman History* 60.24.1). See Wiseman, "Corinth and Rome I," 503.

53. The Corinthian forum measured 656 feet east to west and 328 feet north to south. For a concise description of these monuments, see Sanders, Palinkas, Tzonou-Herbst with Herbst, *Ancient Corinth*, 30–85. Winter, *Divine Honours*, 186, is certainly incorrect that the Archaic Temple "was the only structure the Roman colonists had preserved from Greek Corinth."

54. Mary E. Hoskins Walbank, "The Cults of Roman Corinth: Public Ritual and Personal Belief," in *Society, Economy and Culture under the Roman Empire: Continuity and Innovation*, vol. 3 of *Roman Peloponnese*, ed. A. D. Rizakis and C. E. Lepenioti (Athens: de Boccard, 2010), 357–74, quotation 372, concludes, "The city was able to exploit its ambiguity by identifying with the Greek world yet retaining a Roman identity separate from it."

public identity.[55] Moreover, the colony oversaw the panhellenic Isthmian Games, which brought Greeks from all over the Mediterranean world to the city and its environs (for more on these games, see pp. 196–99). The somewhat hellenized Roman identity of Corinth can be traced to the colony's aristocratic rulers. During the Julio-Claudian period, these consisted of freedmen who were mostly Greek and of Roman *negotiatores* who had lived in the Greek East for generations before making Corinth home. Thus, these latter individuals had much opportunity to be and were influenced by Hellenic culture.[56] Despite this situation, as we will see, imperial divine honors in the colony remained largely Roman in character, which must have been intentional.

Imperial Divine Honors in Corinth

Corinthian inscriptions, coins, statues, and archaeological remains allow for the reconstruction of imperial divine honors in the colony with startling precision. These sources demonstrate that such honors largely followed Roman imperial divine honors with few exceptions. These exceptions, however, kept with the Roman practice of postmortem imperial divine honors. In what follows, I reconstruct the honors in question in Corinth. I begin by presenting the sources for these honors in roughly chronological order of the Julio-Claudians on whom they were bestowed. Then, I explore the identity of the imperial cultic officials in the colony, parsing out who they were and the other public offices that they held in the city. Finally, I address the location where these cultic officials offered imperial sacrifices to the Julio-Claudians as well as how and when these offerings were made.

Divus Julius (Caesar)

The first Julio-Claudian granted divine honors in Corinth was the colony's deceased and divinized founder, Julius Caesar. These honors postdate Caesar's death,

---

55. *RPC* 1.1116–17, 1121, 1125, 1127–28, 1145, 1147, 1162–64, 1166, 1169–73, 1181, 1201.

56. See the excellent studies by Benjamin W. Millis, "The Social and Ethnic Origins of the Colonists in Early Roman Corinth," in *Corinth in Context: Comparative Studies on Religion and Society*, ed. Steven J. Friesen, Daniel N. Schowalter, and James C. Walters (Leiden: Brill, 2010), 13–36; Millis, "The Local Magistrates and Elite of Roman Corinth," in *Corinth in Contrast: Studies in Inequality*, ed. Steven J. Friesen, Sarah A. James, and Daniel N. Schowalter (Leiden: Brill, 2014), 38–53. This situation is somewhat unique to Roman Corinth, because in most colonies, such as Philippi, freedmen were not allowed to hold public offices. Their children, however, were. This means that the freedmen in Corinth were able to enter public office earlier than freedmen in other Roman communities.

Fig. 4.2 Marble base that may have held a statue of *Divus* Julius Caesar from Corinth's theater, Inv. # 2178 | *Photo by author*

but the city may have bestowed them before the Roman Senate's divinization of the slain dictator on January 1, AD 42. Two fragmentary Latin inscriptions and one cultic statue that may have depicted Caesar provide direct evidence for these honors, and one inscription attests to knowledge of his divinization. The latter epigraph is in Greek, inscribed on marble, and dates between AD 43 and 54. Much of its text is missing, because the marble block was probably reused as a doorstep with the letters facing up, resulting in their effacement. It is unclear where in Corinth this epigraph was originally set up, because it was not found in situ or in its original location. This hinders the interpretation of the inscription, and, as we shall see, many other such Corinthian epigraphs that we examine in this chapter. These difficulties notwithstanding, what survives of the inscription contains a list of winners of games for Augustus, Tiberius, and Livia (for more on these games, see pp. 196–200). Its text indicates that the contests were celebrated for Caesar Augustus, "son of a god" (*theou huion*), which is the Greek translation of the Latin phrase *divi filius*. The *theos* in question is *Divus* Julius.[57]

The first epigraph directly attesting to divine honors for Julius Caesar in Corinth is a dedication to the murdered dictator engraved on a marble block, possibly a base that held a statue of him, that was found in Corinth's theater (see

57. "Appendix 1: Inscriptions" §4.1, line 2.

fig. 4.2). The text indicates that something has been consecrated to *"Divus* Julius Caesar" (*divo Iu*[*lio*] *Caesari*).[58] Caesar's name is peculiar in this epigraph and differs from how it appears elsewhere in Corinth and in other Roman sources, such as inscriptions from Philippi that we have already seen.[59] Most often, the divinized ruler is called *Divus* Julius, the official name that the Roman Senate bestowed on him on January 1, 42 BC.[60] This unusual *Divus* Julius Caesar suggests that Corinth granted him divine honors between his death (March 15, 44 BC) and divinization in Rome, after which the name *Divus* Julius became standard.[61] Three reasons support this proposal. First, the Roman Senate had hailed Caesar as *divus* and appointed Antony as his *flamen* in 44 BC before his death.[62] As noted, Antony probably spent time in Corinth between 39 and 36 BC and may have promoted divine honors for Caesar during his visit.[63] Second, Caesar founded Corinth, and the local

58. "Appendix 1: Inscriptions" §4.2. Catherine de Grazia Vanderpool, "Julius Caesar and Divus Iulius in Corinth: Man, Memory, and Cult," in *What's New in Roman Greece? Recent Work on the Greek Mainland and the Islands in the Roman Period*, ed. Valentina Di Napoli et al., Meletemata 80 (Athens: National Hellenic Research Foundation, 2018), 369–78, esp. 369–70, contends that this "block" is a statue base, presumably of *Divus* Julius. Miller, "Imperial Cult," 330, concludes this dedication is "likely" proof of divine honors for *Divus* Julius, even though "this title would not necessitate the existence of the cult." However, he notes that "another inscription" references a "high priest of the first provincial imperial priest of Achaia," which evinces divine honors for the divinized dictator. Miller's reasoning and use of Corinthian sources is flawed. Aside from the fact that "Appendix 1: Inscriptions" §4.2 probably commemorates something consecrated *to Divus* Julius, it is unclear whether the Achaian provincial imperial divine honors involved *Divus* Julius, for they focused on "the Augustan house" (see pp. 214–15). Moreover, Miller's "another inscription" ("Appendix 1: Inscriptions" §4.3) indicates that the person who served as the first provincial imperial high priest also served as *flamen* of *Divus* Julius, a fact he fails to mention.

59. "Appendix 1: Inscriptions" §4.3; 2.2, 3.

60. Suetonius, *Deified Julius*, 88.

61. Mary Walbank, "Evidence for the Imperial Cult in Julio-Claudian Corinth," in *Subject and Ruler: The Cult of the Ruling Power in Classical Antiquity; Papers Presented at a Conference Held in the University of Alberta on April 13–15, 1994, to Celebrate the 65th Anniversary of Duncan Fishwick*, ed. Alastair Small (Ann Arbor: Journal of Roman Archaeology, 1996), 201–2.

62. After Julius Caesar's military victories in winter of 45/44 BC, the Roman Senate voted a number of divine honors to Caesar during his lifetime, which included the title *divus* and a *flaminia* resembling that of Jupiter, Mars, and Quirinus (the divinized Romulus). This priesthood, along with other divine honors that the senate bestowed, appears not to have been inaugurated before Caesar's assassination (Cicero, *Philippics* 2.110–111), because either he refused them or some senators, like Cicero, *Philippics* 13.41; 2.111, realized their impropriety. For a discussion of these honors, see Ittai Gradel, *Emperor Worship and Roman Religion* (Oxford: Clarendon, 2002), 54–72.

63. Walbank, "Evidence for the Imperial Cult," 202, notes, "Corinth was his administrative

aristocrats of the new colony owed their power and prestige to him. Many of these original colonists were Roman freedman who, under normal circumstances, were ineligible to hold public office. Their children, however, could. Caesar appears to have made an exception for these Corinthian freedmen, allowing them to serve in public offices, for which they would have been grateful and his divinization would have been entirely appropriate.[64] Third, Rome had a tradition of honoring divinely its founder, Romulus. According to Roman tradition, Romulus, along with his brother Remus, founded Rome. The former ruled the city until his mysterious disappearance, which some legends interpreted as his ascension into heaven as the new Roman god Quirinus.[65] For these reasons, Corinth probably bestowed cultic honors on Caesar after his death but before his Roman divinization.

The second inscription attesting to divine honors for Julius Caesar in Corinth dates between AD 54 and 58 and is found on a statue base that once held the image of a Corinthian benefactor, an equestrian (the second highest rank in the Roman Empire) named Gaius Julius Spartiaticus, that a Corinthian tribe set up to honor the latter.[66] It is unclear where the colonists placed this monument originally, because archaeologists did not find the base in situ but built into a ramp dating to the Byzantine period. This uncertainty notwithstanding, the inscription provides Spartiaticus's résumé of public offices, one of which was that he was the "*flamen* of *Divus* Julius" (*flam(ini) divi Iuli*).[67] This epigraph is the only evidence for this priesthood in the colony and testifies to the strong affinity that the colonists had for their founder. Most often, divine honors for *Divus* Julius in other Roman communities were subsumed into those of other Julio-Claudians.[68] This was not the case at Corinth, where a priesthood for Caesar is attested almost one hundred years after his divinization.

The statue identified as *Divus* Julius is a marble image over eight feet tall that excavators found in the southern portion of a building called the Julian Basilica, which

---

base for the Peloponnese . . . and Antony's head appears on a Corinthian coin issue between 39 and 36 B.C. It is a reasonable assumption that Antony would have favoured, or perhaps even initiated, the establishment of a cult of Divus Iulius at Corinth."

64. Millis, "Local Magistrates," 38–53.

65. Cicero, *On the Republic* 2.10 (17–18). For more on Quirinus and Romulus, see Herbert Jennings Rose and John Scheid, "Quirinus," *OCD* 1253; Herbert Jennings Rose and John Scheid, "Romulus, Remus," *OCD* 1296–97.

66. For the dating of this inscription, see Antony J. S. Spawforth, "Corinth, Argos, and the Imperial Cult: Pseudo-Julian, *Letters* 198," *Hesperia* 63 (1994): 218–21.

67. "Appendix 1: Inscriptions" §4.3, lines 5–6.

68. Walbank, "Evidence for the Imperial Cult," 202.

Fig. 4.3 Marble statue, probably of *Divus* Julius, from Corinth's Julian Basilica, S-1098 | *Photo by author*

I discuss in detail below, located on the forum's eastern end just north of the South Stoa (see figs. 4.1, 3). The image's head is missing, and only the torso remains. However, what survives resembles the statues of Augustus and probably Claudius from Thessalonica, which depicted these Julio-Claudians in a Zeus-like guise (see figs. 3.6, 9). In similar fashion, the Corinthian statue is nude from the waist up with a toga wrapped around the image's lower half, the excess of which is draped over the left arm, which recalls Jupiter. The image was made in either Augustus's (31 BC–AD 14) or Tiberius's reign (AD 14–37) and thus post-dates Julius Caesar's divinization by some time.[69] As I discuss below, provided that this image is of *Divus* Julius, it was probably the focal point of the Julian Basilica's imperial shrine.[70]

Octavia

The next relative of Augustus whom Corinth divinely honored is his sister and onetime wife of Antony, Octavia. This grant of divine honors is unique for three

69. Catherine de Grazia Vanderpool, "Catalogue of Sculpture," in *The Julian Basilica: Architecture, Sculpture, Epigraphy*, vol. 22 of *Corinth: Results of Excavations Conducted by the American School of Classical Studies at Athens* (Princeton: American School of Classical Studies at Athens, 2022), 327–35, S-7.

70. De Grazia Vanderpool, "Julius Caesar," 370–72, notes that a second marble statue that may have depicted Julius Caesar has been found in Corinth. The image consists of a marble head dating to the Julio-Claudian period, the measurements of which mean that the statue originally stood six and a half feet. The head was found in a drain of the Peirene Fountain (see fig. 4.1), where it had been placed in the sixth century AD. Given this context, it is impossible to know whether this was a cultic image.

reasons. First, she is neither a Julian nor a Claudian. Second, to date, divine honors for her are unattested in any other Roman colony.[71] Third, this is the only example of Corinthian divine honors for someone connected to Augustus that is attested by a surviving literary work. The book in question is by the second-century AD geographer Pausanias, who traveled around mainland Greece and composed a travel guide in Greek known as the *Description of Greece*. One of his stops was Corinth, where Pausanias notes that there was a *naos* of Octavia near the city's forum:

> Now *hyper* the marketplace is the *naos* of Octavia, sister of Augustus who reigned over the Romans after Caesar, the present founder of Corinth.[72]

Several scholars translate the Greek preposition *hyper* as "above" and the Greek noun *naos* as "temple," identifying the *naos* of Octavia as the largest temple complex in Corinth, Temple E (see fig. 4.1).[73] However, Pausanias's Greek is imprecise. When used with the accusative case, the case in question, *hyper* can mean "above," "over," or "beyond."[74] So, where exactly Pausanias meant is unclear. Moreover, the Greek noun *naos* can mean "temple," "shrine," "innermost part of a temple," or "portable shrine."[75] The Latin term frequently used to translate *naos*, *aedes*, carries the same flexibility, and, as we shall see, there was an *aedes* of Augustan Apollo in an area of Corinth known in antiquity as Ten Shops, which was not a large temple but a small shrine. Thus, Pausanias's reference to Octavia's *naos* needs not have been to a literal temple.

Some scholars have concluded that Octavia's *naos* is a temple that some Corinthian coins depict.[76] The coins in question picture a temple with the inscription "(Dedicated to) the Julian Family" (*Gent(i) Iuli*) on its architrave (or horizontal stone block atop columns) on their reverses (see fig. 4.13), while their obverses depict the busts of Augustus, Tiberius, and Livia (for more on this temple, see pp. 204–6). However, because some other Corinthian coins, which do not contain

71. Mary E. Hoskins Walbank, "Pausanias, Octavia and Temple E at Corinth," *ABSA* 84 (1989): 361–94, esp. 370–73, notes there is no evidence for any Roman, not Greek, city bestowing divine honors on Octavia: "no evidence of any cult, altar or temple." Thus, for Walbank, no Corinthian *naos* of Octavia existed: "it is difficult to accept or explain Pausanias's identification."

72. ὑπὲρ δὲ τὴν ἀγορὰν ἐστιν Ὀκταβίας ναὸς ἀδελφῆς Αὐγούστου βασιλεύσαντος Ῥωμαίων μετὰ Καίσαρα τὸν οἰκιστὴν Κορίνθου τῆς νῦν (Pausanias, *Description of Greece* 2.3.1).

73. Georges Roux, *Pausanias en Corinthe (livre II, I à 15): Texte, traduction, commentaire archéologique et topographie* (Paris: Les Belles Lettres, 1958), 112–16.

74. LSJ 1857–58, esp. 1858; BDAG 1030–31, esp. 1031.

75. LSJ 1160; BDAG 665–66.

76. Roux, *Pausanias en Corinthe*, 113; F. Imhoof-Blumer and P. Gardner, "Numismatic Commentary on Pausanias," *JHS* 6 (1885): 50–101, esp. 71. As we shall see below, some scholars even contend that the Julian Family Temple, the *naos* of Octavia, and Temple E are one and the same.

an image of the Julian Family Temple, picture a seated female figure on the obverse (see fig. 4.14), many of these same historians have identified this enthroned woman as Octavia or the Julian family line in the guise of Octavia and gone so far as to conclude that the image on these coins is the cultic image of Octavia's *naos*, even though there is no direct link between the Julian Family Temple and the seated female figure.[77] Establishing a connection between the Julian Family Temple and Octavia from the different sides of unrelated coins is inappropriate methodologically. Hence, such a conclusion is implausible. Moreover, one important bit of biographical information about Octavia argues against any connection between the Julian Family Temple and her: Octavia was not a Julian.

Because of this difficulty, a few scholars dismiss Pausanias's testimony outright, concluding that he is wrong. But the uniqueness and specificity of Pausanias's claim—that Octavia's *naos*, not known in any other Roman colony, existed in Corinth—supports his accuracy. Given the flexibility of the meaning of *naos* and its Latin counterpart *aedes*, Octavia's *naos* was probably a shrine in or near the forum. The reason why it has not been identified is that archaeologists have yet to discover it, yet to identify it (or to identify it correctly), or they will never identify it, because Octavia's *naos* was dismantled sometime after Pausanias visited the city. If my suggestion is correct, it remains unclear whether Corinth erected this shrine while Octavia was alive or after her death in 11 BC. That the colony waited until all Julio-Claudians, even its founder Julius Caesar, died before it granted them divine honors suggests that Octavia's *naos* was erected postmortem. If this is correct, then Corinth broke with the mother city in this regard, for Rome did not divinize Octavia after her death. It is possible that she provided some benefaction for the city on her likely sojourn in Corinth with Antony between 39 and 36 BC or afterward, which may account for this grant of postmortem divine honors.

Gaius Caesar and Lucius Caesar

The second and third Julio-Claudians whom Corinth granted divine honors are Augustus's two adopted sons, Gaius Caesar and Lucius Caesar, Augustus's biological grandsons, the children of his colleague Marcus Agrippa and his daughter Julia. Gaius was born around 20 BC and Lucius 17 BC. Augustus adopted the

---

77. Imhoof-Blumer and Gardner, "Numismatic Commentary on Pausanias," 71, conclude, "The seated lady holding sceptre and patera may be copied from the statue in this temple [the Julian Family Temple]." They go on to suggest that the image is not of Octavia but the personification of the Julian family "in the likeness of Octavia," which may have led Pausanias to deduce that the temple belonged to her.

brothers shortly after the latter's birth. As soon as they were able, they began their public careers in service of the empire. Lucius's first imperial post was a provincial command in Spain. On the way, however, sickness struck him, and he died on August 20, AD 2. Two years later, Augustus sent Gaius to the east to parley with Parthia (a rival empire whose center was in modern-day Iran) and to appoint a new king of Armenia, a kingdom between the Roman and Parthian Empires. This appointment resulted in a revolt by some Armenians that Gaius had to quell. In the process, the young commander neared a walled city to negotiate with its inhabitants. Gaius, however, came too close to the wall, and he was fatally wounded. On February 21, AD 4, he, too, died.[78] The Roman Senate did not divinize these two deceased young men.[79] Nevertheless, sometime between AD 4 and the end of Tiberius's reign, Corinth set up two nude statues of Gaius Caesar and Lucius Caesar in the guise of the two famous Greek twins Castor and Pollux (or Polydeuces as the Greeks called him), the Dioscuri, in the Julian Basilica, probably in a space all their own on the northeastern side of the building (see figs. 4.4, 5).[80]

Fig. 4.4 Marble statue of Gaius Caesar from Corinth's Julian Basilica, S-1080 | *Photo by author*

78. Adrian Goldsworthy, *Augustus: First Emperor of Rome* (New Haven: Yale University Press, 2014), 423–25.

79. At this point in Rome's history, Julius Caesar was the only divinized Julio-Claudian.

80. De Grazia Vanderpool, "Catalogue of Sculpture," 339–43, S-10; 343–46, S-11. Catherine de Grazia Vanderpool, "The Julio-Claudian Family Group," in *The Julian Basilica: Architecture, Sculpture, Epigraphy*, vol. 22 of *Corinth: Results of Excavations Conducted by the American School of Classical Studies at Athens* (Princeton: American School of Classical Studies at Athens, 2022), 276, notes, "There are no known instances where Gaius and Lucius are shown nude during their lifetimes."

In some versions of the Greek myth, Castor and Pollux were two sons of Zeus who were great athletes and shared immortality between them, while in others, they had human parents, but because of their athletic prowess, they were singularly honored by the gods.[81] In each version, because of their love for each other, they alternated living and dying for a day. A fragment of an early Greek epic connected to Corinth indicates that Castor and Pollux competed in the first Isthmian Games (for more on these games, see pp. 196–99). Castor won the foot race (*stadion*), while Pollux won the boxing event (*pygmē*).[82]

When excavators uncovered the image of Gaius on the northeastern side of the Julian Basilica, it contained paint residue, as did the

Fig. 4.5 Marble statue of Lucius Caesar from Corinth's Julian Basilica, S-1065 | *Photo by author*

statue of Augustus from the same location and an image that may be of Augustus that was found in the theater, both of which I discuss below. Thus, the images of Gaius and Lucius were both brightly decorated with paint and not the color of cold marble. Moreover, they were probably the object of postmortem sacrifices, for which no evidence survives.[83] While this is another case in which Corinth appears to have deviated

81. For the first version, see Pindar, *Nemean Odes* 10.49–59. For the second version of the myth, see Homer, *Odyssey* 11.298–304.

82. Christos Tsagalis, "Eumelos of Corinth," in *Early Greek Epic Fragments I: Antiquarian and Genealogical Epic*, ed. Franco Montanari and Antonios Rengakos, Trends in Classics 47 (Berlin: de Gruyter, 2017), 29–30, fragment 23.

83. De Grazia Vanderpool, "Julio-Claudian Family Group," 278, contends, "The fact that the pair may have occupied their own space in the basilica, far from the other statues, suggests the possibility that they were conceptualized separately and served a different function, perhaps as objects of hero cult that paid honors to them in their deaths as a way of honoring the imperial house."

from the Roman practice of divine honors for *divi*, the city's actions may have followed a decree of the Roman Senate, which the colony interpreted in light of its own customs. According to an inscription from the Roman colony of Pisa in northwestern Italy, because the Roman Senate decreed some "honors" (*honores*; exactly which ones are unclear) for Lucius Caesar, Pisa passed a decree of its own, legislating postmortem divine honors for Lucius. In the process, the colony erected an altar dedicated to "his departed spirit" (*manibus eius*). On August 20 (the day that Lucius died) of every year, Pisa's magistrates and *duoviri* dressed in black togas and offered a black bull and ram over which they poured milk, honey, and oil to Lucius's departed spirit on that altar. Moreover, the city permitted any private individual who wished to make "offerings to the deceased" (*inferiae*) to do so.[84] Similarly, after Gaius Caesar died, the colony decreed that its magistrates and *duoviri* had to make public offerings to "his departed spirit" (*manibus eius*) on the anniversary of his death (February 21), too, "in the same place and in the same manner" (*eodem loco eodemque modo*) as it offered sacrifices to Lucius Caesar.[85] It is unclear whether the Roman Senate had made any decree related to Gaius, but given that it did after Lucius passed, it may have. Thus, the honors that Corinth established for Lucius and Gaius may have followed the mother city's senate to some extent, and they, at least the honors for Lucius, appear to have continued into the second century AD. A Corinthian Greek inscription contains a list of victors of imperial games that Corinth hosted (see pp. 197–200), which included an equestrian event that was held "for Lucius Caesar, Augustus's son."[86] While postmortem divine honors for the brothers may stem from a senatorial decree, the depicting of Gaius and Lucius as the Dioscuri may relate to the Corinthian tradition that the latter competed in the first set of the Isthmian Games. If this is the case, then the colony interpreted the Roman Senate's decreed honors for the brothers as divine and in light of its own unique customs.

Divus Augustus

As is the case with Philippi and Thessalonica, most evidence for imperial divine honors in Corinth relates to Augustus. This evidence consists of epigraphs (nine, possibly eleven, to date), one statue that was erected after his death and diviniza-

---

84. *ILS* 139. I am indebted to de Grazia Vanderpool, "Julio-Claudian Family Group," 276, for the reference to the inscriptions from Pisa. Lucius was a patron of Pisa, for another inscription from the colony erected in AD 4 calls him "our patron" (*patroni nostri* [*ILS* 140, line 15]).

85. *ILS* 140.

86. ἐπὶ Λ(ουκίου) Καίσαρις Σεβαστοῦ υ[ἱοῦ] ("Appendix 1: Inscriptions" §4.13, lines 32–33).

Fig. 4.6 Statue base from Corinth's forum that once held the statue of *Divus* Augustus | *Photo by author*

tion (September 14, AD 14), and one image set up after Augustus's passing that may depict him.[87] These two statues, provided that the latter depicts Augustus, may have been used in imperial cultic rituals. I introduce these images here but discuss them further below when I address where Corinthian imperial divine honors were located (see pp. 207–11). With few exceptions, the inscriptions in question are either dedications to *Divus* Augustus or epigraphs acknowledging his divinization. Excavators found most of these in the forum, some of which were in excavated buildings. These inscriptions showcase that Corinth bestowed postmortem divine honors on Augustus after the Roman Senate divinized him.[88] Three of these epigraphs attest to

87. "Appendix 1: Inscriptions" §4.1, 3, 4, 5, 6, 7, 8, 9, 10, and possibly 11, 12.

88. Corinth had its own reasons for establishing postmortem divine honors for *Divus* Augustus. The colony became the capital of the province of Achaia, and it flourished under his reign, especially toward the end of it, as the archaeological records attest to Corinth's expansion and growth. By the mid-first century AD, the city was able to boast of magnificent buildings, such as the Julian Basilica, Temple E, and several others.

Fig. 4.7 The statue base of *Divus* Augustus from Corinth's forum | *Reconstruction by Margaret Laird; used with permission*

knowledge of Augustus's postmortem divinization in Corinth, but not necessarily to divine honors.[89] I will begin with these latter epigraphs, after which I discuss those inscriptions that evidence divine honors for *Divus* Augustus.

89. "Appendix 1: Inscriptions" §4.1, 4, 5.

The first inscription acknowledging the emperor's divinization is composed in Latin, dates to AD 66/67, is engraved on marble, and consists of three fragments, one of which was found in the Julian Basilica. The epigraph appears to commemorate the dedication of an unknown object to the emperor Nero. In the process, it calls

him "the great-great-grandson of *Divus* Augustus" ([...*pro · nepoti ·*] [*divi*] *· Aug(usti)*).[90] The editors of this inscription have restored the title *divus* before Augustus's name, which is probably correct, because after his divinization, *Divus* Augustus was his official title. The second epigraph is a fragmentary Latin inscription inscribed on marble in two fragments, which is another dedication of an unknown object. This one, however, is to the emperor Tiberius.

Fig. 4.8 Bench on the statue of *Divus* Augustus in the forum with its butt grooves | *Photo by author*

Based on Tiberius's imperial title and what letters remain, the editor of the inscription has restored his lineage as "son of *Divus* Augustus" ([... *Tiberio · divi · Au*]*gusti*), which, again, is a probable restoration.[91] The third epigraph that refers to Augustus's postmortem divinization is one that we have already seen, the Greek inscription calling Augustus "son of a god" (*theou huion*). In addition to indirectly acknowledging *Divus* Julius's divine status, the epigraph does the same for *Divus* Augustus, as it calls the emperor Tiberius *theou Sebastou hu[ion]* or "son of the god Augustus," which is the Greek translation of the Latin phrase *divi filius*.[92]

Five of the nine, possibly eleven, inscriptions associated with Augustus directly attest to postmortem divine honors for him as *Divus* Augustus in Corinth.[93] Two of these are sacred dedications to the divinized emperor. Both are composed in

90. "Appendix 1: Inscriptions" §4.4, lines 4–5.
91. "Appendix 1: Inscriptions" §4.5.
92. "Appendix 1: Inscriptions" §4.1, line 5.
93. "Appendix 1: Inscriptions" §4.6, 7, 8, 9, 10.

Latin, fragmentary, engraved on marble, and postdate Augustus's divinization in Rome. The first was found in four pieces in the South Stoa on the forum's southern end (see fig. 4.1) and resembles the dedication to *Divus* Julius Caesar noted above, as it indicates that some object has been dedicated to "*Divus* Augustus" ([*d*]*ivo* [*Au*]*gusto*).[94] The second Latin epigraph consists of four fragments, with three of these being found in the southeastern portion of the forum (see fig. 4.1). When these pieces were assembled, they revealed that the inscription is a "sacred dedication" that a certain Corinthian citizen made to "*Divus* Augustus" ([*divo A*]*ugus*[*to*] [*sac*]*rum*) because of his justice (*ob iustiam*; *iustia* being the Latin equivalent of the Greek *dikaiosynē*).[95] The next Latin epigraph contains the only known reference to a priest of *Divus* Augustus in Corinth. The inscription dates to the emperor Claudius's reign (AD 41–54), was inscribed on limestone, and was found built into a wall in the northwestern part of the forum (see fig. 4.1). Therefore, the epigraph's original location remains unknown. The inscription's text indicates that a client set up a monument for his benefactor, listing the latter's résumé. The public office that most concerns me is that he served as *flamen* of

Fig. 4.9 Marble statue of *Divus* Augustus from Corinth's Julian Basilica, S-1116 | *Photo by author*

Augustus (*fla*[*men*] *Aug*[*usti*]).[96] For reasons unknown, *divus* has been omitted from the epigraph, which may be an error of the person who drafted the text of the inscription or the stonecutter who inscribed it.[97] Nevertheless, it is certain

---

94. "Appendix 1: Inscriptions" §4.6.

95. "Appendix 1: Inscriptions" §4.7.

96. "Appendix 1: Inscriptions" §4.8, line 7.

97. For a discussion of mistakes in inscriptions, see D. Clint Burnett, *Studying the New Testament: An Introduction* (Peabody, MA: Hendrickson, 2020), 16–20.

that the title belongs in the text. The fourth inscription attesting to divine honors for *Divus* Augustus comes from the fragmentary remains of a marble altar that postdates the emperor's death, which archaeologists found in an imperial shrine in the Julian Basilica (see pp. 207–9) (see fig. 4.1) and the building on the eastern end of the forum north of the South Stoa. The epigraph on the altar indicates that some Corinthian citizens dedicated it to "*Divus* Augustus" ([*Divo*] *August*[*o . . .*]) at their own expense.[98]

The final epigraph attesting to post-mortem divine honors for *Divus* Augustus is a fragmentary Latin epigraph, engraved on marble, and dating to Tiberius's reign (AD 14–37) that was connected to a monument that held a statue, probably of bronze, of the divinized emperor that has not survived. The inscription's text acknowledges that a group known as the *Augustales* set up this monument and dedicated it to "*Divus* Augustus" ([*divo A*]*ugus*[*to . . .*]) (for more on the *Augustales*, see pp. 200–202) (see figs. 4.6, 7, 8).[99]

This monument was imposing. Based on the size of the imprint of the statue's right foot, two and a half feet long, the image of *Divus* Augustus was between eight and ten feet tall (see fig. 4.6). Moreover, at the time when this monument was set up, the base itself, which was cylindrical and made of limestone, was probably over eight feet

Fig. 4.10 Marble statue, possibly of *Divus* Augustus, from Corinth's theater, T-389 | *Photo by author*

above the pavement of the forum. This means that the monument's total height was between sixteen and eighteen feet. Along with the bronze of the actual statue, the base was covered with plaster and some kind of revetment, probably marble,

98. "Appendix 1: Inscriptions" §4.9, line 1. This inscription is one that my earlier work on Corinthian imperial divine honors, "Divine Titles," did not consider, because of its fragmentary state, and the identification of it as an altar occurred after my initial research and acceptance of the article for publication in early 2017. Unfortunately, my work did not appear in print until 2020.

99. "Appendix 1: Inscriptions" §4.10.

and there were four benches for sitting at the bottom of it (see fig. 4.7).[100] The monument's orientation, facing westward toward Temple E, means that this giant image of *Divus* Augustus observed the activity associated with that temple (see fig. 4.1) (for more on Temple E, see pp. 211–14).[101] It is unclear whether this statue was associated with imperial cultic ritual. It is possible that this is the case, but the kind of cultic honors that would have occurred before it, sacrifices, leave no trace in the archaeological record.

The statue that unquestionably depicts Augustus and that may have been used in imperial divine honors is a marble image of the emperor. The statue was found in the southwestern portion of the basement (or cryptoporticus) of the Julian Basilica (see figs. 4.1, 9). It is of exquisite quality and pictures Augustus in a pious manner: with his toga pulled atop the back of his head in a posture that we have seen already, *capite velato*, which was one that Romans, not Greeks, assumed when they prayed, prophesied, or sacrificed (cf. 1 Cor 11:2–16).[102] The statue's left and right forearms along with hands are missing, but his right hand probably held a *lituus* or curved wand that Roman augurs used to measure out a space whence to practice augury. Augustus's left hand may have held a scroll.[103] Moreover, when this image was found, there were traces of paint on its eyes and lips. Thus, like the statue of Gaius Caesar, this statue was not the color of cold marble but was vibrantly decorated.[104] While some have dated this image to Augustus's lifetime, the art historian who produced the latest and official publication of this statue, Catherine de Grazia Vanderpool, contends that it was set up during Tiberius's reign.[105] This is important because of the manner in which the statue depicts Augustus. It does not picture him as a *divus* in the guise of Jupiter, as another image, discussed below, may (see fig. 4.10), but as a pious Roman who interprets signs

100. Margaret L. Laird, "The Emperor in a Roman Town: The Base of the *Augustales* in the Forum at Corinth," in *Corinth in Context: Comparative Studies on Religion and Society*, ed. Steven J. Friesen, Dan N. Showalter, and James C. Walters (Leiden: Brill, 2010), 67–116, esp. 67–84.

101. Laird, "Emperor in a Roman Town," 93, observes of this orientation, "If this building was the town's imperial cult center, deified Augustus would observe rituals performed in his honor. However, a more complex relationship would arise if Temple E were the Capitolium. In this case the image of a deified emperor in the guise of Jupiter might gaze towards the cult site of the god to which he was assimilated."

102. Richard E. Oster, "When Men Wore Veils to Worship: The Historical Context of 1 Corinthians 11.4," *NTS* 34 (1988): 481–505.

103. De Grazia Vanderpool, "Catalogue of Sculpture," 299–306, S-1.

104. De Grazia Vanderpool, "Julio-Claudian Family Group," 269–70, notes, "Augustus's eyes were painted with iris and pupil, and his lips given a reddish hue, but the color vanished almost immediately."

105. De Grazia Vanderpool, "Catalogue of Sculpture," 299–306, S-1.

and omens to determine the will of the gods.[106] It is probable, especially given that excavators found the altar dedicated to *Divus* Augustus near this image, that the statue was used in imperial cultic activity. However, if such rituals occurred, they have left no trace in the archaeological record.[107]

The statue that may depict *Divus* Augustus and might have been the object of imperial sacrifice was found in Corinth's theater (see fig. 4.1) in 1926 (see fig. 4.10). It is an over-life-size marble statue of a male figure, which dates between Tiberius's (AD 14–37) and Claudius's reigns (AD 41–54). The image's head, the most important part of a statue for identification purposes, is missing, as well as the feet, the left hand, and the entire right arm. What remains of the statue depicts a half-naked male figure in a Jupiter-like posture. A mantle is wrapped around the image's lower body, the excess of which is draped over his left arm. Astonishingly, there are traces, much in places, of paint on the statue, which indicates that, like the images of Gaius and Augustus Caesar, this one was also decorated. Quite a bit of red pigment remains on the mantle as well as light brown and yellowish brown pigment on the hips and legs. The art historian who published the statue, Mary Sturgeon, proposes that it "very likely represents an emperor" and probably Augustus.[108] Because of the image's high quality, she suggests that the image depicts him as a *divus*.[109] As I discuss below (see pp. 210–11), this statue may have been used in imperial cultic celebrations that possibly occurred in Corinth's theater but have left no trace in the material record.

Alongside the epigraphs attesting to and statuary possibly testifying to postmortem divine honors for *Divus* Augustus, two Corinthian inscriptions may evidence divine honors connected to the emperor while he was alive.[110] The first is composed in Latin, inscribed on three fragments of marble, and dates broadly to the first and second centuries AD. Archaeologists found it in the southern portion of the Julian Basilica, and the epigraph may have been set up in this part of the building (see fig. 4.1). It is a dedication not to Augustus's person but to his *genius* and that of the colony's that a local aristocrat paid for.[111] As we have seen, Romans believed that people, places, and things such as political entities possessed a *genius*, which was

106. De Grazia Vanderpool, "Julio-Claudian Family Group," 237.

107. De Grazia Vanderpool, "Julio-Claudian Family Group," 280–84. For the altar, see "Appendix 1: Inscriptions" §4.9.

108. Mary C. Sturgeon, *Sculpture: The Assemblage from the Theater*, vol. 9, part 3 of *Corinth: Results of Excavations Conducted by the American School of Classical Studies at Athens* (Princeton: American School of Classical Studies, 2004), 66–68, no. 2.

109. Sturgeon, *Sculpture*, 67.

110. "Appendix 1: Inscriptions" §4.11, 12.

111. "Appendix 1: Inscriptions" §4.11.

a creative and protective power (see pp. 43–44). Thus, this inscription is not proof of divine honors for Augustus's person but of the creative protective power that watched over him and Corinth. On the one hand, this inscription is not unusual for a Roman colony. On the other hand, if this epigraph dates to the early Julio-Claudian period, then it deviates from Roman imperial divine honors. Recall chapter 1's discussion that the earliest evidence for public imperial divine honors in Rome associated with the reigning emperor's *genius* dates to AD 55. Such a deviation is unsurprising, because Roman colonies were not carbon copies of Rome. As we have seen, the Roman colony of Philippi granted postmortem divine honors to Tiberius, whom the Roman Senate did not divinize. Nevertheless, any firm conclusions about this Corinthian inscription are impossible because of the lack of precision in its dating. Therefore, it remains unclear whether this dedication was made to Augustus's *genius*, the adopted son of Julius Caesar, or that of another emperor, as all Julio-Claudian emperors were hailed as Augustus.

The second Corinthian epigraph that may attest to divine honors associated with Augustus while he was alive indicates that there was an *aedes* or "shrine" and a *statua* or "cultic statue" connected to Augustus in a commercial area of Corinth. The inscription is from a marble architrave, a horizontal stone piece resting atop the columns on the front of a building, that was found in the village that once existed on the site of Corinth. It broadly dates to the first century AD and refers to "a shrine and statue of *Apollonis Augusti* and Ten Shops" (*aedem · et · statuam · Apollonis Augusti · et · tabernas decem*) that four Corinthian aristocrats had constructed.[112] The interpretation of this inscription is difficult for two reasons. First, its date. It is unclear whether the epigraph dates to or after Augustus's reign, which ended in AD 14. Second, the translation of *Apollonis Augusti*. Literally, the text reads "Augustan Apollo." The question is where does the emphasis lie? Is it with Apollo or with Augustus? If the former, then the inscription identifies Apollo as having some relationship with Augustus. If the latter, then it stresses his identification as Apollo. We should reject the pairing of Augustus's name with Apollo's as identifying the emperor as some form of Apollo, for there was no such thing as the doctrine of the incarnation outside Christianity in the first-century Greco-Roman world.[113] Therefore, it seems most probable that this inscription attests to a relationship between Apollo and Augustus, for Augustus claimed a special connection to and the protection of this particular deity. According to ancient

112. "Appendix 1: Inscriptions" §4.12, line 3.
113. A. D. Nock, "Notes on Ruler-Cult I–IV," *JHS* 48 (1928): 35, notes, "There is not, therefore, in general a definite popular belief that a particular ruler is in a strict sense the reincarnation of a particular deity."

sources, it was rumored that Apollo was Augustus's father,[114] at one point in his life Augustus used a symbol of Apollo, the sphinx, as his personal seal,[115] and the emperor moved a temple of Apollo in Rome from outside the city's boundaries to the confines of his own house.[116] Thus, the Corinthian epigraph is probably not a shrine to Augustus who is identified as Apollo but to Apollo who protects the emperor. If this is correct, then the inscription in question likely dates to Augustus's reign.

Tiberius

Toward the end of Tiberius's life, he did not serve Rome's best interests. He retired to the island of Capri in AD 26, and he spent the rest of his days in gluttonous and homicidal behavior as well as debaucheries.[117] Thus, upon his death on March 16, AD 37, neither the Roman Senate nor Corinth divinized him. However, during his reign (AD 14–37), one Greek Corinthian poet, Honestus of Corinth, composed an epigram that was inscribed on a famous monument to the Muses on Mount Helicon in Thespiae in modern-day mainland Greece, in which he calls this emperor a god. The epigram is an encomium to Livia who, according to Honestus, boasts of "two gods with scepters" and who "has given light to two lights of peace."[118] In the inscription's context, these two gods and lights of peace are *Divus* Augustus and Tiberius. While this epigraph is not direct evidence of divine honors for Tiberius in Corinth, it records the perspective of one Corinthian, albeit a Greek speaking one, who considered Tiberius divine. That is, unless his words are poetic hyperbole. That Honestus thought of Tiberius as a god is interesting in light of the fact that there is no trace of divine honors for him in Corinth. Unfortunately, it is unclear whether any other Corinthians had similar convictions about this emperor and whether they did so while he was alive.

---

114. Suetonius, *Deified Augustus* 94.4; Dio Cassius, *Roman History* 45.1.2.

115. Suetonius, *Deified Augustus* 50; Dio Cassius, *Roman History* 51.3.6–7.

116. Mary Beard, John North, and Simon Price, *Religions of Rome*, 2 vols. (Cambridge: Cambridge University Press, 1998), 1:198–99.

117. Suetonius, *Tiberius* 41, 43–44, 62, 69.

118. ἡ δοιοὺς σκήπτροισι θεοὺς . . . εἰρήνης δισσὰ λέλαμπε φάη ("Appendix 1: Inscriptions" §4.14, lines 1–2). If Honestus thought of the deceased Augustus and reigning Tiberius as gods, it is worth pondering what he thought of Livia, who was married to the former and gave birth to the latter, or, in his words, one who "boasts" of them.

Diva Augusta

The fifth Julio-Claudian whom Corinth divinely honored is the second woman connected to Augustus, Livia. After her husband's death in AD 14, Livia was adopted into his family, and her name was changed to Augusta.[119] She died in AD 29 and was buried with Augustus in his mausoleum in Rome. Many people in Rome wanted the Roman Senate to divinize Augusta, but her son, Tiberius, refused. Therefore, she was not divinized.[120] That changed, however, when Augusta's grandson Claudius became emperor in AD 41. He oversaw her divinization on January 17, AD 42.[121] Soon after this, Corinth established postmortem divine honors for her.[122] To date, three inscriptions, one Greek and two Latin, attest to these postmortem divine honors. The first Latin epigraph is fragmentary, engraved on marble, dates to Claudius's reign, and indicates that the colony dedicated a building or part of one to *"Diva* Augusta" ([*div*]*ae · Aug*[*ustae* . . .]).[123] Like so many inscriptions in Corinth, archaeologists did not find this one in situ, so what exactly the city dedicated to her remains unknown. The other Latin inscription is inscribed on marble, dates to Claudius's reign, and is connected to imperial games that Corinth hosted (see pp. 196–200). As with the former epigraph, excavators did not find this artifact in situ but in a medieval wall that ran across the forum. The inscription's text contains the résumé of a Corinthian aristocrat. The public office that most concerns me is his time as *agōnothetēs* or president of the Isthmian Games and another set of games for the Julio-Claudians, during which time he instituted a poetry contest for *"Diva* Julia Augusta" ([. . . *ad · Iulia*]*m · di-va*[*m · Au*]*g*(*ustam*)).[124] The final epigraph associated with divine honors for *Diva* Augusta is composed in Greek and one that we have already seen. In discussions of *Divus* Julius and *Divus* Augustus, I noted that one inscription related to games that Corinth hosted implicitly acknowledges their divinizations in Rome by re-

119. Suetonius, *Deified Augustus* 101.2; Tacitus, *Annals* 1.8.

120. Tacitus, *Annals* 5.1–2; Dio Cassius, *Roman History* 58.1.1–6.

121. Suetonius, *Deified Claudius* 11.2; Dio Cassius, *Roman History* 60.5.1–5.

122. Corinth probably did not need much prodding to establish these divine honors, because the empress was an informal patroness of the colony. One Corinthian voting tribe was named after her (see table 4.1), and Augusta's image appears on coins that the city minted during her lifetime. On these coins, she is enthroned and holding an array of objects: a patera or shallow bowl whence one pours libations, a scepter (symbolizing her authority), and ears of corn (symbolizing her connection to the colony's fertility) (*RPC* 1.1149–50). Currently, there is no concrete evidence that Livia/Augusta provided a benefaction for the city, though it is likely that she did.

123. "Appendix 1: Inscriptions" §4.15, line 1.

124. "Appendix 1: Inscriptions" §4.16, line 9.

ferring to their respective sons Augustus and Tiberius as a *huios theou*, meaning *divi filius*. This epigraph references Livia's postmortem divinization, as it records that there was a poetry contest for "*thea* Julia Augusta" (*thean I[o]ulian Sebastēn*), *thea* being the Greek translation of *diva*.[125]

Divus Claudius

The sixth Julio-Claudian to whom Corinth probably granted divine honors is the last *divus* in the family, Claudius. I say "probably" because there is no direct evidence that the colony established such honors for him, that is, unless a statue that I discuss below depicts the emperor. After Claudius died and the Roman Senate divinized him on October 14, AD 54, Corinth probably set up divine honors for him when they heard of the senate's decision. While there is no extant evidence for this, during the emperor's lifetime, the colony interpreted Claudius's military achievements as munificent. In AD 43, Claudius sent an invasion force to take Britain. The Romans overwhelmed the Britons, and when word reached the emperor of the impending victory, he set out from Rome to Britain. Once he arrived, Claudius joined the army and engaged the remaining Britons in battle, at which the Romans were victorious. The Roman Senate granted Claudius and one of his sons the title Britannicus, voted Claudius a triumph, decreed a festival to commemorate the victory, and erected triumphant arches commemorating the emperor's victory.[126] Claudius then extended Rome's *pomerium* or "sacred boundary" in an act that demonstrated his expansion of the empire.[127] To show its appreciation for Claudius's victory, Corinth established a cult of *Britannia Victoria* or "Britannic Victory" and appointed a priest to oversee it. Only one such priest is attested in the epigraphic record, so it is unclear how long this cult lasted.[128] All this means that for reasons unknown, Corinth had an affinity for the emperor Claudius. Two Latin inscriptions that we have already examined attest that Corinth knew of Claudius's divinization in Rome, and one cultic statue from the colony may depict *Divus* Claudius. The first epigraph is one that we saw in connection with Corinth's knowledge of Augustus's divinized status: a fragmentary

125. "Appendix 1: Inscriptions" §4.1, line 9.

126. Dio Cassius, *Roman History* 60.19.1–60.22.2.

127. Tacitus, *Annals* 12.23; *CIL* 6.37022, 40416.

128. Carolynn Roncaglia, "Inscriptions," in *The Julian Basilica: Architecture, Sculpture, Epigraphy*, Vol. 22 of *Corinth: Results of Excavations Conducted by the American School of Classical Studies at Athens* (Princeton: American School of Classical Studies at Athens, 2022), no. I-23 (abbreviated Roncaglia, *Corinth* 22 hereafter); A. B. West, ed., *The Latin Inscriptions 1896–1926*, vol. 8, part 2 of *Corinth: Results of Excavations Conducted by the American School of Classical Studies at Athens* (Princeton: American School of Classical Studies at Athens, 1931), nos. 86–90 (abbreviated West, *Corinth* 8.2 hereafter).

inscription that probably is a dedication to the emperor Nero. This epigraph probably calls Nero "*Dīvus* Claudius's son" ([. . . *divi · Claudii · f*(*ilii*) . . .]), as editors have plausibly restored these words in its text.[129] The second inscription is on the statue base of the benefactor Spartiaticus that a Corinthian tribe set up. The epigraph indicates that "*Dīvus* Claudius" (*divo Claudio*) bestowed equestrian status on the tribe's patron.[130] The final piece of evidence that may attest to postmortem divine honors for *Dīvus* Claudius is a marble statue that may be of him that was found in the Julian Basilica. Much of this image, except for its torso, is missing, which makes identification difficult, if not impossible. Given that at least eleven other statues

Fig. 4.11 Coin (*RPC* 1.1208) possibly depicting Nero or Nero's genius in a Corinthian temple | *Courtesy of Yale University Art Gallery*

of Julio-Claudians were set up in this building near this image (see table 4.6), it is probable that this one depicts a Julio-Claudian and possible that it is *Dīvus* Claudius.[131] Therefore, Corinth may have used this statue for imperial cultic rituals, which have left no trace in the archaeological record.

Nero's Genius (?)

The final Julio-Claudian for whom Corinth may have established divine honors is the emperor Nero. If they did, however, these honors were not to his person but to his *genius*. Near the end of his reign in AD 67/68, the colony minted one coin series depicting an unknown temple with four columns, with a wreath on its architrave on the reverse.[132] Inside the temple is a statue that one specialist on Corinthian coins, Michel Amandry, has identified as Nero standing in a toga (see fig. 4.11).[133]

129. "Appendix 1: Inscriptions" §4.4, line 2.

130. "Appendix 1: Inscriptions" §4.3, line 5.

131. De Grazia Vanderpool, "Catalogue of Sculpture," 335–39, S-8, dates this statue to Claudius's reign, but if it is of *Dīvus* Claudius, then it must postdate his reign. If the image dates to Claudius's reign, then it probably depicts the emperor in the guise of Jupiter. After his death and divinization, however, Corinth may have redubbed the statue as that of *Dīvus* Claudius.

132. This identity of the temple is unknown despite Winter's, *Divine Honours*, 188–89, claim that it is Temple E/the *naos* of Octavia.

133. *RPC* 1.1208; Michel Amandry, *Le monnayage des duovirs Corinthiens*, Bulletin de Correspondance Hellénique Supplement 15 (Athens: École française d'Athènes, 1988), 224–25.

Fig. 4.12 Corinthian coin (*RPC* 1.1191), minted during Nero's reign (AD 54–68), depicting Corinth's genius | *Courtesy of Yale University Art Gallery*

The poor quality of the image on surviving coins makes the identification difficult, and it may not necessarily be of Nero. In fact, the original publication of this coin by the British Museum leaves the statue unidentified.[134] If it is of Nero, then it probably is of his *genius*, for the image resembles other depictions of other Roman *genii*, including Corinth's *genius*, which the colony minted on coins (see fig. 4.12).[135]

Provided that my identification of the image is correct, there is nothing unusual about Romans honoring someone's *genius*, and by AD 55, the Roman state was making regular sacrifices to Nero's (see pp. 43–44). Moreover, as noted above, Corinth may have been officially sacrificing to the emperor's *genius* since Augustus's reign.[136] The temple at which this may have happened is probably the Julian Family Temple, which I discuss below, but this is uncertain.

The Julio-Claudian Family

Not only did Corinth establish divine honors for the above individual Julio-Claudians, but also the colony had a cultic affinity for their entire imperial family. Thus, we may say that while the Corinthians established postmortem divine honors for certain Julio-Claudians and one individual connected to them—*Divus*

---

134. Barclay V. Head, ed., *Catalogue of Greek Coins in the British Museum: Corinth, Colonies of Corinth, Etc.* (London: Trustees of the British Museum, 1889), 67, nos. 548–50.

135. *RPC* 1.1189.

136. "Appendix 1: Inscriptions" §4.11.

Julius, Octavia, *Divus* Augustus, Gaius Caesar, Lucius Caesar, *Diva* Augusta, and (probably) *Divus* Claudius—they divinely honored the family line that produced the aforementioned family members (except for Octavia, who was not a Julian). As noted, the Corinthians were divided into tribes, many of which were named after Julio-Claudians (see table 4.1). The coins that the city minted during the Julio-Claudian period demonstrate detailed attention to this imperial family, depicting busts of twenty different Julio-Claudians (see table 4.2).[137]

TABLE 4.2 JULIO-CLAUDIANS DEPICTED ON CORINTHIAN COINAGE

Julio-Claudian	Numismatic Reference
Julius Caesar	*RPC* 1.1116, 1132, 1134
Augustus	*RPC* 1.1132, 1134, 1136, 1138, 1139, 1144, 1151, 1157
Gaius Caesar	*RPC* 1.1136
Lucius Caesar	*RPC* 1.1136
Tiberius	*RPC* 1.1140, 1144, 1145, 1146, 1147, 1148, 1152, 1158
Augustus Postumus	*RPC* 1.1141
Germanicus	*RPC* 1.1142, 1178, 1179
Drusus Minor	*RPC* 1.1143, 1149 (maybe), 1150 (maybe)
Livia	*RPC* 1.1149, 1150, 1153 (maybe), 1154 (maybe), 1155 (maybe), 1156 (maybe), 1159 (maybe), 1160 (maybe), 1161 (maybe)
Caligula	*RPC* 1.1171, 1172, 1173
Tiberius Gemellus	*RPC* 1.1171 (maybe)
Agrippina	*RPC* 1.1174, 1175
Nero Caesar	*RPC* 1.1174, 1175
Drusus Caesar	*RPC* 1.1174, 1175
Antonia Minor	*RPC* 1.1177
Claudius	*RPC* 1.1180, 1181, 1182
Nero	*RPC* 1.1182, 1183, 1184, 1189, 1192, 1195, 1197, 1200, 1201, 1202, 1203, 1204, 1205, 1206, 1207, 1208, 1209
Britannicus	*RPC* 1.1182, 1183, 1184
Agrippina Minor	*RPC* 1.1183, 1184, 1190, 1193, 1196, 1198
Claudia Octavia (Nero's wife)	*RPC* 1.1191, 1194, 1199

137. Walbank, "Evidence for the Imperial Cult," 204, observes, "The Corinthians were, in fact, peculiarly attentive to the Julio-Claudians in this regard [that is, in its coinage], faithfully recording events in the political and domestic life of the imperial family."

As we have seen and shall see below, archaeologists have found the remains of twelve marble statues inside the Julian Basilica, all of which probably depict Julio-Claudians (see table 4.6). The identity of three of these images is known, *Divus* Augustus, Gaius Caesar, and Lucius Caesar, and it is likely that two other statues depicted *Divus* Julius and *Divus* Claudius (see figs. 4.3, 4, 5, 9). These five images were probably used for imperial cultic activity.

Besides these sources, there are four more pieces of evidence attesting to Corinth's bestowal of divine honors on the Julio-Claudian line. First, the city erected a temple to the Julian family that archaeologists have yet to identify and at which the family line was divinely celebrated. I discuss this temple below as I describe where the Corinthians celebrated imperial divine honors in their colony (see pp. 204–6). Second, an inscription dated between AD 54 and 58 honoring Spartiaticus, the benefactor of a Corinthian tribe, calls the Julio-Claudian family "divine" (*divinus*).[138] Third, in the early second century AD, there was an association in Corinth known as "the college of the *Lares* of the divine house" (*collegio · Larum · Domu[s] · Divinae*), to which one freedman of the emperor Hadrian belonged.[139] It is possible but not certain that this group existed in the Julio-Claudian period.

Finally, a fragmentary inscription on marble from the Julian Basilica's northern end dating to the Roman imperial period attests to a dedication, not necessarily divine, to the "Caesars Augusti" (*Cae[sa]ribus · Augustis*) and the colony of Corinth.[140] In this epigraph's original publication, archaeologist Paul Scotton surmised that this inscription was a generic dedication to deceased and living Julio-Claudians.[141] Taking up this interpretation, Winter identified the gods and lords "in heaven" and "on earth" about whom Paul speaks in 1 Cor 8:5–6 as divinized and living Julio-Claudians. This identification of the Caesars Augusti further supports his argument that many problems associated with the Corinthian Christians were connected to imperial divine honors.[142] In the epigraph's official publication, Carolynn Roncaglia concludes that the inscription's date and identity of the Caesars Augusti are far from certain. She rejects Scotton's proposal that this is a generic dedication to living

---

138. "Appendix 1: Inscriptions" §4.3, lines 12–13.

139. "Appendix 1: Inscriptions" §4.17, lines 2–3.

140. "Appendix 1: Inscriptions" §4.18. The epigraph consists of twelve fragments, and all but one were found in this portion of the Julian Basilica. The findspot of this inscription may be of import because, as I discuss below, the Julian Basilica's imperial shrine was located on the building's opposite side, the southern end.

141. Paul D. Scotton, "A New Fragment of an Inscription from the Julian Basilica at Roman Corinth," *Hesperia* 74 (2005): 95–100.

142. Winter, *Divine Honours*, 209–25.

and deceased emperors as unlikely, because, while references to plural Caesars Augusti in epigraphs are rare, almost all other ones have specific Caesars Augusti in mind. By the forms of the letters (a science known as paleography), the epigraph appears to date to the Julio-Claudian period. However, this date is uncertain, mainly because, as Roncaglia notes, there are no examples of two Julio-Claudians being called Caesars Augusti in Julio-Claudian sources. The closest comparisons to the Corinthian epigraph are from periods in Rome's history when two emperors reigned at the same time, that is, the mid-second and early fourth centuries AD. In the end, Roncaglia proposes that the identity of these Caesars Augusti is unknown, but it is "likely" that they are Gaius Caesar and Lucius Caesar. If this is the case, then the inscription may be related to their cultic statues (see figs. 4.4, 5).[143]

Imperial Cultic Officials

Now that we know on whom Corinth bestowed divine honors, the next issue we must address is who offered such honors on behalf of the colony. Evidence for imperial divine honors in the colony attests to three different imperial cultic officials, a traditionally Roman priestly office, *flamen*, and two Romanized-Greek public offices connected to games associated with imperial divine honors, *agonothetae* and *isagogi* (in their respective plural transliterated Latin). From the names of the officials who filled them and other information that we can cull from these epigraphs, such as their careers, that of their family members, and their social statuses in the colony, the individuals who filled these posts were all aristocratic men with Roman citizenship who were at the apex of Corinthian and Achaian provincial society. Thus, they were the most powerful men in the city and the province. One interesting note about Corinth is that to date, no evidence exists for female imperial priests, such as *sacerdotes* in Philippi (see pp. 81–82), in the colony. This may be an accident of the survival of the evidence, however. It is also possible, though less likely in my opinion, that Corinthian men were the only persons who celebrated Julio-Claudian imperial divine honors in the city.

Flamines

The only attested imperial priests in Corinth are *flamines*. These priesthoods or *flaminiae* are traditional Roman ones dating back to the time when kings ruled Rome (753–509 BC). Most often they served only one god, such as the *flamen Di-*

---

143. Roncaglia, *Corinth* 22:376–79, quotation 389, Gaius and Lucius "are the most likely dedicatees."

alis or *flamen* of Jupiter.[144] When the Roman Senate began to divinize deceased Julio-Claudians, individual *flamines* were chosen to serve specific Julio-Claudian *divi*. Corinth followed its mother city in this practice, appointing *flamines* for this purpose, but only those for *Divus* Julius and *Divus* Augustus are attested in the epigraphic record. From these inscriptions, we know of only one *flamen* for each of these, but surely there were more for these *divi* as well as for *Divus* Claudius, provided that he received imperial divine honors, and possibly for Gaius Caesar and Lucius Caesar. Given that there is no evidence for imperial priestesses in Corinth, the colony may have selected *flamines* for *Diva* Augusta and Octavia, too. The earliest known *flamen* is one for *Divus* Augustus, and he is somewhat of a long-lost friend, Gaius Julius Laco, the dynast of Sparta whom we encountered on this book's first pages (for he was the individual whom Gythium honored alongside the deceased Augustus, Tiberius, Livia, Germanicus, Drusus, the Roman general Flamininus, and Laco's father Eurycles; see pp. 1–4). A Latin inscription referenced above attests that Laco served as "*flamen* of Augustus" (*fla(men) · Aug(usti)*).[145] As noted, the epigraph was inscribed on limestone, dates to Claudius's reign, and was not found in situ. Moreover, as we saw, for reasons unknown, *divus* has been omitted from the epigraph, but certainly it belongs in it.

Laco and his family were wealthy aristocrats with direct connections to the Julio-Claudians. His father, Eurycles, had given Caesar Octavian military aid at the battle of Actium (31 BC), for which the emperor bestowed Roman citizenship on him and his descendants.[146] Unfortunately, Eurycles abused his association with Augustus by fomenting unrest in Achaia and some of Rome's client kingdoms such as Judea. Therefore, Augustus banished him from Achaia.[147] Eurycles's sins were not visited upon his family, however. His grandson, Laco's son, Gaius Julius Argolicus, married the daughter of a senator close to Tiberius, and his association to this emperor allowed the family to regain prominence in Achaia.[148] Laco probably fell from Tiberius's grace, however, when the emperor exiled his daughter-in-law.[149] He must have regained his position after Tiberius's death, for the Corinthian inscription attesting to his imperial priesthood indicates that he served in an imperial post under Claudius known as a *procurator*.[150] The specifics of this office are

---

144. Livy, *History of Rome* 1.20.1–4; Varro, *On the Latin Language* 5.84.

145. "Appendix 1: Inscriptions" §4.8, line 7.

146. G. W. Bowersock, "Eurycles of Sparta," *JRS* 51 (1961): 112–18.

147. Josephus, *Jewish Antiquities* 16.300–310; *Jewish War* 1.513–532.

148. Tacitus, *Annals* 6.18, calls Laco and Argolicus "prominent men of the Achaeans" (*e primoribus Achaeorum*). For more information, see Bowersock, "Eurycles," 116–17.

149. Tacitus, *Annals* 6.18; Bowersock, "Eurycles," 117.

150. West, *Corinth* 8.2:47–49. Contra Bowersock, "Eurycles," 117, who concludes that the Gaius

unknown, but it is certain that Laco needed the emperor's approval to hold it.[151] In addition to this imperial office, the epigraph attests that Laco filled four other Corinthian public posts. First, he was one of the colony's augurs and thus was charged with inaugurating or consecrating sacred space, advising the magistrates on the meaning of the flight of birds, and announcing auguries that the gods declared of their own accord (see fig. 4.9 for *Divus* Augustus depicted as an augur).[152] This meant that Laco had a great deal of power in the decision-making process in Corinth. Second, he was a *curio*. The details of this Latin office are obscure, but it appears to have been a public post associated with the organization of and divine honors connected to the Corinthian tribes.[153] Third, Laco held the highest magistracy in the colony, *duovir quinquennalis*, possibly in AD 17/18, which means he was one of the most powerful public figures in Corinth, at least during Tiberius's reign.[154] Finally, he was *agonothete* of the Isthmian Games as well as another set of games in honor of Augustus (for more on these games, see pp. 196–200), possibly in AD 19.[155] As we shall see, to serve in this latter office, he would have needed a substantial amount of capital to oversee the execution of these contests, because on occasion, he may have needed to underwrite some or all the costs.

The other known *flamen* was one of Laco's sons and someone whom we have already met, too, Gaius Julius Spartiaticus, the *flamen* of *Divus* Julius.[156] The epigraph attesting to this post is found in an honorary inscription that a Corinthian tribe set up providing Spartiaticus's résumé. From this epigraph, he followed somewhat in his father Laco's footsteps. Spartiaticus's public career began in the Roman military where he reached the office of military tribune probably during Claudius's reign, and it was this emperor who conferred the rank of equestrian upon him. While Nero was emperor, Spartiaticus served him as a *procurator* (as Laco had done for Claudius). In addition to serving as *Divus* Julius's *flamen* in Corinth, the epigraph in question notes that Spartiaticus held three other offices in the colony. First, he was *pontifex* or "priest" of one or more gods in Corinth, but which god(s) is (are) unclear. Therefore, he was charged with offering tradi-

---

Julius Laco referred to in the inscription in question is the grandson of Eurycles and son of Gaius Julius Laco whom we met on this book's first pages.

151. West, *Corinth* 8.2:49.

152. John Scheid, *An Introduction to Roman Religion*, trans. Janet Lloyd (Bloomington: University of Indiana Press, 2003), 112–13.

153. West, *Corinth* 8.2:40, 49.

154. For a discussion of the dating of Laco's time as *duovir quinquennalis*, see West, *Corinth* 8.2:48–49, who notes that it is "possible" that he served in that public office in AD 17/18, a date that Kent, *Corinth* 8.3:25, seems to accept.

155. Kent, *Corinth* 8.3:30, surmises that Laco served as *agonothete* in AD 19, while West, *Corinth* 8.2:48, places it in AD 39.

156. "Appendix 1: Inscriptions §4.3," lines 5–6.

tional divine honors and thus ensuring that the city gave to the gods what was due them so that the gods might continue to provide the means that Corinth needed to survive and to thrive. Second, Spartiaticus reached the public office of *duovir quinquennalis* not once but twice during Claudius's reign.[157] This means that he must have been a powerful man in Corinth and retained this position for the emperor's thirteen-year reign. Third, he served as *agonothete* of the Isthmian Games and two other sets of games in honor of the Julio-Claudians, one in honor of Augustus and another in honor of the reigning emperor (for more information, see pp. 196–200). Exactly when Spartiaticus served as *agonothete* is unknown, but he must have been a wealthy person, because he oversaw these three sets of games, which meant that, if needs must, he had the ability to underwrite them.[158] Finally, in addition to these Corinthian public offices, he held a provincial office, too. Spartiaticus was the first person to hold the high priesthood of the Augustan family for the province of Achaia. This office, however, did not fall under Corinthian imperial divine honors but under provincial imperial divine honors that I discuss below (see pp. 214–16).

Agonothetae

The next type of public office in Corinth connected to imperial divine honors is that of the *agonothete*, which is the Latin transliteration of the Greek public office of *agōnothetēs*. Originally, this public post had nothing to do with imperial divine honors but was the person who oversaw the Isthmian Games. These contests were founded in the 580s BC in honor of Poseidon and Palaimon, a child whose original name was Melicertes and whose mother drowned him in the sea and whose corpse a dolphin brought to the shores of Isthmia, at which point the Corinthians venerated him as divine. The games, along with the Olympian, Pythian, and Nemean, were known as panhellenic because Greeks from all over the Mediterranean participated in them. They were held every two years in April or May and by the early Roman period consisted of chariot, horse, and foot races; boxing; wrestling; discus and javelin throwing; and musical and poetry contests mainly for men, youths, and boys.[159] To facilitate these activities, the site of Isthmia, which

157. West, *Corinth* 8.2:52, "tentatively" dates Spartiaticus's two terms as *duovir quinquennalis* to AD 42/43 and 47/48; Kent, *Corinth* 8.3:25, to AD 47/48 and 52/53; and Spawforth, "Corinth, Argos, and the Imperial Cult," 219, to AD 46/47 and either 41/42 or 56/57.

158. West, *Corinth* 8.2:52–53, leaves open the date of Spartiaticus's time as *agonothete*, while Kent, *Corinth* 8.3:31, places it in AD 47.

159. West, *Corinth* 8.2:64–65; Kent, *Corinth* 8.3:28–31. For the program of events at the Isthmian Games, see B. D. Meritt, *The Greek Inscriptions 1896–1927*, vol. 8, part 1 of *Corinth: Results of Excavations Conducted by the American School of Classical Studies at Athens* (Cambridge: Ameri-

was about five miles from Corinth, contained a temple complex of Poseidon, a stadium, a theater, and a bath.[160] Since their inception, Corinth oversaw these games. When Mummius sacked the city in 146 BC, Rome transferred oversight of these games to the nearby Greek city of Sicyon, and the contests were held there.[161] Once Roman Corinth was founded (44 BC), administration of the games returned to Corinth. However, the Isthmian Games appear to have been celebrated in the colony, not at Isthmia, for the first one hundred years or so. During Claudius's reign, archaeological and epigraphic evidence indicates that the games returned to Isthmia.[162] For the frequency that these games were held, beginning with Paul's ministry in Corinth and through the remainder of the Julio-Claudian period, see table 4.3.

TABLE 4.3 SCHEDULE OF THE ISTHMIAN, CAESAREAN, AND IMPERIAL GAMES FROM AD 51 TO AD 67

Isthmian Games	Caesarean Games	Imperial Games
AD 51	AD 51	AD 51
AD 53		
AD 55	AD 55	AD 55
AD 57		
AD 59	AD 59	AD 59
AD 61		
AD 63	AD 63	AD 63
AD 65		
AD 67	AD 67	AD 67

After Actium (31 BC) and in 30 BC, Corinth established a second set of games in honor of Caesar Octavian's victory, known as the Caesarean Games. Originally,

---

can School of Classical Studies at Athens, 1931), nos. 14–16 (abbreviated Meritt, *Corinth* 8.1 hereafter). For more information on the games in general, see David Lunt, *The Crown Games of Ancient Greece: Archaeology, Athletes, and Heroes* (Fayetteville: University of Arkansas Press, 2022), 65–82.

160. Lunt, *Crown Games*, 67–79.

161. Pausanias, *Description of Greece* 2.2.2.

162. Elizabeth R. Gebhard, "The Isthmian Games and the Sanctuary of Poseidon in the Early Empire," in *The Corinthia in the Roman Period*, ed. Timothy E. Gregory, Journal of Roman Archaeology Supplement 8 (Ann Arbor: Journal of Roman Archaeology, 1994), 78–94, places the games in Isthmia between AD 50 and 60 in light of the archaeological evidence from the site. Mika Kajava, "When Did the Isthmian Games Return to the Isthmus? (Reading 'Corinth' 8.3.153)," *CP* 97 (2002): 168–78, places the games in Isthmia in AD 43, seven years before Gebhard, in light of his reediting of a Corinthian inscription ("Appendix 1: Inscriptions" §4.16).

they occurred every fourth year after the Isthmian Games.[163] However, sometime in the early first century AD, Corinth reversed this order and began to celebrate the Caesarean Games before the Isthmian.[164] These former contests occurred mostly in Corinth, even after the Isthmian Games returned to Isthmia, and appear to have consisted of encomia and poetry contests.[165] Thus, they were not on the same scale as their Isthmian counterparts. For the celebration of the Caesarean Games from AD 51 to 67, see table 4.3. Sometime in Tiberius's reign, Corinth introduced a third set of games in honor of the reigning emperor named after him, Tiberian for Tiberius, Gaian for Gaius, Claudian for Claudius, and Neronian for Nero. For simplicity's sake, I refer to these games as Imperial. These contests were celebrated every four years, too, probably in Corinth, and their contests resembled their Caesarean counterparts. For the years of Imperial Games from the founding of Christianity in the colony until the end of Nero's reign, see table 4.3. Despite the celebration of these games together, each set appears to have been distinct, because they had their own list of victors, which were engraved on stone.[166]

An *agonothete* was elected every two years to oversee the Isthmian Games, after 30 BC, the Isthmian or Caesarean Games, and beginning in Tiberius's reign, the Isthmian or the Caesarean and Imperial Games. According to the Corinthian sources to date, every person who filled this office during the Julio-Claudian period was a Roman citizen. However, the exact years that these aristocrats held this office is a matter of scholarly contention (see table 4.4). Since each *agonothete* was responsible for the overall production and execution of these contests, including underwriting their cost, if necessary, whoever filled the post of *agonothete* belonged to the wealthiest circles of Corinth.[167] Due to this fact, the Isthmian Games' renown, and their international character, this office was probably the most prized

---

163. One Corinthian Greek inscription containing a list of victors of the Caesarean Games is dated "year 33 from Caesar's victory at Actium [in 31 BC]" (ἔτους · λγ · ἀπὸ τῆς ἐν Ἀκτ[ίῳ] Καίσαρος γίκης; Meritt, *Corinth* 8.1, no. 14, lines 1–2).

164. West, *Corinth* 8.2, no. 81.

165. "Appendix 1: Inscriptions" §4.1 and the comments by Meritt, *Corinth* 8.1:19; Gebhard, "Isthmian Games," 87; Kajava, "When Did the Isthmian Games," 173. See *IG* 12.6.1.340 = PH344104, which is a first-century AD inscription mentioning a person from Samos who won the chariot race (ἅρμα) at the Isthmian and Caesarean Games "in Corinth" (ἐν Κορίνθῳ).

166. Meritt, *Corinth* 8.1, nos. 14–16; "Appendix 1: Inscriptions" §4.1. For a discussion, see West, *Corinth* 8.2:64–66; Kent, *Corinth* 8.3:28–31.

167. Wiseman, "Corinth and Rome I," 500. For a recent discussion, see James R. Harrison, "Paul and the *Agōnothetai* at Corinth," *Roman Corinth*, vol. 2 of *The First Urban Churches*, ed. James R. Harrison and L. L. Welborn, WGRWSup 8 (Atlanta: SBL Press, 2016), 271–326, esp. 281–84. In addition to the *agonothete*, the Isthmian Games were under the oversight of a group of probably ten men known as *Hellanodicae*, presumably elected, who were tasked with judging the various contests. See Wiseman, "Corinth and Rome I," 499–500.

in the colony, even more so than *duovir* and *duovir quinquennalis*.[168] The individuals who held this post also held other public offices in the colony. For example, Cornelius Pulcher held every major public post in Corinth—*aedile, duovir, duovir quinquennalis*—and was twice *agonothete*, once of the Imperial Games only (how this is possible is unclear), and once of the Isthmian and Caesarean Games.[169]

TABLE 4.4 JULIO-CLAUDIAN *AGONOTHETAE* FROM CORINTH[170]

agonothete	Source
Gaius Secundius Dinippus	*SEG* 11.61, lines 5–7
Gaius Heius Pamphilus	Kent, *Corinth* 8.3, no. 150, lines 1–3
Titus Manlius Juvencus	Kent, *Corinth* 8.3, no. 154, lines 5–6; West, *Corinth* 8.2, no. 86, lines 6–8
Gaius Julius Laco	"Appendix 1: Inscriptions" §4.8, lines 5–6
Lucius Castricius Regulus	Kent, *Corinth* 8.3, no. 153, lines 4–7
Aulus Arrius Proclus	Kent, *Corinth* 8.3, no. 156, lines 7–8
[-] Juventius Proclus	*SIG* 802, col. 1, lines 5–6
Cornelius Pulcher	"Appendix 1: Inscriptions" §4.16, lines 4–7
Gaius Julius Spartiaticus	"Appendix 1: Inscriptions" §4.3, lines 7–8
Lucius Rutilius [- - - -]	West, *Corinth* 8.2, no. 82, line 5
M. Pu[- - -]	Kent, *Corinth* 8.3, no. 208, lines 4–5
[- - - -] Bassius	Philostratus, *Life of Apollonius of Tyana* 4.26; *Letters* 36
Tiberius Claudius Dinippus	Kent, *Corinth* 8.3, nos. 158–60, 162–63; West, *Corinth* 8.2, nos. 54, 86–90

Isagogeus

The third public office connected with imperial divine honors in Corinth is that of *isagogeus*. When the Isthmian, Caesarean, and Imperial Games were celebrated together, an *isagogeus* was appointed to assist the *agonothete* with the Imperial,

168. Wiseman, "Corinth and Rome I," 500, points out, "The honor [of being an *agonothete*] was considered the highest that the city could bestow, to judge from its prime place in most of the texts preserving a *cursus honorum* in ascender order." Engels, *Roman Corinth*, 97, notes, "The international character of the games meant that he [the *agonothete*] would receive the honor and esteem of the entire Hellenic world."

169. "Appendix 1: Inscriptions" §4.16.

170. This table is taken from Kent, *Corinth* 8.3:30–31. Because the years in which individual Corinthian aristocrats held this office is debated, I have altered Kent's table by removing his reconstruction of the exact dates when individual Corinthians were *agonothetae*.

not the Isthmian or Caesarean, Games. The office is the Latin transliteration of the Greek title *eisagōgeus*, which was a minor Greek office that differed from city to city.[171] We do not know much about the *isagogi* in Corinth, because, while the title appears four times in the epigraphic record, we know the names of only two *isagogi*, Publius Puticius Rufus and Gaius Rutilius Fuscus.[172] If they were typical *isagogi*, then they were boys or young men when they held the office.[173] Exactly how they came to do so—if by appointment or election and, if the former, by whom—is unknown. In the case of Fuscus, he served as *isagogeus* when his father Lucius Rutilius was *agonothete*. Thus, the father may have appointed the son. According to Plato, *eis-agōgeis* are connected to musical competitions, enroll competitors, assign places to them, and judge the contests.[174] That the Corinthian Imperial Games consisted of musical and poetry contests in honor of the reigning emperor remains consistent with the Platonic description of the role of an *eisagōgeus*, and thus the Corinthian *isagogi* may have functioned similarly. It is clear from epigraphs and coins from Corinth that Rufus and Fuscus were from aristocratic families. During Tiberius's reign (AD 14–37), someone in Rufus's family, possibly his father or grandfather, Publius Puticius Jullus, was an *aedile* in the colony, given the honors of a *duovir*, and Corinth may have acknowledged him as its patron (*patronus*).[175] Individuals from Fuscus's family became *duoviri*—Lucius Rutilius Plancus (in either AD 12/13 or 15/16) and Lucius Rutilius Piso (AD 66/67)—and set up the shrine and statue of Augustan Apollo in the area of Corinth known in antiquity as Ten Shops (see p. 211).[176]

Augustales

In addition to imperial *flamines*, *agonothetae*, and *isagogi*, another set of individuals was connected to imperial divine honors in Corinth, the *Augustales*.[177] In the late first century BC, Latin-speaking communities began to bestow a newly created "rank" on certain wealthy outsiders, *liberti* or "freedman," that is, emancipated slaves, and rich nonaristocrats who were unable to become *decuriones*

---

171. Athens, for example, elected five εἰσαγωγεῖς whose duty it was to introduce cases that were brought to trial (Aristotle, *Athenian Constitution* 52.2).

172. "Appendix 1: Inscriptions" §4.19–22.

173. According to Plato, *Laws* 4.765A, an εἰσαγωγεύς should be under thirty years old.

174. Plato, *Laws* 4.765A.

175. "Appendix 1: Inscriptions" §4.23, line 2. It is possible that one of Rufus's relatives oversaw the Isthmian Games as one of the ten *Hellanodicae*. See the possible reconstruction of Puticius in Meritt, *Corinth* 8.1, no. 18, which may be a list of *Hellanodicae* from the colony. For another Puticius named in a fragmentary inscription found on the Acrocorinth, see *CIL* 3.542.

176. *RPC* 1.1145–48 (for Plancus), 1203–6 (for Piso); "Appendix 1: Inscriptions" §4.12.

177. I am indebted to Laird, "Emperor in a Roman Town," 72–75, for the sources for Corinthian *Augustales* outside Meritt, *Corinth* 8.1, West, *Corinth* 8.2, and Kent, *Corinth* 8.3.

in their respective Latin-speaking communities.[178] The rank was that of *Augustalis* (*Augustales* in the plural) or some variation.[179] These *Augustales* used their riches to promote the honor, not necessarily divine, of Julio-Claudians by setting up public monuments and buildings, underwriting the cost of imperial festivals, and by patronizing and facilitating imperial divine honors.[180] Corinthian epigraphy attests to six *Augustales*, two of whom are *liberti* and another of whom is a *verna* or "imperial slave" born in the emperor's house (see table 4.5). This group went by different names in the colony, *Augustales* of Tiberius Claudius Augustus, *Augustales*, and *collegium* of *Augustales*. They appear first in the epigraphic record in Tiberius's reign and are attested into the second century AD. The Corinthian *Augustales* provided benefactions connected to the Julio-Claudians, such as the erection of the towering monument with a bronze statue of *Divus* Augustus in the forum (see figs. 4.6–8).[181] We do not know of any other connection that *Augustales* in Corinth had with imperial divine honors. If they celebrated any such honors, they probably did so on the private, not public, level. That is, Corinth neither officially sanctioned their actions nor paid for their offerings. They may have performed these imperial divine honors at various places throughout the colony, including at shrines at crossroads as occurred in Rome (see pp. 43–44).

TABLE 4.5 CORINTHIAN *AUGUSTALES*

Name	Title	Servile origin (if known)
Quintus Cispuleius Primus (West, *Corinth* 8.2, no. 77)	*Augustalis* of Tiberius Claudius Augustus	*libertus*
Gnaeus Cornelius Speratus ("Appendix 1: Inscriptions" §4.7, line 3)	*Augustalis*	
Tiberius Claudius Stephanus (*CIL* 3.6099)	*Augustalis*	

178. I have taken the idea of *Augustales* as "wealthy outsiders" from Laird, "Emperor in a Roman Town," 72.

179. The three commonest names of *Augustales* in the Latin West are *Augustales*, *seviri Augustales*, and *seviri*. For a recent, informed discussion of *Augustales*, including their various names, see Gwynaeth McIntyre, *A Family of Gods: The Worship of the Imperial Family in the Latin West* (Ann Arbor: University of Michigan Press, 2016), 111–29.

180. Laird, "Emperor in a Roman Town," 72. The evidence associated with *Augustales* is difficult to interpret, because virtually all of it, except for one reference in one literary work, is from inscriptions that members of this group set up. However, even the one literary reference, Petronius, *Satyricon* 30, is to an inscription!

181. Laird, "Emperor in a Roman Town," 76–97.

Name	Title	Servile origin (if known)
Name unknown (West, *Corinth* 8.2, no. 69)	*Augustalis*	*libertus*
Sargarius Alcimius (*ILS* 1504)	(Member of the) *collegium* of *Augustales*	*verna*

Imperial Cultic Officials as Benefactors

Not only did the *flamines*, *agonothetae*, and *isagogi* administer imperial divine honors, but also they used their wealth to benefit Corinth. Such beneficence had a twofold consequence: (1) it beautified the colony, and (2) it impressed Corinth's *populus* and kept the names of these wealthy individuals (and that of their families) at the forefront of their minds, which aided in securing votes in local Corinthian elections. One Corinthian tribe honored *Divus* Julius's *flamen* Spartiaticus for his *munificentia* or "munificence" to the Julio-Claudians and the colony.[182] Unfortunately, no evidence for any of Spartiaticus's benefactions survive, or that of his father, *Divus* Augustus's *flamen*, Laco. We know from Pausanias that a certain Spartan named Eurycles paid for the construction of a lavish bath in Corinth that was near a statue of Poseidon. According to this ancient travel guide, this was "the most renowned of" (*onomastotaton*) any bath in the city, and Eurycles had decorated it with precious stones from quarries near Sparta.[183] It is possible, even probable, that this Eurycles is the same one that we met in this book's introduction, the father of Laco and grandfather of Spartiaticus whom the emperor Augustus had appointed dynast of Sparta and several nearby cities, including Gythium (see pp. 1–4). Archaeologists in Corinth may have discovered these baths north of Peirene Fountain and east of the Lechaion Road (see fig. 4.1). When excavators examined the site, they found that the earliest phase of its construction dates to Augustus's reign and that the bath's walls had been covered with precious stones from quarries near Sparta.[184] If this Eurycles is Laco's father and Spartiaticus's grandfather, then it increases the probability that these latter two men provided

---

182. "Appendix 1: Inscriptions" §4.3, line 13.

183. Pausanias, *Description of Greece* 2.3.5. Contra Winter, *Divine Honours*, 201, who concludes that "C. Julius Laco . . . built the luxurious bath in Corinth and, according to Pausanias, 'beautified it with various kinds of stone.'" Pausanias, *Description of Greece* 2.3.5, clearly says that Eurycles, not Laco, constructed the bath: "The Spartan man Eurycles made this" (τοῦτο δὲ Εὐρυκλῆς ἐποίησεν ἀνὴρ Σπαρτιάτης).

184. Jane Biers, "*Lavari est vivere* Baths in Roman Corinth," in *The Centenary 1896–1996*, vol. 20 of *Corinth: Results of Excavations Conducted by the American School of Classical Studies at Athens*, ed. Charles Williams II and Nancy Bookidis (Princeton: American School of Classical Studies

similar benefactions for Corinth, which have not been identified, have yet to be discovered, or were dismantled in antiquity and thus will never be discovered.

According to an inscription listing the résumé of a Corinthian *agonothete* named Cornelius Pulcher, he paid for the renovation of (*novo*) the buildings of the *Caesareon*, probably an imperial shrine or temple in Isthmia, and the construction of a building in Corinth, and he provided a banquet for all colonists (*omnibus colonis*), which excluded the *incolae*.[185] Two individuals who were members of the family of one of the two known *isagogi*, Gaius Rutilius Fuscus, paid for the construction of the shrine and cultic statue of Augustan Apollo in Ten Shops (see p. 211).[186] During Tiberius's reign, the *Augustales* erected the bronze statue of *Divus* Augustus atop a base with four benches at the bottom of it in the forum (see figs. 4.6–8). It is evident from the remains of the benches that the people of Corinth sat frequently on them, for they evidence signs of wear or butt grooves (see fig. 4.8).[187] Finally, one particular *Augustalis* dedicated an unknown object, building, or part of a building to *Divus* Augustus because of his *iustitia*.[188]

Location of Imperial Divine Honors

So far we have explored to which Julio-Claudians Corinth granted divine honors and who oversaw and administered them. The question remains, Where did the colony's imperial *flamines* make the public honors in question? The answer to this query is that there was no one location in which these honors occurred but several. To date, Greco-Roman literature, archaeology, statuary, inscriptions, and coins attest to three, possibly five, Corinthian sites at which imperial divine honors were celebrated, and some historians have suggested a sixth location in which they were housed. In addition to these sites of public imperial divine honors, it is possible and even probable that private imperial divine honors occurred in the colony and that some Corinthians placed certain Julio-Claudians among their domestic *Lares* and at shrines at crossroads in Corinth and its environs. This is especially the case when one considers that Latin literary sources attest that aristocratic Romans incorporated imperial divine honors into their domestic shrines (see pp. 51–53), the fascination that the Corinthians had with the imperial family (see tables 4.1, 2), and that there were private imperial shrines at crossroads in

---

at Athens, 2003), 303–19, esp. 305–7; Sanders, Palinkas, Tzonou-Herbst with Herbst, *Ancient Corinth*, 114–15.

185. "Appendix 1: Inscriptions" §4.16, lines 12–13.
186. "Appendix 1: Inscriptions" §4.12.
187. Laird, "Emperor in a Roman Town," 95–96.
188. "Appendix 1: Inscriptions" §4.7.

Rome. To date, no Corinthian evidence attests to such shrines, domestic or at crossroads, however, which means it is fruitless to discuss the notion any further until more evidence is available. In what follows, I discuss each location in which public imperial divine honors occurred or were said to have occurred, in turn describing what we can reconstruct of imperial sacrifices that may have been offered at these Corinthian sites.

Octavia's Naos

The first site of imperial divine honors is Octavia's *naos* that I referenced above (see pp. 172–74). To recap, according to Pausanias, "above" or "beyond" (*hyper*) Corinth's forum there was a *naos* of Octavia, which I propose is probably a small shrine to Octavia that archaeologists have yet to identify, have yet to discover, or will never discover because it has been demolished.[189] If my suggestion is correct, then there was probably an altar connected to this shrine at which cultic officials carried out postmortem sacrifices to Octavia. Given that in Greco-Roman cults, priests tended to serve gods and priestesses goddesses, it is possible that there was a female priesthood for Octavia in Corinth whose main base of operations was Octavia's *naos*. If this is the case, then the priesthood has left no record. If it is not, then priests, maybe *flamines* of *divi* offered such sacrifices.

The Julian Family Temple

The second location of imperial divine honors was a temple known as the Julian Family Temple. From AD 32 to 33 (or possibly AD 33 to 34), Corinth minted eleven coin series picturing a temple with six columns atop a podium, which is a distinctive Roman architectural feature (see fig. 4.13).[190] The architrave of the temple contains the Latin inscription "(Dedicated to) the Julian Family" (*Gent(i) Iuli*), which identifies the temple as one that Corinth set aside for the imperial family.[191] Archaeologists have yet to locate or identify this temple, but some historians

189. Pausanias, *Description of Greece* 2.3.1. Paul D. Scotton, "Form and Function," in *The Julian Basilica: Architecture, Sculpture, Epigraphy*, vol. 22 of *Corinth: Results of Excavations Conducted by the American School of Classical Studies at Athens* (Princeton: American School of Classical Studies at Athens, 2022), 219–21, quotation 221, tentatively suggests that Pausanias's *naos* of Octavia is the Julian Basilica: "One wonders if the basilica, by the time of Pausanias's visit, had become the 'Temple of Octavia,' whatever he meant by that."

190. Greek temples tended not to be built on podia and to have access from all sides, like the temple of Apollo at Corinth.

191. *RPC* 1.1151–61. Contra Miller, "Imperial Cult," 330, who incorrectly identifies the Julian Family Temple as "an imperial temple of Julius Caesar."

Fig. 4.13 Corinthian coin (*RPC* 1.1153) depicting Corinth's Julian Family Temple | *Courtesy of Yale University Art Gallery*

conclude that the Julian Family Temple is Octavia's *naos*.[192] The first historians to make this proposal did so on the shakiest of grounds. Assuming rightly that the Julian Family Temple was imperial, they posited that depictions of a seated female figure on the obverse of other first-century AD Corinthian coins that did not picture the Julian Family Temple (!) depicted the temple's cultic statue of Octavia (see fig. 4.14).[193]

This means that there is no direct evidence linking the Julian Family Temple with Octavia's *naos*. Moreover, the seated female figure on Corinthian coins in question may be not Livia but the Roman goddess Health/Well-being (*Salus*). However, the most compelling evidence against identifying the Julian Family Temple with Octavia's *naos* is that Octavia was not a Julian (or a Claudian); she was an Octavian.[194] The reason that her brother, Octavian, became a Julian was that Julius Caesar adopted him in his will as his son. This act literally made Octavian a Julian, for the Romans took adoption very seriously.

Therefore, the Julian Family Temple was probably a temple devoted to *Divus* Julius, the founder of Roman Corinth, and his family line, which included the combined Julio-Claudian families. Such temples were rare in the Roman world, but they did exist. The closest analogy is the "shrine of the Julian family" (*sacrarium genti Iuliae*) with its "statue of *Divus* Augustus" (*effigiesque divo Augusto*) that the second-century AD Roman historian Tacitus records was constructed in AD 16 in the Italian city of Bovillae.[195] The reason the city set up this temple and cultic image was Bovillae's connection to *Divus* Julius; Bovillae was the ancestral home

---

192. Pausanias, *Description of Greece* 2.3.1.
193. Imhoof-Blumer and Gardner, "Numismatic Commentary," 50–101, esp. 71.
194. Walbank, "Pausanias," 370.
195. Tacitus, *Annals* 2.41.

Fig. 4.14 Corinthian coin (*RPC* 1.1149) depicting a bust of Tiberius on the obverse (*left*) and an enthroned female figure on the reverse (*right*) that some connect with the Julian Family Temple | *With permission of wildwinds.com*

of his family. According to an ancient Roman tradition, a certain Ascanius, the son of Aeneas the Trojan refugee who founded Rome, was also known as Julus. This Ascanius went out and founded a city near Rome named Alba Longa. Sometime later, citizens of Alba Longa founded Bovillae, establishing the link between the two cities and the Julian family.[196] In the same way, Corinth's Julian Family Temple underscored the city's connection with its founder, whom the Roman Senate divinized, and his descendants. Among the eleven coin series depicting the temple, they contain busts of three different Julio-Claudians on their obverses, Augustus, Tiberius, and probably Livia.[197] By the time Corinth minted these coins, it had already established postmortem divine honors for *Divus* Augustus. In my estimation, this was one of the major centers of imperial cultic activity in Corinth, and by the time that Paul composed his first extant letter to the Corinthian Christians (1 Corinthians in AD 56/57), this temple probably housed the cultic statues of *Divus* Julius, *Divus* Augustus, *Diva* Augusta, and *Divus* Claudius, provided that the latter was divinely honored. As for its location, we shall have to wait and see whether archaeologists can confidently identify it.[198]

196. For the identification of Ascanius with Julus, see Virgil, *Aeneid* 1.265–271. For Julius Caesar's speech acknowledging his family line and claiming its descent from Venus, the mother of Aeneas, see Suetonius, *Deified Julius* 6.1. Inscriptions on an altar from Bovillae provide concrete evidence of the Julian family's connection to Bovillae and Alba Longa (*CIL* 1.1439).

197. *RPC* 1.1151–61. Walbank, "Evidence for the Imperial Cult," 202–4. It is unclear why the Julian Family Temple appears on coinage only in AD 32 to 33 (or possibly AD 33 to 34). Walbank proposes that the coinage marks a special anniversary associated with the original dedication of the temple in Corinth: AD 33/34 marked the twentieth anniversary of *Divus* Augustus's death and Tiberius's appointment as emperor (AD 14); the sixtieth anniversary of the Roman Senate's supposed restoration and hailing of Caesar Octavian as Augustus (AD 27); and the fiftieth anniversary of the Secular Games that were held in Rome (AD 17).

198. Walbank, "Cults of Roman Corinth," 364, suggests that the Julian Family Temple was housed in the Archaic Temple, north of the forum (see fig. 4.1).

Fig. 4.15 Remains of Corinth's Julian Basilica | *Photo by author*

Julian Basilica

Several times in the above discussions, I referenced the Julian Basilica as the place where archaeologists found statues of Julio-Claudians and inscriptions attesting to divine honors for them. It is now time to take a closer look at this building that formed the eastern border of the Corinthian forum (see fig. 4.1). The Julian Basilica was a limestone structure with a main floor and a basement area known as a cryptoporticus, which served as an underground support for the upper, main floor. The building was about 126 feet long, seventy-seven feet wide, and about fifty-five feet high. It was constructed on a podium that was about thirteen and a half feet above the forum, so that to enter the Julian Basilica from the forum, one had to ascend a staircase. Though the building went through several phases during the imperial period, the first began during Augustus's reign between 2/1 BC and AD 4/5. While not much remains today (see fig. 4.15), when Paul first visited Corinth in AD 50/51, marble revetment probably covered most of the Julian Basilica's interior walls (see fig. 4.16).[199]

The building's main purpose appears to have been to serve the judicial and administrative needs of the province of Achaia, to be the tribunal or seat of Roman legal power for the Roman governor who lived in the colony, and as an imperial

---

199. Paul D. Scotton, "Reconstruction," in *The Julian Basilica: Architecture, Sculpture, Epigraphy*, vol. 22 of *Corinth: Results of Excavations Conducted by the American School of Classical Studies at Athens* (Princeton: American School of Classical Studies at Athens, 2022), 119–64.

Fig. 4.16 Reconstruction of Corinth's Julian Basilica (1st century AD) | *Courtesy of the Trustees of the American School of Classical Studies at Athens; used with permission*

shrine that was located in an exedra or recess in a wall on its southern end.[200] It was near this shrine that excavators found the remains of the statues of Gaius Caesar, Lucius Caesar, *Divus* Augustus, and probably of *Divus* Julius and *Divus* Claudius as well as remains of seven other statues whose identities are unknown, but they are certainly of Julio-Claudians (see table 4.6).[201]

TABLE 4.6 JULIO-CLAUDIAN STATUARY FROM CORINTH'S JULIAN BASILICA

Julio-Claudian	Reference
Divus Augustus	de Grazia Vanderpool, "Catalogue of Sculpture," 299–306, S-1
Nero Caesar (not the emperor Nero)	de Grazia Vanderpool, "Catalogue of Sculpture," 306–11, S-2

200. Scotton, "Form and Function," 217–19.

201. Some of these statues had been intentionally moved, others had been reused in later building projects, and still others had fallen into the Julian Basilica's cryptoporticus, where they remained until their discovery. See de Grazia Vanderpool, "Catalogue of Sculpture," 299–351.

Julio-Claudian	Reference
Britannicus (maybe)	de Grazia Vanderpool, "Catalogue of Sculpture," 211, 311–15, S-3
Unknown Julio-Claudian	de Grazia Vanderpool, "Catalogue of Sculpture," 315–18, S-4
Germanicus (maybe)	de Grazia Vanderpool, "Catalogue of Sculpture," 318–25, S-5
Drusus II (maybe)	de Grazia Vanderpool, "Catalogue of Sculpture," 211, 325–27, S-6
Divus Julius (probably)	de Grazia Vanderpool, "Catalogue of Sculpture," 327–35, S-7
Divus Claudius (probably)	de Grazia Vanderpool, "Catalogue of Sculpture," 335–39, S-8
Unknown Julio-Claudian	de Grazia Vanderpool, "Catalogue of Sculpture," 335–39, S-9
Gaius Caesar	de Grazia Vanderpool, "Catalogue of Sculpture," 339–43, S-10
Lucius Caesar	de Grazia Vanderpool, "Catalogue of Sculpture," 343–46, S-11
Diva Livia (maybe)	de Grazia Vanderpool, "Catalogue of Sculpture," 347–51, S-12

These statues are of high-quality marble from the famous Athenian quarry on Mount Pentelicus. The image probably of *Divus* Julius is the tallest of all surviving statues, and it was found directly in front of the tribunal or a raised platform on which the provincial governor would sit and render judgment. Therefore, it is probable that this statue was the focal point of imperial cultic activities, as it probably stood on a dais in the exedra in front of the tribunal.[202] In addition to the statues, several inscriptions related to imperial divine honors, discussed above, have come from the Julian Basilica; the most important for identifying the building as a site of imperial divine honors are the altar dedicated to *Divus* Augustus and the dedication to an Augustus's *genius*, which may be the emperor Augustus or another emperor who went by that title.[203] Thus, the Julian Basilica

---

202. De Grazia Vanderpool, "Julio-Claudian Family Group," 255–66; de Grazia Vanderpool, "Catalogue of Sculpture," 327–35, S-7.

203. "Appendix 1: Inscriptions" §4.9, 11.

underscores how interconnected imperial divine honors were to the judicial and administrative affairs not only of Corinth but also of Achaia.

The Theater

The only direct evidence that our next site, the Corinthian theater (see fig. 4.1), was a center of imperial divine honors in the colony is the remains of a statue that probably depicts *Divus* Augustus (see fig. 4.10). Corinth's theater was first built around 415 BC with stone seats and a wooden stage area. The Greek Corinthians renovated this structure in the late fourth century BC and built a new orchestra or place whence plays were conducted. In the early first century AD, the Roman colonists began to Romanize the Greek theater. They modified its seating and built a *scaenae frons* or decorated stone background for the theater's stage. During the early second century AD, the *scaenae frons* was renovated into a three-story structure with numerous niches in which statues were placed.[204] At that time, the statue in question was probably placed in one of these niches at the stage's eastern end, near where archaeologists found it in 1926.[205] Like the images from the Julian Basilica, this statue is made of high-quality marble from the famous Athenian quarry on Mount Pentelicus. This, along with the Jupiter-like posture of the image, suggests that it may have served as an object of imperial divine honors in the mid-first century AD. There was no set standard cultic statue in the Roman world, and any divine image could function as a cultic statue, especially to receive smaller sacrifices of wine and incense. Moreover, it is clear that Roman theaters and even the Colosseum in Rome, which was built after the Julio-Claudian period, were places in which imperial cultic images were set up.[206] It is important to note that it is unclear where the statue, which dates to Tiberius's or Claudius's reign, was displayed immediately after it was erected. It was probably in the theater, and the image may have been in a more accessible location than the second-century Corinthians placed it, in a niche in the *scaenae frons*. Recall that the first inscription attesting to divine honors for *Divus* Julius that I discussed is from a marble block,

204. Richard Stillwell, *The Theatre*, vol. 2 of *Corinth: Results of Excavations Conducted by the American School of Classical Studies at Athens* (Princeton: American School of Classical Studies, 1952), 131–41; Sanders, Palinkas, Tzonou-Herbst with Herbst, *Ancient Corinth*, 120–25.

205. Sturgeon, *Sculpture*, 67. She notes that it is probable that a statue of *Diva* Augusta served as a companion to this image in Corinth's theater and that it was set up in an opposite niche in the *scaenae frons*, although no evidence exists for such a statue.

206. See Nathan T. Elkins, "The Procession and Placement of Imperial Cult Images in the Colosseum," *Papers of the British School at Rome* 82 (2014): 73–107.

which possibly served as a statue base, from Corinth's theater (see fig. 4.2).[207] If this block is a statue base, then it is possible that a statue resembling the one that may depict *Divus* Augustus once stood atop it, an image that has not been found or has been destroyed before the modern period. Provided that this is the case, then the statue that may be of *Divus* Augustus may have been displayed near a statue of *Divus* Julius on a similar statue base. On balance, there is circumstantial, but not concrete, evidence that suggests that Corinth's theater was a site of imperial cultic activity for *Divus* Julius and *Divus* Augustus. The most logical time for this to occur would have been during the celebration of the Caesarean and Imperial Games, which, given that they consisted of poetry and encomia contests, were probably held in Corinth's theater.[208]

Ten Shops (?)

As noted in our discussion of divine honors for *Divus* Augustus, a marble architrave with an inscription attests to an *aedes* and a *statua* of Augustan Apollo in a Corinthian building known as Ten Shops (*tabernae decem*), the location of which is unknown.[209] As mentioned above, it is unclear whether the inscription was set up during Augustus's reign or afterward and whether it attests to divine honors for the living Augustus. For reasons already stated, it is probable that the epigraph attests to a shrine of Apollo who protected Augustus that was erected during the emperor's lifetime. Thus, this site is evidence not for imperial divine honors but of a deity who looks after the emperor. Therefore, this shrine of Apollo showcases that Corinth paired its commercial interests to the emperor's well-being. However, if I am wrong and Augustus has been assimilated with Apollo, then this epigraph attests to a shrine dedicated to Augustus, possibly during his lifetime, in the midst of a commercial area in Corinth. Either way, this shrine bespeaks the intertwining of the colony's economy with Augustus.

Temple E

The final place that some scholars have suggested imperial divine honors occurred is the largest temple in Corinth, Temple E, which formed the western boundary of the Corinthian forum (see fig. 4.1). This temple was built between AD 14 and 41

---

207. "Appendix 1: Inscriptions" §4.2.

208. I have been unable to locate any scholarly discussion about the role that this statue may have played in Corinthian imperial divine honors.

209. "Appendix 1: Inscriptions" §4.12.

Fig. 4.17 Remains of Archaic Temple; the caption is Remains of Corinth's Archaic Temple with its Doric columns | *Photo by author*

and renovated in the late first century AD after an earthquake struck Corinth in AD 77 and damaged it. Originally, Temple E was made of limestone and built atop a platform that measured 144 by 77 feet, roughly a fourth of an American football field. The exact dimensions of the temple at this point are unknown, but it had six columns of Doric order across its front, which resemble the columns that were erected in Corinth's Archaic Temple (see fig. 4. 17).

Temple E proper was placed at the western end of the sanctuary or boundary of the sacred limits of the temple complex, which consisted of a wall to the west (against which the temple abutted) and a stoa to the temple's north and south. After the earthquake, the temple was rebuilt of marble atop the distinctive Roman podium. Temple E's sacred boundary was extended, which left the temple in the middle of the temple complex, not at the temple complex's western end. Please note that the site map that I have used in this chapter depicts Temple E as it would have looked after the earthquake of AD 77, not before it.[210]

210. Sarah Elizabeth Freeman, "Temple E," in *Architecture*, vol. 1, part 2 of *Corinth: Results of Excavations Conducted by the American School of Classical Studies at Athens* (Cambridge: Harvard University Press, 1941), 166–236; Charles K. Williams III, "A Re-evaluation of Temple E and the West End of the Forum," in *The Greek Renaissance in the Roman Empire*, ed. S. Walker

During excavations, archaeologists found nothing concrete to identify to whom the Corinthians dedicated Temple E. A few historians interpret Pausanias's reference to Octavia's *naos* as referring to Temple E.[211] As we have seen, this is improbable, for this latter building was probably a small shrine dedicated to Octavia. Other scholars identify Temple E as Octavia's *naos* but stress that it was the location of imperial divine honors in general, not just those for Octavia in particular. Charles Williams, the former director of Corinth Excavations at the American School of Classical Studies at Athens, posits that "the logical interpretation" of Pausanias's text and "the safest assumption is that Temple E was built to house the Imperial Cult."[212] If this is the case, Williams surmises, then "one is tempted to see in this evidence that the emphasis in official religion [in Corinth] turned from the Olympian gods in the course of the first century A.D. towards the Imperial Cult."[213]

While Williams's identification is possible, it remains conjecture, for no archaeological evidence corroborates it. However, comparative evidence from other Roman colonies argues against his thesis. Remains of Roman communities demonstrate that often temples to Jupiter were in Roman forums and that they were the largest such buildings in colonies.[214] As we have seen, it is probable that the upper terrace of Philippi's forum contained such a temple (see pp. 87–88). The first-century Roman architect Vitruvius (circa 80–15 BC) designed a Roman forum in the Roman colony of Fano on the northeastern side of Italy in which he placed a basilica with a shrine to Augustus directly across the forum from the city's temple of Jupiter.[215] This arrangement, which resembles the layout of Corinth's forum, suggests that across from the Corinthian Julian Basilica, one would expect to find

---

and A. Cameron, BICS 55 (London: Oxford University Press, 1989), 156–62; Sanders, Palinkas, Tzonou-Herbst with Herbst, *Ancient Corinth*, 30–32.

211. Pausanias, *Description of Greece* 2.3.1; Roux, *Pausanias en Corinthe*, 112–16.

212. Charles K. Williams II, "The Refounding of Corinth: Some Roman Religious Attitudes," in *Roman Architecture in the Greek World*, ed. Sarah Macready and F. H. Thompson, SALOP 10 (London: Society of the Antiquaries, 1987), 26–37, quotation 29.

213. Williams, "Refounding of Corinth," 29. Winter, *Divine Honours*, 186–89, follows Williams on this point, because it fits into his larger portrait of early Christianity at odds with imperial divine honors in Corinth.

214. Ian M. Burton, "Capitoline Temples in Italy and the Provinces (Especially Africa), *ANRW* 12.1:259–372.

215. Vitruvius, *On Architecture* 5.1.6–7, notes in passing that in the construction of the basilica in Fano, he omitted two columns in front of the imperial shrine so that the statue of Augustus in the shrine could look out into the forum and see the temple of Jupiter on its opposite end. I am indebted to Scotton, "Form and Function," 199–21, and de Grazia Vanderpool, "Julio-Claudian Family Group," 280–84, for this reference to Vitruvius's work. They do not, however, use this

Jupiter's temple. The fact that the temple directly across from the Julian Basilica is Temple E argues in favor of an identification of the temple as Jupiter's.[216] Consequently, Temple E was probably not an imperial temple. This does not mean, however, that imperial sacrifices did not occur there occasionally, for as we have seen and I shall stress below, the intertwining of traditional and imperial divine honors means that offerings to both groups were made on altars dedicated to gods and *divi*.

Provincial Imperial Divine Honors

A comprehensive treatment of imperial divine honors in Corinth would be remiss without a discussion of such honors for a portion of the province that were housed in the colony but were celebrated for certain cities in Achaia. These provincial divine honors were unique in the Greek East, because for most of the Julio-Claudian period, Achaia did not have a *koinon* uniting all the cities in the province, as was the case in the Roman provinces of Asia, Galatia, and Bithynia.[217] Rather, Achaia had several local *koina* that consisted of clusters of Greek cities.[218] In the mid-50s AD, however, some *koina* united to form a single grant of provincial divine honors for Nero, which was based in Corinth, the provincial capital of Achaia. Unlike the provinces of Asia, Galatia, and Bithynia, these united *koina* in the province did not build an imperial temple for Nero or, for as long as the Roman province existed, any emperor for that matter.[219] The earliest evidence for this grant of Neronian provincial imperial divine honors consists of an inscription that records the résumé of the Corinthian benefactor, Spartiaticus. He served as "high priest of the Augustan house for life and [was] the first of the Achaians (to hold this office)"

---

literary testimony to argue for the identity of Temple E but to support their convincing thesis that the Julian Basilica contained an imperial shrine.

216. One of Temple E's original excavators and the person who published its official report, Freedman, "Temple E," 232–36, posits that the temple was dedicated to Jupiter, and an inscription, Kent, *Corinth* 8.3, no. 152, attests to a priest of Jupiter Capitolinus in early first-century AD Corinth. See also Walbank, "Pausanias," 361–94. In Corinth's official site guide, Sanders, Palinkas, Tzonou-Herbst with Herbst, *Ancient Corinth*, 32, echo the uncertainty of Temple E's identity, noting that it may have been dedicated to Octavia, Jupiter, or imperial cultic activity.

217. Francesco Camia, "Between Tradition and Innovation: Cults for Roman Emperors in the Province of Achaia," in *Kaiserkult in den Provinzen des Römischen Reiches: Organisation, Kommunikation, und Repräsentation*, ed. Anne Kolb and Marco Vitale (Berlin: de Gruyter, 2016), 255–83.

218. These *koina* were named the following: Boeotian, Euboian, Phocidian, Locrian, and Dorian. See Camia and Kantiréa, "Imperial Cult in the Peloponnese," 398.

219. Barbara Burrell, *Neokoroi: Greek Cities and Roman Emperors* (Leiden: Brill, 2004), 17–85, 147–62, 166–74. See the lack of discussion of Achaian temples in Burrell, *Neokoroi*.

(*archieri Domus Aug(ustae)* [*in*] *perpetuum, primo Achaeon*).[220] It is clear that this priesthood was under the auspices of the Achaian *koinon*, because a Greek inscription from Athens on a statue base of Spartiaticus dating between AD 54 and 68 provides the Greek translation of this priesthood—"high priest of the Augustan gods and the house of the Augusti . . . for life [and] first of the Achaians (to hold this office) forever"—and places this office in the realm of divine honors associated with "the *koinon* of Achaia."[221]

There is, however, one striking difference between these two epigraphs, which highlights the Roman character of imperial divine honors in Corinth. The Corinthian inscription notes that Spartiaticus was "high priest of the Augustan house for life," while the Athenian epigraph indicates that he was not only high priest of "the house of the Augusti . . . for life" but also "high priest of the Augustan gods." The Corinthian inscription omits this latter reference, probably because it referred to a public office that Spartiaticus held in Athens, not Corinth. In the Roman colony, the divine title by which Julio-Claudians were divinely honored was *divi*, not *dei* or "gods." The exact duties of the high priest of the Augustan house for the Achaian *koinon* are uncertain. Given that there were no imperial temples for the *koinon*, they probably consisted of sacrifices. It is possible that they included wild-beast fights and gladiatorial combats in honor of the Julio-Claudian line. A first-century AD letter that may date to the Julio-Claudian period notes that the city of Argos, near Corinth, complains about the tribute that Corinth had recently started collecting from Argos and other Greek cities.[222] These taxes, the letter states, are onerous. Moreover, according to the missive, Corinth was using these taxes to fund what appears to be an annual "festival that is neither Greek nor ancient" consisting of "a foreign spectacle" in which wild-beast fights occur in the colony's theaters (*sic*). In the letter, Argos objected to this tribute and sent ambassadors to the governor of Achaia asking for remittance for paying it.[223] Wild-beast fights were Roman, not Greek, in nature and were almost always put on in the context of imperial divine honors.[224] It is possible but uncertain that these contests were part of the imperial divine honors for the Achaian *koinon* that were

220. "Appendix 1: Inscriptions" §4.3, lines 8–9; Spawforth, "Corinth, Argos," 218–21.

221. ἀρχιερέα θε[ῶν] Σεβαστῶν κ[αὶ] [γέ]νους Σε[β]αστῶν, ἐκ τοῦ κοινοῦ τῆ[ς] Ἀχαίας διὰ βίου πρῶτον τῶν ἀπ' αἰῶνος ("Appendix 1: Inscriptions" §4.24, lines 2–7).

222. This letter has been mistakenly placed in a collection of missives related to the fourth-century AD Roman emperor Julian the Apostate. See Spawforth, "Corinth," 211–32.

223. οὐδὲ πρὸς Ἑλληνικὴν οὐδὲ παλαιὰν πανήγυριν . . . ξενικῇ θέᾳ (Julian, *Letters* 28); Spawforth, "Corinth," 211–30.

224. Simon R. F. Price, *Rituals and Power: The Roman Imperial Cult in Asia Minor* (Cambridge: Cambridge University Press, 1984), 89, notes, "animal fights [along with gladiatorial

housed in Corinth's theater (see fig. 4.1).[225] If this is correct, then any divine honors were directed toward the Julio-Claudian line, not to individual Julio-Claudians, for Spartiaticus was "high priest of the Augustan house."

Aspects of Imperial Divine Honors

Now that we know where imperial divine honors were housed, we must explore certain aspects of these honors, namely, of what they consisted and when and how imperial *flamines* in Corinth made them. Unfortunately, we cannot reconstruct these particulars from Corinthian evidence alone, but we must draw on data from Rome, other Roman colonies, and documents associated with Roman imperial administration. Once again, the best evidence to address these questions is the *Acts of the Arval Brothers* and the Roman military calendar known as the *Feriale Duranum* (for discussions of these sources, see pp. 42, 91–93). These two documents attest that state-sponsored imperial sacrifices included bulls, male cows, and female cows, which were offered to Julio-Claudian *divi*, and that beginning in AD 55 bulls were sacrificed to the reigning emperor's *genius*. It is most probable that Corinthian imperial *flamines* offered these animals to *Divus* Julius, Octavia, Gaius Caesar, Lucius Caesar, *Divus* Augustus, *Diva* Augusta, and probably to *Divus* Claudius. In contrast to the *Acts of the Arval Brothers*, an inscription from Corinth suggests that the colony may have made offerings to the reigning emperor's *genius*, beginning with Augustus. If this is the case, then it is probable that this practice continued throughout the Julio-Claudian period.[226] In addition to animal sacrifices, the *Feriale Duranum* attests another type of sacrifice, one of wine and incense known as a *supplicatio*. This type of offering was probably made before the images of the Julio-Claudian *divi*, Octavia, Gaius Caesar, Lucius Caesar, and Nero's *genius* on the altar dedicated to *Divus* Augustus that was a part of the imperial shrine in the Julian Basilica.[227] Animal sacrifices and *supplicationes* were probably offered in Corinth regularly on altars before Octavia's shrine, the Julian Family Temple, and, though unattested in the Corinthian evidence, on altars in Corinth's theater before, during, or after the poetry and encomia contests for Julio-Claudians during the Caesarean and Imperial Games or on other celebratory occasions, provided that such imperial festivities occurred there.

---

combats], which spread from Rome . . . were put on almost exclusively in connection with the imperial cult."

225. Camia and Kantiréa, "Imperial Cult in the Peloponnese," 388–89.

226. "Appendix 1: Inscriptions" §4.11.

227. "Appendix 1: Inscriptions" §4.9; "Appendix 2: Reconstructed Julio-Claudian Imperial Calendar in Philippi and Corinth."

Given that imperial sacrifices mentioned in the *Acts of the Arval Brothers* and the *Feriale Duranum* were the same as those offered to the Roman gods, that is, bulls, bovines, wine, and incense, we can reconstruct how such sacrifices were carried out in Corinth. These offerings would have been offered for the benefit of the entire colony and performed in public view. Sacrifices of wine and incense would have been carried out without much work and need not have occurred on the imperial altars in the aforementioned places but before images, painted or statues, of Julio-Claudian *divi*, Octavia, Gaius Caesar, Lucius Caesar, and the reigning emperor's *genius* set up anywhere in the colony. On the other hand, blood sacrifices would have occurred at the end of sacred processions like the one in Gythium that opened this book but in the Roman custom of processions (see pp. 1–4). This means that imperial *flamines* would have led in procession local elites, musicians, and *victimarii*, or special slaves who killed the sacrificial animals, winding their way through the city to the altar that was being used for the ritual in question.

Once the imperial procession arrived at the altar, the imperial *flamen* would have washed his hands with water, burned incense, and poured a libation of wine to the Julio-Claudian *divi*, Octavia, Gaius Caesar, Lucius Caesar, or the emperor's *genius*.[228] These sacred rites completed, the imperial *flamen* would have poured wine and some special flour atop the sacrificial animal's head as well as run his knife down the beast's back.[229] These acts functioned to transfer ownership of the bull or cow from the imperial *flamen* and thus Corinth's *populus* to the object of sacrifice, the Julio-Claudian *divi*, Octavia, Gaius Caesar, Lucius Caesar, or the emperor's *genius*. At this point, the animal was supposed to nod its head, thereby giving consent to be slaughtered.[230] Whereupon, the *victimarius* would have struck the animal on its head to stun it, cut its throat, and drained its blood.

Once the beast was dead, a special cultic official known in Latin as a *haruspex* would have inspected its entrails (liver, lungs, gall bladder, the peritoneum, and heart) to ensure that the Julio-Claudian *divi*, Octavia, Gaius Caesar, Lucius Caesar, or the emperor's *genius* had accepted the offering. If no abnormalities were found, the object was believed to have been acceptable to the divine being to whom it was offered.[231] After such confirmation, the entrails of the animal would have

228. Valerie M. Warrior, *Roman Religion* (Cambridge: Cambridge University Press, 2006), 21–22.

229. In Rome, the Vestal Virgins made this flour, which was mixed with other ingredients and called *mola salsa*. There is no evidence, however, that *mola salsa* was used in Roman sacrifices outside Rome. Thus, the people of Corinth may have used something else. See Scheid, *Introduction*, 81, 83.

230. Scheid, *Introduction*, 83.

231. No *haruspices* (the Latin plural of *haruspex*) are attested (yet?) in Corinth, but given

been boiled in a pot. This finished, the *flamen* would have dumped them, along with more wine and special flour, onto the fires of the altar where they would have been consumed. Finally, the remainder of the animal would have been divided among the participants and eaten near the imperial altar by the *flamen* and participants in the procession. Thus, not every citizen or denizen of Corinth would have eaten meat or drunk wine from imperial sacrifices. This fact is probably why the Corinthian *agonothete* Cornelius Pulcher boasted in an inscription that he provided a banquet (*epulum*) to "all colonists" (*omnibus colonis*), not just a small number of aristocrats participating in the ritual.[232] Any meat that was not consumed at such a sacrifice was taken to the *macellum* or "meat market" and sold (1 Cor 10:25).

The *Acts of the Arval Brothers* provide us with another way that imperial sacrifices would have been offered in Corinth, in conjunction with those offered to traditional Roman gods. According to one specialist of Roman imperial divine honors, Ittai Gradel, the *Acts of the Arval Brothers* that date to the Julio-Claudian period indicate that sacrifices were almost always offered to the gods, Julio-Claudian *divi*, and beginning in AD 55, the reigning emperor's *genius*, with one major exception: the commemoration of the day on which the temple of *Divus* Augustus in Rome was founded. In this case, sacrifices to the gods were omitted.[233] This suggests that imperial sacrifices in Corinth probably were associated with traditional sacrifices. To provide an example, on January 3, AD 38, the president of the Arval Brothers vowed to sacrifice cows and to donate a certain weight of gold and silver to Jupiter, Juno, Minerva, Dea Dia, *Salus* (the personification of public health, security, and well-being), and *Divus* Augustus, provided that these divine beings continued to preserve Caligula, maintain his well-being, and keep him safe from any assassination plots.[234]

This combination of Corinth's gods and the Julio-Claudians is clear from Corinthian material. Soon after the city was refounded and gained control of the Isthmian Games in honor of Poseidon, it added the Caesarean Games in honor of Augustus and during Tiberius's reign the Imperial Games in honor of the reigning emperor. Both sets of these games were celebrated in Corinth originally after or then before the Isthmian Games, and they were overseen by the same public official who administered the Isthmian Games, an *agonothete*. When the Isthmian,

---

that they were active in other Roman colonies, they probably were in Corinth, too. *Lex Coloniae Genetivae* 62 stipulates that every *duovir* has the right to have a *haruspex*, among several other attendants.

232. "Appendix 1: Inscriptions" §4.16, lines 12–13.
233. Gradel, *Emperor Worship*, 179–80.
234. "Appendix 1: Inscriptions" §2.16.

Caesarean, and Imperial Games were held together, the colony selected an *isago-geus* to aid the *agonothete*. Provided that the identification of the statues of *Divus* Julius, *Divus* Augustus (from Corinth's theater), and *Divus* Claudius are correct, the Corinthians depicted these divinized emperors in the guise of Jupiter.[235] It is possible that the statue of *Divus* Augustus that the *Augustales* erected in the forum pictured him similarly. At the very least, the image of *Divus* Augustus faced Temple E with its back to the Julian Basilica, the judicial and administrative center of the province. Provided that Temple E was dedicated to Jupiter, then the divinized emperor who claimed piety as one of his virtues watched over the sacrifices to the god that occurred in front of his image.[236] Consequently, Corinthian imperial divine honors did not compete with traditional divine honors, contrary to what some New Testament scholars contend, for imperial divine honors were associated with and wedded to traditional divine honors either directly or indirectly in a symbiotic relationship.[237] This means that sacrifices to Julio-Claudian *divi*, Octavia, Gaius Caesar, Lucius Caesar, and the reigning emperor's *genius* need not have occurred only on imperial altars. Because the gods and the Julio-Claudians in question and Octavia worked together, sacrifices may have been offered to them on altars of the traditional gods (even the altar[s] in the temple complex of Temple E) with offerings being directed to both groups.

The final aspect of imperial sacrifices that we must reconstruct is when they were offered. Once again, the *Acts of the Arval Brothers* and *Feriale Duranum* are most helpful, for they provide the exact days when the Arval Brothers and those Roman soldiers stationed at Dura Europos, Syria offered sacrifices.[238] Both texts show that imperial offerings were made to imperials who were *divi* on their birthdays and anniversaries of special occasions throughout the year, especially for the reigning emperor. To provide the reader with an idea, appendix 2 lists the imperial sacrifices that the Arval Brothers offered in Rome for the year AD 59, the most complete year among the *Acts of the Arval Brothers* that date to the Julio-Claudian period, and the days throughout the year that the soldiers in Dura Europos made offerings to Julio-Claudian *divi*. Given that Paul visited Corinth for the first time

---

235. The area of Ten Shops contained an *aedes* and *statua* of Apollo who protects Augustus: "Appendix 1: Inscriptions" §4.12.

236. *Res gestae divi Augusti* 19.1–2; 20.1, 4; 34.2.

237. Gradel, *Roman Religion*, 275–76, notes that the Arval Brothers honored the Roman gods and *divi* at the same time, and "there was evidently no question of rivalry, and the old gods had nothing to fear from the newcomer [i.e., deified imperials]." Walbank, "Cults of Roman Corinth," 364, concludes of divine honors for imperials in Corinth, "Worship of the imperial family flourished alongside and in conjunction with local civic cults."

238. "Appendix 2: Reconstructed Julio-Claudian Imperial Calendar in Philippi and Corinth."

in AD 50/51, the second in the mid-50s AD, the third in the late 50s AD, and that he probably wrote the various letters to the Corinthians in the mid-50s AD, the list of birthdays of Julio-Claudian *divi* and the reigning emperor that would have been celebrated in Corinth were the following: *Divus* Julius's (July 12), *Divus* Augustus's (September 23), (maybe) *Diva* Augusta's (January 30), *Divus* Claudius's (August 1), and Nero's (December 15) (this latter sacrifice would have been to his *genius*). The birthdays of Octavia and Gaius Caesar and Lucius Caesar are unknown, but they may have been celebrated, too. Besides anniversaries of births, imperial sacrifices in Corinth would have commemorated important milestones associated with Julio-Claudian *divi*, such as anniversaries of their ascensions to the imperial throne, military victories such as the cult of *Britannia Victoria* (see p. 188), granting of offices, like consul of Rome, or titles, such as "father of the fatherland," and their safe return to Rome after traveling. Thus, these days probably witnessed imperial festivals and processions that ended in sacrifice, as discussed above.

Synthesis and Conclusion

To conclude this discussion of imperial divine honors in Corinth, I will synthesize and summarize our findings. The colony established postmortem divine honors for Julio-Claudian *divi*—*Divus* Julius, *Divus* Augustus, *Diva* Augusta, and (probably) *Divus* Claudius—and for three individuals connected to Augustus, Gaius Caesar and Lucius Caesar, the emperor's adopted sons, and Octavia, Augustus's sister. In addition to these honors, Corinth offered sacrifices to the reigning emperor's *genius* maybe from Augustus's reign onward. The evidence indicates that Corinth appointed special Roman priests (to date no imperial priestesses are attested) known as *flamines* to administer those sacrifices and to oversee the cults of these Julio-Claudians and Octavia, although to date only *flamines* of *Divus* Julius and *Divus* Augustus are attested. For how long these imperial *flaminiae* lasted is unclear. The first and only attestation of *Divus* Julius's *flaminia* dates between AD 54 and 58, almost one hundred years after the establishment of divine honors for him in Corinth. Similarly, the only evidence for *Divus* Augustus's priesthood in Corinth dates to AD 66/67, nearly fifty years after his death and divinization in Rome.

Such priests were drawn from wealthy local aristocratic Corinthian families, some of whom had connections throughout the province of Achaia and the Roman imperial bureaucracy (e.g., Laco and Spartiaticus). During the time when Paul established early Christianity in the colony, these men either had held, were holding, or would go on to hold the most prestigious public offices in Corinth, *duovir*, *duovir quinquennalis*, and *agonothete* of the Isthmian, Caesarean, and Imperial Games, as they served in their imperial cultic posts. In some cases (as with Laco and Spartiaticus), the holding of these imperial cultic posts was a family affair. Corinth's *flamines* offered oxen, male cows, female cows, bulls, incense, or wine to the above Julio-Claudians, Octavia, and the reigning emperor's *genius* on altars in front of Octavia's shrine, the Julian Family Temple, and possibly on altars before the images of *Divus* Julius and *Divus* Augustus in the Corinthian theater. Sacrifices of incense and wine were probably made to specific Julio-Claudians and the Julio-Claudian family on the imperial altar in the Julian Basilica's shrine. These sacrifices were offered in view of the public and on behalf of Corinth. The larger sacrifices of animals occurred at the conclusion of imperial processions that imperial *flamines* led on special days connected to the Julio-Claudians that were celebrated annually or spontaneously upon hearing news of momentous events in the lives of the Julio-Claudians. In addition to these offerings at imperial cultic sites, sacrifices were probably offered to the above Julio-Claudians, Octavia, and the reigning emperor's *genius* on altars of various Corinthian gods and in conjunction with these latter deities. Besides priests, Corinth appointed two more imperial cultic posts, that of *agonothete* and *isagogeus*, both of which were connected to games in Corinth associated with Augustus and the reigning emperor. Not only did these imperial cultic officials oversee imperial sacrifices, games, or both, but also they provided concrete benefactions to Corinth such as building projects and paying for banquets for all colonists. Such acts increased their own reputations and that of their families and ultimately served to promote their public careers in the colony and, if they were lucky, in the province and in the empire. A group of freedmen and wealthy outsiders known as *Augustales* were active in Corinth and provided munificence connected to the Julio-Claudians in the colony. They may have offered divine honors to the Julio-Claudians, especially on shrines of *Lares* of Corinthian crossroads. If such offerings were made, they were on the private, not public, level. Finally, it is possible and even probable that some Corinthians assimilated certain Julio-Claudians into their domestic hearths and made other private offerings to them, for which no evidence has survived.

IMPERIAL DIVINE HONORS AND EARLY CHRISTIANITY IN CORINTH

We are now able to bring this contextual reconstruction of imperial divine honors in Corinth to bear upon what relationship, if any, these honors had with early Christianity in the colony. It is evident that such honors had a prominent place in the city and that early Corinthian Christians would have been aware of them.[239] When Paul made his first, second, or third visits to the city between AD 50 and 57 (Acts 18:1–18; 2 Cor

---

239. Contra Miller, "Imperial Cult," 314–32, esp. 329–31.

2:1; 12:14, 21; 13:1–3; Acts 20:2–3), he would have seen Octavia's *naos*, the Julian Family Temple, the Julian Basilica with its imperial shrine and statues, the massive bronze statue of *Divus* Augustus in the forum (see figs. 4.1, 6–7, 13, 15–16), and the images of *Divus* Julius (provided that one existed) and *Divus* Augustus (provided that it has been correctly identified) in Corinth's theater (see figs. 4.2, 10). The Corinthian Christians and possibly Paul would have seen, heard, and smelled imperial processions and sacrifices as they winded their way through the colony during imperial celebrations throughout the year.[240] Christians in Corinth who could read would have noticed imperial titles on inscriptions attached to monuments such as the statue base of *Divus* Augustus in the forum (see figs. 4.6, 7), the Julian Family Temple identifying it as such (see fig. 4.13), the altar dedicated to *Divus* Augustus in the Julian Basilica, and on statue bases and sarcophagi honoring imperial *flamines*, which would have been on funerary monuments directly outside Corinth. Paul's converts would have seen the Latin legend and image of the Julian Family Temple on coins (not to mention the busts of twenty Julio-Claudians; see table 4.2) that these Christians used to buy their daily bread and wine, including for their eucharistic meals, and that they contributed to the collection for the saints in Jerusalem (1 Cor 16:1–4; 2 Cor 8:1–9:15). In short, early Christians in Corinth could not have escaped imperial divine honors. Thus, the scholarly consideration of them to interpret Paul's letters to the Corinthian Christians is appropriate.[241] However, the question remains, How should we use divine honors for Julio-Claudians in reading 1 (and maybe 2) Corinthians?

As noted above, some New Testament scholars contend that the relationship of divine honors for Julio-Claudians with nascent Christianity in Corinth was one of direct opposition. From an identification of Temple E as imperial and the *theoi* and *kyrioi* "in heaven," "on earth," or both (1 Cor 8:5–6) as Julio-Claudians, these exegetes conclude that such honors were the most important cultic honors in first-century AD Corinth and thus the biggest competitor to early Christianity. Thus, Paul sought to counteract their influence upon his converts in the composition of mainly 1 Corinthians.[242] The difficulty with this reconstruction is that the Corinthian sources for imperial divine honors do not support it. While Temple E's identity is debated, it seems likely that it was dedicated to Jupiter, not to any Julio-Claudian(s). Moreover,

---

240. These processions, which included human participants and the sacrificial animals, would have winded their way through the city to imperial altars to offer sacrifices to Julian-Claudian *divi*, Octavia, Gaius Caesar, Lucius Caesar, or the emperor's *genius*.

241. To quote Deissmann, *Light from the Ancient East*, 340, on this point, "It must not be supposed that St. Paul and his fellow-believers went through the world blindfolded, unaffected by what was then moving through the world of men in great cities."

242. Winter, *Divine Honours*, 166–225; Wright, *Paul and the Faithfulness of God*, 1:311–47, esp. 332; Finney, "Christ Crucified," 20–33.

there is no indication that Corinth hailed any Julio-Claudian, living or dead, as *kyrios*. Although Greek speakers would have called Julio-Claudian *divi "theoi,"* they were probably aware that this was the translation of *divus*, for which there was no corresponding Greek term or concept.[243] Hence, Greek-speaking Corinthians probably knew that in their city, *theos* did not equal *divus*. The former were gods, but the latter were humans who had died and whom the Roman Senate had decreed had been translated into the heavenly sphere. If my reconstruction is correct, then there is no evidence from the Corinthian correspondence that supports direct conflict between early Christians and their pagan counterparts in the colony that stemmed from divine honors for Julio-Claudians, as some New Testament scholars propose.

This lack of strife is surprising when one considers two things. First, 1 Corinthians is filled with numerous references to pagan Corinthians interacting with Christians.[244] This letter attests that some Christians sued their brothers and sisters in Christ and had their cases heard before pagan Corinthian judges (1 Cor 6:1–8). Some believers in the colony visited prostitutes who were, presumably, non-Christian (1 Cor 6:12–20). Not a few Corinthian Christians, both male and female, were married to pagan Corinthians and remained so even after their conversion; at least that was Paul's wish for them (1 Cor 7:12–16). Believers visited pagan temple complexes and dined on food that priests had offered to Corinth's gods and divinities (1 Cor 8:7–13; 10:14–22), they entered the homes of their pagan counterparts for repasts even on food that had been offered to idols (1 Cor 10:23–30), and the Corinthian Christians purchased meat offered to pagan gods in Corinth's meat market (*makellon*) (1 Cor 10:25). Because of the prominence of imperial divine honors in the colony and that they were embedded into traditional divine honors, such meat may have been offered to the Julio-Claudian *divi*, Octavia, Gaius Caesar, Lucius Caesar, and even the emperor's *genius*, which means that in a way, imperial divine honors were part of the problem that Paul attempted to address in 1 Corinthians. Finally, pagan Corinthians entered Christian assemblies at will (1 Cor 14:16, 22–25). Despite this frequent interaction between Christians and pagans in Corinth, our sources show no evidence of conflict associated with imperial divine honors.[245]

---

243. For an example of this from Corinth, see "Appendix 1: Inscriptions" §4.1.

244. See John M. G. Barclay, "Thessalonica and Corinth: Social Contrasts in Pauline Christianity," *JSNT* 47 (1992): 49–74, esp. 57–72; James C. Walters, "Civic Identity in Roman Corinth and Its Impact on Early Christians," in *Urban Religion in Roman Corinth: Interdisciplinary Approaches*, ed. Daniel N. Schowalter and Steven J. Friesen, HTS 53 (Cambridge: Harvard University Press, 2005), 397–417.

245. In the words of Barclay, "Thessalonica and Corinth," 57, "one of the most significant, but least noticed, features of Corinthian church life is the absence of conflict in the relationship between Christians and 'outsiders.'"

Second, imperial, along with traditional, divine honors contributed to the mistreatment of Christians in Philippi and Thessalonica. In the former, believers' refusal to participate in these two types of divine honors that were wedded to each other and that were hallmarks of what it meant to be a good *colonus* of the Roman colony, and their proclamation of a new, non-Roman deity resulted in the suffering and even imprisonment of some Philippian Christians (Phil 1:27–30). Paul's establishment of the church in Thessalonica and the Thessalonian Christians' subsequent aggressive evangelistic activity produced such persecution that Paul feared that his converts had apostatized from the faith (1 Thess 3:1–5). There is nothing in 1 or 2 Corinthians that approaches anything similar to these cases. Thus, the most appropriate question for us to ponder is, considering the prominence of imperial divine honors for Julio-Claudians in Corinth, which is much more than in Philippi and Thessalonica (hence the size of this chapter compared to the previous two), and the frequent interaction between pagans and Christians, Why do we not possess evidence for a clash between imperial divine honors and early Christianity? The answer to this question can be found in the contextual reconstructions of Julio-Claudian Corinth, imperial divine honors, and 1 Corinthians.

As a prosperous trading center and master of two harbors, Corinth was not the small socially conservative Roman colony that Philippi was. To put it into perspective, every *colonus* of Philippi was registered into one voting tribe, the Voltinia (see p. 80), while the *coloni* of Corinth were scattered among twelve of them with ten tribes probably dating to the Julio-Claudian period (see table 4.1). The aristocrats who ruled Corinth consisted of Greeks who had been given Roman citizenship, such as Laco and Spartiaticus, Greek slaves whom their Roman masters had emancipated and to whom they had given Roman citizenship, Roman *negotiatores* who had lived and traded in the Greek East for some time, and the male descendants of these three groups. This situation differed markedly from Philippi, where the same group of socially conservative Roman *coloni* from Italy and their male descendants maintained control of the colony for three hundred years (see pp. 100–104). The impact that local leaders had on Philippi and Corinth is evident in the official languages of the two colonies. While Latin was the official language of Corinth and Philippi after their founding as Roman colonies, by the early second century AD, Corinth began to use Greek as an official language, whereas Philippi did not adopt Greek until the third century.[246] Moreover, Corinth was a city with a storied past whose influence loomed over the Roman colony. The early colonists assimilated parts of the Greek city into their new Roman community, which was not the case in Philippi. Consequently, because of Corinth's Greek past and status as the provincial capital of Achaia, the city and its ethos were more

246. See Kent, *Corinth* 8.3:18–19.

open to non-Roman influences than its Macedonian sister colony, Philippi. We can see the result that Greek influence made in Roman Corinth when we compare Corinthian imperial divine honors with those in Philippi. While both colonies celebrated Roman imperial divine honors, Corinth established the Caesarean and Imperial Games within the context of the panhellenic Isthmian Games; the city appears to have honored divinely Lucius Caesar and Gaius Caesar as Dioscuri in keeping with a local Greek tradition about the two twins; and beginning in Nero's reign, the colony created a provincial imperial cultic priesthood for "the Augustan house" in which cities in the Achaian *koinon* participated. There is no evidence that Philippi did any of these things, however.

In addition to the openness of Corinth to foreign non-Roman customs, including on its imperial divine honors, a close reading of 1 Corinthians suggests that Christians in the colony did not clash with their pagan counterparts over imperial divine honors or traditional divine honors, for that matter, because pagans, like many Christians, in the city did not grasp the Jewish apocalyptic nature of the gospel.[247] According to Paul, the message of the cross was utter foolishness to pagans in Corinth (1 Cor 1:18, 23), for it consisted of divine wisdom that had been revealed through the gospel that was alien to the cosmopolitan culture of Corinth (1 Cor 1:19–21, 27–31), and even to the cosmic powers who rule the present evil age (1 Cor 2:6–8).[248] Many of Paul's converts did not grasp this key countercultural aspect of the gospel. Because of the preponderance of spiritual gifts operative among the Corinthian Christians (1 Cor 1:7; 12:1–14:40) and what appears to be an overrealized spiritualized eschatology, they considered themselves already reigning, as though Christ's triumphant return had already occurred (1 Cor 4:8–13).[249] The world could continue as it always had with no difficulties for the Corinthians in Christ, because they in some sense had transcended it. One consequence of this attitude was that some Corinthian Christians were consuming meat and foodstuffs that had probably been sacrificed to pagan gods *and* to one or more Julio-Claudian(s), the entire Julio-Claudian line, or even to the reigning emperor's *genius*, at the same time (1 Cor 8:7–13; 10:14–22, 23–30).[250]

---

247. Barclay, "Social Contrasts," 57–72. For an informed discussion of Paul as an apocalyptic thinker and 1 Corinthians, see Alexandra Brown, *The Cross and Human Transformation: Paul's Apocalyptic Word in 1 Corinthians* (Minneapolis: Fortress, 1995).

248. Unlike some interpreters, I conclude that the rulers of 1 Cor 2:6–8 are cosmic powers, not Julio-Claudians.

249. Fitzmyer, *1 Corinthians*, 209–28. Yet Barclay, "Thessalonica and Corinth," 64, raises the possibility that the Corinthian Christians did not have an overrealized eschatology and that what appears in 1 Corinthians is Paul's perspective on the situation, which is colored by Paul's apocalyptic worldview.

250. For this reason, Paul probably considered imperial and traditional divine honors as

Consequently, it is probable that most pagans in Corinth did not take seriously these overzealous spiritualized Corinthian Christians, because they did not grasp the gospel's meaning, as Paul proclaimed it, for two reasons. First, nonbelieving Corinthians may have dismissed Christians as fanatics of a *superstitio*, a dysfunctional and unsanctioned cult, that had washed up on their shores, which, as a double-port city, such *superstitiones* were wont to do. For this reason, the pagan Corinthians did not react with the same fervor that their fellow Philippian colonists did in attempting to eradicate Christianity in their colony. Second, as John M. G. Barclay plausibly suggests, the Corinthian Christians who considered themselves to be spiritual may have acted upon their belief only in Christian assemblies. Outside such gatherings, these believers may have behaved "as they wished" and thus continued to act as they always had before being in Christ.[251] Therefore, there may not have been a difference between the pre- and post-Christian behavior of some Corinthians in Christ for the pagan Corinthians to observe. Provided that Barclay is correct, in 1 Corinthians, Paul seeks to counter this perspective. The fascinating thing to consider is that if the apostle was successful, then this would have led to conflict between his converts and their pagan counterparts, as we find to varying degrees in Philippi and Thessalonica. Nevertheless, there is no direct literary evidence to know whether Paul was successful in this venture, for there is a gap of about fifty years in our knowledge of the Corinthian church. The next time we meet the Corinthian Christians (1 Clement), conflict is still a problem in the church, but, like in 1 Corinthians, this is inner conflict among Christians, not harassment or persecution from outsiders.

Conclusion

To summarize, imperial divine honors in the Roman colony of Corinth were Roman in nature and consisted of postmortem cultic acts that the Corinthians gave to *Divus* Julius, *Divus* Augustus, *Diva* Augusta, probably *Divus* Claudius; the deceased but not divinized Octavia, Gaius Caesar, and Lucius Caesar; and to the reigning emperor's *genius*, which may have begun in Augustus's reign. In addition to such honors, the colony had an affinity for the entire Julio-Claudian line and appears

---

"idolatry" (1 Cor 10:19), and it is possible that he thought of the *divi* and the deceased Gaius Caesar, Lucius Caesar, and Octavia as demons, as he believed such was the case with sacrifices to the traditional gods (1 Cor 10:20–22). As John M. G. Barclay, "Paul, Roman Religion and the Emperor," in *Pauline Communities and Diaspora Jews* (Grand Rapids: Eerdmans, 2016), 345–62, quotation 355, notes, Paul does not distinguish between imperial and traditional divine honors but "lumps together" all pagan cultic activity in idolatry.

251. Barclay, "Thessalonica and Corinth," 70–71.

to have honored it in a way similar to the emperor's *genius*. The divine honors in question consisted of divine titles, cultic statues, an imperial altar, one temple, one *naos*, one imperial shrine, and sacrifices that local Roman *flamines* offered to the aforementioned Julio-Claudians and Octavia. Moreover, there were two other Corinthian offices, that of *agonothete* and *isagogeus*, which were Romanized Greek public offices connected to imperial divine honors. The former was the president of games associated with Augustus, the Caesarean Games, and the reigning emperor, the Imperial Games, which were wedded to but distinct from the panhellenic Isthmian Games. When all three games were celebrated together, an *isagogeus* was appointed or elected to aid the *agonothete* in his duties. Alongside these imperial cultic officials, there was a group of rich freedmen and wealthy outsiders known as *Augustales* who promoted Julio-Claudian rule in the colony, erected monuments associated with imperial divine honors, and may have offered private, not public, imperial sacrifices. In addition to these honors, beginning in Nero's reign, Corinth was the site of provincial imperial divine honors for the Julio-Claudian line, the Augustan house. These honors, however, were small and approached nothing like the massive imperial temples and festivals that we find in provinces of Asia, Bithynia, and Galatia but consisted of sacrifices for the Julio-Claudian family.

The Corinthian imperial *flamines* (to date there are no priestesses attested), *agonothetae*, and *isagogi* not only administered the above divine honors but also filled the highest public offices, including priesthoods of traditional gods, in the colony before, during, or after their tenure as imperial cultic officials. Thus, these imperial divine honors, like all forms of divine honors, were embedded into the public life of Corinth. Despite the pervasiveness of the former in the colony, there is no evidence that these honors came into direct conflict with early Christianity, even though Corinthian pagans frequently interacted with their Christian counterparts, and some of the latter even participated in traditional pagan and imperial sacrifices. The above reconstruction of Corinth and a critical reading of 1 Corinthians provide a reason for this. As a port city of two harbors that hellenized Romans controlled, Corinth was open to non-Roman influences such as Christianity. Moreover, the pagan Corinthians, like some Christian Corinthians, probably misunderstood the apocalyptic nature of the gospel because they did not take time to understand its meaning, or they were ignorant of the gospel's content because of the failure of some Corinthian Christians to live it out in the colony, or both. Either way, those Corinthians in Christ were able to live peaceably in the city.

Conclusion

Throughout this book, we have seen that imperial divine honors in Philippi, Thessalonica, and Corinth were woven into Philippian, Thessalonian, and Corinthian public life, what today we would call the political, religious, social, and economic spheres of each city. On the one hand, these various grants of imperial divine honors resembled each other in five respects. First, they consisted of the same types of honors, though differing in degree, that these communities offered to their gods: temples, altars, processions, cultic images, priests or priestesses, sacrifices, prayers, hymns and encomia, divine titles, festivals, games, and the like.[1] Second, imperial divine honors in Philippi, Thessalonica, and Corinth resulted from the legal decisions of bodies politic in these cities. These political entities supported them, that is, paid for them with civic funds, and when these honors were celebrated, they were given on behalf of the citizens of these respective communities. Third, when the motivation(s) for the imperial divine honors in Philippi, Thessalonica, and Corinth is (are) known, benefaction was one of the key contributing factors to the creation of grants of these honors for Julio-Claudians. Thessalonica bestowed the honors in question most often on living Julio-Claudians to show gratitude for munificence as well as to court future beneficence from the Julio-Claudians who provided benefaction. Philippi and Corinth most often established divine honors for deceased Julio-Claudians whom the Roman Senate divinized, *divi*, to show appreciation for their beneficent rule while they were alive. Fourth, the individuals whom these communities chose to oversee the celebration of imperial divine honors were local aristocrats who held other Philippian, Thessalonian, and Corinthian public offices and used their wealth and influence to promote such honors, as well as Julio-Claudian rule and, of course, themselves, in these cities. Finally, imperial divine honors were embedded into and celebrated with traditional divine honors in Philippi, Thessalonica, and Corinth.

---

1. However, all three cities probably offered sacrifices to, not on behalf of, Julio-Claudians.

On the other hand, Philippian, Thessalonian, and Corinthian imperial divine honors differed markedly from each other in three major ways that can be traced to the status of these communities in the Roman Empire and their unique local contexts. First, the objects of divine honors varied from city to city. Thessalonica was a Greek city that practiced its own form of Greek civic imperial divine honors with some influence from Roman imperial divine honors due to Roman patrons of these honors in the city.[2] To this end, Thessalonica tended to bestow divine honors on living Julio-Claudians, Julius Caesar being the exception. Augustus's wife Livia notwithstanding, the city waited until the deaths of Augustus and Claudius before hailing them as *theoi*, the Greek translation of the Latin term and concept *divi* (*divus* in the singular). Philippi and Corinth were Roman colonies and thus miniature Romes. They tended to bestow divine honors on deceased Julio-Claudians whom the Roman Senate divinized, *Divus* Julius, *Divus* Augustus, *Diva* Augusta, and *Divus* Claudius, and to sacrifice to the reigning emperor's *genius*, not his person, although when this began in each colony appears to have differed.[3] Philippi and Corinth varied from each other in the granting of postmortem divine honors for non-Julio-Claudian *divi*. For reasons unknown, Philippi bestowed divine honors on the deceased Tiberius, and Corinth established such honors for Octavia (who was not a Julio-Claudian), Gaius Caesar, and Lucius Caesar after their deaths.

Second, the imperial cultic officials in Philippi, Thessalonica, and Corinth differed. In the Greek city of Thessalonica, a Greek imperial *hiereus*, or "priest," who was also "president" of a set of Greek imperial games, or *agōnothetēs*, appears to have overseen most imperial divine honors in the city. In Philippi and Corinth, however, traditional male Roman priests, *flamines*, tended to individual Julio-Claudian *divi*, while in Philippi, Roman priestesses, *sacerdotes*, celebrated divine honors for the sole female Julio-Claudian *diva*, Augusta. To date, there is no extant evidence that suggests that such priestesses were active in Corinthian imperial divine honors. Finally, because of local histories and customs, the execution of imperial divine honors varied from city to city. Philippi was a Greek city that had existed only for about three hundred years before it was founded and then refounded as a Roman colony in 42 BC and 30 BC, respectively, two acts that obliterated the Greek city's existence. The early colonists of Roman Philippi consisted of disenfranchised Italians and discharged soldiers with a keen desire to

---

2. Because Thessalonica had earned the coveted status of being a "free city" in the Roman Empire, it did not participate in Greek provincial imperial divine honors in the period we have considered, the mid-first century AD.

3. While there is no direct evidence in Philippi, such sacrifices may have begun in Nero's reign, and the evidence from Corinth raises the possibility that offerings began in Augustus's reign.

maintain their distinctive Roman customs. Therefore, aside from postmortem divine honors for Tiberius, Philippi's Julio-Claudian imperial divine honors perfectly mirrored the honors in question in Rome. Thessalonica was a Greek city that, although founded after Greek Philippi in 316/315 BC, had a tradition of bestowing divine honors on living benefactors, at least since 148 BC but perhaps earlier. In keeping with this custom, the city did not establish divine honors for every Julio-Claudian but only those who aided Thessalonica in some way, Julius Caesar, Augustus, Livia, and probably Claudius and Nero. Unlike the aforementioned cities, Corinth had an illustrious past. Founded as a Greek city as early as the tenth century BC, Corinth had a storied history and oversight of one of the Greek world's most famous set of games, the Isthmian. Despite Rome's eradication of Corinth as a political entity in 146 BC and founding as a Roman colony in 44 BC, the Greek city continued to influence the Roman colony even to the point of affecting its imperial divine honors. While Roman Corinth followed the Roman Senate in establishing divine honors for Julio-Claudian *divi*, the city bestowed postmortem divine honors on three individuals whom the senate did not divinize, Octavia, Gaius Caesar, and Lucius Caesar. The colony honored these latter two personages in the guise of the famous Greek twins, Castor and Pollux, who, according to a Greek Corinthian tradition, competed in and won competitions in the first set of Isthmian Games. It was to these distinguished contests that Corinth wedded two sets of games connected to the Julio-Claudians, the Caesarean and Imperial Games, and at the beginning of Nero's reign, the colony became the site of limited provincial imperial divine honors for the Julio-Claudian line, which consisted of a priesthood and sacrifices.

Because of the contextual nature of imperial divine honors in Philippi, Thessalonica, and Corinth and the uniqueness of the Christian communities in these cities, the relationship between Christianity and the honors in question differed from city to city. In Philippi, which cultivated an atmosphere of conservative Roman values, imperial divine honors were bestowed almost exclusively on *divi*, Tiberius being the one exception. These cultic acts were embedded into the colony's public life, including traditional divine honors. To this end, the early Christian proclamation of a non-Roman deity, the God of Israel, and his divinely chosen vice-regent to whom all the cosmos would give obeisance, Jesus the Messiah, to the former's glory conflicted with imperial and traditional Philippian divine honors resulting in the mistreatment of Christians, including the imprisonment of some (Phil 1:27–30). Thessalonica's somewhat Romanized Greek imperial divine honors for living and deceased Julio-Claudians meant that the city interpreted its peace, prosperity, and "free" status as a divine gift and evidence that Thessalonica's gods had chosen and worked through the Julio-Claudian line. However, the aggressive evangelistic activity of Thessalonian Christians heralding the God of Israel's imminent kingdom and his divinely chosen viceroy, the Messiah Jesus, jeopardized Thessalonica's "free" status. To bring their wayward compatriots back into the fold of traditional and imperial divine honors, the Thessalonians harassed and mistreated Christians in their city. While Corinth mainly practiced Roman imperial divine honors, the influence of the Greek city on the Roman colony meant that Corinth established divine honors, albeit postmortem, for non-Julio-Claudian *divi* (and in one case a relative of Augustus's) more than its Macedonian counterpart, Philippi. However, the colony, no less than Philippi and Thessalonica, wedded imperial divine honors to Corinthian traditional divine honors to the point that the former pervaded public life in the city. This suffusion of divine honors for Julio-Claudians into Corinthian society notwithstanding, because of the Jewish apocalyptic nature of the gospel and the possible un-Christian behavior of some believers, many pagan Corinthians failed to grasp the gospel's countercultural essence. All of this is despite the fact that Christians and pagan Corinthians interacted frequently. Coincidentally, this ignorance of the gospel's true nature and power resulted in a situation in which Christians in Corinth were able to live peaceably with their pagan counterparts.

These above conclusions differ markedly from some Pauline interpreters who contend that the relationship between early Philippian, Thessalonian, and Corinthian Christianity and imperial divine honors was one of conflict mainly between Christ and Caesar. For many scholars, the *euangelion* of *kyrios* Jesus opposed, sometimes openly, at other times covertly, that of *kyrios* Caesar. These exegetes often try to discover ways around Paul's positive comments about Greco-Roman governing authorities in Rom 13:1–7 (discussed below; see pp. 234–38). For example, N. T. Wright, claiming that Paul's use of *kyrios* and *euangelion* echoes "imperial rhetoric" and that Caesar is guilty of "giving himself divine honors," contends that while believers are to pay taxes and render obedience to governing authorities, Paul desires to show in Rom 13:1–7 that Caesar is not divine:

> reading Romans 13 against the backdrop of the extravagant claims made within the burgeoning imperial cult highlights one point in particular. According to Paul (and the Jewish tradition in which he stands) the rulers are not themselves divine; they are set up by the one God, and they owe this God allegiance. Romans 13 constitutes a severe demotion of arrogant and self-divinizing rulers.[4]

4. N. T. Wright, "Romans," *NIB* 10:719. For a more concise presentation of Wright's thoughts, see N. T. Wright, "Paul and Empire," in *The Blackwell Companion to Paul*, ed. Stephen Westerholm (Malden, MA: Wiley-Blackwell, 2011), 291–95.

For Wright, this is especially the case when one takes Rom 13:1–7 into the larger context of Romans, where Paul's goal is to show that the gospel upstages, out-flanks, delegitimates, and subverts "the 'gospel' of Caesar and Rome."[5]

The problem with Wright's portrait is that such an anti-imperial reading of Rom 13:1–7 lacks support in our ancient sources. As we have seen throughout this book, there is no evidence that *kyrios* and *euangelion* were imperial terms in mid-first-century AD Philippi, Thessalonica, or Corinth. As I have shown elsewhere, the earliest evidence of *kyrios* being used for a Roman emperor in mainland Greece dates to AD 67, a few years after Paul's probable martyrdom in Rome.[6] Moreover, direct evidence from the abovementioned cities refutes Wright's portrait of the Roman emperor "giving himself divine honors." In each case, Philippian, Thessalonian, and Corinthian aristocrats bestowed such honors on certain Julio-Claudians of their own free will most often to show apprecia-tion for imperial benefaction. Thessalonica established divine honors almost ex-clusively for living Julio-Claudians, while Philippi and Corinth for deceased and most often Julio-Claudian *divi*. Aside from Gaius (Caligula), there is no evidence that Julio-Claudians demanded divine honors in Rome, the location whither Paul composed his letter to the Romans.[7] For example, the second-century AD Roman historian Tacitus records that in AD 65, Nero survived an assassination plot. To show gratitude to the gods for his escape, the Roman Senate voted sacrifices to be made to certain deities and a temple to the divine personification of Safety (*Salus*) be constructed in Rome.[8] One sycophantic senator, however, put forth a motion acclaiming Nero as a *divus* and asking that a temple be built for him. Before the senate considered the matter, the emperor vetoed it. The reason, according to Tac-itus, was that Nero's advisors interpreted the motion as a harbinger of his death, "for the honor of a god is not performed for the first citizen [i.e., the emperor] until he has ceased to live among humans."[9]

---

5. N. T. Wright, *Paul and the Faithfulness of God* (Minneapolis: Fortress, 2013), 2:1271–1319, esp. 1306; Wright, "Romans," *NIB* 10:717–23. For a more concise presentation of Wright's thoughts, see "Paul and Empire," 291–95.

6. D. Clint Burnett, *Studying the New Testament through Inscriptions: An Introduction* (Pea-body, MA: Hendrickson, 2020), 58–76.

7. Philo, *On the Embassy to Gaius*.

8. Tacitus, *Annals* 15.68–74.

9. *nam deum honor principi non ante habetur, quam agere inter homines desierit* (Tacitus, *Annals* 15.74). This does not mean, however, that private individuals did not divinely honor Julio-Claudians in Rome. See Ittai Gradel, *Emperor Worship and Roman Religion* (Oxford: Clar-endon, 2002), 375–79.

If we take a step back from Philippi, Thessalonica, Corinth, and Rome and look to other places in the Roman Empire, it is evident that most Julio-Claudians tried to curb such honors for themselves from communities under their dominion while they were alive.[10] When Gythium sent an embassy to Rome to inform Tiberius of the imperial festival that it had decreed, he praised the city for the divine honors for the deceased Augustus but refused those for himself, saying, "I praise you for these things accepting it as fitting that in general all people and your own city should cherish as remarkable the greatness of my father's benefactions for the entire world as honors fitting for the gods. However, I am satisfied with those honors more appropriate for humans."[11] When Germanicus, Tiberius's adopted son, was proconsul of Egypt in AD 19, some Egyptians awarded his adopted father, Livia, and him divine honors. Germanicus, however, issued an edict, preserved on a papyrus, halting the honors for himself: "I accept your goodwill that you always exhibit when you see me. However, I deprecate altogether your godlike acclamations as enviable to me, for they are fitting only to the one who is truly the savior and benefactor of the entire human race: my father [Tiberius] and his mother, my grandmother [Livia]."[12] When Claudius ascended to the imperial throne in AD 41, the Alexandrians passed several cultic and noncultic honors for the newly crowned emperor. In a letter that Claudius composed, which is also found on a papyrus, he accepted the noncultic honors but refused the cultic ones, noting, "I deprecate a high priest and shrines dedicated to me. I wish not to be vulgar to my contemporaries, and I judge in every age sanctuaries and such singular gifts have been given to the gods only."[13] Finally, after Nero became emperor in October AD 54, a community in a region of Egypt known as the Arsinoite nome sent him a golden crown and informed him of their decision to build a *naos* to him. The emperor responded in a missive preserved on papyrus declining both honors: "I deprecate your *naos*, because this honor is rightly assigned by humans to the

---

10. M. P. Charlesworth, "The Refusal of Divine Honors: An Augustan Formula," *Papers of the British School at Rome* 15 (1939): 1–10.

11. ['Ε]φ' οἷς ὑμᾶς ἐπαινῶν προσήκειν ὑπ<ο>λαμβάνω{ι} καὶ κοινῇ πάντας ἀνθρώπους καὶ ἰδίᾳ τὴν ὑμετέραν πόλιν ἐξαιρέτους φυλάσσειν τῶι μεγέθει τῶν τοῦ ἐμοῦ πατρὸς εἰς ἅπαντα τὸν κόσμον εὐεργεσιῶν τὰς θεοῖς πρεσπούσας τιμάς, αὐτὸς δὲ ἀρκοῦμαι ταῖς μετριωτέραις τε καὶ ἀνθρωπείοις ("Appendix 1: Inscriptions" §I.3, lines 17–20).

12. τὴν μὲν εὔνοιαν ὑμῶν, ἣν αἰεὶ ἐπιδείκνυσθε, ὅταν με εἴδητε, ἀποδέχομαι, τὰς δὲ ἐπιφθόνου[ς] ἐμοὶ καὶ ἰσοθέους ἐκφωνήσεις ὑμῶν ἐξ [ἅ]παντος παραιτοῦμαι. πρέπουσι γὰρ μόνῳ τῶι σωτῆρι ὄντως καὶ εὐεργέτη τοῦ σύνπαντος τῶν ἀνθρώπων γένους, τῷ ἐμῷ πατρὶ καὶ τῇ μητρὶ αὐτοῦ, ἐμῇ δὲ μάμμῃ (*Sel. Pap.* 2.211, lines 33–42).

13. ἀρχιερέα δ' ἐμὸν καὶ ναῶν κατασκευὰς παρετοῦμε, οὔτε φορτικὸς τοῖς κατ' ἐμαυτὸν ἀνθρόποις βουλόμενος εἶναι τὰ ἱερὰ δὲ καὶ τὰ τοιαῦτα μόνοις τοῖς θεοῖς ἐξέρετα ὑπὸ τοῦ παντὸς αἰῶνος ἀποδεδόσθαι κρίν[ω]ν (*Sel. Pap.* 2.212, lines 48–51).

gods only, and I send back the gold crown that you have given, because I do not wish to burden you at the beginning of my government."[14]

I am not suggesting that Julio-Claudians did not take full advantage of what today we would call the political and religious capital of communities in the empire bestowing such honors on them while they were alive. However, exploiting the traditions of Greco-Roman communities for their own advantage is a far cry from Wright's claim that these emperors demanded and gave themselves divine honors in Rome and elsewhere in the empire. What is more, there were limits to Roman propriety that emperors were not to transgress, and when they did, they paid for it with their lives. Some Roman officials assassinated Gaius (Caligula) on January 24, AD 41, and the Roman Senate declared Nero an enemy of the state before he committed suicide on June 9, AD 68.[15] The reason for the demise of these two Julio-Claudians lay in their erratic and un-Roman behavior, and with the case of Gaius in particular, the divine honors that he demanded for himself.[16]

If Roman emperors most often did not claim divine honors for themselves, then this portion of Wright's reading of Rom 13:1–7 is untenable.[17] In fact, it is questionable even if the passage calls out the Roman emperor explicitly. Instead, Paul seems to have in mind the numerous public officials of Rome that kept the city going and the Roman imperial bureaucracy, neither of which needed the full attention of the Roman emperor.[18] In support of this reading, the apostle exhorts the Roman Christians "to subject themselves to *higher authorities*" in the plural, and he says that "*these*" authorities "*are* appointed by God" (Rom 13:1).[19]

---

14. τόν τε ναόν σου παρητησάμην, δειὰ τὸ θεοῖς μόνοις ταύτην τὴν τειμὴν ὑπ᾽ ἀν[θ]ρ[ώ]πων δεικαίως ἀπονέ[με]ϲθαι, καὶ τὸν χρυσοῦν στέ[φαν]ον ἔπεμψά γε χαρισθή[σεσ]θε, μὴ βουλόμενος ἐν ἀρ[χῇ τ]ῆς ἡγεμονίας ἐπειβαρε[ῖν ὑ]μᾶς (Orsolina Montevecchi, "Nerone a una polis e ai 6475," *Aegyptus* 50 [1970]: 5–33, column 1, lines 2–10).

15. Suetonius, *Gaius Caligula* 52–59; *Nero* 26–29; Dio Cassius, *Roman History* 59.29.1–7; 63.22.1–63.29.2.

16. Suetonius, *Gaius Caligula* 22.2–4; Dio Cassius, *Roman History* 59.4.4.

17. For a thorough review of scholarship on Rom 13:1–7, see Robert Jewett, *Romans: A Commentary*, Hermeneia (Minneapolis: Fortress, 2006), 780–803.

18. This is evident in that Rome's empire functioned despite the emperor Tiberius moving to the island of Capri in AD 26, where he remained for the rest of his reign (until AD 37), and his incompetent successor, Gaius (Caligula) who reigned from AD 37 to 41.

19. ἐξουσίαις ὑπερεχούσαις ὑποτασσέσθω ... αἱ δὲ οὖσαι ὑπὸ θεοῦ τεταγμέναι εἰσίν. See the much-neglected German article by August Strobel, "Zum Verständnis von Rm 13," *ZNW* 47 (1956): 67–93, which demonstrates that Paul's Greek vocabulary in Rom 13:1–7 translates Roman administrative and constitutional terminology. For similar perspectives in English, see Joseph A. Fitzmyer, *Romans: A New Translation with Introduction and Commentary*, AB 33 (New York: Doubleday, 1993), 661–76, and Jewett, *Romans*, 788, who notes, "Since the participle οἱ ὑπερέχοντες, as well as the noun ἐξουσίαι, can be used to refer to government officials, their somewhat redundant

Paul probably is thinking of this multitude of officials when he says in Rom 13:2, "that the one who resists *the authority* opposes *the* appointment by God."[20] These two definite articles (*tē*) are more than likely anaphoric and thus look back to Rom 13:1's higher authorities. Thus, we should probably translate them as "such": "the one who resists such authority opposes such an appointment by God." In Rom 13:3, yet again Paul refers to more than one ruler as he tells his audience that "*rulers are* not a terror to the good work but to evil (work)."[21] Finally, the apostle calls these higher authorities "*public ministers* attending to this very purpose," which is probably weal or the common good (Rom 13:6).[22] On the other hand, Paul's reference to fearing "the authority" (*tēn echousian*), receiving praise "from it" (*ex autēs*) (Rom 13:3), that the authority is "God's minister" (*theou diakonos*), and an "avenger" (*ekdikos*) bearing "the sword" (*tēn machairan*) (Rom 13:4) probably refers to the larger Roman imperial bureaucracy. This is especially the case with his latter reference to capital punishment, because the emperor's permission was not needed for the execution of non-Romans, as is clear from the gospel narratives (Matt 27:1–2, 24–26 // Mark 15:1–15 // Luke 23:1, 13–25; John 18:28–32; 19:13–16). Paul's pluralistic description of authorities in Rome and his reference to the Roman bureaucratic system gain greater importance in light of 1 Pet 2:13–17, where the author clearly has the emperor in mind: "Submit yourselves to every human institution because of the Lord: whether the king [*basilei*] as a higher [authority], the governor as sent by him for punishing criminals. . . . Honor all people. Love the brotherhood. Fear God. Honor the king [*basilea*]." It is evident from first-century AD Greek sources, including one connected to Thessalonica, that *basileus* was a common title for the Roman emperor (John 19:12; Acts 17:7; Rev 17:12).[23] Paul could easily have used this term in Rom 13:1–7 had he intended

---

combination here has a cumulative sense that encompasses a range of officials placed in superior positions of political authority, duly appointed to their tasks and currently exercising their power." One of the reasons that commentators do not point this out to the degree to which they should is that many are preoccupied with either supporting or refuting the notion that ἐξουσίαι in Rom 13:1–7 refers to angels, spiritual beings, or both.

20. ὥστε ὁ ἀντιτασσόμενος τῇ ἐξουσίᾳ τῇ τοῦ θεοῦ διαταγῇ ἀνθέστηκεν.

21. οἱ γὰρ ἄρχοντες οὐκ εἰσὶν φόβος τῷ ἀγαθῷ ἔργῳ ἀλλὰ τῷ κακῷ.

22. λειτουργοὶ γὰρ θεοῦ εἰσιν εἰς αὐτὸ τοῦτο προσκαρτεροῦντες. On the one hand, Wright, "Romans," *NIB* 10:720, seems to agree with this assessment, because he concludes that "Romans 13:1–7 is about the running of civic communities." On the other hand, he spends most of his discussion of Rom 13:1–7 focused on the Roman emperor and the Roman Empire: Wright, "Romans," *NIB* 10:716–23.

23. As we have seen in chapter 3, Antipater of Thessalonica, *Greek Anthology* 10.25, calls Augustus "my brave king" (τὸν ἐμὸν βασιλῆα τὸν ἄλκιμον) and asks him to be kind to Antipater's patron, Piso.

to single out the emperor, but he did not.[24] As emphasized, most often he refers to a plurality of authorities.

What is striking about the apostle's choice of words is that throughout this book, we have seen that these authorities, not the Roman emperor, were the individuals who promoted imperial (as well as traditional) divine honors in the cities of the Roman Empire, including its capital. Such honors in Rome have not formed this book's main focus, but we have seen that in the mid-first century AD, they consisted of postmortem divine honors for *Divus* Julius, *Divus* Augustus, *Diva* Augusta, *Divus* Claudius, and, beginning in AD 55, Nero's *genius* (see pp. 41–45).[25] To provide an example, the college of the Arval Brothers, which consisted of Roman senators, offered regular sacrifices to Julio-Claudian *divi* and, beginning in AD 55, the emperor's *genius*. One particular Arval Brother was Taurus Statilius Corvinus, who, as vice president (*promagister*) of this college for AD 38, offered on September 21 of that same year a sacrificial victim "to *Divus* Augustus at his new temple," among all the other regular sacrifices that he made in AD 38.[26] In addition to serving as *promagister* of the Arval Brothers, Corvinus was a consul in Rome in AD 45 and a member of the college of the *quindecemviri* (literally, "fifteen men") who kept and consulted Rome's Sibylline Oracles.[27] Thus, these "higher authorities" to which Paul exhorts the Roman Christians to submit themselves were the very ones who sponsored and performed imperial (as well as traditional) divine honors in Rome. The real question then becomes this: How can the apostle, who abominates all forms of idolatry (cf. 1 Cor 10:20–21), ask Christians in Rome to submit to the instigators and celebrants of imperial divine honors?

The answer to this question lies in Paul's apocalyptic theology and the Jewish and burgeoning Christian tradition of God's complete sovereignty over the nations, which, to be fair, is an aspect of Wright's interpretation of Paul and

24. Dieter Georgi, *Theocracy in Paul's Praxis and Theology*, trans. David E. Green (Minneapolis: Fortress, 1991), 81–102, quotation 102, who adopts a more anti-imperial reading of Romans than I, acknowledges, "Yet Paul, in this letter to the citizens of the capital, never mentions the *princeps* [or emperor] or the special status of Rome."

25. It is the case that the Roman Senate divinized Gaius Caligula's sister and Nero's second wife and infant daughter after their deaths. However, divine honors for them appear not to have been a regular part of Roman public divine honors, and after the ignominious deaths of these two emperors, the honors in question for these *divae* ceased.

26. *ad templum novom divo Augusto unam* ("Appendix 1: Inscriptions" §1.2, lines 87–88).

27. For Corvinus as consul, see Dio Cassius, *Roman History* 60.25.1. For him as a *quindecemvir*, see *CIL* 6.32447. For more information on Corvinus's public career, see Klaus Wachtel, "Taurus Statilius Corvinus," *Prosopographia Imperii Romani Saec. I. II. III.*, part 7, fascicle 1, 2nd ed. (Berlin: de Gruyter, 1999), §822. For a discussion of this college, see John Scheid, *An Introduction to Roman Religion*, trans. Janet Lloyd (Bloomington: University of Indiana Press, 2003), 121–23.

Rom 13:1–7 with which I agree.[28] This Jewish perspective is clearest in the prophetic apocalyptic work of Daniel.[29] Several times, the prophet articulates an aspect of apocalyptically revealed wisdom: human governments rise and fall at God's discretion (Dan 2:20–23, 31–45; 4:25).[30] These kingdoms rule because God desired them to do so, even though some of their subjects offer divine honors to their kings. Thus, in Dan 6 when Babylonian aristocrats grow jealous of Daniel and his success in the Babylonian imperial administration, they plot his demise by instigating Darius to sign into law that all the monarch's subjects must offer him only divine honors for a month (Dan 6:1–9). The text stresses that when Daniel knew that the king had signed the order, he continued to pray to Israel's God alone, as he had always done.[31] The conspirators found the prophet disobeying Darius's order, for which he is thrown into the lions' den, despite the king's protestations (Dan 6:10–18). Once Daniel emerges unscathed from the den of lions, Darius has his enemies thrown in, at which point the lions devour them (Dan 6:19–24). This event prompts the monarch to decree that everyone in the Babylonian Empire must give divine honors to Daniel's god, the God of Israel (Dan 6:25–28).

Nowhere in the story does Daniel accuse Darius of blasphemy because he desired divine honors for himself. Nor does the king's decree that his subjects must give the God of Israel divine honors suggest that for Darius he is the only god. Rather, Daniel's God is one before whom all people in the monarch's dominion are to fear (Dan 6:26). In short, in this story, Daniel found a way to serve the Babylonian king and to live within an empire that promoted divine honors for pagan gods (cf. Dan 3:1–30) and human rulers, sometimes even at the monarch's command. All the while, Daniel maintained his distinctive devotion to the God of Israel. I suggest that the apostle Paul functioned similarly in the Roman Empire.[32] To this end, in Rom 13:1–7, Paul, fully aware of the complexity of imperial (as well as traditional) divine honors and their embeddedness into the public life of every city in the Roman Empire, including Rome, encourages the Roman

28. Wright, "Romans," *NIB* 10:718–19.

29. For the connection between Rom 13:1–7 and Daniel, see James D. G. Dunn, *Romans 9–16*, WBC 38B (Nashville: Nelson, 1988), 770–71. John J. Collins, *Daniel: A Commentary on the Book of Daniel*, Hermeneia (Minneapolis: Fortress, 1993), 228, notes, "God's power over the kings of the earth is a theme of the collected tales of Daniel 1–6."

30. This same perspective, though not from an apocalyptic perspective, is found in Jer 27:1–22; 29:1–23; Isa 45:1–7; Wis 6:1–25.

31. This indicates that for the author of Daniel, Darius expected that his subjects pray only to him for a month.

32. Given that Paul does not single out imperial divine honors, he must have considered them on par with traditional divine honors, and thus they were forms of idolatry.

Christians to submit themselves to these authorities in general and in the payment of taxes, tribute, and honor, though not divine, in particular (Rom 13:6–7). There are, however, limits to this submission. As Victor Furnish points out, "*submitting oneself to the governing authorities is compatible with serving God insofar as those authorities faithfully discharge their responsibility to be God's agents for the common good.*"[33] It is of import that the apostle does not say "obey" (*hypakouō*) the governing authorities. When it comes to obedience for him, humanity is divided into two camps. There are those humans who are slaves of Sin and those who are slaves of righteousness. The former "obey" that cosmic power, not the imperial authorities, while the latter have "obeyed" the gospel (*hypakoē*; *hypakouō* [Rom 6:1–17, esp. 6:16–17]). Paul's desire is for all, both Jew and gentile, to be in the latter camp (*hypakoē*; *hypakouō* [Rom 1:5; 10:16; 15:18]). Moreover, Robert Jewett perceptively points out that the apostle's call for the submission of Christians to rulers in Rom 13:1–7 occurs in the context of his admonition of the Roman believers' nonconformity to "this age" (*aiōni toutō*) and to the transformation of their mind (singular) by its renewal so that they may approve what God's will is (Rom 12:2).[34] Therefore, like in Daniel, the apostle knew that there may come a time when the Roman Christians must "disobey" (*parakouō*) a command of the governing authorities who are under the cosmic power of Sin, especially if that command was to offer divine honors to anyone or anything other than the God of Israel. In such a case, Paul would have wanted the Roman Christians' obedience to righteousness above their submission to their local authorities.[35]

As I bring this book to a close, I wish to emphasize that I have no desire to be an apologist for imperial divine honors or the Roman Empire, for that matter. What I do want is to reconstruct the world of early Christianity, including the honors in question, as accurately as possible. When I was a square supervisor on an excavation in Israel, I used to tell the volunteers whom I directed that we had one chance to tell the story of the people whose lives we were digging up. Therefore, we had a duty to tell that story as accurately as possible not only for the sake of those real persons who once occupied the site at which we were excavating but also because we would want others in the future to do the same for us. For this reason, I believe that even imperial divine honors and the individuals who participated in them deserve to have their story told accurately. I do not think it serves the church or the academy or advances the gospel to mispresent any facet

33. Victor Paul Furnish, *The Moral Teachings of Paul: Selected Issues*, 3rd ed. (Nashville: Abingdon, 2009), 157.

34. Jewett, *Romans*, 789.

35. See the excellent discussion by Frank Matera, *Romans*, Paideia (Grand Rapids: Baker Academic, 2010), 301–4.

of imperial divine honors. Rather, it seems to me that such misrepresentation does nothing but build up a strawman for the gospel to easily knock down. In my opinion, and one to which I think Paul would consent with a wholehearted "amen," the apocalyptically revealed gospel of Jesus the Messiah needs no strawman to demonstrate its otherworldly life-giving and life-altering power, for such a gospel and the Triune God from whom it generates have the ability to effect salvation for any person at any point in history in a way that is incomparable to anything that exists in this age. The reason is that the gospel is anchored in and sourced from the age to come (Rom 1:16–17).

APPENDIX 1

Inscriptions

§I.1 GYTHIUM'S SACRED LAW (*HIEROS NOMOS*)

PROVENANCE: GYTHIUM (found near the city's theater)
DATE: AD 15
LANGUAGE: GREEK
SOURCE: *SEG* 11.923[1]

1   ------------------------ ἐπιτιθέτω ... ων --------
    [ἐπὶ μὲν τὴν πρώτην θεοῦ Σεβαστοῦ Καίσ]αρος τοῦ πατρός, ἐπὶ δὲ τὴν ἐχ
    δ[ε]ξιῷ[ν]
    [δευτέραν Ἰουλίας τῆς Σεβα]στῆς, ἐπὶ δὲ τὴν τρίτην Αὐτοκράτορος Τιβερίου
    Κα[ίσα]-
    [ρος τ]οῦ Σεβαστοῦ, τ[ὰ]ς εἰκόνας παρεχούσης αὐτῷ τῆς πόλεως. Προτιθέσ[θω]
5   [δὲ κ]αὶ τράπεζα ὑπ' αὐτοῦ ἐν μέσῳ τῷ θεάτρῳ καὶ θυμιατήριον ἐπικείσθω κα[ὶ]
    [ἐπι]θυέτωσαν πρὶν εἰσιέναι τὰ ἀκροάματα ὑπὲρ τῆς τῶν ἡγεμόνων σωτηρία[ς]
    οἵ τε σύνεδροι καὶ αἱ συναρχίαι πᾶσαι. Ἀγέτω δὲ τὴν μὲν πρώτην ἡμέραν θεοῦ
    Καίσ[α]-
    ρος θεοῦ υἱοῦ Σεβαστοῦ Σωτῆρος Ἐλευθερίου, τὴν δὲ δευτέραν Αὐτοκράτορος [Τι]-
    βερίου Καίσαρος Σεβαστοῦ καὶ πατρὸς τῆς πατρίδος, τὴν δὲ τρίτην Ἰουλίας
    Σεβαστῆ[ς]
10   τῆς τοῦ ἔθνους καὶ πόλεως ἡμῶν Τύχης, τὴν δὲ τετάρτην Γερμανικοῦ Καίσαρος
    τῆς Ν[ί]-
    κης, τὴν δὲ πέμπτην Δρούσου Καίσαρος τῆς Ἀφροδείτης, τὴν δὲ ἕκτην Τίτου
    Κοϊνκτίο[υ]

1. I have followed *SEG* 11.923 over the *editio princeps* of the first printed edition of this inscription: S. B. Kougeas, "*Epigraphikai ek Gytheiou symbolai ein tēn istorian tis Lakonis kata tous
chronous tēs Rōmaikēs Autokratorias*," *Hellenika* 1 (1928): 16–38.

Φλαμενίνου καὶ ἐπιμελείσθω τῆς τῶν ἀγωνιζομένων εὐκοσμίας. Φερέ{ρε}τω δὲ καὶ πά-

σης τῆς μισθώσεως τῶν ἀκροαμάτων <καὶ> τῆς διοικήσεως τῶν ἱερῶν χρημάτων τὸν λόγον τῇ πόλ[ει]

μετὰ τὸν ἀγῶνα τῇ πρώτῃ ἐκκλησίᾳ· κἂν εὑρεθῇ νενοσφισμένος ἢ ψευδῶς λογογραφῶν ἐξελε[γ]-

15 χθείς, μηκέτι μηδεμίαν ἀρχὴν ἀρξάτω καὶ ἡ οὐσία αὐτοῦ δημευέσθω. Ὧν δ' ἂν ποτε δημευθῇ τὰ ὄντα,

ταῦτα <τὰ> χρήματα ἱερὰ ἔστω καὶ ἐξ αὐτῶν προσκοσμήματα ὑπὸ τῶν κατ' ἔτος ἀρχόντων κατασκε[υ]-

αζέσθω. Ἐξέστω δὲ τῷ βουλομένῳ Γυθεατῶν παντὶ περὶ τῶν ἱερῶν ἐκδικεῖν χρημάτων ἀθῴῳ ὄ[ν]-

τι. *vacat* Ἐπεισαγέτω δὲ ὁ ἀγορανόμος μετὰ τὸ τὰς τῶν θεῶν καὶ ἡγεμόνων ἡμέρας τελέσαι τῶν θυ-

μελικῶν ἀγώνων ἄλλα[ς δύ]ο ἡμέρας τὰ ἀκροάματα, μίαν μὲν εἰς μνήμην Γαΐου Ἰουλίου Εὐρυκλέου[ς]

20 εὐεργέτου τοῦ ἔθνους καὶ τῆς πόλεως ἡμῶν ἐν πολλοῖς γενομένου, δευτέραν δὲ εἰς τειμὴν Γα-

ΐου Ἰουλίου Λάκωνος κηδεμόνος τῆς τοῦ ἔθνους καὶ τῆς πόλεως ἡμῶν φυλακῆς καὶ σωτηρία[ς]

ὄντος. Ἀγέτω δὲ τοὺς ἀγῶνας ἀπὸ τῆς θεοῦ ἐν αἷς ἂν ᾖ δυνατὸν ἡμέραις αὐτῶι· ὅταν δὲ τῆς ἀρχῆς

ἐξίῃ, παραδιδότω τῷ ἀντιτυνχάνοντι ἀγορανόμωι διὰ γραφῆς δημοσίας τὰ εἰς τοὺς ἀγῶνας χρη[στή]-

ρια πάντα καὶ λαμβανέτω{ι} χειρόγραφον παρὰ τοῦ παραλαβόντος ἡ πόλις. Ὅταν ὁ ἀγορανόμος τοὺ[ς]

25 [ἀγῶ]νας ἄγῃ τοὺς θυμελικούς, πομπὴν στελλέτω ἐκ τοῦ ἱεροῦ τοῦ Ἀσκληπιοῦ καὶ τῆς Ὑγιεία[ς],

πομπευόντων τῶν τε ἐφήβων καὶ τῶν νέων πάντων καὶ τῶν ἄλλων πολειτῶν ἐστεμμένων δάφν[ης]

στεφάνοις καὶ λευκὰ ἀμπεχομέν<ω>ν. Συμπομπευέτωσαν δὲ καὶ αἱ ἱεραὶ κόραι καὶ αἱ γυναῖκες ἐν

[τ]αῖς ἱεραῖς ἐσθῆσιν. Ὅταν δὲ ἐπὶ τὸ Καισάρηον ἡ πομπὴ παραγένηται, θυέτωσαν οἱ ἔφοροι ταῦ-

[ρ]ον ὑπὲρ τῆς τῶν ἡγεμόνων καὶ θεῶν σωτηρίας καὶ ἀϊδίου τῆς ἡγεμονίας αὐτῶν διαμονῆς κα[ὶ]

30 [θ]ύσαντες ἐπανανκασάτωσαν τά τε φιδείτια καὶ τὰς συναρχίας ἐν ἀγορᾷ
θυσιάσαι. Εἰ δὲ ἢ μὴ τε-

[λ]έσουσιν τὴν πομπὴν ἢ μὴ θύσουσιν ἢ θύσαντες μὴ ἐπανανκάσουσι θυσιάζειν
ἐν ἀγορᾷ τὰ

[φ]ιδείτια καὶ τὰς συναρχίας, ἐκτεισάτωσαν ἱερὰς τοῖς θεοῖς δραχμὰς δισχιλίας.
Ἐξέστω δὲ τῶι

βουλομένῳ Γυθεατῶν κατηγορεῖν αὐτῶν. *vacat* Οἱ ἔφοροι οἱ ἐπὶ Χαίρωνος
στρατηγοῦ καὶ ἱερέως θε-

ου Σεβαστοῦ Καίσαρος οἱ περὶ Τερέντιον Βιάδαν ἐγδότωσαν τρεῖς γραπτὰς
εἰκόνας τοῦ θε-

35 ου Σεβαστοῦ καὶ Ἰουλίας τῆς Σεβαστῆς καὶ Τιβερίου Καίσαρος τοῦ Σεβαστοῦ
καὶ τὰ διὰ θέατρον

ἴκρια τῷ χορῷ καὶ θύρας μιμικὰς τέσσερας καὶ τῇ συνφωνίᾳ ὑποπόδια.
Στησάτωσαν δὲ καὶ στή-

λην λιθίνην χαράξαντες εἰς αὐτὴν τὸν ἱερὸν νόμον καὶ εἰς τὰ δημόσια δὲ
γραμματοφυλάκια θέτω-

σαν ἀντίγραφον τοῦ ἱεροῦ νόμου, ἵνα καὶ ἐν δημοσίωι καὶ ἐν ὑπαίθρῳ καὶ πᾶσιν
ἐν φανερῷ κείμενος ὁ νό-

μος [διηνε]κῆ τὴν τοῦ δήμου τοῦ Γυθεατῶν εὐχαριστίαν εἰς {σ} τοὺς ἡγεμόνας
παρέχῃ πᾶσιν ἀνθρώ-

40 ποις. Εἰ δὲ ἢ μὴ ἐνχαράξουσι τοῦτον τὸν νόμον, ἢ μὴ ἀναθήσουσιν τὴν στήλην
πρὸ τοῦ ναοῦ ἢ μὴ γρά-

[ψουσι τὸ ἀντίγραφον - -]

. . . Let the (*agoranomos*)[2] . . . on the first (pedestal an image) of his father the
god Augustus Caesar, on the second (pedestal) to the right (an image) of Julia
(Livia) Augusta, and on the third (pedestal an image) of the victorious general
Tiberius Augustus Caesar, the images that the city gave to him [the *agoranomos*].
Let a table be set by him in the midst of the theater and a censer be laid on it.
Before the contests start, let the councilors and all the magistrates burn incense
on behalf of the well-being of the rulers. Let (the *agoranomos*) celebrate the first
day for the god, savior, and liberator Caesar Augustus son of a god, the second
day for the victorious general Tiberius Augustus Caesar who is the "father of the
fatherland," the third day for Julia Augusta the Good Fortune of our nation and

2. In a Greek city, this was the official who oversaw the marketplace, the food supply, and
buildings therein.

city, the fourth for Victory of Germanicus Caesar, the fifth for Aphrodite of Drusus Caesar, and the sixth for Titus Quinctius Flamininus.[3]

Let (the *agoranomos*) have charge of the good behavior of the competitors. Let him present an account of every payment for the performances and administration of the sacred funds to the city in the first assembly after the competition. If it is found that he has embezzled or kept false accounts and if he is convicted, let him no longer hold any office and let his possessions be seized as public property. Whatever possessions have been seized as public property at that time, let these things become sacred funds and, from these, let decorations be furnished by the annual *archontes*. Let it be permitted for any of the Gytheates who desires to bring a case about the sacred funds without there being retribution.

After the days for the gods and rulers have been completed, let the *agoranomos* celebrate two other days of theatrical contests and performances, the first for the memory of Gaius Julius Eurcyles who was the benefactor of our nation and city in many ways and the second for the honor of Gaius Julius Laco protector of the security and well-being of our nation and city. Let him celebrate the contests of the goddess on which days it be possible for him.

Whenever he leaves office, let the city hand over to the next *agoranomos* via a public document all the sacrifices in the contests and let him receive a handwritten document from the one who receives it. Whenever the *agoranomos* celebrates the theatrical contests, let him begin the procession from the temple complex of Aesculapius and Health with the *ephebes*, all the young men, and the other citizens processing, wearing white, and being crowned with crowns of sweet bay leaves. Let the sacred girls and the women process in sacred garments. When the procession arrives at the *Kaisarēon*, let the *ephoroi* sacrifice a bull on behalf of the well-being of the rulers and gods and the eternal continuance of their governance and let him force the members of the common mess[4] and all the collective magistrates to sacrifice in the marketplace. If they do not conduct the procession or sacrifice or, after sacrificing, they do not force the members of the common mess and all the collective magistrates to sacrifice in the marketplace, let them pay two thousand sacred drachmas to the gods. Let it be permitted for any Gytheate who desires to denounce them.

Let the *ephoroi* in office during the time when Chairon is *stratēgos* and priest of the god Augustus Caesar—those with Terentius Biades—provide (money) for the three painted pictures of the god Augustus, Julia Augusta, and Tiberius Augustus Caesar and for the theater a stage for the chorus, four doors for stage performances, and footstools for the orchestra. Let them set up a stone stele and

3. The exact relationship of Victory and Aphrodite to Germanicus and Drusus is unclear.
4. This is a distinctive office found in the Greek city of Sparta and those cities over which Sparta had control at one point and time in its history, such as Gythium.

engraved on it this sacred law and let them put a copy of the sacred law in the public archives so that this ordained law—in public, in the open air, and evident to all—may demonstrate to all people the gratitude of the citizen body of the Gytheates for their rulers. Now if they do not engrave this law or set up the stele before the temple or to write a copy....

§I.2 Dedication to Livia as *Thea Tychē*

PROVENANCE: GYTHIUM (found near the city's theater)
DATE: AD 15
LANGUAGE: GREEK
SOURCE: KOUGEAS, *"EPIGRAPHIKAI EK GYTHEIOU,"* 44

1   [... Γυθεατ]ῶν πό-
   λεως τὸ ἄγαλμα
   ἀνέθηκεν τῇ ἐ-
   πιφανεστάτῃ
   θεᾷ Τύχῃ[5] τῆς πό-
5   λεως

... the city of the Gytheates dedicated this cultic statue to the most manifest goddess Good Fortune of the city (Livia).

§I.3 Tiberius's Letter to Gythium

PROVENANCE: GYTHIUM (found near the city's theater)
DATE: AD 15
LANGUAGE: GREEK
SOURCE: *SEG* 11.922[6]

1   - - γ
   - - γο

---

5. In the *editio princeps* of this epigraph, Kougeas, *"Epigraphikai ek Gytheiou,"* 44, fails to place iota subscripts on the dative article, superlative, and nouns: τῇ ἐ|πιφανεστάτῃ| θεᾷ Τύχῃ.

6. I have followed *SEG* 11.922 over the inscription's *editio princeps*: Kougeas, *"Epigraphikai ek Gytheiou,"* 38–43.

- - ες καὶ

- - - εἰ δέ τις

5 [- - ἔ]σεσθαι κυρι

- - μήτε ψήφισμα

- - ἔκαπονδος ἔστω

[- - ἡ οὐσία] αὐτοῦ καθιερούσθω τοῖς ἡ-

[γεμόσι - - τ]ὰς τῶν θεῶν τειμὰς ἁλοῦς

10 [- - ὡς ἐναγὴς ἀπολλύσθω ἀκρίτου ὄ]ντος τοῦ κτείναντος αὐτόν.

['Επιστολὴ τοῦ Τιβερ]ίου.

[Τιβέριος Καῖσαρ, θεοῦ Σεβ]αστοῦ υἱὸ[ς, Σ]εβαστός, ἀρχιερεύς, δημαρχικῆς

ἐξουσίας

[τὸ ἑκκαιδέκατο]ν Γυθεατῶν ἐφόροις καὶ τῇ πόλει χαίρειν. Ὁ πεμφθεὶς ὑπ' ὑμῶν

[πρὸς τ]ε ἐμὲ καὶ τὴν ἐμὴν μητέρα πρεσβευτὴς Δέκμος Τυφφάνιος Νεικάνωρ

15 [ἀνέδ]ωκέν μοι τὴν ὑμετέραν ἐπιστολήν, ᾗ προσεγέγραπτο τὰ νομοθετηθέν-

[τα ὑπ' ὑ]μῶν εἰς εὐσέβειαν μὲν τοῦ ἐμοῦ πατρός, τιμὴν δὲ τὴν ἡμετέραν.

['Ε]φ' οἷς ὑμᾶς ἐπαινῶν προσήκειν ὑπ<ο>λαμβάνω{ι} καὶ κοινῇ πάντας ἀνθρώ-

πους καὶ ἰδίᾳ τὴν ὑμετέραν πόλιν ἐξαιρέτους φυλάσσειν τῶι μεγέθει τῶν τοῦ

ἐμοῦ πατρὸς εἰς ἄπαντα τὸν κόσμον εὐεργεσιῶν τὰς θεοῖς πρεσπούσας

20 τιμάς, αὐτὸς δὲ ἀρκοῦμαι ταῖς μετριωτέραις τε καὶ ἀνθρωπείοις ·ἡ μέντοι ἐμὴ μη-

τηρ τόθ' ὑμῖν ἀποκρινεῖται, ὅταν αἴσθηται παρ' ὑμῶν ἥν ἔχετε περὶ τῶν εἰς αὐτὴν

τιμῶν

κρίσιν.

[The first ten lines of the stone are too fragmentary to translate but they contained a decree of some kind] Letter of Tiberius. Tiberius Augustus Caesar—son of the god Augustus, high priest, holding tribunician power for the sixteenth time—to the *ephoroi* and the city of the Gytheates, greetings. The ambassador, Decimus Tyrannius Nicanor, sent by you to my mother and me gave me your letter in which the laws ordained by you were prescribed for the piety of my father and our honor. I praise you for these things accepting it as fitting that in general all people and your own city should cherish as remarkable the greatness of my father's benefactions for the entire world as honors fitting for the gods. However, I am satisfied with those honors more appropriate for humans. Notwithstanding, my mother will answer you when she learns from you what judgment you have made for the honors for her.

§1.1 Mytilene's Decree of Divine Honors for Augustus

PROVENANCE: MYTILENE

DATE: 29 BC–AD 11

LANGUAGE: GREEK

SOURCE: *OGIS* 456 = *IGR* 4.39 = *IG* 12.2.58 (In cases where these editions differ, I have followed *IG*)

Column A

1   –]ν δὲ κα-

–]δας ἱερὰ

–]εσθαι ἐν τε-

–] γραψόντων εἰς α-

5   [– τὸν ὑμν]ηθέντα ὕμνον ὑπὸ

[– ἐ]ν ταῖς γινομέναις θέαις

[– – – – – – – – τιθέναι δὲ κατὰ πενταετηρ]ίδα ἀγῶνας θυμελικοὺς

[– – – – – – – – – – – – – – τοῖς νικήσ]ασιν ἆθλα ὅσα ὁ Διακὸς νόμος πε-

[ριέχει – – – τοῦ ἐπὶ τῶν στεφ]άνων(?) καὶ τοῦ ἀρχιερέως καὶ τοῦ στεφανη-

10   [φόρου – – – – – πέμψαι δὲ – – –]ς καταγγελεῖς τῶν πρώτων ἀ<χθ>ησο-

[μένων ἀγώνων – – – ταῖς ἐπισ]ημοτάταις πόλεσιν. ἀναθεῖναι δὲ δέλτου[ς]

[ἢ στήλας τοῦδε τοῦ ψηφίσματος ἐχούσας τὸ ἀντίγραφον ἐν τῷ ναῷ τῷ

κατασ]κευαζομένῳ αὐτῷ ὑπὸ τῆς Ἀσίας ἐν Περγάμῳ κα[ὶ]

[– – – καὶ Μυτιλήνῃ – – –]ῳ καὶ Ἀκτίῳ καὶ Βρεντεσίῳ καὶ Ταρραχῶνι καὶ Μα[σ]-

[σαλίᾳ καὶ – – – – καὶ Ἀν]τιοχήᾳ τῇ πρὸς τῇ Δάφνῃ. τὰς δὲ κατ' ἐνιαυτὸν

15   [θυσίας – – – ἐν τῷ ναῷ τοῦ Διὸ]ς καὶ ἐν τῷ τοῦ Σεβαστοῦ. ὅρκον δὲ εἶναι τῶν δι-

[καζόντων καὶ τῶν – – – ὀμνυ]ομένων σὺν τοῖς πατρίοις θεοῖς καὶ τὸν Σεβασ-

[τόν. – – – ἐν τῷ ναῷ τοῦ Διὸς καὶ ἐν τῷ τῆς Ἀφροδί]της τὴν εἰκόνα τοῦ

θεοῦ. τὰς δὲ τῶν γανων

– – – – – – – – – – – – τεμένους εἶναι καὶ τἆλλα δίκαια καὶ τίμι[α]

[– – – – – – – – – – – – κ]ατὰ δύναμιν τὴν ἑαυτοῦ. ἱερῶν δὲ ἐπὶ <τ>ράπε]-

20   [ζαν – – – – – – – – – κατ]ὰ μῆνα ἐν τῇ γενεθλίῳ αὐτοῦ ἡμέρᾳ καὶ π[α]-

[ρατιθέναι — — — — — τῶν] αὐτῶν θυσιῶν ὡς καὶ τῷ Διῒ παρίσταται. τρέ-
[φεσθαι δὲ τὰ ἱερεῖα — — — βόας — — —]ς ἐφελιωμένους ὡς καλλίστους καὶ με[τὰ]

[— — — μὲν ὑπὸ τῶν κατ' ἐνια]υτὸν στρατηγ<ῶ>ν, δύο δὲ ὑπὸ τῶν [ἐπ]ι[σ]-
[τατῶν(?) — — — — — —] δὲ ὑπὸ τῶν ἀγορανόμων, τρία δὲ ὑπὸ τοῦ ἀρχιερέως

25　[— — — — — — — — — — — — — — — — — τοῦ] δημοσίου δραχμὰς ἑκάστῳ τετρα-
[κοσίας — — — — — — — — — — — — — δ]είκνυσθαι δὲ τοὺς τραφέντας
[— — — — — — — — — τά τεθυσόμενα ἐν τ]οῖς ἀγῶσιν τρέφεσθαι τὸν ἴσο[ν]
[χρόνον — — — — — — — — — — — — — —] τὴν γενέθλιον ἡμέραν αὐτο[ῦ]

μηδενὶ διδομένου

30　[— — — — — — — — — — — — — — — — — τῷ σ]τεφανηφόρω καὶ τ[ῷ]

καθ'] ἕκαστον ἔτος ἐν

— — — —αι τίθεσθαι ἐπ[ὶ]

— — — — — —ενα— — —

Column B

1　εὐεργεσιῶν νομισ. . . . . . εὐχαριστίαν. ἐπιλογίσασθαι δὲ τῆς
οἰκείας μεγαλοφροσύνης ὅτ[ι]
τοῖς οὐρανίου τετε[υ]χόσι δό-
5　ξης καὶ θεῶν ὑπεροχὴν καὶ
κράτος ἔχουσιν οὐδέποτε δύ-
ναται συνεξισωθῆναι τὰ καὶ
τῇ τύχῃ ταπινότερα καὶ τῇ φύ-
σει. εἰ δέ τι τούτων ἐπικυδέσ-
10　τερον τοῖς μετέπειτα χρό-

νοις εὑρεθήσεται, πρὸς μη[δὲ]-
[ν] τῶν θεοποιεῖν αὐτὸν ἐπὶ [πλέ]-
ον δυνησομένων ἐλλείψει[ν]
τὴν τῆς πόλεως προθυμίαν
15 καὶ εὐσέβειαν. παρακαλεῖν
δὲ αὐτὸν συγχωρῆσαι ἐν τῇ [οἰ]-
κίᾳ αὐτοῦ δέλτον ἀναθεῖνα[ι]
καὶ ἐν τῷ Καπετωλίῳ δέ[λτον]
ἢ στήλην τοῦδε τοῦ ψηφ[ίσμα]-
20 τος ἔχουσαν τὸ ἀντίγραφ[ον].
εὐχαριστῆσαι δὲ περὶ αὐτο[ῦ]
τοὺς πρέσβεις τῇ τε συγ[κλή]-
τῳ καὶ ταῖς ἱερήαις τῆς Ἑσ[τί]-
ας καὶ Ἰουλίᾳ τῇ γυναικὶ αὐτοῦ
25 καὶ Ὀκταΐᾳ τῇ ἀδελφῇ καὶ τοῖς
τέκνοις καὶ συγγενέσι καὶ φί-
λοις. πεμφθῆναι δὲ καὶ στέφα-
νον ἀπὸ χρυσῶν δισχιλίων, ὃν
καὶ ἀναδοθῆναι ὑπὸ τῶν πρέσ-
30 βεων. εὐχαριστῆσαι δὲ ἐπ' αὐτοῦ καὶ τῇ συγκλήτῳ τοὺς πρέσβεις προσενηνεγμένης αὐτῆς
τῇ πόλει συμπαθέστατα καὶ
τῆς πατρίου χρηστότητος
35 οἰκείως.

Column A

[the first three lines are too fragmentary to translate] . . . of the things written
for . . . the hymn sung by . . . in the spectacles that occur . . . to put in the theatric
contests every fifth year . . . the prizes for the victors, as many as the law pertain-
ing to Zeus encompasses . . . on the crowns (?) and of the high priest and of the
crown bearer now to send . . . heralds of the first contests that are held . . . among
the most distinguished cities to set up writing tablets or stelae having the copy
of this decree in the temple that is being built for him by Asia in Pergamum and
. . . in Mytilene . . . and in Actium, Brundisium, Tarraco, and Massalia . . . and in
Antioch that is near Daphne. Now the yearly sacrifices . . . in the temple of Zeus

and in the temple of Augustus. Now the oath of the judges and of . . . those who swear with the ancestral gods and Augustus . . . in the temple of Zeus and in the temple of Aphrodite the image of the god. Now that of the . . . to be sanctuaries and the other rights and honors . . . according to his own power. Now on the table of the sacrifices . . . according to the month on his birthday and to place beside . . . the same sacrifices as are provided to Zeus. Now the sacrifices are to be full grown . . . oxen . . . chosen as the most beautiful and with . . . by the *stratēgoi* of that year, now two by the presidents (?) . . . , now two by the clerks of the *agora*, now three by the chief priest . . . four hundred drachmas to each from the public funds . . . Now to bring forth the full grown (oxen ?) . . . that are sacrificed during the contests are to be grown for the same amount of time . . . his birthday . . . of what is given to no one . . . to the crown bearer and to . . . every year . . . to be placed on . . .

Column B

Of the benefactions . . . a thanksgiving. Now that it conforms to the greatness of mind to consider that those who have profited from heavenly glory and those who have the supremacy and power of the gods can never be made equal with things that are by fortune and by nature humbler. But if thereafter in the future anything more distinguished than these will be found, the eagerness and piety of the city will not fall short of the possibilities to make him a god even more. That he [Augustus] is encouraged to grant that a writing table be set up in his house and a writing tablet or a stele in the Capitolium[7] having a copy of this decree. That the ambassadors are to give thanks for him to the summoned council [the Roman Senate], the priestesses of Hestia [the Vestal Virgins], Julia his wife [*sic*],[8] Octavia his sister, his children, his relatives, and to his friends. That a crown of two thousand gold pieces, which is to be presented by the ambassadors, is to be sent. That the ambassadors are to give thanks to him and to the summoned council [the Roman Senate] for the latter having had sympathy for our city and for its dutiful ancestral kindness.

§1.2 ARVAL BROTHERS' SACRIFICE ON SEPTEMBER 21, AD 38 IN ROME

PROVENANCE: ROME (found in the temple complex of Dea Dia, five miles outside Rome)

---

7. This is the temple of Jupiter Best and Greatest that stood on Rome's Capitoline Hill.
8. Livia, not Julia, was Augustus's wife. Julia was his daughter.

DATE: SEPTEMBER 21, AD 38

LANGUAGE: LATIN

SOURCE: *ACTS OF THE ARVAL BROTHERS* 12C LINES 83–92

83   (*vacat*) A(nte) d(iem) (undecimum) k(alendas) Octobres (*vacat*)
Taurus Statilius Corvinus promagister collegii fratrum arv[ali]um
85   nomine, quod eo die C. Caesar Augustus Germanicus conș[ensu]
senatus delatum sibi patris patriae nomen recepisset in Cạ[pitlio]
Iovi, Iunoni, Minervae hostias maiores (tres) inmolavit et ad templum
novom divo Augusto unam. (*vacat*).
Adfuerunt Paullus Fabius Persicus, M. Furius Camillus, Appius Iunius
90   [Silanus, P. Me]m̦miuș [Reg]ụlụș, C̦. C̦aẹcịnạ, Ḷ. Ạnnịuș Vịnịc̦ịanụ[s,]
[C. Calpurniu]s Piso. (*vacat*)

On the eleventh day before the Calends of October;[9] since on that day Gaius
Caesar Augustus Germanicus received the title "father of the fatherland," which
was conferred on him by the senate's decree, the vice president Taurus Statilius
Corvinus sacrificed in the name of the college of the Arval Brothers three full-
grown victims to Jupiter, Juno, and Minerva on the Capitoline Hill and a full-grown
victim to *Divus* Augustus at his new temple. Paullus Fabius Persicus, Marcus Furius
Camillus, Appius Junius Silanus, Publius Memmius Regulus, Gaius Caecina (Lar-
gus), and Lucius Annius Vinicianus, and Gaius Calpurnius Piso were present.

§2.1 INSCRIPTION ATTESTING TO PHILIP'S SHRINE

PROVENANCE: PHILIPPI (found reused in the window of Basilica A, a
Byzantine church in the city; see fig. 2.1, no. 4)

DATE: 350–300 BC

LANGUAGE: GREEK

SOURCE: PILHOFER 2.161

Column I	Column II
1 Φιλίππου Ε[--]ΦΙ[-]ΤΕ[- - 5- -]ΟΛ[-]Υ	[-]Τ[...]
τῆς πελεθρια[ί]ας δραχμὰς [...]	ΗΔ[...]
χιλίας διακοσίας πεντήκοντα	[-]ΑΥΡΟ
καὶ ἐπώνιον δραχμὰς [...]	ἐπώ[νιον]

9. That is, September 21.

5   εἴκοσι ὀβολόν τεταρτημόριον·   [. . .]
      καὶ ἄλλου τεμένους Φιλίππου   [-]Ο[. . .]
      χιλίας δέκα ἐπώνιον [δραχμὰς]   ΔΡΑΣΗ[. . .]
      εἴκοσι ὀβολόν τεταρτημόριον   ἐπών[ιον]
      Ἄρεως πεντήκοντα [δραχμάς]   Ποσειδ[ῶνος]
10   ἐπώνιον δραχμὴν [. . .].   ἐπών[ιον]
      Ἡρώων πεντήκοντα [δραχμὰς]   ΣΤΕ[. . .]
      [ἐπ]ώνιον δραχμὴν [. . .]   ἐπώνι[ον].

. . . of Philip Ε[--]ΦΙ[-]ΤΕ[- - 5- -]ΟΛ[-]Υ [-]Τ[. . .]. of one thousand square feet . . .
drachmas [. . .] ΗΔ[. . .] 1,250 (drachmas) [-]ΑΥΡΟ and a tax of . . . drachmas . . .
a tax of twenty (drachmas) and one-fourth an obol . . . , and the other shrine of
Philip [-]Ο[. . .] 1,010 (drachmas) and a tax of . . . drachmas ΔΡΑΣΗ[. . .] twenty
(drachmas) and one-fourth an obol. The (shrine) of Ares, a tax of fifty drachmas.
The (shrine) of Poseidon, a tax of . . . drachma . . . The (shrine) of the Hero, a tax
of fifty drachmas. ΣΤΕ[. . .] a tax of . . . drachma . . . a tax.

§2.2 MONUMENT OF JULIO-CLAUDIANS IN PHILIPPI'S FORUM

PROVENANCE: PHILIPPI (found reused in Basilica B, a Byzantine church
    in the city; see fig. 2.1, no. 7)
DATE: AD 16–37
LANGUAGE: LATIN
SOURCE: *CIPH* 2.1.8A = PILHOFER 2.282

1   A[---]
      Ti(berius) · C[aesa]r · divi · Augusti · f(ilius)
      divi [Iuli] n(epos) · trib(unicia) · potest(ate) XXXIIX
      Dru[sus] Caesar · Ti̱(berii) Aug(usti) · f(ilius)
5   divi · A̱[ug(usti) n(epos)] divi · Iuli pro[n(epos)] tṟ(ibunicia) pot(estate) · II ·
      vacat
      Caḏ[m]us · Atimetus · Martia̱[lis]
      C(aii) · Iuli̱ [A]ugusti · liberati̱ · MO+[---][10]

A . . . Tiberius Caesar son of *Divus* Augustus, grandson of *Divus* Julius, holding

---

10. Pilhofer 2.282, restores the end of the epigraph to read *mo(numentum) ḏ(e) [s(uo)]* [*f*(a-
ciendum) *c*(*uraverunt*)].

tribunician power for the twenty-eighth time. Drusus Caesar, son of Tiberius Augustus, grandson of *Divus* Augustus, great-grandson of *Divus* Julius, holding tribunician power twice. Cadmus, Atimetus, and Martialis, sons of Gaius Julius, freedmen of Augustus . . . [11]

§2.3 STATUE BASE OF *FLAMEN* OF *DIVUS* JULIUS, GAIUS ANTONIUS RUFUS

> PROVENANCE: ALEXANDRIA TROAS (there are a total of four statue bases of Rufus that the second, seventh, eighth, and ninth *vicus* or "neighborhood" of the Roman colony of Alexandria Troas set up, the texts of which are identical except for the names of the *vici*. Two bases remain at Alexandria Troas, one is in the British Museum, London, England, and the other in the Kunsthistoriches Museum in Vienna, Austria)
>
> DATE: MID-FIRST CENTURY AD
>
> LANGUAGE: LATIN
>
> SOURCE: MARIJANA RICI, *THE INSCRIPTIONS OF ALEXANDREIA TROAS*, INSCHRIFTEN GRIECHISCHER STÄDTE AUS KLEINASIEN 53 (Bonn: Habelt, 1997), no. 36 = *CIPh* 2.1 (appendix 4, no. 4) = Pilhofer 2.700[12]

```
1    Divi · Iuli(i) · flamini
     C(aio) · Antonio ·
     M(arci) · f(ilio) · Volt(inia tribu) · Rufo ·
     flamini · Divi · Aug(usti) ·
5    Col(oniae) · Cl(audiae) · Aprensis · et ·
     Col(oniae) · Iul(iae) · Philippens(is) ·
     eorundem · et · principi ·
     item · Col(oniae) · Iul(iae) · Parianae,
     trib(uno) · mil(itum) · coh(ortis) · XXXII · volun-
10   tarior(um) · trib(uno) · mil(itum) · leg(ionis) · XIII ·
     Gem(inae) · praef(ecto) · equit(um) · alae · I ·
     Scubulorum,
     vic(us) II
```

---

11. The criterion for determining that this inscription attests to a monument is the Latin case of the names of Julio-Claudians in the text, which are nominative and thus they cannot be the ones to whom anything is dedicated.

12. For the other three inscriptions, see Pilhofer 2.701–3.

(This monument was set up by the members of the) second *vicus* (of Alexandria Troas) to the *flamen* of *Divus* Julius, Gaius Antonius Rufus, son of Marcus, from the Voltinian tribe; *flamen* of *Divus* Augustus in the Claudian Colony of the Aprians and in the Julian Colony of the Philippians; first citizen of the aforementioned colonies as well as of the Julian Colony of the Parians; military tribune of the thirty-second cohort of volunteers; military tribune of the thirteenth legion Gemina; and prefect of the cavalry of the first Ala Scubulorum.

§2.4 DEDICATION MEMORIALIZING THE BENEFICENCE OF LUCIUS ATIARIUS SCHOENIAS

> PROVENANCE: PHILIPPI (found in the ruins of the Octagon or church
> dedicated to Paul; see fig. 2.1, no. 6)
> DATE: AD 41–54
> LANGUAGE: LATIN
> SOURCE: *CIPH* 2.1.6

1   *vacat* Pro · salu̜[te ---] [--- in h]o̜no̜[rem ---] [---] coniu̜[gis ---] [---]que ·
     Ti̜[(berii) ---]
     vacat Germani[ci ---] [--- libe]rorumqu̜[e ---] [[---]] [---]M̜ *vacat* L(ucius) ·
     Atiariu[s ---]
     vacat Schoenia[s ---] [--- f]lamen · divi · A[ugusti ---] [--- fl]a̜men · Ti(berii)
     · Caesaris [Aug(usti) ---] [---iud]e̜x · in · quinque · dec̜[urias adlectus ---]
     vacat trib(unus) · mil(itum) · leg(ionis) · V [---] [--- trib(unus)] cohortium
     · pr̜[aet(oriarum) ---] [--- prim(us)] pil(us) · leg(ionis) · XXI · Rapacis ·
     CV+[---] [---]arum · VII · et · VIII · praef(ectus) · C[---]
5   *vacat* signa · aenea · I+ [---] [---]que · dedicatio[---] [---]M · basim · mar-
     moream [---] [---] v̜iritim · populo · promis[erat ---]
     vacat paganis · et · milita[ribus ---] [---] A̜ugusta[libus ---] [---]S · triclin-
     ior(um) · decurion̜[ibus ---] [--- eorum]que · coniugib(us) · ac · liberis
     [---]
     vacat in · balineis · ad · AR[---] --- [---]M · eorum · gratuitum · fe̜[cit ---] [---]
     t̜iae · P(ublii) · f(iliae) · Paullae *vacat*
     vacat idem · duo · V[³ letters]+[---] [--- a]d̜itum · lapi̜deis · GR+[---] *vacat*

For the well-being of . . . in honor of . . . his wife . . . and of Tiberius Germanicus . . . and freedmen . . . M . . . Lucius Atiarius Schoenias . . . *flamen* of *Divus* Augustus . . . *flamen* of Tiberius Caesar Augustus . . . named as a judge in five divisions . . . tribune of a military fifth legion ... tribune of a praetorian cohort ... first centurion of the twenty-first legion Rapax ... CV ... prefect of the seventh and eighth ... C ... a bronze sign I ... and a dedication ... M a marble base ... he promised for the *populus* individually ... the villagers, the soldiers ..., and the *Augustales* ... S ... banquets for the *decuriones* ..., their wives, and their freedmen ... in the baths to AR ... M he showed his gratitude ... Paula daughter of Publius ... the same two ... stone stairs....

§2.5 Inscription from Monument Honoring Gaius Oppius Montanus

PROVENANCE: PHILIPPI (reused in building projects in Philippi's forum)
DATE: FIRST PART OF THE SECOND CENTURY AD
LANGUAGE: LATIN
SOURCE: *CIPH* 2.1.60 = PILHOFER 2.235A

Caio · Oppio · Ç(aii) [f(ilio)]
Vol(tinia) · Monta[no]
eq(uiti) · R(omano) · fil(io) · col(oniae) · or[nam(entis)]
dec(urionalibus) · II vir(aliciis) · q(uin) · q(uennaliciis) · ho[nor(ato)]
5   irenarc(hae) · IIvir(o) · mu[ner(ario)]
pontif(ici) · flamen(i) [divi Aug(usti)]
principi · et · patṛ[ono col(oniae)]
Philipp(iensium) · decuṛ[iones or-]
namenta Ṛ[---]
10   *vacat* + [---]

For Gaius Oppius Montanus, son of Gaius, from the Voltinian tribe; Roman equestrian; son of the colony; given the honor of the ornaments belonging to the *decuriones*, to the *duoviri*, and to the *duoviri quinquennales*; peace officer; *duovir*; *munerarius*; *pontifex*; *flamen* of *Divus* Augustus; first citizen and patron of the colony of the Philippians. The ornaments belonging to the *decuriones*....

§2.6 Dedication of the Pavement of Philippi's Forum

PROVENANCE: PHILIPPI (found engraved on the lower forum's pavement; see figs 2.1, no. 5; 7)
DATE: AD 14–67

LANGUAGE: LATIN
SOURCE: *CIPH* 2.1.66

[---]ḶVS · trib(unus) · mil(itum) · [---]III · fla(men) · divi · Aug(usti) · d(e) ·
s(ua) · p̣[(ecunia) f(ecit)].

. . . LUS, military tribune . . . III, and *flamen* of *Divus* Augustus paved (the forum)
at his own expense.

§2.7 Inscription from a Funerary Altar or Statue Base of Gaius Oppius Montanus

PROVENANCE: VASSILAKI, A VILLAGE CLOSE TO PHILIPPI
DATE: AD 100–150
LANGUAGE: LATIN
SOURCE: *CIPH* 2.1.130 = PILHOFER 2.031

1   C(aius) Oppiụs[13]
     Montanus
     patronus · col(oniae)
     [f]lam(en) · divi · Aug(usti)
5   ---

Gaius Oppius Montanus, patron of the colony, *flamen* of *Divus* Augustus. . . .

§2.8 Inscription from a Statue Base of a *Duovir Quinquennalis*

PROVENANCE: PHILIPPI (in the forum; see figs 2.1, no. 5; 7)
DATE: FIRST TO SECOND CENTURY AD
LANGUAGE: LATIN
SOURCE: *CIPH* 2.1.152 = PILHOFER 2.241

1   ---
     [pon]ṭif(ici) · fḷaṃịn(i) [---][14]

13. Pilhofer 2.031 reads O[ppiu]s.
14. In my opinion, it is probable that this inscription contained the Latin genitive *divi* before *Augusti*.

[A]ugusti · II · vi̠r(o) [iur(e) dic(undo) II vir(o)]
[qui]n̠q(uennali) · II · *vacat*
5   [---]ÇVM[---]

... *pontifex, flamen* of (*Divus?*) Augustus, *duovir* with jurisdictional power, *duovir quinquennalis* ... CVM. ...

§2.9 INSCRIPTION POSSIBLY ATTESTING TO THE DEDICATION OF A BUILDING IN PHILIPPI'S FORUM

PROVENANCE: RAKTCHA, A VILLAGE NEAR PHILIPPI

DATE: AD 14–37

LANGUAGE: LATIN

SOURCE: *CIPH* 2.1.2 = PILHOFER 2.088

1   [--- Ti(berius) Cae]sar · div(i) · Aug(usti) · [f(ilius) Aug(ustus) - - -][15]

... Tiberius Caesar Augustus son of *Divus* Augustus ...

§2.10 INSCRIPTION FROM STATUE BASE OF *SACERDOTES* OF *DIVA* AUGUSTA

PROVENANCE: PHILIPPI (in the northeast portion of the forum's lower
    terrace, part of which was in situ; see figs 2.1, no. 5; 7)

DATE: AD 66–99

LANGUAGE: LATIN

SOURCE: *CIPH* 2.1.126 = PILHOFER 2.226

Inscription A
1   [Iu]lia̠e C(aii) · f(iliae) ·
Auru̠ncinae
sa̠ce̠rdoti · divae ·
vacat A̠ug(ustae). *vacat*

Inscription B
1   Iulia̠e [.] f̠(iliae)

15. Pilhofer 2.088 reads [... *Cae*]*sar · div*(*i*) *· Aug*(*usti*) *· [...].

Modiae
sacerd(oti) [divae Aug(ustae)].

Inscription C

1   [---]CV+++[---][16]
     [sacerd(oti) divae][17]
     Aug(ustae).

Inscription D

1   Maeciae · C(aii) · f(iliae)
     Auruncinae
     Calavianae · sacerd(oti) ·
     vacat · divae · Aug(ustae) · *vacat*

Inscription E

1   Octaviae · P(ublii) · f(iliae) ·
     vacat Pollae · *vacat*

Inscription F

1   [*vacat*] Maecia · C(aii) f(ilia) Auruncin[a Cal]aviana · fecit · *vacat*

Inscriptions A–F

Maecia Auruncina Calaviana, daughter of Gaius, set up (this monument) for Julia
Auruncina, daughter of Gaius, *sacerdos* of *Divus* Augusta; Julia Modia, daughter
of . . . *sacerdos* of *Divus* Augusta, . . . CV . . . *sacerdos* of *Divus* Augusta; Maecia
Auruncina Calaviana, daughter of Gaius, *sacerdos* of *Divus* Augusta; and Octavia
Polla, daughter of Publius.

§2.11 Inscription on Sarcophagus of Cornelia Asprilla, *Sacerdos* of *Diva* Augusta

PROVENANCE: KAVALA, FORMERLY KNOWN AS NEAPOLIS (Acts 16:11)
DATE: AD 80–90
LANGUAGE: LATIN
SOURCE: *CIPH* 2.1.118 = PILHOFER 2.002

---

16. Pilhofer 2.226 reads [. . .]CVLAE.
17. Pilhofer 2.226 reads [. . .].

1   Cornelia · P(ublii) · fil(ia) · Asprilla · sac(erdos) · divae ·
     vacat Aug(ustae) · ann(orum) · XXXV · h(ic) · s(ita) · e(st). *vacat*

Here is laid Cornelia Asprilla, daughter of Publius, *sacerdos* of *Diva* Augusta. She lived thirty-five years.

§2.12 INSCRIPTION FROM SARCOPHAGUS OF PUBLIUS CORNELIUS ASPER ATIARIUS MONTANUS, *FLAMEN* OF *DIVUS* CLAUDIUS

PROVENANCE: KAVALA, FORMERLY KNOWN AS NEAPOLIS (Acts 16:11)
DATE: AFTER AD 54
LANGUAGE: LATIN
SOURCE: *CIPH* 2.1.53 = PILHOFER 2.001

1   <u>P(ublius) · Cornelius · Asper · Atiarius · Montanus</u>
     <u>equo · publico · honoratus · item · ornamentis · decu-</u>
     rionatus · et · IIviralicis · pontifex · flamen · divi · Claudi · Philippis ·
     vacat · ann(orum) · XXIII · h(ic) · s(itus) · e(st) · *vacat*

Here is laid Publius Cornelius Asper Atiarius Montanus, honored as a public knight and with the ornaments belonging to the *decuriones* and the *duoviri*; *pontifex*; and *flamen* of *Divus* Claudius in Philippi. He lived twenty-three years.

§2.13 SEAT OF THE *AUGUSTALES* IN PHILIPPI'S THEATER

PROVENANCE: PHILIPPI (found in situ in the theater; see fig 2.1, no. 3)
DATE: ROMAN IMPERIAL PERIOD
LANGUAGE: LATIN
SOURCE: PILHOFER 2.145

1   Aug(ustales).

(*Place belonging to the*) Augustales.

§2.14 Dedication for Philippi's *Curia*

> PROVENANCE: PHILIPPI (in the northwestern portion of the forum; see
> figs 2.1, no. 5; 7)
>
> DATE: AD 161–176
>
> LANGUAGE: LATIN
>
> SOURCE: *CIPH* 2.1.16 = PILHOFER 2.201

1   [In hono]ṛẹm · ḍivinae · domus · et · col(oniae) · Iul(iae) · Aug(ustae) ·
      Phiḷ[ipp(iensium)]¹⁸
      [--- ex] ṿoluntate · sua · a divo [A]ntonino · ex epulis ·
      [---¹⁹ C(aio) Modio Laeto Rufiniano q(uaestore) pr(o) p]r(aetore)
        · provinc(iae) · Maced(oniae) · curat̲[o]ṛe · r(ei) · p(ublicae) ·
      Philipp(iensium). *vacat*

In honor of the divine house and the Julian Augustan Colony of the Philippians
... from his own will. To *divus* Antoninus for public banquets ... by Gaius Modius
Laetus Rufinianus, *quaestor propraetor* of the Macedonian province and *curator*
of the *res publica* of the Philippians.

§2.15 Dedication from Philippi's Imperial Temple

> PROVENANCE: PHILIPPI (in the northeastern portion of the forum; see
> figs 2.1, no. 5; 7)
>
> DATE: AD 161–176
>
> LANGUAGE: LATIN
>
> SOURCE: *CIPH* 2.1.19 = PILHOFER 2.228

1   [In honorem divinae domus et col(oniae) Iul(iae) Aug(ustae)
      Philipp(iensium)]²⁰
      CVR[---]ANA Proba [ex] ṿoḷ[u]ṇṭaṭ[e sua resti]ṭuit²¹

---

18. Pilhofer 2.201 reads, *Phil̦[ipp(iensis) . . .*].

19. Pilhofer 2.201 restores [*. . . curante C(aio) Modio Laeto Rufiniano q(uaestore) pr(o) p*]
within the brackets.

20. Pilhofer 2.228 omits this line from his edition of the epigraph.

21. Pilhofer 2.228 reads *CVR* at the beginning of line three: *CVR*[--- *C(aius) Modius Laetus
Rufi*]*nianus q(uaestor) pr(o) pr(aetore) et curat*[*or r(ei) p(ublicae) Philipp(iensium) . . .*].

vacat [--- C(aius) Modius Laetus Rufi]nianus q(uaestor) pr(o) pr(aetore) et curat[or r(ei) p(ublicae) Philipp(iensium)]. *vacat*

Gaius Modius Laetus Rufinianus, *quaestor pro praetor* and *curator* of the *res republica* of the Philippians restored (this temple) CVR . . . ANA Proba . . . from his own testament in honor of the divine house and the Julian Augustan Colony of the Philippians.[22]

§2.16 Arval Brothers' Sacrifice on January 3, AD 38 in Rome

PROVENANCE: ROME (found in the temple complex of Dea Dia, five
 miles outside Rome)
DATE: JANUARY 3, AD 38
LANGUAGE: LATIN
SOURCE: *ACTS OF THE ARVAL BROTHERS* 12A LINES 1–15

[M. Aquila Iuliano, P. Nonio Asprenate co(n)s(ulibus), C. Caesar Augustus
 Germanicus mag(ister) fratr(um) arval(ium)]
[a(nte) d(iem) (tertium) non(as) Ianuar(ias)]
[Taurus Statilius Corvinus promag(ister) collegii fratrum arvalium nomine]
[vota nuncupavit pro salute C. Caesaris Augusti Germanici, pont(ificis) max-
 (imi), trib(unicia), pot(estate), co(n)s(ulis), p(atris) p(atriae), victimis]
[immolatis in Capitolio, quae superioris anni magister voverat, persoluit
 et in]
[proximum annum nuncupavit, praeunte - - - in]
[eadem verba, quae infra scripta sunt: *vacat*]
["Iuppiter o(ptime) m(axime), si. C. Caesar Augustus Germanicus - - -,]
[quem me sentio dicere, vivet domusque eius ? incolumis erit a(nte) d(iem)
 (tertium) non(as) Ian(uarias), quae proximae p(opulo) R(omano) Q(uir-
 itibus) rei p(ublicae)]
[p(opuli) R(omani) Q(uiritium) erunt fuerint, eumque diem eosque (eumque ?) salvos servaueris]
[ex periculis, si qua sunt eruntue ante eum diem eventumque bonum ita,
 uti me sentio dicere,]
[dederis eosque (eumque ?) in eo statu, quo nunc sunt (est ?)]
1   [aut eo meliore servaueris,] astu [ea ita faxis, tum tibi collegii]

---

22. It is unclear how "*CVR*[---]*ANA Proba*" fits into this inscription.

fratrum arvali[um nomine bove aurato voveo esse futurum.]

Iuppiter o(ptime) m(axime), quae in ver[ba tibi bove aurato vovi esse fu-
  tur]um, [quod]

hoc die vovi, ast tu ea ita fa[xis, tum tibi donum] auri p(ondo) (viginti
  quinque)

5   argenti p(ondo) (quinquaginta quinque) ex pecunia fratrum [ar]valium
  nomine eoru[m]

positum iri voveo. *vacat*

Iuno regina, quae in verba Iovi o(ptimo) m(aximo) bove aurato vovi esse
  futurum, quod hoc die vovi, ast tu ea ita faxis, tum tibi colle[gii]

fratrum arvalium nomine bove aurata voveo esse future[m.]

10   Minerva, quae in verba Iovi o(ptimo) m(aximo) bove aurato vovi esse
  futur[um,]

ast tu ea ita faxis, tum tibi collegii fratrum arvalium n[omine]

bove aurata voveo esse fu<tu>rum."

In eadem verba vovit deae Diae, Saluti, divo Augusto. *vacat*

Adfuerunt Paullus Fabius Persicus, Cn. Domitius Ahenobar[bus]

15   M. Furius Camillus. *vacat*

When Marcus Aquila Julianus and Publius Nonius Asprenas were consuls and
Gaius Caesar Augustus Germanicus was the president of the Arval Brothers, on the
third day before the Nones of January,[23] the vice president Taurus Statilius Corvinus formerly pronounced vows in the name of the college of the Arval Brothers for
the well-being of Gaius Caesar Augustus Germanicus, *pontifex maximus*, holding
tribunician power, consul, and "father of the fatherland." Having sacrificed victims
on the Capitoline Hill, he fulfilled (the vows) that the president of the previous
year had vowed and he formerly pronounced (new vows) for the coming year . . .
dictating in the same terms that are written below: "Jupiter Best and Greatest, if
Gaius Caesar Augustus Germanicus . . . whom I hereby name, remains alive and his
house is unharmed on the third day before the Nones of January of the following
year[24] that will be and will have been next for the Roman people, the Quirites,
the Republic of the Roman people, the Quirites; if, as I hereby name, on this day
you have preserved them (maybe "him") safe from perils and as they are (now)
in good fortune; if you have granted them (maybe "him") the same state as they
are now or you have preserved them in a better state; if you have accomplished
these things in this manner, then I solemnly promise that I will sacrifice an ox
with gilded horns to you in the name of the college of the Arval Brothers. Jupiter

23. That is, January 3.
24. That is, January 3, AD 39.

Best and Greatest, in the terms that I solemnly have promised that I will sacrifice an ox with gilded horns to you, what I solemnly have promised today, if you have accomplished these things in this manner, then I solemnly promise that a gift of twenty-five pounds of gold and fifty-five pounds of silver will be deposited for you from the money of the Arval Brothers in their name. Queen Juno, in the terms that I solemnly have promised to sacrifice an ox with gilded horns to Jupiter Best and Greatest, what I solemnly have promised today, if you have accomplished these things in this manner, then I solemnly promise that I will sacrifice a cow with gilded horns to you in the name of the college of the Arval Brothers. Minerva, in the terms that I solemnly have promised to sacrifice an ox with gilded horns to Jupiter Best and Greatest, if you have accomplished these things in this manner, then I solemnly promise that I will sacrifice a cow with gilded horns to you in the name of the college of the Arval Brothers." He solemnly promised Dea Dia, *Salus*, and *Divus* Augustus with the same terms. Paullus Fabius Persicus, Gnaeus Domitius Ahenobarbus, and Marcus Furius Camillus were present.

§3.1 Statue Base of Quintus Caecilius Metellus

> PROVENANCE: THESSALONICA (found near the Cassander Gate; see fig. 3.1, no. 6)
> DATE: 148–146 BC
> LANGUAGE: GREEK
> SOURCE: *IG* 10.2.1 134

1   Κόϊντον Καικέ[λιον Κοίντου Μέτελλον]
    στρατηγὸν ἀ[νθύπατον Ῥωμαίων]
    τὸν αὐτῆς σω[τῆρα καὶ εὐεργέτην]
    ἡ π[όλις]

The city (set up this statue of) Quintus Caecilius Metellus, son of Quintus, general, proconsul of the Romans, and her savior and benefactor.

§3.2 Honorary Inscription for Paramonus Son of Antiogonus

> PROVENANCE: THESSALONICA (found near the Church of Saint Demetrius)
> DATE: 95 BC

LANGUAGE: GREEK
SOURCE: *IG* 10.2.1.4 = *IG* 10.2.1S.4

1   οἱ νέοι

Ἀθηναγόρας Ἀπολλοδώρου, Πύρρος Κλειτομάχο[υ],

Νεικόστρατος Ν[ε]ικομάχου, Διογένης Ἐπιγένου,

Στράτων Ξένωνος, Ν[ε]ικήρατος Ἀνδροκλέους

5   εἶπαν·

ἐπεὶ Παράμονος Ἀντιγόνου αἱρεθεὶς γυμνασίαρ[χος]

εἰς τὸ ᵛ τρίτον ᵛ καὶ ᵛ πεντηκοστὸν ᵛ ἔτος πολλὴν π[ροση]-

νέγκατο προθυμίαν [ε]ἰς [τ]ὸ προστατῆσαι τῆς ἀρχῆς εὐ[σχη]-

μόγως, ἔν τε τοῖς χορηγουμένοις ἄπασιν ἐκτενῆ π[αρα]-

10   σκευάζων ἑαυτὸν καὶ τὰς ἠθισμένας τειμὰς Γ‒ ‒ ‒ ⁵⁻⁶‒ ‒ ‒ .

τοῖς τε θεοῖς καὶ Ῥωμαίοις εὐεργέταις ἐπαύξων· π[ρονο]-

ούμενος δὲ καὶ τῆς εὐταξίας τῆς ἐν τῶι τόπωι κ[αὶ κα]-

θόλου στοχαζό[μ]ενος ἐμ πᾶσι τοῦ πρέποντος, οὐ τ[ὴν δα]-

π<ά>νην τὴν προσήκουσαν παραλέλοιπεν, ἀλλὰ τ[ὸν]

15   χρόνον τῆς ἀρχῆς δὶς τῆς ἡμέρας²⁵ τιθεὶς τὸ ἄλε[ιμμα δι]-

ατε<τέ>λεκεν· δίκαιον δὲ ἐστιν τοὺς φιλοδόξῳ προα[ιρέ]-

σει χρωμένους τῶν καθηκουσῶν τιμῶν τυνχάνε[ιν],

ἵνα καὶ ἕτεροι, θεωροῦντες τὰς γινομένας τιμὰς

ὑπὸ τῶν νέων, τῶν ὁμοίων ζηλωταὶ γίνωνται·

20   ἔδοξεν τοῖς ἀπὸ τοῦ γυμνασίου ἐπαινέσαι τ[ε]

τὸν Παράμονον ἐπὶ τῆι προαιρέσει καὶ στεφανῶσ[αι]

θαλλοῦ στεφάνωι καὶ εἰκόνι χαλκῆ καὶ γραπτῆι τ[ε]-

λείαι, τὸ δὲ ψήφισμα ἀναγραφὲν εἰστήλην λιθίνη[ν]

τεθῆναι προφανὲς ἐν τῶι γυ<μ>νασίωι, χορηγηθέ[ν]-

25   τος ὑπὸ τῶν ταμιῶν κατὰ τὸ παρὸν τοῦ τε εἰς τὴ[ν]

γραπτὴν εἰκόνα καὶ στήλην ἀναλώματος. vacat

ἐπεχειροτονήθη ᵛ ἔτους γ′ ᵛ καὶ ᵛᵛ ν′, vacat

[Ὑπ]ερβερταίου ᵛᵛ δεκάτηι [[Ε]] ἀπιόντος. vacat

25. I have followed the reading of *IG* 10.2.1S.4 over *IG* 10.2.1.4, which reads χρόνον τῆς ἀρχῆς. . . .
ΤΗΣΙ. . . . . ΑΣ.

The *neoi*—Athenagoras son of Apollodorus, Pyrrus son of Clitomachus, Nicostratus son of Nicomachus, Diogenes son of Epigenus, Straton son of Xenon, and Niceratus son of Androcleus—said, "Since Paramonus son of Antiogonus, who was chosen to be gymnasiarch for the fifty-third year,[26] applied himself with much eagerness so that he presided over his office with dignity, he himself provided splendidly by defraying all costs, he increased the accustomed honors G . . . for the gods and the Roman benefactors, he took thought of good order that is in this place, in general he endeavored in all things what was fitting, he did not neglect the associated cost but continued to pay for oil twice a day during the time of his office. It is right that those who desire a reputation of loving glory receive proper honors so that others, when they observe these honors given by the *neoi*, they might become zealous imitators of similar actions. It seemed good to those from the gymnasium to praise Paramonus because of his reputation, to crown him with an olive crown, and to furnish him with a bronze life-sized painted statue. This decree is to be engraved publicly on a stone stele that is to be displayed in a conspicuous place in the gymnasium, and the expense for the painted image and the stele is to be paid for by the treasurers where possible." (This decree) was sanctioned in the year fifty-three, on the tenth day before the end of Hyperbertaius.

§3.3 Honorary Decree of Publius Salarius Pamphilus and Manius Salarius

PROVENANCE: THESSALONICA
DATE: 39/38 BC
LANGUAGE: GREEK
SOURCE: *IG* 10.2.1.109

1   ἔτους · γ′ · [[Ἀντωνίου]]
     Πόπλιος · Σαλάριος Πάμφιλος
     καὶ Μάνιος · Σαλάριος Ποπλίου · υἱὸς
     τὸ Ὀσιριῆον καὶ τὸ ἐν αὐτῷ περίστυλον
5   καὶ τὸ διδυμαφόριον Ὀσίριδι καὶ τοῖς
     ἄλλοις θεοῖς τοῖς ἐντεμενίοις πᾶσι

26. Year 1 of the Macedonian provincial calendar was 148 BC (see pp. 115–16), which dates this inscription to 95 BC.

καὶ πάσαις ᵛᵛ πολιταρχούντων
Ἀριστάρχου τοῦ Ἀριστάρχου, Νικίου τοῦ
Θεοδώρου, Ξεννέου τοῦ Σιμίου, Θεοδώρου
10   τοῦ Εὐτύχου, Δημητρίου τοῦ Ἀντιγόνου,
ταμίου τῆς πόλεως Στίλβωνος τοῦ Διονυσο-
φάνους, νεοκοροῦντος Διοδώρου τοῦ Κραμβαί(ου).

In year three of [[the era of Antony]], Publius Salarius Pamphilus and Manius
Salarius son of Publius (dedicated) the *Osiriēon*,[27] the peristyle that is in it, and
the *didumaphorion* (?) to Osiris and the all the other male and female gods in the
same temple complex when Aristarchus son of Aristarchus, Nicias son of Theodorus, Xenneas son of Simias, Theodorus son of Eutychus, and Demterius son of
Antigonus were politarchs; Stilbon son of Dionysophanes was treasurer of the city;
and Diodorus son of Crambaius was the temple custodian.

§3.4 Inscription Commemorating Temple of Caesar Augustus

PROVENANCE: THESSALONICA (rubble of Cassander Gate; see figs. 3.1,
        no. 6; 5)
DATE: 27 BC–AD 14
LANGUAGE: GREEK
SOURCE: *IG* 10.2.1.31

1   – – – –
        – – ᶜ·³⁻⁴ – –ΒΟΣΑ – – – – – – – – –
        ἀ[ν]θύπατος – – – – ᶜ·⁷⁻⁸ – – – –
        λατομίας ἐπόησ[εν τὸν]
            Καίσαρος να[όν].
5   ἐπὶ ἱερέως καὶ ἀγων[οθέτου · Αὐ]-
        τοκράτορος · Καίσα[ρος · Θεοῦ]
        υἱοῦ Σεβασ{βασ}το[ῦ – – – – ᶜ·⁷⁻⁸ – – – –]
        ὡς τοῦ Νεικοπόλ[εως · ἱερέως]
        δὲ τῶν θεῶν · Δω[– – – ᶜ·⁵⁻⁶ – – – τοῦ – – ᶜ·⁴⁻⁵ – – –]
10   που, Ῥώμης δὲ κ[αὶ Ῥωμαίων]
        εὐεργετῶν · Νεικ[– – – – ᶜ·⁶⁻⁸ – – – – τοῦ]

27. That is, the temple complex of Osiris.

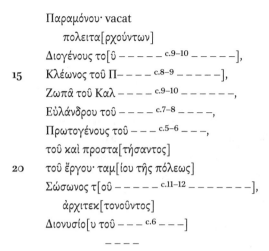

Παραμόνου· vacat

πολειτα[ρχούντων]

Διογένους το[ῦ – – – – – c.9–10 – – – – –],

15 Κλέωνος τοῦ Π– – – – c.8–9 – – – – –],

Ζωπᾶ τοῦ Καλ – – – – c.9–10 – – – – – –,

Εὐλάνδρου τοῦ – – – – c.7–8 – – – –,

Πρωτογένους τοῦ – – – c.5–6 – – –,

τοῦ καὶ προστα[τήσαντος]

20 τοῦ ἔργου· ταμ[ίου τῆς πόλεως]

Σώσωνος τ[οῦ – – – – – c.11–12 – – – – – – –],

ἀρχιτεκ[τονοῦντος]

Διονυσίο[υ τοῦ – – – c.6 – – –]

– – – –

... BOSA.... The proconsul ... made Caesar's temple of quarried stone when ... the priest and *agōnothetēs* for the victorious general Augustus Caesar son of a god ... –us son of Nicopolis; priest of the gods Do– ... son of ... –pus; Roma and the Roman benefactors Nic– ... son of Paramonus; and when Diogenes son of ... Cleon son of ... Zopas son of Cal– ... Eulandrus son of ... Protogenes son of ... were politarchs ... and supervised the work; Sosonus son of ... was treasurer of the city ... Dionysus son of ... was the architect.

§3.5 INSCRIPTION FROM TEMPLE OF AUGUSTUS, HERCULES, AND THESSALONICA

PROVENANCE: ENVIRONS OF THESSALONICA (Loutra Sedes)

DATE: 12 BC–AD 14

LANGUAGE: GREEK AND LATIN

SOURCE: *IG* 10.2.1S.1650

1 Αὐτοκράτορι Καίσαρι θεοῦ υἱῶι

Σεβαστῶι καὶ Ἡρακλεῖ καὶ τῆι πόλει

Αὐία Αὔλου θυγάτηρ Πώσιλλα τὸν

ναὸν καὶ τὰ θερμὰ καὶ τὴν δεξαμενὴν

5 καὶ τ[ὰ]ς περει[κειμέν]ας στοὰς τῶι ὕδατι ἐκ τοῦ ἰδίου.

vacat

Imp(eratori) · Caesari · divi · f(ilio) · Aug(usto) · pontif(ici) · max(imo)

et · Herculi et civitati Thessalonicensium
Avia A(uli) · f(ilia) · Posilla · aedem · aquas · piscinam · et
porticus · circa · piscinam de suo

Avia Posilla daughter of Aulia (dedicated) this temple, the bath, the cistern, and
the stoas surrounding the water to the victorious general Augustus Caesar son of
a god, Hercules, and the city from her own funds. Avia Posilla daughter of Aulia
(dedicated) this temple, the bath, the pool, and the portico around the pool to
victorious general Caesar Augustus, son of the *divus*, and *pontifex maximus*, Hercules, and the city of the Thessalonians from her own funds.

§3.6 Dedication to Livia

> PROVENANCE: THESSALONICA (found reused in the Church
>   of Saint Demetrius)
> DATE: AD 14–29
> LANGUAGE: GREEK
> SOURCE: *IG* 10.2.1S.1060

1   [θεᾷ Ἰουλίᾳ Σεβαστῇ]
         [γυναι]κὶ θεοῦ Σεβαστοῦ Καίσα[ρος]
         [καὶ μ]ητρὶ Τιβερίου Καίσαρος
            [Σε]βαστοῦ· ἡ πόλις

The city (dedicated this) to the goddess Julia Augusta, wife of the god Augustus
Caesar and mother of Tiberius Caesar Augustus.

§3.7 Dedication to Nero

> PROVENANCE: THESSALONICA
> DATE: AD 54–68
> LANGUAGE: GREEK
> SOURCE: *IG* 10.2.1S.131

1   [. .] [[Νέρωνος]] Κλαυ-
         [δί]ου, θεοῦ [Σ]εβα[στοῦ]

[Κλα]υδίου υἱοῦ, Γερμανικ[οῦ]
[Καί]σαρο[ς] υἱωνοῦ, Τιβε[ρίου]
5 [Καίσ]αρος [Σε]βαστοῦ υἱων[οῦ]
[υἱοῦ, θεου Σεβαστοῦ] υἱων[ου] υἱωνοῦ,
[Καίσαρος Σεβ]αστο[ῦ Γερμανικοῦ ἀρ]χιερέω[ς]
[μεγίστου, δημαρχικῆς ἐ]ξουσ[ίας τὸ., αὐ]τοκρά[τορος τὸ.],
[– ἐ]τοῦς · β[– –]
10 – ΛΗ– –
– ἸΕΡΗ– –
– CI – –
– –

... of [[Nero]] Claudius Caesar Augustus Germanicus, son of the god Augustus Claudius, grandson of Caesar Germanicus, great-grandson of Tiberius Caesar Augustus, great-great-grandson of the god Augustus, high priest, holding tribunician power for ... time, victorious general for the ... time ... year B ... LE ... IERH ... CI. ...

§3.8 Decree from Calindoia

PROVENANCE: CALINDOIA (found in a field)
DATE: AD 1
LANGUAGE: GREEK
SOURCE: *SEG* 35.744

1 ἔτους · η′ καὶ μ′ · καὶ · ρ′·
οἱ πολιτάρχαι προβουλευσα-
μένων τῶν βουλευτῶν
καὶ γενομένης ἐκκλησίας εἶ-
5 παν ἐν τῶι δήμωι· ἐπεὶ Ἀ-
πολλώνιος Ἀπολλωνίου
τοῦ Κερτίμμου γενόμε-
νος ἀνὴρ ἀγαθὸς καὶ πάσης
τειμῆς ἄξιος, ἐπιδεξάμενος
10 αὐθαίρετον ἱερατήαν Διὸς καὶ Ῥώμης
καὶ Καίσαρος θεοῦ υἱοῦ Σεβαστοῦ τοσαύτην
εἰσηνέγκατο μεγαλοφροσύνην ἀξίως καὶ τῆς τῶν προ-

γόνων καὶ τῆς ἰδίας ἀρετῆς φιλοδοξήσας, ὥστε μηδεμίαν ὑπερβολὴν καταλιπεῖν τῶν εἰς τοὺς θεοὺς καὶ τὴν
15　　πατρίδα δαπανημάτων, τάς τε γὰρ παρ' ὅλον τὸν ἐνιαυτὸν
ἐκ τῆς πόλεως κατὰ μῆνα γεινομένας Διὶ καὶ Καίσαρι Σεβαστῶι θυσίας ἐκ τοῦ ἰδίου παριστὰς καὶ τοῖς θεοῖς τὰς
τειμὰς πολυτελεῖς προσηνέγκατο καὶ τοῖς πολείταις τὴν
ἑστίασιν καὶ εὐωχίαν μεγαλομερῆ παρέσχετο καὶ λαϊ-
20　　κῶς πανδημεὶ δειπνίζων καὶ κατὰ τρίκλεινον[28] καὶ τὴ[ν]
ἐπὶ τῆς πανηγύρεως πομπὴν ποικίλην καὶ ἀξιοθ[έατον]
σκευάσας καὶ τοὺς ἀγῶνας Διὶ καὶ Καίσαρ[ι τῶ]ι Σεβ[αστῶι]
πολυτελεῖς θέμενος καὶ ἀξίους τ[– – – – – ca. 19 – – – – – – – –]
οὐ μόνον πρὸς τὴν τῆς εὐωχίας [. .]ονῶν [– – – – ca. 14 – – – –]
25　　τὴν θέαν καὶ τὴν ἀπά[τη]ν [καὶ τὴν διά]χυσιν τῆς ψ[υχῆς]
ἐφιλανθρώπησεν τοὺς πολείτας τάς τε ἐκ τῆς π[όλε]-
ως ἐν τῆι πανηγύρει δημοτελεῖς γεινομένας θυσίας Διὶ
καὶ Καίσαρι τῶι Σεβαστῶι καὶ τοῖς λοιποῖς εὐεργέταις παραι-
τησάμενος τὴν πατρίδα ταῖς ἰδίαις δαπάναις παρέστη-
30　　σεν καὶ βουθυτήσας καὶ ἰδία<ι> καθ' ἕκαστον τῶν πολειτῶν
τὴν πᾶσαν ἑορτὴν εὐώχησεν ἐν τοῖς τρικλείνοις καὶ
κατὰ τὸ κοινὸν ταῖς φυλαῖς ἐπιδόσεις ἐποιήσατο λαμ-
προτάτας, ἵνα, ὅποι ποτ' ἂν ἥδεσθαι βούλωνται, τὴν αὐτοῦ χάριν ἑστιῶνται, τὸ δὲ παράπαν πάσης δαπάνης
35　　ἀφειδήσας καὶ Καίσαρος ἄγαλμα κατεσκεύασεν ἐκ τοῦ
ἰδίου καὶ ἀναθεὶς αἰώνιον ὑπόμνημα τῆς εἰς πάντας ἀνθρώπους εὐεργεσίας τοῦ Σεβαστοῦ καὶ
τῆι πατρίδι τὸ προσκόσμημα καὶ τῶι θεῶι τὴν
καθήκουσαν τειμὴν καὶ χάριν ἔνειμεν. δι' ἃ δεδό-
40　　χθαι τῆι βουλῆι καὶ τῶι δήμωι ἐπαινέσαι τε αὐτὸν ἐπὶ τῆ<ι> λανπρότητι τῆς ψυχῆς καὶ τῆς εἰς
τὴν πατρίδα φιλοδοξίας καὶ στεφανῶσαι θαλλοῦ στεφάνωι καὶ ἐψηφίσθαι αὐτοῦ καὶ τοῦ πατρὸς αὐτοῦ Ἀπολλωνίου καὶ τῆς μητρὸς αὐτοῦ Στραττοῦς ἑκάστου ἄγαλμα λίθινον,
45　　σταθῆναι δὲ τὰ ἀγάλματα καὶ τὸ ψήφισμα τοῦτο ἔνθ' ἂν αὐτὸς ὁ ἀγω-

---

28. τρίκλεινον here and in line 31 is the Greek transliteration of the Latin term *triclinium*. For more on Greek and Roman dining practices, see D. Clint Burnett, *Studying the New Testament through Inscriptions: An Introduction* (Peabody, MA: Hendrickson, 2020), 90–95.

νοθέτης ἐπισημοτάτω‹ι› τῆς ἀγορᾶς αἱρῆται τόπωι, ἵνα καὶ οἱ λοιποὶ τῶν πολειτῶν ἀποθεωροῦντες εἰς τὴν εὐχαριστίαν τῆς πόλεως πρόθυμοι γεί-
νωνται φιλοδοξεῖν καὶ τῆι πατρίδι προσφέρεσθαι φιλανθρώπως· καὶ ἐπι-
χειροτονηθέντος τοῦ ψηφίσματος Ἀπολλώνιος τὰς μὲν τειμὰς
50   καὶ τὴν ἐκ τῆς πατρίδος χάριν ἐδέξατο, τοῦ [δ]ὲ δαπανήματος ἀπέλυ-
σεν τὴν πόλιν. vacat Ἐπεχειροτονήθη Δαι[σί]ου ιδ'.

Year 148.[29] The politarchs, after the councilors deliberated and the assembly met,
said to the citizen body, "Since Apollonius, son of Apollonius and grandson of Cer-
timmus, being a good man and worthy of all honor, having voluntarily accepted
the priesthood of Zeus, Roma, and Caesar Augustus son of a god, has worthily
introduced such greatness of mind and having sought the honor of his forebears
and his own virtue, so that he left no excess of expenses for the gods and his fatherland, for: he paid for from his own funds for the entire year the monthly sacrifices from the city to Zeus and Caesar Augustus; he offered expensive honors to
the gods; he furnished sumptuous feasting and entertainment for the citizens; he
provided a banquet for all the people together and by groups on dining couches;
he arranged a procession at the festival assembly that was varied and well worth
seeing; he put on expensive contests for Zeus and Caesar Augustus; he . . . worthy
. . . not only for the . . . of feasting . . . ονῶν . . . the goddess, the fraud (?), and the
diffusion of life; he was benevolent to the citizens by obtaining permission from
the city to offer at the festal assembly the public sacrifices to Zeus, Caesar Augustus, and the remaining benefactors and by furnishing them for his home city
at his own expense; he, having sacrificed oxen, entertained for the entire festival
from his own funds each one of the citizens by groups on dining couches; and in
general, he provided magnificent gifts to the tribes so that wherever they wished
to delight, they feasted on his *charis*; altogether he was unsparing with every expense; he prepared a cultic statue of Caesar from his own funds, dedicated it as
an everlasting memorial of the beneficence of Augustus for all humans, and freely
bestowed it as an additional adornment for his home city and a proper honor and
charis for the god [Augustus]. For these reasons, it seemed good to the council and
the citizen body to praise him for the enlightenment of his soul and his love of
honor for his home city and to crown him with an olive crown and to decree for
him, for his father Apollonius, and for his mother Stratto a marble statue of each
one, to set up these statues and this decree in the most distinguished place in the

29. Year 1 of the Macedonian provincial calendar was 148 BC (see pp. 115–16), which places
this inscription in AD 1.

agora wherever the *agōnothetēs* himself [Apollonius] chooses, so that the rest of the citizens, observing the gratitude of the city, might become eager to love honor and to provide benevolently for their home city." When the decree was approved, Apollonius accepted the honors and *charis* from his home city, but relieved the city of the expense. It was approved on the fourteenth day of Daisius.[30]

§3.9 STATUE BASE OF LIVIA

PROVENANCE: THASOS
DATE: 19–12 BC
LANGUAGE: GREEK
SOURCE: *IG* 12.8.381B

Fragment B
5   ὁ δῆμος
      Λειβιαν Δρου[σιλλ]αν τ[ὴ]ν τοῦ Σεβαστοῦ Καίσαρος
      γυναῖκαν θεὰν εὐεργέτιν.

Fragment B

The citizen body (set up this statue of) Livia Drusilla, wife of Caesar Augustus, the benefactor goddess.

§3.10 DECREE MENTIONING THE WILL OF AN UNKNOWN THESSALONIAN

PROVENANCE: THESSALONICA
DATE: BEFORE AD 19[31]
LANGUAGE: GREEK
SOURCE: *IG* 10.2.1.133 = *IG* 10.2.1S.133

---

30. That is, April or May 14, AD 1.

31. In the *editio princeps*, Edson dated the inscription to AD 153–154 and restored line 5 as [Τι(βερίου) · Ἰουλίου · Ῥοιμη]τάλκου, Tiberius Julius Rhoemetalces who reigned over the client kingdom of Bosporus from AD 131 to 154. After the work of Louis Robert, "Les inscriptions de Thessalonique," *RevPhil* 48 (1974): 212–15, and his restoration of the line as [Γ(αΐου) · Ἰουλίου · Ῥοιμη]τάλκου, most epigraphers date the inscription to the early first century AD; see *IG* 10.2.1s 133.

1   [ᵛ ἔτους ᵛ . ᵛ καὶ ᵛ . ᵛ καὶ ᵛ .] ᵛ Σεβαστοῦ. ᵛ

    [κατὰ · τὸ · δόξαν · τῇ · βουλῇ ? ·] καὶ · τοῖς · νέοις · Π · Κερ-

    [– – – – – – – – – c. 16 – – – – – – – δ]ιὰ διαθήκην · ἱερέως · καὶ ἀγω-

    [νοθέτου · Αὐτοκρά]τορος · Καίσαρος · θεοῦ · υἱοῦ · Σεβαστοῦ

5   [Γ(αΐου) · Ἰουλίου · Ῥοιμη]τάλκου · δυνάστου · ἀνταγωνοθε-

    [τοῦντος · ? Ἡλιοδώ]ρου · τοῦ · Ἡλιοδώρου · ἱερέως · θεῶν

    [– – – – c. 8 – – – – το]ῦ Φ[ίλ]ωνος · Ῥώμης δὲ καὶ Ῥωμαίων εὐεργετῶν

    – – – c. 7 – – – – γος · το[ῦ ·] Διονυσίου · πολειταρχούντων

    – – c.4 – – δώρου · τοῦ [· Ν]εικάνδρου · Ἀσκληπιοδώρου · τοῦ

10   Ἀσκληπιοδώρου · [Σω]σιπάτρου · τοῦ · Εἰσιδώρου · Ζωΐλου

    τοῦ · Ζωΐλου · τοῦ · Λυσιπόνου · Ἀθηνογένους · τοῦ

    Πλουσίας · γυμνασιαρχοῦντος · Μενελάου

    τοῦ · Ἀντιγόνο[υ ·] ἐφηβαρχοῦντος Νεικολάου

    τοῦ · Ἐπιμένο[υ]ς · ταμίου · τῆς πόλεως · Γ · Ἀγιλ-

15   ληΐου Ποτείτου · ἀρχιτ[έ]κτονος · Λ · Εἰουλείου · Φύρμου (!),

           ταμιευόντων ᵛ τῶν

        νέων [[– – – – – – c.13 – – – – – – – Υ]]

           Τ Μεμμίου Ζωσίμου

           – – – –

The year . . . of Augustus. According to the council's and the *neoi*'s judgment and according to the will of Publius Cer– . . . when the dynast Gaius Julius Rhoemetalces was priest and *agōnothetēs* of the victorious general Caesar Augustus son of a god; Heliodorus son of Heliodorus was vice-*agōnothetēs*; . . . son of Philon was priest of the gods; . . . –nus son of Dionysus was . . . of Roma and the Roman benefactors; when . . . –dorus son of Nicandrus, Asclepiodorus son of Asclepiodorus, Sosipater son of Isidorus, Zoilus son of Zoilus and grandson of Lusiponus, and Athenogenes son of Plousia were politarchs; Menelaus son of Antigonus was gymnasiarch; Nicolaus son of Epimenes was the ephebarch; Gaius Agilleius Potitus was city treasurer; Lucius Julius Firmus was architect; and Titus Memmius Zosiomus and . . . treasurers of the *neoi*. . . .

§3.11 DEDICATION HONORING THESSALONIAN BENEFACTOR

PROVENANCE: THESSALONICA (found in debris of the Church of Saint Demetrius)

DATE: BEFORE END OF FIRST CENTURY AD

LANGUAGE: GREEK
SOURCE: *IG* 10.2.1.32 = *IG* 10.2.1S.32

1   ἡ πόλις κ[αὶ οἱ συμπραγματευόμενοι]
    Ῥωμαῖο[ι, ἐπὶ ἱερέως καὶ ἀγωνοθέ]-
    του Αὐτ[οκράτορος Καίσαρος Θε]-
    οῦ υἱοῦ [θεοῦ Σεβαστοῦ] Γαῖου
5   Ἰουλίου [– – – – c.8 – – – –, ἱερέ]ως Διὸς
    Ἐλευθε[ρίου καὶ Ῥώμης Ζ]ωΐλου,
    φύσει δ[ὲ [– – – – c.8 – – – – θεῶ]ν Ἀντι-
    δότο[υ τοῦ – – – – c.8–9 – – – – –]ς, Ῥώμης
    καὶ Ῥω[μαίων εὐεργετῶν Θε]οδώρου³²
10 τοῦ Ἰλ[άρου ?, πολιταρχ]ούντων
    Ἐπικ[τήτου τοῦ – – c. 4–5 – – –]δος, Σω–

    – – –

The city and the Roman *negotiatores* (dedicated) ... to ... when Gaius Julius ...
was the priest and *agōnothetēs* of the victorious general the god Caesar Augustus son of a god, ... Zolius was priest of Zeus the Deliverer and Roma. Now by nature ... of gods, Antidotus son of ... –s, when Theodorus son of Hilaros was ... of Roma and the Roman benefactors and Epictetus son of ... –dos, So– ... were politarchs.

§3.12 DECREE HONORING THESSALONIAN BENEFACTOR

PROVENANCE: THESSALONICA (found in the *agora*; see fig. 3.1, no. 4)
DATE: 27 BC–AD 14
LANGUAGE: GREEK
SOURCE: *IG* 10.2.1S.1059

1   [ἡ πόλις καὶ οἱ συμπρ]αγματευόμε-
    [νοι Ῥωμαῖ]οι Μᾶρκον Πάπιον Μάρ-
    [κου υἱ]ὸν Μάξιμον, ἐπὶ ἱερέως
    [κ]αὶ ἀγωνοθέτου Καίσαρος θεοῦ

---

32. *IG* 10.2.1.32 reads καὶ Ῥω[μαίων ? Διονυσ]οδώρου. However, the most logical reading of the epigraph is found in *IG* 10.2.1s.32, which I have adopted.

5   υἱοῦ Σεβαστοῦ Νικολάου Δη-
         μητρίου τοῦ καὶ Κλιτομάχου.

The city and the Roman *negotiatores* (set up this statue of) Marcus Papius Maximus son of Marcus when Nicolaus son of Demetrius also known as Clitomaxus was the priest and *agōnothetēs* of Caesar Augustus son of a god.

§3.13 DECREE OF SARDIS DIVINELY HONORING GAIUS

PROVENANCE: SARDIS (found near the temple of Artemis)
DATE: APRIL 5 BC
LANGUAGE: GREEK
SOURCE: *SARDIS* 7.1.8 = *IGR* 4.1756, LINES 1–20

1   τὸ κοινὸν
        τῶν ἐπὶ τῆς Ἀσίας
        Ἑλλήνων καὶ ὁ δῆμος ὁ Σαρδι-
        ανῶν καὶ ἡ γερουσία ἐτίμησαν Μηνογέ-
5   νην Ἰσιδώρου τοῦ Μηνογένους τοῖς ὑπογεγραμμένοις·
        εἰσαγγειλάντων Μητροδώρου Κόνωνος καὶ Κλεινίου καὶ Μουσαίου καὶ Διονυσίου
        στρατηγῶν·
        ἐπεὶ Γάϊος Ἰούλιος Καῖσαρ ὁ πρεσβύτατος τῶν τοῦ Σεβαστοῦ παίδων τὴν
        εὐκταιοτάτην
        ἐκ περιπορφύρου λαμπρὰν τῷ παντὶ κό<σ>μῳ ἀνείληφε τήβεννον, ἥδονταί
        τε πάντες
        ἄνθρωποι συνδιεγειρομένας ὁρῶντες τῷ Σεβαστῷ τὰς ὑπὲρ τῶν παίδων εὐχάς,
        ἥ τε ἡ-
10   μετέρα πόλις ἐπὶ τῇ τοσαύτῃ εὐτυχίᾳ τὴν ἡμέραν τὴν ἐκ παιδὸς ἄνδρα
        τελεοῦσα[ν]
        αὐτὸν ἱερὰν ἔκρινεν εἶναι, ἐν ᾗ κατ᾽ ἐνιαυτὸν ἐν λαμπραῖς <ἐ>σθῆσιν
        στεφανηφορεῖν ἅπαντας, θ[υ]-
        σίας τε παριστάν<αι> τοῖς θεοῖς τοὺς κατ᾽ ἐνιαυτὸν στρατηγοὺς καὶ κατευχὰς
        ποιεῖσθαι διὰ τῶν
        ἱεροκηρύκων ὑπὲρ τῆς σωτηρίας αὐτοῦ, συνκαθιερῶσαι τε ἄγαλμα αὐτοῦ τῷ
        τοῦ πατρὸς ἐν-

ἱδρύοντας ναῶι, ἐν ᾗ τε εὐανγελίσθη ἡ πόλις ἡμέρᾳ καὶ τὸ ψήφισμα ἐκυρώθη
       καὶ ταύτην στε-

15   φ<αν>ηφορῆσαι τὴν ἡμέραν καὶ θυσίας τοῖς θεοῖς ἐκπρεπεστάτας ἐπιτελέσαι,
       πρεσβήαν τε

       ὑπὲρ τούτων στεῖλαι τὴν ἀφιξομένην εἰς Ῥώμην καὶ συνχαρησομένην αὐτῶι τε
       καὶ τῶι Σε-

       [β]αστῶι· δεδόχθαι τῇ βουλῇι καὶ τῶι δήμωι ἐξαποσταλῆναι πρέσβεις ἐκ τῶν
       ἀρίστων ἀν-

       δρῶν τοὺς ἀσπασομένους τε παρὰ τῆς πόλεως καὶ ἀναδώσοντας αὐτῶι τοῦδε
       τοῦ δό-

       γματος τὸ ἀντίγραφον ἐσφραγισμένον τῇ δημοσίᾳ σφραγῖδι, διαλεξομένους τε
       τῶι Σε-

20   βαστῶι περὶ τῶν κοινῇ συμφερόντων τῇ τε Ἀσίᾳι καὶ τῆι πόλει. καὶ ἡρέθησαν
       πρέσβεις Ἰόλλας Μητροδώρο[υ]

       καὶ Μηνογένη<ς> Ἰσιδώρου τοῦ Μηνογ<έ>νους.

The *koinon* of the Greeks of Asia and the citizen body and the *gerousia* of the
Sardians honored Menogenes son of Isidorus grandson of Menogenes in the following undermentioned ways: at the motion of the *stratēgoi* Metrodorus son of
Konon, Clenias, Musaius, and Dionysius: since the eldest of the sons of Augustus,
Gaius Julius Caesar, took up the white toga, which is the most prayed for by the
entire world, instead of the purple edged toga, all humans delighted when they
saw that their prayers on behalf of the children rose together to Augustus. Because of such a fortuitous event, our city has decided that the day on which he
[Gaius] transitioned to a man from a child should be holy and that on that day
every year all will wear wreaths in white garments; when the *stratēgoi* of each year
make offerings to the gods, they will make prayers through the sacred heralds on
behalf of his [Gaius's] well-being; they will set up a cultic statue of him [Gaius]
and dedicate it in his father's temple; the city, on the day in which it was told the
good news and the decree was confirmed, on this day they will wear crowns and
offer the most remarkable sacrifices to the gods; and that they send an embassy
about these things to Rome and that it rejoices with him [Gaius] and Augustus.
It seemed good to the council and citizen body to dispatch as ambassadors some
of the best men who will bring greetings from the city, who will deliver to him
a sealed copy of this decree with the public seal, and who will converse with
Augustus about the events that have occurred in the Asian *koinon* and the city.
The ambassadors chosen were Iollas son of Metrodorus and Menogenes son of
Isidorus and grandson of Menogenes.

§3.14 Building Dedication from Calindoia

PROVENANCE: CALINDOIA

DATE: 27 BC

LANGUAGE: GREEK

SOURCE: SEBASTIAN PRIGNITZ, "EIN AUGUSTUSPRIESTER DES JAHRES 27 V. CHR.," *ZPE* 178 (2011): 210–14

1   ἔτους   Κ καὶ Ρ
    Ἀρριδαῖος καὶ Κότυς οἱ Σωπάτρου καὶ
    Σώπατρος Κότυος τὴν ἐξέδραν
    καὶ τὸ βουλευτήριον καὶ τὴν στοὰν
5   τῆι πόλει, ἐπὶ ἱερέως Διὸς καὶ
    Ῥώμης καὶ Αὐτοκράτορος Καίσαρος
    θεοῦ υἱοῦ Σεβαστοῦ, Ἀρριδαίου
    τοῦ Σωπάτρου.

Year 120.[33] Arridaeus and Cotys sons of Sopater and Sopater son of Cotys (dedicated) the exedra, the *bouleutērion*, and the stoa to the city when Arridaeus son of Sopater was priest of Zeus, Roma, and the victorious general Caesar Augustus son of a god.

§3.15 List of Benefactions Connected to Imperial Divine Honors from Eresus

PROVENANCE: ERESUS

DATE: AFTER AD 14

LANGUAGE: GREEK

SOURCE: *IG* 12, SUPPL. 124

1   [— —
    — — — — — — — — — —]
    [— — — — — —]εσαμεν[— — — — — — — — — — — — — —
    — — — — — — — —]

---

33. Year 1 of the Macedonian provincial calendar was 148 BC (see pp. 115–16), which places this inscription in 28/27 BC. However, the fact that Caesar Octavian is hailed as Augustus in January 27 BC firmly dates the epigraph to 27 BC.

[ἐβουθύτη]σε μὲν ὑπὲρ ὑγιήα[ς — — — — — — — — — — — — — —
ἐπετέλεσσε δὲ]

[γλύ]κισμον τοῖς τε πολίταις [κ]αὶ ['Ρ]ω[μαίοις καὶ παρο]ί[κ]οις. ἔν τ[ε
προτάνει]

5   [Κλα]υδίω Νέρωνι τὰ μὲν Νεδάμ[εια καὶ Σέβ]αστα τὸ πρῶ[τον] ἐ[βουθύτησεν,
ἐπε]-

[τέλ]εσσε δὲ καὶ γλύκισμον τοῖς [τε πολ]είταις καὶ ['Ρ]ωμαίοις καὶ [παροίκ]οις
[καὶ]

[τοῖς] Καισαρήοις ταῖς σωτηρίοις [ἀμέραις] τῶ Σεβάστω Κ[αί]σα[ρος ἔδ]ωκε
[τοῖς προ]-

[γεγρ]αμμένοις ὑπὸ τὰν εὐωχίαν [καὶ] ἀνά[κ]λισιν ἄρνα καὶ κερά[μιον οἴνω καὶ
ἄρτω]

[μνα]ὶς τρεῖς. ἐν δὲ προτάνει Γαΐω Καίσαρι τῶ παῖδι τῶ Σεβάστ[ω ἀ]γίμονι [τὰς
νεό]-

10   [τατ]ος ἐβουθύτησε μὲν πάλιν τὰ Νεδάμεια καὶ Σέβαστα, ἐπε[τέλε]σ[σε]ν δὲ
[γλύκισ]-

[μον] τοῖς τε πολείταις καὶ 'Ρωμαίοις [καὶ παρ]οί[κο]ις. ἔν τε πρυτ[άνει
Ἀ]π[ολ]λων[ο]-

[δό]τω προσαγγελίας γενομένας ἐπὶ σαωτηρία καὶ νίκα τῶ Σεβάστω ἐβουθ[ύτη]-
[σε]ν ἐπὶ τοῖς εὐαγγελίοις τοῖς θέοις πάντεσσι καὶ παίσαις [καὶ ἀνέκλι]νε
μὲ[ν ἐπὶ]

[τ]ὰν βουθυσίαν τοῖς τε πολίταις [καὶ 'Ρ]ωμαίοις καὶ παροίκοις, [ἐπέδ]ω[κ]ε
δὲ [τοῖς]

15   [προ]γεγραμμένοις καὶ εἰς τὰν ε[ὐωχ]ίαν οἴνω [κ]εράμιον καὶ ἄ[ρτω μναὶ]ς τρεῖς.
[καθ]-

[ιέρ]ωσε δὲ καὶ τοῖς παίδεσσι τῶ Σεβ[άστ]ω τέμενός τε καὶ να[ῦον ἐκ] τῶν
ἰδ[ίων]

[ἐν τ]ῶ ἐπιφανεστάτω τόπω τᾶς ἀγόρας, ὅπποι καὶ ἐπιγέγραπται, [βουλό]μενος
[ἐνδεί]-

[κνυ]σθαι τὰν εἰς πάντα τὸν οἶκον εὐχαριστίαν αὕτω καὶ εὐσέβ[εια]ν. ἔχων
[δὲ χωρί]-

[ον ἰ]διόκτητον ἐν τῶ ἐπιφανεστ[ά]τω τᾶ πόλι κατεσκεύασε[ν καὶ] ἐν τούτ[ω
τέμε]-

20   [νός] τε καὶ ναῦον καὶ προγραψάμενος ἐπὶ τᾶς βόλλ{λ}ας ἀνέθηκ[ε Λιο]υ[ία]
Σεβ[άστα]

[Προ]νοία τᾶ γύναικι τῶ Σεβάστω θέω Καίσαρος, καθόττι καὶ ἁ ἐπι[γράφα
π]εριέ[χει. ἰδρύ]-

[σα]το δὲ καὶ ἐπὶ τῷ λίμενι τῷ ἐμ[πορί]ῳ [να]ῦον τῷ Σεβάστῳ θέ[ῳ Καίσαρι],
ὅπ[πως μή]-

[δε]ις τόπος ἐπίσαμος ἀπολίπη[ται τᾶς ε]ἰς τὸν θέον ἐξ αὗτω ε[ὐνοίας] καὶ
εὐ[σεβεί]-

[α]ς. κατεσκεύασεν δὲ ναῦον τῷ Σεβά[στῳ θ]έῳ Καίσαρι καὶ ἐπὶ
[— — — — — — — — — με]-

25   [τὰ] τᾶς γύναικος αὗτω Ἀμμίω τᾶς Ἀπ[ολλ]οφάνη, οὐ μόνον τ[ὰν πόλι]ν ἀλ[λὰ
καὶ τὰν]

[λο]ίπαν ἐπαρχήαν μάρτυρα ποήμενος τᾶς εἰς τὸν θέον εὐσε[βεία]ς.

He sacrificed oxen on behalf of the well-being . . . he distributed sweet meats and
wine to the citizens, the Romans, and the resident aliens. During the presidency of
Claudius Nero, first he sacrificed oxen at the Nedameia and Augustea Games, and
he distributed sweet meats and wine to the citizens, the Romans, and the resident
aliens. During the days of the Caesars who are saviors, he gave in honor of Augustus Caesar to the aforementioned individuals a symposium and feast of a lamb,
a jar of wine, and three minas of bread. During the presidency of Gaius Caesar,
son of Augustus, prince of the youth, again he sacrificed oxen at the Nedameia
and Augustea Games, and he distributed sweet meats and wine to the citizens,
the Romans, and the resident aliens. During the presidency of Apollonodotus at
the good news of the well-being and victory of Augustus, he sacrificed oxen at
all the good news gods and goddesses, and at the sacrifice of oxen, he provided a
symposium for the citizens, the Romans, and the resident aliens. At the feast, he
gave to the aforementioned individuals a jar of wine and three minas of bread. He
dedicated a temple complex and a temple to the sons of Augustus from his own
funds in the most conspicuous place in the *agora*. By what has been inscribed, he
wished to demonstrate his gratitude and piety for the entire house (of Augustus).
Having private property in the most conspicuous place in the city, he prepared
in this place a temple complex and a temple. Having provided a written notice to
the councilors, he dedicated (the temple complex and temple) to Livia Augusta
Pronoia,[34] wife of the god Augustus Caesar, as the epigraph (from the temple
complex) attests. He consecrated a temple to the god Augustus Caesar at the
harbor's market so that no notable place is left without goodwill and piety for the
god in it. He prepared a temple for the god Caesar Augustus and for . . . with his
wife Ammion, daughter of Apollophanes, he demonstrated his piety for the god
not only in the city but also in the rest of the province (of Asia).

34. That is, the goddess Providence.

§4.1 VICTOR LIST FROM CAESAREAN GAMES

PROVENANCE: CORINTH (reused as a Byzantine capital and probably
   also as doorstep)
DATE: AFTER AD 42
LANGUAGE: GREEK
SOURCE: MERITT, *CORINTH* 8.1, NO. 19

1   οἱ νεικήσαντες τὰ Καισάρει[α· εἰς]
      Καίσαρα θεοῦ υἱὸν Σεβαστὸν
      λογικῶι Ἐνκωμίωι
      Γάιος Ἰούλιος "Ιων Κορίνθιος, ὁ καὶ Ἀ[ργεῖος(?)]
5   εἰς Τιβέριον Καίσαρα θεοῦ Σεβαστοῦ υ[ἱὸν]
            Σεβαστὸν
         λογικῶι Ἐνκωμίωι
      Γάιος Ἰούλιος "Ιων Κορίνθιος, ὁ καὶ Ἀρ[γεῖος(?)]
      εἰς θεὰν Ἰ[ο]υλίαν Σεβαστὴν
10   Ποιήματι
      Γάιος Κ[ά]σσιος Φλάκκος Συρα[κόσιος]

The victors at the Caesarean Games: an elegant encomium for Caesar Augustus
son of a god, the Corinthian Gaius Julius Jon also known as Argius; an elegant
encomium for Tiberius Augustus Caesar son of the god Augustus, the Corinthian
Gaius Julius Jon also known as Argius; a poem for the goddess Julia Augusta, the
Syracusean Gaius Cassius Flaccus.

§4.2 POSSIBLE STATUE BASE OF *DIVUS* JULIUS CAESAR

PROVENANCE: CORINTH (found in the theater; see fig. 4.2)
DATE: AFTER MARCH 15, 44 BC
LANGUAGE: LATIN
SOURCE: KENT, *CORINTH* 8.3, NO. 50

1   divo Iu[lio]
      Caesari
      [sacrum]

Sacred to *Divus* Julius Caesar.

§4.3 STATUE BASE OF GAIUS JULIUS SPARTIATICUS

PROVENANCE: CORINTH (reused in pavement of a Byzantine ramp)
DATE: AD 54–59[35]
LANGUAGE: LATIN
SOURCE: WEST, *CORINTH* 8.2, NO. 68

1   C(aio) · Iulio · Laconis · f(ilio)
      Euryclis · n(epoti) · Fab(ia) · Spartiati[co]
      [p]rocuratori · Caesaris · et · Augustae
      Agrippinae · trib(uno) · mil(itum) · equo · p[ublico]
5   [ex]ornato a divo · Claudio · flam(ini)
      divi · Iuli · pontif(ici) · IIvir(o) · quinq(uennali) · iter(um)
      agonothetę · Isthmion · et · Caese(reon) ·
      [S]ebasteon · archieri · domus · Aug(ustae)
      [in] perpetuum · primo · Achaeon
10   ob v[i]rtutem · eius · et · animosam
      f[usi]ṣṣ[im]amque · erga · domum
      divinam · et · erga · coloniam nostr(am)
      munificientiam · tribules
      tribu[s] · Calpurnia[e]
15   [pa]trono.

The tribesmen of the Calpurnian tribe (set up this statue) of their patron Gaius Julius Spartiaticus—son of Laco and grandson of Eurycles, from the Fabian tribe, *procurator* of Caesar (Nero) and Augusta Agrippina, military tribune, adorned with a public knighthood by *Divus* Claudius, *flamen* of *Divus* Julius, *pontifex*, twice *duovir quinquennalis*, *agonothete* of the Isthmian and Caesarean Augustan Games, high priest for life of the Augustan house and first Achaian (to hold this office)— because of his virtue and most undaunted outpouring beneficence for the divine family and our colony.

---

35. A. B. West, ed., *The Latin Inscriptions 1896–1926*, vol. 8, part 2 of *Corinth: Results of Excavations Conducted by the American School of Classical Studies at Athens* (Princeton: American School of Classical Studies at Athens, 1931), no. 68, dates the inscription between Claudius's death on October 13, AD 54 and AD 55. However, I follow Antony J. S. Spawforth's, "Corinth, Argos, and the Imperial Cult: Pseudo-Julian, *Letters* 198," *Hesperia* 63 (1994): 218–19, redating of the epigraph between Nero's accession to the imperial throne in AD 54 and Agrippina's murder in AD 59.

§4.4 Dedication of Monument for Nero

> PROVENANCE: CORINTH (found in the Julian Basilica; see figs. 4.1, 15, 16)
> DATE: AD 66/67
> LANGUAGE: LATIN
> SOURCE: RONCAGLIA, *CORINTH* 22, NO. I-8 = KENT, *CORINTH* 8.3, NO. 81[36]

1   [- - - Neroni C]lạ[udio - - -]
     [- - - divi Claudii f(ilii) Germanici]
     [Caes(aris)] n(epoti) Tị(beri) Cae[s(aris) Aug(usti) pro nepoti]
     [divi] Aug(usti) ab n[epoti Caesari Aug(usto)]
5   [Germ(anico) po]nt(ifici) max(imo) trib(unicia) [pot(estate) - - -]
     Unknown number of lines[37]
     [- - - P. Memmi- C]leandr[- - -]
     [- - -] Valer P P
     P

(This monument was set up)...for Nero Claudius Caesar Augustus Germanicus, son of *Divus* Claudius, grandson of Germanicus Caesar, great-grandson of Tiberius Caesar Augustus, great-great-grandson of *Divus* Augustus, *pontifex maximus*, holding tribunician power for the...time, Publius Memmius Cleander and VALER P P P.

§4.5 Dedication to Tiberius

> PROVENANCE: CORINTH (found in the forum near South Basilica; see fig. 4.1)
> DATE: AUGUST AD 14–JUNE AD 18
> LANGUAGE: LATIN
> SOURCE: KENT, *CORINTH* 8.3, NO. 72

1   [Tiberio · divi · Au]gusti · [f(ilio) · Caes]ari · co(n)s(uli) ·
     − − − − − trib(unicia) · p]otest(ate) · XV− − − −

36. I follow Roncaglia's reconstruction in *Corinth* 22, no. I-8.

37. Kent, *Corinth* 8.3, no. 81, reconstructs the following two lines after line 5, which are not found in Roncaglia, *Corinth* 22, no. I-8:
[*Imp* · − − · *cos* · − − ·]
[*curam · agentibus · II · viris · P. · Memmmio* ·]

To Tiberius Caesar son of *Divus* Augustus consul . . . holding tribunician power for the . . . time.

§4.6 DEDICATION TO *DIVUS* AUGUSTUS

PROVENANCE: CORINTH (found in the South Stoa; see fig. 4.1)
DATE: AFTER AD 14
LANGUAGE: LATIN
SOURCE: KENT, *CORINTH* 8.3, NO. 51

1   [d]ịvo [Au]gusto [sacrum]

(This is) sacred to *Divus* Augustus.

§4.7 DEDICATION TO *DIVUS* AUGUSTUS

PROVENANCE: CORINTH (fragments found in the forum and South Basilica; see fig. 4.1)
DATE: AFTER AD 14
LANGUAGE: LATIN
SOURCE: KENT, *CORINTH* 8.3, NO. 52

1   [divo A]ugus[to]
[sac]rum.
Cṇ(aeus) · [Corneliu]s · Speratus · Aug(ustalis) ·
ob · ị[ustitia]m

(This is) sacred to *Divus* Augustus. The *Augustalis* Gnaeus Cornelius Speratus (set this monument up) because of his (*Divus* Augustus's) justice.

§4.8 MONUMENT OF GAIUS JULIUS LACO

PROVENANCE: CORINTH (found built into a wall in the Northwest Shops)
DATE: AD 41–54
LANGUAGE: LATIN
SOURCE: WEST, *CORINTH* 8.2, NO. 67

1   Ti(beri) · Claudi · Caesar(is) ·
    Aug(usti) · Germanici
    procuratori ·
    C(aio) · Iulio · C(ai) · f(ilio) · Fab(ia) · Laconi
5   augur(i) · agonothet(ae)
    Isthm(ion) · et · Caesareon
    IIvir(o) · quinq(uennali) · cur(ioni) · fla(mini) · Aug(usti)
    Cydichus · Simonis
    Thisbeus · b(ene) · m(erito)

Cydichus Thisbeus son of Simon[38] (set up this monument) for the well-deserving *procurator* of Tiberius Claudius Germanicus Caesar Augustus, Gaius Julius Laco, son of Gaius, from the Fabian tribe, *augur*, *agonothete* of the Isthmian and Caesarean Games, *duovir quinquennalis*, *curio*, and *flamen* of (*Divus*) Augustus.

§4.9 ALTAR OF *DIVUS* AUGUSTUS

> PROVENANCE: CORINTH (found in the Julian Basilica; see figs. 4.1, 15, 16)
> DATE: AFTER SEPTEMBER 14, AD 14
> LANGUAGE: LATIN
> SOURCE: RONCAGLIA, *CORINTH* 22, NO. 1-6

1   [Divo] August[o sacrum]
    Cn(aeus) Cn(aeus) Cn(aeus) [nomen]
    Pius Ŗom[- - -]
    Mosc[hus]
    [d(e)] s(uis) p(ecunias) [f(aciendum) c(uraverunt)]

Sacred to *Divus* Augustus. Gnaeus . . . Pius, Gnaeus Rom . . . , and Gnaeus Moschus managed the construction of this altar from their own money.

---

38. West, *Corinth* 8.2:49, "In a Latin inscription, the phrase *Cydichus Simonis* would normally mean Cydichus, the slave of Simon. Here we suspect, however, that the expression is a direct translation of a common Greek method of indicating the relationship of father and son."

§4.10 Inscription from Monument of *Divus* Augustus

PROVENANCE: CORINTH (found in the forum)

DATE: AFTER AD 14

LANGUAGE: LATIN

SOURCE: MARGARET L. LAIRD, "THE EMPEROR IN A ROMAN TOWN: THE BASE OF THE *AUGUSTALES* IN THE FORUM AT CORINTH," IN *CORINTH IN CONTEXT: COMPARATIVE STUDIES ON RELIGION AND SOCIETY*, ED. STEVEN FRIESEN, DAN SHOWALTER, AND JAMES WALTERS (Leiden: Brill, 2010), 67–116 = Kent, *Corinth* 8.3, no. 53[39]

1   [divo A]ụgus[to sacr(um)]
[nomen nomen][40]
[Au]ġustales [ob h(onorem) d(ecreto) d(ecurionum)]][41]

The *Augustales* (dedicated this monument) as sacred to *Divus* Augustus in honor of (*Divus* Augustus) by decree of the *decuriones*.

§4.11 Dedication to the *Genius* of Augustus

PROVENANCE: CORINTH (found in the Julian Basilica; see figs. 4.1, 15, 16)

DATE: FIRST TO SECOND CENTURY AD

LANGUAGE: LATIN

SOURCE: RONCAGLIA, *CORINTH* 22, NO. I-1

1   [- - -]ịnique Genio Augus[ti]
[- - -]rum L(audis) I(uliae) C(orinthiensis)
sacrum A(ulus) [M]iniatius Q(uinti) f(ilius)
[- - -]
5   [or]nament(is) decurion[alibus or]natus p(ecunia) [s(ua)]

Sacred to . . . and . . . Augustus's *genius* . . . of the Renowned Julian (Colony) of the Corinthians. Aulus Minatius, son of Quintus . . . who was given the ornaments belonging to the *decuriones*, (dedicated this) from his own money.

---

39. I follow Laird's reconstruction of the epigraph.
40. Kent, *Corinth* 8.3, no. 53, does not reconstruct this line.
41. Kent, *Corinth* 8.3, no. 53, reconstructs only [*Au*]*gustales* in this line.

§4.12 Commemoration of Augustan Apollo's Shrine and Statue

PROVENANCE: CORINTH
DATE: JULIO-CLAUDIAN PERIOD
LANGUAGE: LATIN
SOURCE: WEST, *CORINTH* 8.2, NO. 120

1   L(ucius) · Hermidius Celsus · et · L(ucius) · Rutilius [– – – – – – sacerdotes
    Apollinis(?)]
    Augusti · et · L(ucius) · Hermid[ius] Maximus et L̤(ucius) · Hermidius
    [– – – – – –]
    aedem · et · statuam · Apoḷḷinis Augusti · et · tabeṛṇaṣ ḍeçẹṃ

Lucius Hermidius Celsus and Lucius Rutilius . . . priests of Augustan Apollo and
Lucius Hermidius Maximus and Lucius Hermidius . . . (dedicated) this shrine,
statue of Augustan Apollo, and the Ten Shops.

§4.13 List of Winners from the Isthmian Games

PROVENANCE: CORINTH
DATE: LATTER HALF OF THE SECOND CENTURY AD (AD 150–199)
LANGUAGE: GREEK
SOURCE: MERITT, *CORINTH* 8.1, NO. 15 LINES 31–33

31   Γ(άϊος) Κλώδιος Φίλων Κορίνθ[ιος]
    ἀποβατικὸν ἐπὶ Λ. Καίσαρις
    Σεβαστοῦ υ[ἱοῦ]

The Corinthian Gaius Clodius Philon (won) the equestrian event for Lucius Caesar
son of Augustus.

§4.14 Statue Base of Livia Augusta

PROVENANCE: THESPIAE
DATE: AD 14–37

LANGUAGE: GREEK

SOURCE: CHRISTOPHER P. JONES, "EPIGRAPHICA VIII–IX," *ZPE* 146 (2004): 93–98, esp. 93–95

1   ἡ δοιοὺς σκήπτροισι θεοὺς αὐχοῦσα Σεβαστὴ
    Καίσαρας, εἰρήνης δισσὰ λέλαμπε φάη·
    ἔτρεψεν δὲ σοφαῖς Ἑλικωνιάσιν πινυτρόφων
    σύγχορος, ἧς γε νόος κόσμον ἔσωσεν ὅλον.

Augusta, wife of Caesar, who boasts of two gods with scepters and who has given light to two lights of peace. It is fitting for you to be a choir-sharer with the Wise Muses of understanding (because) her mind has saved the entire world.

§4.15 DEDICATION TO *DIVA* AUGUSTA

PROVENANCE: CORINTH (found in a Roman era building south of the original excavation dig house, the Oakley House)

DATE: AD 42–54 (after *Diva* Augusta's divinization on January 17, AD 42)

LANGUAGE: LATIN

SOURCE: KENT, *CORINTH* 8.3, NO. 55

1   [div]ạe · Aug[ustae · av]ạe
    [Ti(beri) · C]ḷaudi · Caẹ[saris]
    [Aug]ụ[sti · Germani]ci

(This building or this part of this building is dedicated) to *Diva* Augusta, grandmother of Tiberius Claudius Germanicus Caesar Augustus.

§4.16 MONUMENT OF GNAEUS CORNELIUS PULCHER (?)

PROVENANCE: CORINTH (found reused in a Byzantine wall in the forum)

DATE: BETWEEN AD 42 (after *Diva* Augusta's divinization on January 17, AD 42) and 68

LANGUAGE: LATIN

SOURCE: MIKA KAJAVA, "WHEN DID THE ISTHMIAN GAMES RETURN TO

THE ISTHMUS? (Reading 'Corinth' 8.3.153)," *CP* 97 (2002): 168–78 =
Kent, *Corinth* 8.3, no. 153[42]

1   [Cn. Cornelio]
    [Cn. f. ---? Pulchro,][43]
    [aedili, praef(ecto) i(ure) d(icundo), II]vịṛ(o) ẹṭ ỊỊ[vir(o)]
    [quinquennali,] agonothete Tib-
5   [ereon Claudi]eon[44] Sebasteon eṭ
    [agonothete I]sthmiọṇ et Caesar-
    [eon, qui Isthm]ia ad Isthmum egit
    [primus omniu]m[45] col(onia) Laud(e) Iul(ia) Cor(inthiensi),
    [carmina ad Iulia]m diva[m Au]g(ustam) virgi-
10   [numque certame]n insṭi[t]ụ[it e]t omnib-
    [us caerimoniis ?[46] Cae]sareon novatis Co-
    [rinthi sacra vo?]to peregit epulumq(ue)
    [omnibus co]lonis dedit,
    [fil(ius) ? Cornel]ius[47] Regulus
    [pat]ri,
15   [d(ecreto)] d(ecurionum).

To Gnaeus Cornelius Pulcher, son of Gnaeus . . . *aedile*, prefect *iure dicundo*,[48]
duovir, duovir quinquennalis, *agonothete* of the Tiberea Claudiea Augustan Games,
and *agonothete* of the Isthmian and Caesarean Games, who was the first of all
to preside over the Isthmian Games at the Isthmus under the authority of the
Renowned Julian Colony of the Corinthians. He instituted poems for *Diva* Julia
Augusta and a chariot race for the young women.[49] He renovated the *Caesareon*
(or the program of the Caesarean Games) for all the sacred rites, he completed

42. I follow Kajava's reconstruction of this epigraph.
43. Kent, *Corinth* 8.3, no. 153, reconstructs the first two lines as follows:
[*L. · Castricio*]
[*f · (tribu) · Regulo*].
44. Kent, *Corinth* 8.3, no. 153, reconstructs [. . . *Caesar*]eon . . .
45. Kent, *Corinth* 8.3, no. 153, reconstructs [*primus · sub · cura*]m . . .
46. Kent, *Corinth* 8.3, no. 153, reconstructs *aedificiis* here.
47. Kent, *Corinth* 8.3, no. 153, reconstructs the name *Castricius*.
48. A Roman official responsible for interpreting and dispensing justice for Roman citizens.
49. Kajava, "When Did the Isthmian Games," 173, points to a parallel inscription from Delphi dating to the mid-first century AD that attests that a certain woman named Hedea won an
"armed chariot race" (ἐνόπλι|ον ἅρματι) when Cornelius Pulcher was ἀγωνοθέτης of the Isthmian
Games (*SIG* 802 = PH239224).

the sacred vows of the Corinthians, and he gave a banquet for all the colonists. His son . . . Cornelius Regulus (erected this monument) for his father by the decree of the *decuriones*.

§4.17 Dedication to Monument of the College of *Lares* of the Divine (Imperial) House

> PROVENANCE: CORINTH (found in the forum)
> DATE: AD 120
> LANGUAGE: LATIN
> SOURCE: KENT, *CORINTH* 8.3, NO. 62

1   – – – – – – – – – – – – – – – – – – –
[decernente] · ꝯ̣ọllegio · Larum · Domụ[s]
  · Divinae ·
curam · agentibus · collegianị[s]
primi<s> · T(ito) · Flavio · Aug(usti) · lib(erti) · Antiọ[cho]
5   et · Ti(berio) · Claudio · Primigenio

(This monument was set up) by the decision of the college of the *Lares* of the divine house. Those chosen to manage (the monument's erection) were the first among the members of the college, Titus Flavius Antiochus, freedman of Augustus, and Tiberius Claudius Primigenius.

§4.18 Dedication to the Augustan Caesars

> PROVENANCE: CORINTH (found in the Julian Basilica; see figs. 4.1, 15, 16)
> DATE: FIRST TO THIRD CENTURY AD
> LANGUAGE: LATIN
> SOURCE: RONCAGLIA, *CORINTH* 22, NO. 1-2[50]

1   Caẹ[sa]ribus Augustis
[e]t coḷ(onia) [La]ud(i) Iu[l(iae) C(orinthiensis)]

---

50. For former, incomplete publications of this epigraph, see West, *Corinth* 8.2, no. 13; Paul D. Scotton, "A New Fragment of an Inscription from the Julian Basilica at Roman Corinth," *Hesperia* 74 (2005): 95–100.

[- - -]AV[- - -]
[- - -]NS F[---]

For the Caesars Augusti[51] and the Renowned Julian Colony of the Corinthians . . .
AV . . . NS F. . . .

§4.19 Monument of the *Isagogeus* Publius Puticius Rufus

PROVENANCE: CORINTH (found in the forum)
DATE: AD 59
LANGUAGE: LATIN
SOURCE: KENT, *CORINTH* 8.3, NO. 208

1   P(ublio) · Puṭicio
     P(ubli) · f(ilio) · Aem(ilia) · Ṛ[ufo] ·
     isagogi · Caesạ[reon]
     Neron[e]ọn · ag[onoth(ete)] ·
5   Ṃ(arci) · Pụ – – – – – –
        – – – – – – –

. . . (set up this monument) for Publius Puticius Rufus, son of Publius, of Aemilian
tribe. (He was) *isagogeus* of the Caesarean Neronean Games when Marcus . . . Pu
. . . was *agonothete*.

§4.20 Monument of the *Isagogeus* Gaius Rutilius Fuscus

PROVENANCE: CORINTH (found in the pavement east of Lechaeum
      Road)
DATE: AD 59
LANGUAGE: LATIN
SOURCE: WEST, *CORINTH* 8.2, NO. 82

1   C(aio) · Rutilio · L(uci) · f(ilio)
     Aem(ilia) Fusco, isagogi

51. Roncaglia, *Corinth* 20, 389, notes, "If specific, then the periods between 6 B.C. and A.D. 14 (Gaius and Lucius), A.D. 161 and 169 (Marcus Aurelius and Lucius Verus), and A.D. 176 and 180 (Marcus Aurelius and Commodus) are the most probable contexts."

Ti̱bereon Claudieon
Cae[s]a[reon Seba]s̱teon
5   [agonothetae L(uci)] Ruti̱li̱
L(uci) f̱(ili)[– – – – p]a̱tṟis
[– – – – – – –]

For Gaius Rutilius Fuscus, son of Lucius, from the Aemilian tribe, *isagogeus* of the Tiberian Claudian Caesarean Augustan Games when his father Lucius Rutilius . . . son of . . . was *agonothete*.

§4.21 MONUMENT OF THE *ISAGOGEUS* GAIUS RUTILIUS FUSCUS

PROVENANCE: CORINTH (found in the Julian Basilica; see figs. 4.1, 15, 16)
DATE: AD 59 (?)
LANGUAGE: LATIN
SOURCE: WEST, *CORINTH* 8.2, NO. 83

1   [– –] a̱nnon[ae curatori isagogi]
[Tibe]ṟeon Clau[dieon Caesareon]
[Sebasteon] a̱go̱ṉo̱[thetae – – –]

. . . *curator annonae*[52] and *isagogeus* of the Tiberian Claudian Caesarean Augustan Games when . . . was *agonothete*.

§4.22 MONUMENT OF THE *ISAGOGEUS* GAIUS RUTILIUS FUSCUS

PROVENANCE: CORINTH (found in the western part of the forum)
DATE: ?
LANGUAGE: LATIN
SOURCE: WEST, *CORINTH* 8.2, NO. 84

1   A̱e̱m̱(ilia)(?) [– – – – – –]
isagog[i – Rutili]

52. This was the individual in charge of the import and distribution of grain during times of famine and great need. According to Dio Cassius, *Roman History* 60.11, there was a famine in Achaia in AD 42, and, according to Josephus, *Jewish Antiquities* 20.101, and *Jewish War* 2.220, another between AD 45 and 48.

Fusci a(*?*)[gonothetae]
Iṣṭḥm[ion – – – –]

... of the Aemilian tribe, *isagogeus* of ... when Rutilius Fuscus was *agonothete* of
the Isthmian Games. ...

§4.23 MONUMENT TO PUBLIUS PUTICIUS JULLO

> PROVENANCE: CORINTH (found in the Peribolus of Apollo, which is
> a colonnaded courtyard north of the Peirene Fountain; see fig. 4.1)
> DATE: AD 14–37
> LANGUAGE: LATIN
> SOURCE: WEST, *CORINTH* 8.2, NO. 106

1   P(ublio) Puticio, M(arco) f(ilio), Aem(ilia)
     Iullo pạteṛno[53]
     aedil(iciis) et [IIvi]ṛ ọr-
     namẹ[ntis] [d(ecreto)] d(ecurionum) hono]
5   ṛạt[o – – – –]

(This monument was set up) for Publius Puticius Jullo, son of Marcus, from the
Aemilian tribe, father (or patron), *aedile* and given the ornaments belonging to a
duovir by the decree of the *decuriones*.

§4.24 STATUE BASE OF GAIUS JULIUS SPARTIATICUS FROM ATHENS

> PROVENANCE: ATHENS
> DATE: AD 54–68
> LANGUAGE: GREEK
> SOURCE: *IG* 2^2 3538

1   Γά · Ἰούλιον Σπαρτια-

---

53. This reading is nonsensical to me, because there is no room for the name of the father in
the inscription. Moreover, the picture of the epigraph and the approximate size of the letters,
including those that are missing, seem to suggest to me that a better reading may be something
like *pạṭṛno*, which might mean that Iullus was a patron of the colony.

τικὸν ἀρχιερέα θε-
[ῶν] Σεβαστῶν κ[αὶ]
[γέ]νους Σε[β]αστῶν,
5   ἐκ τοῦ κοινοῦ τῆ[ς]
Ἀχαίας διὰ βίου πρῶ-
τον τῶν ἀπ' αἰῶνος,
ὁ ἱερεὺς Ποσειδῶνο[ς]
Ἐρεχθέος Γαιηόχου
10   Τι · Κλαύδιος Θεογένη[ς]
Παιανιεὺς τὸν ἑαυτοῦ
φίλον.

Gaius Julius Spartiaticus, high priest of the Augustan gods and (high priest) of the Augustan family from the Achaian *koinon* for life, first of (the Achaians) from the age (to hold this office). The priest of Poseidon Erechtheus Earthholder and Tiberius Claudius Theogenes Paianieus, his own friend, (set up this statue).

Reconstructed Julio-Claudian Imperial Calendar in Philippi and Corinth

Acts of the Arval Brothers **for AD 59**

January 3: vow of two cows to Jupiter, two cows to Juno, two cows to Minerva, two cows to Public *Salus*, two cows to *Divus* Augustus, two cows to *Diva* Augusta, and two cows to *Divus* Claudius if they keep Nero healthy and well during the upcoming year

March 4: cow to Jupiter, cow to Juno, cow to Minerva, and a bull to Nero's *genius* because of the emperor's consulship

March 5: cow to Jupiter, cow to Juno, cow to Minerva, and a bull to Nero's *genius* because the emperor became *pontifex*

April 5: cow to Jupiter, cow to Juno, cow to Minerva, a cow to Public *Salus*, a cow to Providence, a bull to Nero's *genius*, and a cow to *Divus* Augustus for the emperor's well-being

Feriale Duranum

July 12: an ox to *Divus* Julius on his birthday

June 23: cow to Jupiter, cow to Juno, cow to Minerva, a cow to Public *Salus*, a cow to Felicity, a cow . . . , a cow to *Divus* Augustus, a cow to *Diva* Augusta, a cow to *Divus* Claudius, a bull to Mars Ultor, a bull to Nero's *genius* for the emperor's well-being and return to Rome

August 1: an ox to *Divus* Claudius on his birthday

September 11: cow to Jupiter, cow to Juno, cow to Minerva, a bull to Nero's *genius*, a cow to Public *Salus*, a cow to the household gods for the emperor's well-being and return to Rome

September 23: an ox to *Divus* Augustus on his birthday

October 12: Augustalia in Rome, a cow to *Divus* Augustus, a cow to *Diva* Augusta, and a cow to *Divus* Claudius

October 13: a cow to Jupiter, a cow to Juno, a cow to Minerva, a cow to Publica Felicity, a bull to Nero's *genius*, a cow to *Divus* Augustus, a cow to *Diva* Augusta, and a cow to *Divus* Claudius because of the anniversary of Nero's accession to the imperial throne (*imperium*)[1]

December 15: a cow to Jupiter, a cow to Juno, a cow to Minerva, a cow to Publica *Salus*, a cow to Felicity, and a bull to Nero's *genius* because of the emperor's birthday

---

1. I have reconstructed the sacrifices for October 13, AD 59, from those that occurred on October 13, AD 58.

Bibliography

Adam-Veleni, Polyxeni. "Entertainment and Arts in Thessaloniki." Pages 263–81 in *Roman Thessaloniki*. Edited by D. V. Grammenos. Translated by David Hardy. Thessaloniki Archaeological Museum Publication 1. Thessaloniki: Thessaloniki Archaeological Museum, 2003.

————. "Institutions . . . Inscribed on Marble." Pages 107–10 in *Kalindoia: An Ancient City in Macedonia*. Edited by Polyxeni Adam-Veleni. Thessaloniki: Archaeological Museum of Thessaloniki, 2008.

————. "Thessaloniki: History and Town Planning." Pages 121–76 in *Roman Thessaloniki*. Edited by D. V. Grammenos. Translated by David Hardy. Thessaloniki Archaeological Museum Publication 1. Thessaloniki: Thessaloniki Archaeological Museum, 2003.

Aland, Barbara, Kurt Aland, Eberhard Nestle, Erwin Nestle, and Holger Strutwolf, eds. *Novum Testamentum Graece*. 28th rev. ed. Stuttgart: Deutsche Bibelgesellschaft, 2012.

Allamani-Souri, Victoria. "Brief History of Imperial Thessaloniki." Pages 80–91 in *Roman Thessaloniki*. Edited by D. V. Grammenos. Translated by David Hardy. Thessaloniki Archaeological Museum Publication 1. Thessaloniki: Thessaloniki Archaeological Museum, 2003.

————. "The Imperial Cult." Pages 98–119 in *Roman Thessaloniki*. Edited by D. V. Grammenos. Translated by David Hardy. Thessaloniki Archaeological Museum Publication 1. Thessaloniki: Archaeological Museum, 2003.

————. "The Province of Macedonia in the Roman Imperium." Pages 67–79 in *Roman Thessaloniki*. Edited by D. V. Grammenos. Translated by David Hardy. Thessaloniki Archaeological Museum Publication 1. Thessaloniki: Thessaloniki Archaeological Museum, 2003.

Amandry, Michel. *Le monnayage des duovirs Corinthiens*. Bulletin de Correspondance Hellénique Supplement 15. Athens: École française d'Athènes, 1988.

Amandry, Michael, et al. *From the Death of Caesar to the Death of Vitellius (44 BC–AD 69)*. Vol. 1 of *Roman Provincial Coinage*. London: British Museum Press, 1992.

"Ancient Corinth." American School of Classical Studies at Athens. https://www.ascsa.edu.gr/excavations/ancient-corinth.

Appian. *Roman History*. Translated by Horace White and Brian McGing. 5 vols. LCL. Cambridge: Harvard University Press, 1912–2020.

Aristotle. *Athenian Constitution. Eudemian Ethics. Virtues and Vices*. Translated by H. Rackham. LCL. Cambridge: Harvard University Press, 1935.

Augustine. *City of God*. Translated by George E. McCracken et al. 7 vols. LCL. Cambridge: Harvard University Press, 1957–1972.

Aulus Gellius. *Attic Nights*. Translated by J. C. Rolfe. 3 vols. LCL. Cambridge: Harvard University Press, 1927.

Barclay, John M. G. "Conflict in Thessalonica." *CBQ* 55 (1993): 512–30.

———. "Paul, Roman Religion and the Emperor." Pages 345–62 in *Pauline Communities and Diaspora Jews*. Grand Rapids: Eerdmans, 2016.

———. *Paul and the Gift*. Grand Rapids: Eerdmans, 2015.

———. "Thessalonica and Corinth: Social Contrasts in Pauline Christianity." *JSNT* 47 (1992): 49–74.

Barrett, Anthony. *Livia: First Lady of Imperial Rome*. New Haven: Yale University Press, 2002.

Bauckham, Richard. *Jesus and the God of Israel: God Crucified and Other Studies on the New Testament's Christology of Divine Identity*. Grand Rapids: Eerdmans, 2008.

Beard, Mary. "Writing and Ritual: A Study of Diversity and Expansion in the Arval Acta." *Papers of the British School at Rome* 53 (1985): 114–62.

Beard, Mary, John North, and Simon Price. *Religions of Rome*. 2 vols. Cambridge: Cambridge University Press, 1998.

Behm, Johannes. "θύω, θυσία, θυσιαστήριον." *TDNT* 3:180–90.

Bickerman, Elias J. "*Consecratio*." Pages 3–37 in *Le culte des souverains dans l'Empire romain*. Edited by Willem den Boer. Geneva: Fondation Hardt, 1973.

Biers, Jane. "*Lavari est vivere* Baths in Roman Corinth." Pages 303–19 in *The Centenary 1896–1996*. Vol. 20 of *Corinth: Results of Excavations Conducted by the American School of Classical Studies at Athens*. Edited by Charles Williams II and Nancy Bookidis. Princeton: American School of Classical Studies at Athens, 2003.

Bilabel, Friedrich. "Fragmente aus der Heidelberger Papyrussammlung." *Phil* 80 (1925): 339–40.

Blümel, Wolfgang, ed. *Die Inschriften von Knidos*. Vol. 1. Inschriften griechischer Städte aus Kleinasien 41. Bonn: Habelt 1992.

The Book of Common Prayer and Administration of the Sacraments. Huntington Beach, CA: Anglican Liturgy, 2019.

Bormann, Lukas. *Philippi: Stadt und Christengemeinde zur Zeit des Paulus*. Leiden: Brill, 1995.

Bouffartigue, Jean, and Michel Patillon. *Livres II et III*. Vol. 2 of *De l'abstinence*. Paris: Les Belles Lettres, 1979.

Bowersock, G. W. "Eurycles of Sparta." *JRS* 51 (1961): 112–18.

Brélaz, Cédric. "First-Century Philippi." Pages 153–88 in *Roman Philippi*. Vol. 4 of *The First Urban Churches*. Edited by James R. Harrison and L. L. Welborn. WGRW-Sup 13. Atlanta: SBL Press, 2018.

———, ed. *La colonie romaine: La vie publique de la colonie*. Vol. 2, part 1 of *Corpus des Inscriptions grecques et latines de Philippes*. Athens: École française d'Athènes, 2014.

———. *Philippes, colonie romaine d'Orient: Recherches d'histoire institutionelle et sociale*. Bulletin de correspondance hellénique Supplément 59. Athens: École française d'Athènes, 2018.

———. "Philippi: A Roman Colony within Its Regional Context." Pages 163–82 in *Les communautés du Nord égéen au temps de l'hégémonie romaine: Entre ruptures et continuités*. Edited by Julien Fournier and Marie-Gabrielle G. Parissaki. Meleth-mata 77. Athens: Institute of Historical Research, 2018.

Bremmer, Jan N. *Greek Religion*. GRNSC 24. Oxford: Oxford University Press, 1994.

Brocke, Christoph vom. *Thessaloniki—Stadt des Kassander und Gemeinde des Paulus*. WUNT 2/125. Tübingen: Mohr Siebeck, 2001.

Brown, Alexandra. *The Cross and Human Transformation: Paul's Apocalyptic Word in 1 Corinthians*. Minneapolis: Fortress, 1995.

Brown, Raymond E. *An Introduction to the New Testament*. ABRL. New York: Doubleday, 1997.

Burkert, Walter. *Greek Religion*. Translated by John Raffan. Cambridge: Harvard University Press, 1985.

Burnett, D. Clint. *Christ's Enthronement at God's Right Hand and Its Greco-Roman Cultural Context*. BZNW 242. Berlin: de Gruyter, 2021.

———. "Divine Titles for Julio-Claudian Imperials in Corinth." *CBQ* 82 (2020): 437–55.

———. "Going through Hell: TARTAROΣ in Greco-Roman Culture, Second Temple Judaism, and Philo of Alexandria." *JAJ* 4 (2013): 352–78.

———. "Imperial Divine Honors in Julio-Claudian Thessalonica and the Thessalonian Correspondence." *JBL* 139 (2020): 570–72. Repr. pages 63–92 in *Thessalonica*. Vol. 7 of *The First Urban Churches*. Edited by James R. Harrison and L. L. Welborn. WGRWSup 21. Atlanta: SBL Press, 2022.

———. "The Interplay between Indigenous Cults and Imperial Cults in the New Testament World." In *Inscriptions, Graffiti, Documentary Papyri*. Edited by James R. Harrison and E. Randolph Richards. Grand Rapids: Zondervan, forthcoming.

————. "'Seated in God's Temple': Illuminating 2 Thess 2:4 in Light of Inscriptions and Archaeology Related to Imperial Divine Honors." *LTQ* 48 (2018): 69–94.

————. *Studying the New Testament through Inscriptions: An Introduction.* Peabody, MA: Hendrickson, 2020.

Burrell, Barbara. *Neokoroi: Greek Cities and Roman Emperors.* Leiden: Brill, 2004.

Burton, Ian M. "Capitoline Temples in Italy and the Provinces (Especially Africa)." *ANRW* 12.1:259–372. Part 2, *Principat,* 12.1. Edited by H. Temporini and W. Haase. New York: de Gruyter, 1982.

Cagnat, René, J. Touvain, Pierre Jouguet, and Georges Lafaye, eds. *Inscriptiones graecae ad res romanas pertinentes.* 4 vols. Paris: Leroux, 1901–1927.

Calandra, Elena, and Maria Elena Gorrini. "Cult Practice of a Pompé in the Imperial Age: S. E. G. XI.923." *Sparta* 4 (2008): 3–22.

Camia, Francesco. "Between Tradition and Innovation: Cults for Roman Emperors in the Province of Achaia." Pages 255–77 in *Kaiserkult in den Provinzen des Römischen Reiches: Organisation, Kommunikation, und Repräsentation.* Edited by Anne Kolb and Marco Vitale. Berlin: de Gruyter, 2016.

————. "The *THEOI SEBASTOI* in the Sacred Landscape of the *Polis*: Cult Places for the Emperors in the Cities of Mainland Greece." Pages 9–23 in *Im Schatten der Alten? Ideal und Lebenswirklichkeit im römischen Griechenland.* Edited by Johannes Fouquet and Lydia Gaitanou. Studien zur Archäologie und Geschichte Griechenlands und Zyperns 71. Mainz: Rutzen, 2016.

Camia, Francesco, and Maria Kantiréa. "The Imperial Cult in the Peloponnese." Pages 375–406 in *Society, Economy and Culture under the Roman Empire: Continuity and Innovation.* Vol. 3 of *Roman Peloponnese.* Edited by A. Rizakis and C. Lepenioti. Meletemata 63. Athens: Diffusion de Boccard, 2010.

Carter, Warren. "Paul and the Roman Empire: Recent Perspectives." Pages 9–40 in *Paul Unbound: Other Perspectives on the Apostle.* Edited by Mark D. Given. Atlanta: SBL Press, 2022.

Chaniotis, Angelos. "Festivals and Contests in the Greek World." Pages 3–172 in *Thesaurus Cultus et Rituum Antiquorum (ThesCRA) VII: Festivals and Contests.* Edited by Antoine Hermary. Los Angeles: The J. Paul Getty Museum, 2011.

Charlesworth, M. P. "The Refusal of Divine Honors: An Augustan Formula." *Papers of the British School at Rome* 15 (1939): 1–10.

Chrysostom, John. *The Homilies of S. John Chrysostom Archbishop of Constantinople on the Epistles of S. Paul the Apostle to the Philippians, Colossians, and Thessalonians.* Rev. ed. A Library of Fathers of the Holy Catholic Church Anterior to the Division of the East and West. Translated by Members of the English Church. Oxford: Parker, 1879.

Cicero. *Letters to Atticus.* Translated by D. R. Shackleton Bailey. 4 vols. LCL. Cambridge: Harvard University Press, 1999.

———. *On Duties*. Translated by Walter Miller. LCL. Cambridge: Harvard University Press, 1913.

———. *On the Nature of the Gods. Academics*. Translated by H. Rackham. LCL. Cambridge: Harvard University Press, 1933.

———. *On the Republic. On the Laws*. Translated by Clinton W. Keyes. LCL. Cambridge: Harvard University Press, 1928.

———. *Philippics*. Translated by D. R. Shackleton Bailey. Revised by John T. Ramsey and Gesine Manuwald. 2 vols. LCL. Cambridge: Harvard University Press, 2010.

———. *Pro Caelio. De Provinciis Consularibus. Pro Balbo*. Translated by R. Gardner. LCL. Cambridge: Harvard University Press, 1958.

———. *Pro Milone. In Pisonem. Pro Scauro. Pro Fonteio. Pro Rabirio Postumo. Pro Marcello. Pro Ligario. Pro Rege Deiotaro*. Translated by N. H. Watts. LCL. Cambridge: Harvard University Press, 1931.

———. *Pro Quinctio. Pro Roscio Amerino. Pro Roscio Comoedo. On the Agrarian Law*. Edited by J. H. Freese. LCL. Cambridge: Harvard University Press, 1930.

———. *Tusculan Disputations*. Translated by J. E. King. LCL. Cambridge: Harvard University Press, 1927.

Coarelli, Filippo. *Rome and Environs: An Archaeological Guide*. Translated by James J. Clauss and Daniel P. Harmon. Berkeley: University of California Press, 2008.

Cohick, Lynn H. "Philippians and Empire." Pages 166–82 in *Jesus Is Lord, Caesar Is Not: Evaluating Empire in New Testament Studies*. Edited by Scot McKnight and Joseph B. Modica. Downers Grove, IL: InterVarsity Press, 2013.

Collins, John J. *Daniel: A Commentary on the Book of Daniel*. Hermeneia. Minneapolis: Fortress, 1993.

Conzelmann, Hans. *1 Corinthians: A Commentary on the First Epistle to the Corinthians*. Translated by James W. Leitch. Hermeneia. Philadelphia: Fortress, 1975.

Cooley, Alison E. Res gestae divi Augusti*: Text, Translation, and Commentary*. Cambridge: Cambridge University Press, 2009.

———. *The* Senatus Consultum de Cn. Pisone Patre*: Text, Translation, and Commentary*. Cambridge: Cambridge University Press, 2023.

Corpus Inscriptionum Latinarum. https://cil.bbaw.de.

Cosby, Michael R. "Hellenistic Formal Receptions and Paul's Use of ΑΠΑΝΤΗΣΙΣ in 1 Thessalonians 4:17." *BBR* 4 (1994): 15–34.

Crawford, Michael, ed. *Roman Statutes*. 2 vols. London: Institute of Classical Studies, 1996.

Crossan, John Dominic, and Jonathan L. Reed. *In Search of Paul: How Jesus's Apostle Opposed Rome's Empire with God's Kingdom*. San Francisco: HarperCollins, 2004.

Danker, Frederick W., Walter Bauer, William F. Arndt, and F. Wilbur Gingrich. *Greek-English Lexicon of the New Testament and Other Early Christian Literature*. 3rd ed. Chicago: University of Chicago Press, 2000.

Daubner, Frank. "Macedonian Small Towns and Their Use of Augustus." *RRE* 2 (2016): 391–414.

Daux, George. "Chronique des fouilles et découvertes archéologiques en Grèce en 1957." *BCH* 82 (1958): 644–800.

Deissmann, Adolf. *Licht vom Osten: Das Neue Testament und die neuentdeckten Texte der hellenistisch-römischen Welt*. 4th ed. Tübingen: Mohr Siebeck, 1923.

———. *Light from the Ancient East: The New Testament Illustrated by Recently Discovered Texts of the Graeco-Roman World*. Translated by Lionel R. M. Strachan. 4th ed. New York: Hodder & Stoughton, 1910. Repr., Grand Rapids: Baker Books, 1978.

Despinis, G., T. Stefanidou-Tiveriou, and E. Voutyras, eds. Κατάλογος γλυπτών του Αρχαιολογικού Μουσείου Θεσσαλονίκης. Thessaloniki: Morphotiko Hidryma Ethnikes Trapezes, 2003.

Dessau, Hermann, ed. *Inscriptiones latinae selectae*. 3 vols. Berlin: Weidmannos, 1892–1916.

Diehl, Judith A. "Anti-imperial Rhetoric in the New Testament." Pages 38–81 in *Jesus Is Lord, Caesar Is Not: Evaluating Empire in New Testament Studies*. Edited by Scot McKnight and Joseph B. Modica. Downers Grove, IL: InterVarsity Press, 2013.

Dio Cassius. *Roman History*. Translated by Earnest Cary. 9 vols. LCL. Cambridge: Harvard University Press, 1914–1927.

Diodorus Siculus. *Library of History*. Translated by C. H. Oldfather and Francis R. Walton. 12 vols. LCL. Cambridge: Harvard University Press, 1933–1967.

Dionysius of Halicarnassus. *Roman Antiquities*. Translated by Earnest Cary. 2 vols. LCL 319. Cambridge: Harvard University Press, 1937–1950.

Dittenberger, Wilhelm, ed. *Inscriptiones Atticae aetatis romanae*. Vol. 3 of *Inscriptiones Graecae*. Parts 1–2. Berlin: de Gruyter 1878–1882.

———, ed. *Inscriptiones Megaridis, Oropiae, Boeotiae*. Vol. 7 of *Inscriptiones Graecae*. Berlin: de Gruyter, 1892.

———, ed. *Orientis Graeci Inscriptiones Selectae*. 2 vols. Leipzig: Hirzel, 1903–1905.

Dittenberger, Wilhelm, and Freiherr Friedrich Hiller von Gaertringen. *Sylloge inscriptionum graecarum*. 4 vols. 3rd ed. Leipzig: Hirzel, 1915–1924.

Dittenberger, Wilhelm, and Karl Purgold. *Die Inschriften von Olympia*. Olympia 5. Berlin: Asher, 1896.

Donfried, Karl Paul. "The Cults of Thessalonica and the Thessalonian Correspondence." *NTS* 31 (1985): 336–56.

Dunn, James D. G. *Romans 9–16*. WBC 38B. Nashville: Nelson, 1988.

Edson, Charles, ed. *Inscriptiones Epiri, Macedoniae, Thraciae, Scythiae*. Part 2.1. *Inscriptiones Thessalonicae et viciniae*. Vol. 10 of *Inscriptiones Graecae*. Berlin: de Gruyter, 1972.

Elkins, Nathan T. "The Procession and Placement of Imperial Cult Images in the Colosseum." *Papers of the British School at Rome* 82 (2014): 73–107.

Elliger, Karl, and Wilhelm Rudolph, eds. *Biblia Hebraica Stuttgartensia*. 4th ed. Stuttgart: Deutsche Bibelgesellschaft, 1997.

Elliott, Neil. "Paul and Empire 1: Romans, 1 Corinthians, 2 Corinthians." Pages 143–63 in *An Introduction to Empire in the New Testament*. Edited by Adam Winn. Atlanta: SBL Press, 2016.

Engels, Donald. *Roman Corinth: An Alternative Model for the Classical City*. Chicago: University of Chicago Press, 1990.

Epplett, Christopher. *Gladiators: Deadly Arena Sports of Ancient Rome*. New York: Skyhorse, 2017.

Errington, R. M. "Achaean Confederacy." *OCD* 4–5.

Fantin, Joseph A. *The Lord of the Entire World: Lord Jesus, a Challenge to Lord Caesar?* New Testament Monographs 31. Sheffield: Sheffield Phoenix, 2011.

Fee, Gordon D. *Paul's Letter to the Philippians*. NICNT. Grand Rapids: Eerdmans, 1995.

Finney, Mark. "Christ Crucified and the Inversion of Roman Imperial Ideology in 1 Corinthians." *BTB* 35 (2005): 20–33.

Fishwick, Duncan. *The Imperial Cult in the Latin West: Studies on the Ruler Cult of the Western Provinces of the Roman Empire*. 3 vols. Leiden: Brill, 1987–2002.

Fitzmyer, Joseph A. *First Corinthians: A New Translation with Introduction and Commentary*. AYB 32. New Haven: Yale University Press, 2008.

———. *Romans: A New Translation with Introduction and Commentary*. AB 33. New York: Doubleday, 1993.

Fränkel, Max, ed. *Die Inschriften von Pergamon*. Altertümer von Pergamon 8.1, 2. Berlin: Spemann, 1890–1895.

Fredriksen, Paula. *Paul: The Pagans' Apostle*. New Haven: Yale University Press, 2017.

Freeman, Sarah Elizabeth. "Temple E." Pages 166–236 in *Architecture*. Vol. 1, part 2 of *Corinth: Results of Excavations Conducted by the American School of Classical Studies at Athens*. Cambridge: Harvard University Press, 1941.

Friesen, Steven J. *Imperial Cults and the Apocalypse of John: Reading Revelation in the Ruins*. Oxford: Oxford University Press, 2001.

———. *Twice Neokoros: Ephesus, Asia and the Cult of the Flavian Imperial Family*. RGRW 116. Leiden: Brill, 1993.

Furnish, Victor Paul. *The Moral Teachings of Paul: Selected Issues*. 3rd ed. Nashville: Abingdon, 2009.

Gaertringen, Friedrich Hiller von, ed. *Inschriften von Priene*. Berlin: Reimer, 1906.

Garland, David E. *1 Corinthians*. BECNT. Grand Rapids: Baker Academic, 2003.

Gebhard, Elizabeth R. "The Isthmian Games and the Sanctuary of Poseidon in the Early Empire." Pages 78–94 in *The Corinthia in the Roman Period*. Edited by

Timothy E. Gregory. Journal of Roman Archaeology Supplement 8. Ann Arbor: Journal of Roman Archaeology, 1994.

Gellius. *Attic Nights*. Translated by J. C. Rolfe. LCL. 3 vols. Cambridge: Harvard University Press, 1927.

Georgi, Dieter. *Theocracy in Paul's Praxis and Theology*. Translated by David E. Green. Minneapolis: Fortress, 1991.

Goldsworthy, Adrian. *Augustus: First Emperor of Rome*. New Haven: Yale University Press, 2014.

———. *Caesar: Life of a Colossus*. New Haven: Yale University Press, 2006.

———. *The Complete Roman Army*. London: Thames & Hudson, 2003.

———. *Pax Romana: War, Peace, and Conquest in the Roman World*. New Haven: Yale University Press, 2016.

Goodrich, John K. "Erastus, *Quaestor* of Corinth: The Administrative Rank of ὁ οἰκονόμος τῆς πόλεως (Rom 16:23) in an Achaean Colony." *NTS* 56 (2010): 90–115.

Gorman, Michael J. *Apostle of the Crucified Lord: A Theological Introduction to Paul and His Letters*. 2nd ed. Grand Rapids: Eerdmans, 2017.

Gounaropoulou, Loukretia, and Miltiades B. Hatzopoulou, eds. *Επιγραφές Κάτω Μακεδονίας: Μεταξύ του Βερμίου όρους και του Αξιού ποταμού; Τεύχος Α´ Επιγραφές Βέροιας*. Athens: Diffusion de Boccard, 1998.

Gradel, Ittai. *Emperor Worship and Roman Religion*. Oxford: Clarendon, 2002.

———. "Roman Apotheosis." Pages 186–99 in *Purification Initiation Heroization, Apotheosis Banquet Dance Music Cult Images*. Vol. 2 of *Thesaurus Cultus et Rituum Antiquorum (ThesCRA)*. Edited by Vassilis Lambrinoudakis and Jean Ch. Balty. Los Angeles: The J. Paul Getty Museum, 2004.

Grazia Vanderpool, Catherine de. "Catalogue of Sculpture." Pages 299–371 in *The Julian Basilica: Architecture, Sculpture, Epigraphy*. Vol. 22 of *Corinth: Results of Excavations Conducted by the American School of Classical Studies at Athens*. Princeton: American School of Classical Studies at Athens, 2022.

———. "The Julio-Claudian Family Group." Pages 231–91 in *The Julian Basilica: Architecture, Sculpture, Epigraphy*. Vol. 22 of *Corinth: Results of Excavations Conducted by the American School of Classical Studies at Athens*. Princeton: American School of Classical Studies at Athens, 2022.

———. "Julius Caesar and Divus Iulius in Corinth: Man, Memory, and Cult." Pages 369–78 in *What's New in Roman Greece? Recent Work on the Greek Mainland and the Islands in the Roman Period*. Edited by Valentina Di Napoli, Francesco Camia, Vasilis Evangelidis, Dimitris Grigoropoulos, Dylan Rogers, and Stavros Vlizos. Meletemata 80. Athens: National Hellenic Research Foundation, 2018.

The Greek Anthology. 5 vols. Translated by W. R. Paton. Revised by Michael A. Tueller. LCL. Cambridge: Harvard University Press, 1917–2014.

Green, Gene J. *The Letters to the Thessalonians*. PNTC. Grand Rapids: Eerdmans, 2002.

Gupta, Nijay K. *1 and 2 Thessalonians*. Grand Rapids: Zondervan, 2019.

Habicht, Christian. "Die augusteische Zeit und das erste jahrhundert nach Christi Geburt." Pages 41–88 in *Le culte des souverains dans l'Empire romain*. Edited by Willem den Boer. Geneva: Fondation Hardt, 1973.

———. *Divine Honors for Mortal Men in Greek Cities: The Early Cases*. Translated by John Noël Dillon. Ann Arbor: Michigan Classical Press, 2017.

Hallof, Klaus, and Angelos P. Matthaiou, eds. *Inscriptiones insularum maris Aegaei praeter Delum, 6: Inscriptiones Chii et Sami cum Corassiis Icariaque*. Vol. 12, parts 1–2 of *Inscriptiones Graecae*. Berlin: de Gruyter, 2000, 2003.

Hansen, G. Walter. *The Letter to the Philippians*. PNTC. Grand Rapids: Eerdmans, 2009.

Harmon, Austin M., Alfred R. Bellinger, Henry T. Rowell, and Robert O. Fink. "The *Feriale Duranum*." Pages 1–222 in Yale Classical Studies 7. New Haven: Yale University Press, 1940.

Harrill, J. Albert. "Paul and Empire: Studying Roman Identity after the Cultural Turn." *EC* 2 (2011): 281–311.

———. *Paul the Apostle: His Life and Legacy in Their Roman Context*. Cambridge: Cambridge University Press, 2012.

Harrison, James R. "Excavating the Urban and Country Life of Roman Philippi and Its Territory." Pages 1–61 in *Roman Philippi*. Vol. 4 of *The First Urban Churches*. Edited by James R. Harrison and L. L. Welborn. WGRWSup 13. Atlanta: SBL Press, 2018.

———. *Paul and Imperial Authorities at Thessalonica and Rome: A Study in the Conflict of Ideology*. WUNT 273. Tübingen: Mohr Siebeck, 2011.

———. "Paul and the *Agōnothetai* at Corinth." Pages 271–326 in *Roman Corinth*. Vol. 2 of *The First Urban Churches*. Edited by James R. Harrison and L. L. Welborn. WGRWSup 8. Atlanta: SBL Press, 2016.

Harter-Uibopuu, Kaja. "Trust Fund of Phaenia Aromation (IG V.1 1208) and Imperial Gytheion." *Studia Humaniora Tartuensia* 5 (2004): 1–17.

Hays, Richard B. *First Corinthians*. IBC. Louisville: Westminster John Knox, 1997.

Head, Barclay V., ed. *Catalogue of Greek Coins in the British Museum: Corinth, Colonies of Corinth, Etc*. London: Trustees of the British Museum, 1889.

———. *A Catalogue of the Greek Coins in the British Museum: Macedonia, Etc*. London: Trustees of the British Museum, 1879.

Heen, Erik M. "Phil 2:6–11 and Resistance to Local Timocratic Rule: *Isa theō* and the Cult of the Emperor in the East." Pages 125–53 in *Paul and Empire: Religion and Power in Roman Imperial Society*. Edited by Richard A. Horsley. Harrisburg, PA: Trinity Press International, 1997.

Heilig, Christoph. *The Apostle and the Empire: Paul's Implicit and Explicit Criticism of Rome*. Grand Rapids: Eerdmans, 2022.

———. *Hidden Criticism? The Methodology and Plausibility of the Search for a Countercultural Subtext in Paul*. Tübingen: Mohr Siebeck, 2015.

Hellerman, Joseph H. *Reconstructing Honor in Roman Philippi:* Carmen Christi *as* Cursus Pudorum. SNTSMS 132. Cambridge: Cambridge University Press, 2005.

Hendrix, Holland Lee. "Thessalonica." *ABD* 6:523–27.

———. "Thessalonicans Honour Romans." ThD diss., Harvard University, 1984.

Hengel, Martin. *Christ and Power*. Translated by Everett R. Kalin. Philadelphia: Fortress, 1977.

Herodotus. *The Persian Wars*. Translated by A. D. Godley. 2 vols. LCL. Cambridge: Harvard University Press, 1920, 1925.

Homer. *Iliad*. Translated by A. T. Murray. Revised by William F. Wyatt. 2 vols. LCL. Cambridge: Harvard University Press, 1924, 1925.

———. *Odyssey*. Translated by A. T. Murray. Revised by George E. Dimock. 2 vols. LCL. Cambridge: Harvard University Press, 1919.

Hopkins, Keith. *A World Filled with Gods: The Strange Triumph of Christianity*. New York: Plume, 2001.

Horsley, G. H. R. "The Politarchs." Pages 419–31 in *The Book of Acts in Its Graeco-Roman Setting*. Edited by David W. J. Gill and Conrad Gempf. Vol. 2 of *The Book of Acts in Its First Century Setting*. Grand Rapids: Eerdmans, 1994.

Horsley, Richard A. *First Corinthians*. ANTC. Nashville: Abingdon, 1998.

———, ed. *Paul and Empire: Religion and Power in Roman Imperial Society*. Harrisburg, PA: Trinity Press International, 1997.

———, ed. *Paul and Politics: Ekklesia, Israel, Imperium, Interpretation: Essays in Honor of Krister Stendahl*. Harrisburg, PA: Trinity Press International, 2000.

———, ed. *Paul and the Roman Imperial Order*. Harrisburg, PA: Trinity Press International, 2004.

Hoskins Walbank, Mary E. "The Cults of Roman Corinth: Public Ritual and Personal Belief." Pages 357–74 in *Society, Economy and Culture under the Roman Empire: Continuity and Innovation*. Vol. 3 of *Roman Peloponnese*. Edited by A. D. Rizakis and C. E. Lepenioti. Athens: de Boccard, 2010.

———. "Evidence for the Imperial Cult in Julio-Claudian Corinth." Pages 201–13 in *Subject and Ruler: The Cult of the Ruling Power in Classical Antiquity; Papers Presented at a Conference Held in the University of Alberta on April 13–15, 1994, to Celebrate the 65th Anniversary of Duncan Fishwick*. Edited by Alastair Small. Ann Arbor: Journal of Roman Archaeology, 1996.

———. "The Foundation and Planning of Early Roman Corinth." *JRA* 10 (1997): 95–130.

———. "Pausanias, Octavia and Temple E at Corinth." *ABSA* 84 (1989): 361–94.

Hunt, A. S. *The Oxyrhynchus Papyri*. Part 7. London: Egypt Exploration Fund, 1910.

Hunt, A. S., C. C. Edgar, and D. L. Page, eds. *Select Papyri*. 3 vols. LCL. Cambridge: Harvard University Press, 1932–1942.

Imhoof-Blumer, F., and P. Gardner. "Numismatic Commentary on Pausanias." *JHS* 6 (1885): 50–101.

"Inscriptiones Graecae." Berlin-Brandenburgische Akademie der Wissenschaften. http://telota.bbaw.de/ig/.

Iossif, Panagiotis, and Catharine Lorber. "More Than Men, Less Than Gods: Concluding Thoughts and New Perspectives." Pages 691–710 in *More Than Men, Less Than Gods: Studies on Royal Cult and Imperial Worship*. Edited by Panagiotis P. Iossif, Andrezj Chankowski, and Catharine Lorber. Leuven: Peeters, 2011.

Jacoby, Felix, ed. *Die Fragmente der griechischen Historiker: Geschichte von Staedten und Voelkern (Horographie und Ethnographie), B, Autoren ueber einzelne Staedte (Laender) Nr. 297–607*. Brill, Leiden, 1964.

Jewett, Robert. *Romans: A Commentary*. Hermeneia. Minneapolis: Fortress, 2006.

———. *The Thessalonian Correspondence*. Philadelphia: Fortress, 1986.

Jones, A. H. M. *The Greek City from Alexander to Justinian*. Oxford: Clarendon, 1940.

Jones, Christopher P. "The Earthquake of 26 BCE in Decrees of Mytilene and Chios." *Chiron* 45 (2015): 101–22.

———. "Epigraphica VIII–IX." *ZPE* 146 (2004): 93–98.

Josephus. Translated by Louis H. Feldman, Ralph Marcus, Henry St. J. Thackeray, and Allen Wikgren. 10 vols. LCL. Cambridge: Harvard University Press, 1926–1965.

Julian. *Letters. Epigrams. Against the Galilaeans. Fragments*. Translated by Wilmer C. Wright. LCL. Cambridge: Harvard University Press, 1923.

Kajava, Mika. "When Did the Isthmian Games Return to the Isthmus? (Reading 'Corinth' 8.3.153)." *CP* 97 (2002): 168–78.

Kent, John H., ed. *The Inscriptions 1926–1950*. Vol. 8, part 3 of *Corinth: Results of Excavations Conducted by the American School of Classical Studies at Athens*. Princeton: American School of Classical Studies at Athens, 1966.

Kienast, Dietmar. *Römische Kaisertabelle: Grundzüge einer römischen Kaiserchronologie*. 2nd ed. Darmstadt: Wissenschaftliche Buchgesellschaft, 1996.

Kolbe, Walter, ed. *Inscriptiones Laconiae et Messeniae*. Vol. 5, part 1 of *Inscriptiones Graecae*. Berlin: de Gruyter, 1913.

Kougeas, S. B. "*Epigraphikai ek Gytheiou symbolai ein tēn istorian tis Lakonis kata tous chronous tēs Rōmaikēs Autokratorias.*" *Hellenika* 1 (1928): 7–44.

Koukouli-Chrysantaki, Chaido. "Amphipolis." Pages 409–36 in *Brill's Companion to Ancient Macedon: Studies in the Archaeology and History of Macedon, 650 BC–300 AD*. Edited by Robert J. Lane Fox. Leiden: Brill, 2011.

———. "Colonia Iulia Augusta Philippensis." Pages 5–35 in *Philippi at the Time of Paul and after His Death*. Edited by Charalambos Bakirtzis and Helmut Koester. Harrisburg, PA: Trinity Press International, 1998.

Kristiansen, Kristian. "The Discipline of Archaeology." Pages 3–46 in *Oxford Handbook of Archaeology*. Edited by Barry W. Cunliffe, Chris Gosden, and Rosemary A. Joyce. Oxford: Oxford University Press, 2009.

Ladstätter, Sabine, with Barbara Beck-Brandt, Martin Steskal, and Norbert Zimmermann. *Terrace House 2 in Ephesos: An Archaeological Guide*. Translated by Nicole M. High with Emma Sachs. Istanbul: Homer Kitabevi, 2013.

Laird, Margaret L. "The Emperor in a Roman Town: The Base of the *Augustales* in the Forum at Corinth." Pages 67–116 in *Corinth in Context: Comparative Studies on Religion and Society*. Edited by Steven J. Friesen, Dan N. Showalter, and James C. Walters. Leiden: Brill, 2010.

Lemerle, Paul. "Chronique des fouilles et découvertes archéologiques en Grèce en 1939." *BCH* 63 (1939): 285–324.

Liddell, Henry George, Robert Scott, Henry Stuart Jones. *A Greek-English Lexicon*. 9th ed. with revised supplement. Oxford: Clarendon, 1996.

Lindsay, Wallace M., ed. *Sexti Pompei Festi De verborum significatu quae supersunt cum Pauli epitome*. Leipzig: Teubner, 1913.

Livy. *History of Rome*. Translated by B. O. Foster, Frank Gardner Moore, Evan Taylor Sage, Alfred C. Schlesinger, and Russel M. Geer. 14 vols. LCL. Cambridge: Harvard University Press, 1919–1959.

Long, Fredrick J. "'The God of This Age' (2 Cor 4:4) and Paul's Empire-Resisting Gospel at Corinth." Pages 219–70 in *Roman Corinth*. Vol. 2 of *The First Urban Churches*. Edited by James R. Harrison and L. L. Welborn. WGRWSup 8. Atlanta: SBL Press, 2016.

Lopez, Davina. *The Apostle to the Conquered: Reimagining Paul's Mission*. Paul in Critical Context. Minneapolis: Fortress, 2008.

Lozano, Fernando. "The Creation of Imperial Gods: Not Only Imposition versus Spontaneity." Pages 475–519 in *More Than Men, Less Than Gods: Studies on Royal Cult and Imperial Worship*. Edited by Panagiotis P. Iossif, Andrezj Chankowski, and Catharine Lorber. Leuven: Peeters, 2011.

———. "*Divi Augusti* and *Theoi Sebastoi*: Roman Initiatives and Greek Answers." *ClQ* 57 (2007): 139–52.

Lunt, David. *The Crown Games of Ancient Greece: Archaeology, Athletes, and Heroes*. Fayetteville: University of Arkansas Press, 2022.

Matera, Frank. *Romans*. Paideia. Grand Rapids: Baker Academic, 2010.

McDonough, Christopher, ed. *Servius' Commentary on Book Four of Virgil's Aeneid*. Mundelein, IL: Bolchazy-Carducci, 2004.

McIntyre, Gwynaeth. *A Family of Gods: The Worship of the Imperial Family in the Latin West*. Ann Arbor: University of Michigan Press, 2016.

———. *Imperial Cult*. Leiden: Brill, 2019.

McLean, B. H. *An Introduction to Greek Epigraphy of the Hellenistic and Roman Periods from Alexander the Great down to the Reign of Constantine (323 B.C.–A.D. 337)*. Ann Arbor: University of Michigan Press, 2002.

Meeks, Wayne. *The First Urban Christians: The Social World of the Apostle Paul*. 2nd ed. New Haven: Yale University Press, 2003.

Meritt, Benjamin D., ed. *The Greek Inscriptions 1896–1927*. Vol. 8, part 1 of *Corinth: Results of Excavations Conducted by the American School of Classical Studies at Athens*. Cambridge: American School of Classical Studies at Athens, 1931.

Metcalf, William E. "Numismatics." Pages 135–45 in *The Oxford Handbook of Roman Studies*. Edited by Alessandro Barchiesi and Walter Scheidel. Oxford: Oxford University Press, 2010.

Millar, Fergus. "Two Augustan Notes." *Classical Review* 18 (1968): 264–65.

Miller, Colin. "The Imperial Cult in the Pauline Cities of Asia Minor and Greece." *CBQ* 72 (2010): 314–32.

Millis, Benjamin W. "The Local Magistrates and Elite of Roman Corinth." Pages 38–53 in *Corinth in Contrast: Studies in Inequality*. Edited by Steven J. Friesen, Sarah A. James, and Daniel N. Schowalter. Leiden: Brill, 2014.

———. "The Social and Ethnic Origins of the Colonists in Early Roman Corinth." Pages 13–36 in *Corinth in Context: Comparative Studies on Religion and Society*. Edited by Steven J. Friesen, Daniel N. Schowalter, and James C. Walters. Leiden: Brill, 2010.

Mitchell, Charles, Edward W. Bodnar, and Clive Ross, eds. *Cyriac of Ancona: Life and Early Travels*. The I Tatti Renaissance Library. Cambridge: Harvard University Press, 2015.

Momigliano, Arnaldo. "How Roman Emperors Became Gods." *American Scholar* 55 (1986): 181–93.

Mommsen, Theodore, et al., ed. *Corpus inscriptionum latinarum*. Berlin: de Gruyter, 1893–.

Montevecchi, Orsolina. "Nerone a una polis e ai 6475." *Aegyptus* 50 (1970): 5–33.

Nicolaus of Damascus. *The Life of Augustus and the Autobiography: Edited with Introduction, Translations, and Historical Commentary*. Translated and edited by Mark Toher. Cambridge: Cambridge University Press, 2017.

Nigdelis, Pantelis M. *Inscriptiones Epiri, Macedoniae, Thraciae, Scythiae: Inscriptiones Thessalonicae et viciniae; Supplementum primum, Tituli inter A. MCMLX et MMXV reperti*. Vol. 10, part 2.1 of *Inscriptiones Graecae*. Berlin: de Gruyter, 2017.

Nock, A. D. "Notes on Ruler-Cult I–IV." *JHS* 48 (1928): 21–43.

———. "Religious Developments from the Close of the Republic to the Death of Nero." Pages 481–503 in *The Augustan Empire 44 B.C.–A.D. 69*. Vol. 10 of *Cambridge Ancient History*. Edited by S. A. Cook, F. E. Adcock, and M. P. Charlesworth. Cambridge: Cambridge University Press, 1934.

Oakes, Peter. *Philippians: From Letter to People*. SNTSMS 110. Cambridge: Cambridge University Press, 2001.

———. "Re-mapping the Universe: Paul and the Emperor in 1 Thessalonians and Philippians." *JSNT* 27 (2005): 301–22.

Oster, Richard E. "Numismatic Windows into the Social World of Early Christianity: A Methodological Inquiry." *JBL* 101 (1982): 195–223.

———. "When Men Wore Veils to Worship: The Historical Context of 1 Corinthians 11.4." *NTS* 34 (1988): 481–505.

Ovid. *Metamorphoses*. Translated by Frank Justus Miller. Revised by G. P. Goold. 2 vols. LCL. Cambridge: Harvard University Press, 1916.

———. *Tristia. Ex Ponto*. Translated by A. L. Wheeler. Revised by G. P. Goold. LCL. Cambridge: Harvard University Press, 1924.

Paton, William R., ed. *Inscriptiones insularum maris Aegaei praeter Delum, 2: Inscriptiones Lesbi, Nesi, Tenedi*. Vol. 12 of *Inscriptiones Graecae*. Berlin: de Gruyter, 1899.

Papakonstantinou-Diamantourou, Depoina, Elena Martín Gonzálex, and Klaus Hallof, eds. *Inscriptiones Epiri, Macedoniae, Thraciae, Scythiae: Inscriptiones Thessalonicae et viciniae; Supplementum alterum, Addenda, Indices, Tabulae*. Vol. 10, part 2.1 of *Inscriptiones Graecae*. Berlin: de Gruyter, 2021.

Papazoglou, Fanoula. "Macedonia under the Romans." Pages 192–207 in *Macedonia: 4,000 Years of Greek History and Civilization*. Edited by M. B. Sakellariou. Athens: Ekdotike Athenon, 1983.

Pausanias. *Description of Greece*. Translated by W. H. S. Jones, H. A. Ormerodm, and R. E. Wycherley. 5 vols. LCL. Cambridge: Harvard University Press, 1918–1935.

Peterson, Erik. "Die Einholung des *Kyrios*." *ZST* 7 (1930): 682–702.

Petronius and Seneca. *Satyricon. Apocolocyntosis*. Translated by Gareth Schmeling. LCL. Cambridge: Harvard University Press, 2020.

Pettegrew, David K. *The Isthmus of Corinth: Crossroads of the Mediterranean World*. Ann Arbor: University of Michigan Press, 2016.

Philo. Translated by F. H. Colson, Ralph Marcus, and G. H. Whitaker. 10 vols. LCL. Cambridge: Harvard University Press, 1929–1953.

Pilhofer, Peter. *Die erste christliche Gemeinde Europas*. Vol. 1 of *Philippi*. WUNT 87. Tübingen: Mohr Siebeck, 1995.

———. *Katalog der Inschriften von Philippi*. Vol. 2 of *Philippi*. 2nd ed. WUNT 119. Tübingen: Mohr Siebeck, 2009.

Pillar, Edward. *Resurrection as Anti-imperial Gospel: 1 Thessalonians 1:9b–10 in Context.* Minneapolis: Fortress, 2013.

Pindar. *Nemean Odes. Isthmian Odes. Fragments.* Translated by William H. Race. LCL. Cambridge: Harvard University Press, 1997.

Plato. *Laws.* Translated by R. G. Bury. 2 vols. LCL. Cambridge: Harvard University Press, 1926.

Pleket, H. W. "An Aspect of Emperor Cult: Imperial Mysteries." *HTR* 58 (1965): 331–47.

Pleket, Henry W., Ronald S. Stroud, Angelos Chaniotis, and Johan H. M. Strubbe, eds. *Supplementum Epigraphicum Graecum.* Vol. 45. Amsterdam: Brill, 1998.

Pliny. *Natural History.* Translated by H. Rackham, D. E. Eichholz, and W. H. S. Jones. 10 vols. LCL. Cambridge: Harvard University Press, 1938–1962.

Pliny the Younger. *Letters.* Translated by Betty Radice. 2 vols. LCL. Cambridge: Harvard University Press, 1969.

Plutarch. *Agis and Cleomenes. Tiberius and Gaius Gracchus. Philopoemen and Flamininus.* Vol. 10 of *Lives.* Translated by Bernadotte Perrin. LCL. Cambridge: Harvard University Press, 1921.

———. *Demosthenes and Cicero. Alexander and Caesar.* Vol. 7 of *Lives.* Translated by Bernadotte Perrin. LCL. Cambridge: Harvard University Press, 1919.

———. *Dion and Brutus. Timoleon and Aemilius Paulus.* Vol. 6 of *Lives.* Translated by Bernadotte Perrin. LCL. Cambridge: Harvard University Press, 1918.

———. *Fragments.* Vol. 15 of *Moralia.* Translated by F. H. Sandbach. LCL. Cambridge: Harvard University Press, 1969.

———. *Love Stories. That a Philosopher Ought to Converse Especially with Men in Power. To an Uneducated Ruler. Whether an Old Man Should Engage in Public Affairs. Precepts of Statecraft. On Monarchy, Democracy, and Oligarchy. That We Ought Not to Borrow. Lives of the Ten Orators. Summary of a Comparison between Aristophanes and Menander.* Vol. 10 of *Moralia.* Translated by Harold North Fowler. LCL. Cambridge: Harvard University Press, 1936.

———. *Theseus and Romulus. Lycurgus and Numa. Solon and Publicola.* Vol. 1 of *Lives.* Translated by Bernadotte Perrin. LCL. Cambridge: Harvard University Press, 1914.

Price, Simon R. F. "From Noble Funerals to Divine Cults: The Consecration of the Roman Emperor." Pages 56–105 in *Rituals of Royalty: Power and Ceremonial in Traditional Societies.* Edited by David Cannadine and Simon Price. Cambridge: Cambridge University Press, 1987.

———. "God and Emperors: The Greek Language of the Roman Imperial Cult." *JHS* 104 (1984): 79–95.

———. *Religions of the Ancient Greeks.* Cambridge: Cambridge University Press, 1999.

———. *Rituals and Power: The Roman Imperial Cult in Asia Minor*. Cambridge: Cambridge University Press, 1984.

Prignitz, Sebastian. "Ein Augustuspriester des Jahres 27 v. Chr." *ZPE* 178 (2011): 210–14.

Rahlfs, Alfred, and Robert Hanhart, eds. *Septuaginta*. Rev. ed. Stuttgart: Deutsche Bibelgesellschaft, 2006.

Rapske, Brian. *The Book of Acts and Paul in Roman Custody*. Vol. 3 of *The Book of Acts in Its First Century Setting*. Grand Rapids: Eerdmans, 1994.

Rathmayr, Elisabeth. "New Evidence for Imperial Cult in Dwelling Unit 7 in Terrace House 2 in Ephesos." Pages 9–35 in *Ephesos as a Religious Center under the Principate*. Edited by Allen Black, Christine M. Thomas, and Trevor W. Thompson. WUNT 488. Tübingen: Mohr Siebeck, 2022.

Reisch, Emil. "*Agonothetes*." PW 1:870–77.

Reumann, John. *Philippians: A New Translation with Introduction and Commentary*. AYB 33B. New Haven: Yale University Press, 2008.

Reynolds, Joyce, Charlotte Roueché, and Gabriel Bodard. *Inscriptions of Aphrodisias*. 2007. https://insaph.kcl.ac.uk/insaph/iaph2007/index.html.

Rici, Marijana, ed. *The Inscriptions of Alexandreia Troas*. Inschriften griechischer Städte aus Kleinasien 53. Bonn: Habelt, 1997.

Robert, Louis. *Les gladiateurs dans l'Orient grec*. Limoges: Bontemps, 1940. Repr., Amsterdam: Hakkert, 1970.

———. "Les inscriptions de Thessalonique." *RevPhil* 48 (1974): 180–246.

Romano, David Gilman. "Urban and Rural Planning in Roman Corinth." Pages 25–60 in *Urban Religion in Roman Corinth: Interdisciplinary Approaches*. Edited by Daniel N. Schowalter and Steven J. Friesen. HTS 53. Cambridge: Harvard University Press, 2005.

Roman Provincial Coinage Online. https://rpc.ashmus.ox.ac.uk.

Roncaglia, Carolynn. "Inscriptions." Pages 375–419 in *The Julian Basilica: Architecture, Sculpture, Epigraphy*. Vol. 22 of *Corinth: Results of Excavations Conducted by the American School of Classical Studies at Athens*. Princeton: American School of Classical Studies at Athens, 2022.

Rose, Herbert Jennings, and John Scheid. "Quirinus." *OCD* 1253.

———. "Romulus, Remus." *OCD* 1296–97.

Roux, Georges. *Pausanias en Corinthe (livre II, I à 15): Texte, traduction, commentaire archéologique et topographie*. Paris: Les Belles Lettres, 1958.

Rubin, Benjamin. "Ruler Cult and Colonial Identity: The Imperial Sanctuary at Pisidian Antioch." Pages 33–60 in *Building a New Rome: The Roman Colony of Pisidian Antioch (25 BC–300 AD)*. Edited by Elaine K. Gazda and Diana Ng. Ann Arbor: Kelsey Museum, 2011.

Salmon, Edward Togo. *Roman Colonization under the Republic*. London: Thames & Hudson, 1969.

Sanders, Guy D. R., Jennifer Palinkas, and Ioulia Tzonou-Herbst with James Herbst. *Ancient Corinth: Site Guide.* 7th ed. Princeton: American School of Classical Studies at Athens, 2018.

Scheid, John. *Commentarii fratrum Arvalium qui supersunt: Les copies épigraphiques des protocoles annuels de la confrérie arvale (21 av.–304 ap. J.-C.).* Rome: École Française de Rome, 1998.

——. *The Gods, the State, and the Individual: Reflections on Civic Religion in Rome.* Translated by Clifford Ando. Philadelphia: University of Pennsylvania Press, 2016.

——. *An Introduction to Roman Religion.* Translated by Janet Lloyd. Bloomington: University of Indiana Press, 2003.

——. "The Religious Roles of Roman Women." Pages 377–408 in *From Ancient Goddesses to Christian Saints.* Vol. 1 of *A History of Women in the West.* Edited by Pauline Schmitt Pantel. Cambridge: Harvard University Press, 1992.

——. "To Honour the *Princeps* and Venerate the Gods: Public Cult, Neighbourhood Cults, and Imperial Cult in Rome." Pages 275–99 in *Augustus.* Edited by Jonathan Edmondson. Edinburgh: Edinburgh University Press, 2009.

Scott, Kenneth. "Emperor Worship in Ovid." *Transactions and Proceedings of the American Philological Association* 61 (1930): 43–69.

Scotton, Paul D. "Form and Function." Pages 199–21 in *The Julian Basilica: Architecture, Sculpture, Epigraphy.* Vol. 22 of *Corinth: Results of Excavations Conducted by the American School of Classical Studies at Athens.* Princeton: American School of Classical Studies at Athens, 2022.

——. "A New Fragment of an Inscription from the Julian Basilica at Roman Corinth." *Hesperia* 74 (2005): 95–100.

——. "Reconstruction." Pages 119–64 in *The Julian Basilica: Architecture, Sculpture, Epigraphy.* Vol. 22 of *Corinth: Results of Excavations Conducted by the American School of Classical Studies at Athens.* Princeton: American School of Classical Studies at Athens, 2022.

"Searchable Greek Inscriptions." Packard Humanities Institute. https://epigraphy.packhum.org.

Servius Honoratus, Maurus. *Servii grammatici qui ferunter in Vergilii carmina commentarii.* Edited by Georgius Thilo and Hermannus Hagen. Leipzig: Teubner, 1881.

Sève, Michel. "The Forum at Philippi: The Transformation of Public Space from the Establishment of the Colony to the Early Byzantine Period." Pages 13–35 in *Philippi, from Colonia Augusta to Communitas Christiana: Religion and Society in Transition.* Edited by Steven J. Friesen, Michalis Lychounas, and Daniel N. Schowalter. NovTSup 186. Leiden: Brill, 2022.

Sève, Michel, and Patrick Weber. *Guide du forum de Philippes.* Sites et Monuments 18. Athens: École française d'Athènes, 2012.

———. "Le côté Nord du forum de Philippes." *BCH* 110 (1986): 531–81.

Sherk, Robert K., ed. *The Roman Empire: Augustus to Hadrian*. Translated Documents of Greece and Rome 6. Cambridge: Cambridge, 1988.

Siekierka, Przemyslaw, Krystyna Stebnicka, and Aleksander Wolicki, eds. *Women and the Polis: Public Honorific Inscriptions for Women in the Greek Cities from the Late Classical to the Roman Period*. 2 vols. Berlin: de Gruyter, 2021.

Sismanides, Kostas. "The Sevasteion Building Complex (Rooms A–E)." Pages 124–31 in *Kalindoia: An Ancient City in Macedonia*. Edited by Polyxeni Adam-Veleni. Thessaloniki: Archaeological Museum of Thessaloniki, 2008.

Spawforth, Antony J. S. "Corinth, Argos, and the Imperial Cult: Pseudo-Julian, *Letters* 198." *Hesperia* 63 (1994): 211–30.

———. "Roman Corinth: The Formation of a Colonial Elite." Pages 167–82 in *Roman Onomastics in the Greek East*. Edited by A. D. Rizikis. Athens: de Boccard, 1996.

Stefanidou-Tiveriou, Theodosia. "Art in the Roman Period, 168 BC–337 AD." Pages 563–84 in *Brill's Companion to Ancient Macedon: Studies in the Archaeology and History of Macedon, 650 BC–300 AD*. Edited by Robert J. Lane Fox. Leiden: Brill, 2011.

Still, Todd D. *Conflict at Thessalonica: A Pauline Church and Its Neighbours*. JSNTSup 183. Sheffield: Sheffield Academic, 1999.

Stillwell, Richard. *The Theatre*. Vol. 2 of *Corinth: Results of Excavations Conducted by the American School of Classical Studies at Athens*. Princeton: American School of Classical Studies, 1952.

Strabo. *Geography*. Translated by Horace Leonard Jones. 8 vols. LCL. Cambridge: Harvard University Press, 1917–1932.

Strobel, August. "Zum Verständnis von Rm 13." *ZNW* 47 (1956): 67–93.

Sturgeon, Mary C. *Sculpture: The Assemblage from the Theater*. Vol. 9, part 3 of *Corinth: Results of Excavations Conducted by the American School of Classical Studies at Athens*. Princeton: American School of Classical Studies, 2004.

Suetonius. *The Lives of the Caesars*. Translated by J. C. Rolfe and K. R. Bradley. 2 vols. LCL. Cambridge: Harvard University Press, 1914.

Sutherland, C. H. V., and R. A. G. Carson, eds. *From 31 BC to AD 69*. Vol. 1 of *The Roman Imperial Coinage*. London: Spink & Son, 1984.

Tacitus. *Annals*. Translated by Clifford H. Moore and John Jackson. 2 vols. LCL. Cambridge: Harvard University Press, 1931, 1937.

Taylor, Lily Ross. *Divinity of the Roman Emperor*. Philological Monographs 1. Middletown, CT: American Philological Association, 1931.

Thonemann, Peter. "The Calendar of the Roman Province of Asia." *ZPE* 196 (2015): 123–41.

Tsagalis, Christos. "Eumelos of Corinth." Pages 15–174 in *Early Greek Epic Fragments I*.

Edited by Franco Montanari and Antonios Rengakos. Trends in Classics 47. Berlin: de Gruyter, 2017.

Varro. *On the Latin Language*. Translated by Roland G. Kent. 2 vols. LCL. Cambridge: Harvard University Press, 1938.

Velleius Paterculus. *Compendium of Roman History. Res Gestae Divi Augusti*. Edited by Frederick W. Shipley. LCL. Cambridge: Harvard University Press, 1924.

Vénencie, Jacques, Séraphin Charitonidis, and Demetrios Pallas. "Inscriptions trouvées à Solômos, près de Corinthe." *BCH* 83 (1959): 498–508.

Verhoef, Eduard. *Philippi: How Christianity Began in Europe; The Epistle to the Philippians and the Excavations at Philippi*. London: Bloomsbury T&T Clark, 2013.

Virgil. *Aeneid: Books 7–12. Appendix Vergiliana*. Translated by H. Rushton Fairclough. Revised by G. P. Goold. LCL. Cambridge: Harvard University Press, 1918.

———. *Eclogues. Georgics. Aeneid: Books 1–6*. Translated by H. Rushton Fairclough. Revised by G. P. Goold. LCL. Cambridge: Harvard University Press, 1916.

Vitruvius. *On Architecture*. Translated by Frank Granger. 2 vols. LCL. Cambridge: Harvard University Press, 1931, 1934.

Vos, Craig Steven de. *Church and Community Conflicts: The Relationship of the Thessalonian, Corinthian, and Philippian Churches with Their Wider Civic Communities*. SBLDS 168. Atlanta: Scholars Press, 1999.

Wachtel, Klaus. "Taurus Statilius Corvinus." *Prosopographia Imperii Romani Saec. I. II. III*. Part 7, fascicle 1. 2nd ed. Berlin: de Gruyter, 1999.

Walters, James C. "Civic Identity in Roman Corinth and Its Impact on Early Christians." Pages 397–417 in *Urban Religion in Roman Corinth: Interdisciplinary Approaches*. Edited by Daniel N. Schowalter and Steven J. Friesen. HTS 53. Cambridge: Harvard University Press, 2005.

Warrior, Valerie. *Roman Religion*. Cambridge: Cambridge University Press, 2006.

Wengst, Klaus. Pax Romana *and the Peace of Jesus Christ*. Translated by John Bowden. London: SCM, 1987.

West, Allen B., ed. *The Latin Inscriptions 1896–1926*. Vol. 8, part 2 of *Corinth: Results of Excavations Conducted by the American School of Classical Studies at Athens*. Princeton: American School of Classical Studies at Athens, 1931.

Wilken, Robert Louis. *The Christians as the Romans Saw Them*. 2nd ed. New Haven: Yale University Press, 2003.

Williams, Charles K., III. "A Re-evaluation of Temple E and the West End of the Forum." Pages 156–62 in *The Greek Renaissance in the Roman Empire*. Edited by S. Walker and A. Cameron. BICS 55. London: Oxford University Press, 1989.

———. "The Refounding of Corinth: Some Roman Religious Attitudes." Pages 26–37 in *Roman Architecture in the Greek World*. Edited by Sarah Macready and F. H. Thompson. SALOP 10. London: Society of the Antiquaries, 1987.

Williams, Charles K., III, Nancy Bookidis, and Kathleen W. Slane with Stephen Tracy. "From the Destruction of Corinth to Colonia Laus Iulia Corinthiensis." Pages 258–87 in *The Destruction of Cities in the Ancient Greek World: Integrating the Archaeological and Literary Evidence*. Edited by Sylvian Fachard and Edward M. Harris. Cambridge: Cambridge University Press, 2021.

Winter, Bruce W. *Divine Honours for the Caesars: The First Christians' Responses*. Grand Rapids: Eerdmans, 2015.

Wiseman, James. "Corinth and Rome I: 228 B.C.–A.D. 267." *ANRW* 7.1:438–548. Part 2, *Principat*, 7.1. Edited by H. Temporini and W. Haase. New York: de Gruyter, 1980.

Woolf, Greg, and Miguel John Versluys. "Empire as a Field of Religious Actions." Pages 25–42 in *Religion in the Roman Empire*. Edited by Jörg Rüpke and Greg Woolf. Die Religionen der Menschheit. Stuttgart: Kohlhammer, 2021.

Wright, N. T. *Paul: A Biography*. San Francisco: HarperCollins, 2018.

———. "Paul and Empire." Pages 285–97 in *The Blackwell Companion to Paul*. Edited by Stephen Westerholm. Malden, MA: Wiley-Blackwell, 2011.

———. *Paul and the Faithfulness of God*. 2 vols. Minneapolis: Fortress, 2013.

———. *Paul in Fresh Perspective*. Minneapolis: Fortress, 2005.

———. "Paul's Gospel and Caesar's Empire." Pages 160–83 in *Paul and Politics: Ekklesia, Israel, Imperium, Interpretation; Essays in Honor of Krister Stendahl*. Edited by Richard A. Horsley. Harrisburg, PA: Trinity Press International, 2000.

———. "Romans." *NIB* 10:393–770.

Zetzel, James E. G. "New Light on Gaius Caesar's Eastern Campaign." *GRBS* 11 (1970): 259–66.

Index of Authors

Index of Subjects

Index of Ancient Persons

Index of Scripture

Index of Other Ancient Sources